Bob Dylan
The Day I Was There

Neil Cossar

All rights reserved. No part of this publication may be reproduced, stored in a retrieval system, or transmitted in any form or by any means, electronic, electrostatic, recording, magnetic tape, mechanical, photocopying or otherwise, without prior permission in writing from the publisher.

The publisher makes no representation, express or implied, with regard to the accuracy of the information contained in this publication and cannot accept any responsibility in law for any errors or omissions.

The right of Neil Cossar to be identified as author of this work has been asserted by him in accordance with sections 77 and 78 of the Copyright, Designs and Patents Act 1988.

No part of this book may be reproduced in any form without permission from the publisher except for the quotation of brief passages in reviews.
A catalogue record for this book is available from the British Library

Originally published by This Day In Music Books 2018
This edition © Spenwood Books 2025
ISBN: 978-1-915858-48-1

Spenwood Books
1 Totnes Road
Manchester
M21 8XF

richard@spenwoodbooks.com

Seen Dylan? Email
iwasatthatgig@gmail.com

Editorial management: Neil Cossar
Cover design: Oliver Keen

CONTENTS

PREFACE
14
DULUTH ARMORY
19
31 JANUARY, 1959, DULUTH, IOWA
CRYSTAL BALLROOM
20
1959, FARGO, NORTH DAKOTA
GERDES FOLK CITY
24
GREENWICH VILLAGE, MANHATTAN, NEW YORK
TEN O' CLOCK SCHOLAR
28
OCTOBER 1959, MINNEAPOLIS, MINNESOTA

1960

PIZZA VILLA
30
MARCH 1960, NEW YORK CITY, NEW YORK

1961

CAFÉ WHA?
32
24 JANUARY, 1961, NEW YORK CITY, NEW YORK
CAFÉ WHA?
34
FEBRUARY 1961, NEW YORK CITY, NEW YORK
IDA NOYES HALL
35
SPRING 1961, CHICAGO, ILLINOIS
GERDES FOLK CITY
36
11 APRIL, 1961, NEW YORK CITY, NEW YORK
GERDES FOLK CITY
44
MAY 1961, NEW YORK CITY, NEW YORK
CAFFÈ LENA
45
JUNE 1961, SARATOGA SPRINGS, NEW YORK

CAFÉ ESPRESSO
45
SUMMER 1961, WOODSTOCK, NEW YORK

1962

FOLKLORE MUSIC FESTIVAL
50
21 APRIL, 1962, MICHIGAN

UNION BALLROOM
51
22 APRIL, 1962, ANN ARBOR, MICHIGAN

THE GASLIGHT CAFÉ
52
SEPTEMBER 1962, NEW YORK CITY, NEW YORK

THE KING AND QUEEN
57
21 DECEMBER, 1962, LONDON

SINGERS CLUB
57
22 DECEMBER, 1962, LONDON

THE KING AND QUEEN
58
23 DECEMBER, 1962, LONDON

THE TROUBADOUR
60
29 DECEMBER, 1962, London

1963

JONES STREET
61
FEBRUARY 1963, NEW YORK CITY, NEW YORK

FRETTED INSTRUMENTS
63
SPRING 1963, NEW YORK CITY, NEW YORK

THE BEAR
64
25 APRIL, 1963, CHICAGO, ILLINOIS

FOLK CITY
66
SPRING, 1963, NEW YORK CITY, NEW YORK

MASTERTONE RECORDING STUDIO
67
APRIL 1963, NEW YORK CITY, NEW YORK

THE ED SULLIVAN SHOW
68
12 MAY, 1963, NEW YORK CITY, NEW YORK

MONTEREY FOLK FESTIVAL
69
18 MAY, 1963, MONTEREY, CALIFORNIA

MONTEREY FOLK FESTIVAL
73
27 MAY, 1963, MONTEREY, CALIFORNIA

CAFÉ EXPRESSO
73
WOODSTOCK, NEW YORK

COLUMBIA STUDIO A
74
6 AUGUST, 1963, NEW YORK CITY, NEW YORK

YALE'S WOOLSEY HALL
75
OCTOBER 1963, NEW HAVEN, CONNECTICUT

1964

THE CAGE UMASS
76
26 April, 1964, AMHERST, MASSACHUSETTS

CAFÉ ESPRESSO
78
JULY 1964, WOODSTOCK, NEW YORK

SAVOY HOTEL
81
8 MAY, 1964, LONDON

ROYAL FESTIVAL HALL
82
17 MAY, 1964, LONDON

NEWPORT FOLK FESTIVAL
84
24 JULY, 1964, RHODE ISLAND

WOODSTOCK
85
AUGUST 1964, NEW YORK STATE

THE DELMONICO HOTEL
87
28 AUGUST, 1964, NEW YORK CITY, NEW YORK

ANN ARBOR HIGH SCHOOL
88
19 SEPTEMBER, 1964, MICHIGAN

INDIAN NECK FOLK FESTIVAL
91
14 NOVEMBER, 1964, NEW HAVEN, CONNECTICUT

MEMORIAL GYMNASIUM
92
8 NOVEMBER, 1964, ORONO, MAINE

WILSON HIGH SCHOOL
92
5 DECEMBER, 1964, LONG BEACH, CALIFORNIA

1965

COLUMBIA RECORDING STUDIOS
96
14 JANUARY, 1965, NEW YORK CITY, NEW YORK

WHISKY A GO-GO
97
JANUARY 1965, LOS ANGELES, CALIFORNIA

COLUMBIA STUDIOS
99
20 JANUARY, 1965, HOLLYWOOD, CALIFORNIA

CAPITOL THEATRE
101
21 MARCH, 1965, OTTAWA, ONTARIO, CANADA

CIVIC AUDITORIUM
103
27 March, 1965, SANTA MONICA, CALIFORNIA

LONDON
103
APRIL 1965

THE OVAL
105
30 APRIL, 1965, CITY HALL, SHEFFIELD

THE ODEON, LIVERPOOL
106
1 MAY, 1965, LIVERPOOL

DE MONTFORT HALL
112
2 MAY, 1965, LEICESTER

CITY HALL
112
6 MAY, 1965, NEWCASTLE UPON TYNE

FREE TRADE HALL
113
7 MAY, 1965, MANCHESTER

ROYAL ALBERT HALL
118
9-10 MAY, 1965, LONDON

COLUMBIA STUDIO A
124
15 JUNE, 1965, NEW YORK CITY, NEW YORK

WOODSTOCK
125
JUNE 1965, NEW YORK STATE

NEWPORT FOLK FESTIVAL
126
25 JULY, 1965, RHODE ISLAND

FOREST HILLS STADIUM
129
28 AUGUST, 1965, QUEENS, NEW YORK

HOLLYWOOD BOWL
135
3 SEPTEMBER, 1965, LOS ANGELES, CALIFORNIA

COLUMBIA STUDIO A
142
OCTOBER 1965, NEW YORK CITY, NEW YORK

VETERANS MEMORIAL AUDITORIUM
143
19 NOVEMBER, 1965, COLUMBUS, OHIO

BURLINGTON
146
23 NOVEMBER, 1965, VERMONT

ARIE CROWN THEATER
148
27 NOVEMBER, 1965, CHICAGO, ILLINOIS

KQED
150
3 DECEMBER, 1965, BERKELEY, CALIFORNIA

CIVIC CENTER
151
12 DECEMBER, 1965, SAN JOSE, CALIFORNIA

1966

WBAI FM
153
27 JANUARY, 1966, NEW YORK CITY, NEW YORK

THE GASLIGHT
154
1966, NEW YORK CITY, NEW YORK

THE KETTLE OF FISH
155
GREENWICH VILLAGE, NEW YORK

COLUMBIA STUDIO A
158
14 FEBRUARY, 1966, NASHVILLE, TENNESSEE

OTTAWA AUDITORIUM
161
19 FEBRUARY, 1966, ONTARIO, CANADA

COLUMBIA STUDIO A
162
10 MARCH, 1966, NASHVILLE

KIEL OPERA HOUSE
164
11 MARCH, 1966, ST. LOUIS, MISSOURI

QUEEN ELIZABETH THEATRE
165
26 MARCH, 1966, VANCOUVER, CANADA

RIVERSIDE COLLEGE
165
APRIL 1966, ORANGE COUNTY, CALIFORNIA

THE WHISKY A GO GO
166
8 APRIL, 1966, LOS ANGELES, CALIFORNIA

SYDNEY STADIUM
167
13 APRIL, 1966, SYDNEY, AUSTRALIA

PALAIS THEATRE
171
22 APRIL, 1966, ADELAIDE, AUSTRALIA

CAPITOL THEATRE
174
23 April, 1966, PERTH, AUSTRALIA

ADELPHI CINEMA
176
5 MAY, 1966, DUBLIN, IRELAND

ABC
179
6 MAY, 1966, BELFAST, NORTHERN IRELAND

COLSTON HALL
181
10 MAY, 1966, BRISTOL

CAPITOL THEATRE
183
11 MAY, 1966, CARDIFF, WALES

ODEON THEATRE
185
12 MAY, 1966, BIRMINGHAM

ODEON THEATRE, LIVERPOOL
190
14 MAY, 1966, LIVERPOOL

DE MONFORT HALL
194
15 MAY, 1966, LEICESTER

GAUMONT THEATRE
198
16 MAY, 1966, SHEFFIELD

FREE TRADE HALL
206
17 MAY, 1966, MANCHESTER

GLASGOW ODEON
218
19 MAY, 1966, GLASGOW, SCOTLAND

HOTEL GEORGE V
220
23 MAY, 1966, PARIS, FRANCE

L'OLYMPIA
221
24 MAY, 1966, PARIS, FRANCE

ROYAL ALBERT HALL
222
26 MAY, 1966, LONDON

ROYAL ALBERT HALL
227
27 MAY, 1966, LONDON

375 WEST STREET
236
NEW YORK CITY, NEW YORK

1967

THE PRESIDIO THEATER
241
17 MAY, 1967, SAN FRANCISCO, CALIFORNIA

BIG PINK
242
JUNE 1967, WOODSTOCK, NEW YORK

1969

COLUMBIA STUDIO A
246
14 FEBRUARY, 1969, NASHVILLE, TENNESSEE

COLUMBIA STUDIO A
249
15 FEBRUARY, 1969, NASHVILLE, TENNESSEE

RYMAN AUDITORIUM
250
1 MAY, 1969, NASHVILLE, TENNESSEE

WOODSIDE BAY
251
29-31 AUGUST, 1969, WOOTTON, ISLE OF WIGHT

WOODSTOCK
291
LATE 1969, NEW YORK

1970

COLUMBIA STUDIOS
292
JUNE 1970, NEW YORK CITY, NEW YORK

PRINCETON UNIVERSITY
295
9 JUNE, 1970, NEW JERSEY

1971

MADISON SQUARE GARDEN
297
1 AUGUST, 1971, NEW YORK CITY, NEW YORK

COLUMBIA STUDIOS
304
OCTOBER 1971, NEW YORK CITY, NEW YORK

ACADEMY OF MUSIC
306
31 DECEMBER, 1971, NEW YORK

1972

ROGER'S RESTAURANT
307
SUMMER 1972, EAST HAMPTON, NEW YORK

1973

SHANGRI-LA STUDIOS
309
AUGUST 1973, MALIBU, CALIFORNIA

VILLAGE RECORDER
310
NOVEMBER 1973, LOS ANGELES, CALIFORNIA

1974

CHICAGO STADIUM
318
3 JANUARY, 1974, CHICAGO, ILLINOIS

THE SPECTRUM
319
6 JANUARY, 1974, PHILADELPHIA, PENNSYLVANIA

THE FORUM
320
11 JANUARY, 1974, MONTREAL, CANADA

CAPITAL CENTRE
321
15 JANUARY, 1974, LANDOVER, MARYLAND

HOLLYWOOD SPORATORIUM
325
19 JANUARY, 1974, PEMBROKE PINES, CALIFORNIA

MID-SOUTH COLISEUM
326
23 JANUARY, 1974, MEMPHIS, TENNESSEE

MADISON SQUARE GARDEN
328
31 JANUARY, 1974, NEW YORK CITY, NEW YORK

CRISLER ARENA
335
2 FEBRUARY, 1974, ANN ARBOR, MICHIGAN

ASSEMBLY HALL
336
3 FEBRUARY, 1974, BLOOMINGTON, INDIANA

ST LOUIS ARENA
338
4 FEBRUARY, 1974, ST LOUIS, MISSOURI

DENVER COLISEUM
338
6 FEBRUARY, 1974, DENVER, COLORADO

CENTER COLISEUM
338
9 FEBRUARY, 1974, SEATTLE, WASHINGTON

FRIENDS OF CHILE BENEFIT
340
9 MAY, 1974, FELT FORUM, NEW YORK CITY, NEW YORK

A&R RECORDING
341
SEPTEMBER 1974, NEW YORK CITY, NEW YORK

THE BITTER END
346
26 JUNE, 1975, NEW YORK CITY, NEW YORK

COLUMBIA RECORDING STUDIOS
347
28 JULY, 1975, NEW YORK CITY, NEW YORK

COSTELLO GYMNASIUM
354
2 NOVEMBER, 1975, UNIVERSITY OF MASSACHUSETTS, LOWELL

SPRINGFIELD CIVIC CENTER
356
6 NOVEMBER, 1975, MASSACHUSETTS

PATRICK GYM
357
8 NOVEMBER, 1975, BURLINGTON, VERMONT

CONVENTION CENTER
361
15 NOVEMBER, 1975, NIAGARA FALLS, NEW YORK

WORCESTER MEMORIAL AUDITORIUM
362
19 NOVEMBER, 1975, WORCESTER, MASSACHUSETTS

MUSIC HALL
363
21 NOVEMBER, 1975, BOSTON, MASSACHUSETTS

MAPLE LEAF GARDENS
368
2 DECEMBER, 1975, TORONTO, CANADA

MADISON SQUARE GARDEN
368
8 DECEMBER, 1975, NEW YORK CITY, NEW YORK

1976

LAKELAND CIVIC CENTER
373
18 APRIL, 1976, LAKELAND, FLORIDA

FLORIDA FIELD
373
25 APRIL, 1976, GAINESVILLE, FLORIDA

LSU ASSEMBLY CENTER
374
4 MAY, 1976, BATON ROUGE, LOUISIANA

1978

RUNDOWN STUDIOS
379
JANUARY 1978, SANTA MONICA, CALIFORNIA

WESTERN SPRINGS STADIUM
378
9 MARCH, 1978, AUCKLAND, NEW ZEALAND

MYER MUSIC BOWL
391
20 MARCH, 1978, MELBOURNE, AUSTRALIA

ENTERTAINMENT CENTRE
383
27 MARCH, 1978, PERTH, AUSTRALIA

SYDNEY SHOWGROUND
391
1 APRIL, 1978, SYDNEY, AUSTRALIA

UNIVERSAL AMPHITHEATER
395
1-7 JUNE, 1978, LOS ANGELES, CALIFORNIA

EARLS COURT EXHIBITION CENTRE
397
15-20 JUNE, 1978, LONDON

ZEPPELINFELD
408
1 JULY 1978, NUREMBERG, GERMANY

SCANDINAVIUM
409
12 JULY 1978, GOTHENBERG, SWEDEN

THE PICNIC AT BLACKBUSHE AERODROME
411
15 JULY, 1978, CAMBERLEY, SURREY

NASSAU VETERANS MEMORIAL COLISEUM
435
27 SEPTEMBER, 1978, UNIONDALE

MAPLE LEAF GARDENS
435
12 OCTOBER, 1978, TORONTO, CANADA

CHICAGO STADIUM
436
17 OCTOBER, 1978, CHICAGO, ILLINOIS

THE SUMMIT
439
26 NOVEMBER, 1978, HOUSTON, TEXAS

LSU ASSEMBLY CENTER
439
29 NOVEMBER 1978, BATON ROUGE, LOUISIANA

1979

MUSCLE SHOALS SOUND
441
APRIL – MAY, ALABAMA

SCANDINAVIUM
442
11 JULY, 1979, GOTHENBURG, SWEDEN

VINEYARD CHURCH
442
1979, SANTA MONICA, CALIFORNIA

FOX WARFIELD THEATRE
443
15 NOVEMBER, 1979, SAN FRANCISCO, CALIFORNIA

Photo credits:	448
Credits:	448

PREFACE

I existed in a hermetically sealed world when I worked as *Melody Maker's* American Editor, based in New York between 1973 and 1977. I was going to gigs three or four nights a week, writing all hours of the day, mixing only with fellow music writers, musicians and industry types. I didn't really know anyone outside the music industry apart from the neighbour I'd see collecting her mail or the man at the newsagents where I picked up yesterday's British newspaper. In 1975 I didn't think much about the fuel crisis, the Irish Troubles or even the kidnapping of Patty Hearst. World affairs didn't concern me. I dwelt on where The Who were headed after the loss of momentum in 1974, or what David Bowie would look like the next time I saw him, or who was going to replace Mick Taylor in the Stones.

It came as something of a shock, therefore, when one day in early November the phone rang in my 78th Street apartment and the girl at the IPC office whose task it was to relay telex messages from London informed me that editor Ray Coleman wanted me to cover the 'Bob Die Lon' tour.

'Who?' I asked.
'Bob Die Lon.'
'Bob who?'
'Die Lon.'
'Never heard of him.'

So immersed was I in the world of rock that it never occurred to me in my wildest dreams than an American, not much younger than myself, could be so unfamiliar with Bob Dylan as to be unable to pronounce his name correctly, as if it rhymed with 'nylon'. To me this was like being unable to count to ten, or recite the alphabet. Never having heard Dylan's name pronounced in this way before, I was genuinely mystified as to the identity of the artist whose tour Ray wanted me to cover.

'Can you spell the name for me?' I asked.
'D-Y-L-A-N.'

'Oh, you mean Dylan,' I responded incredulously, pronouncing it correctly.

'Oh, that's how you say it,' she replied. 'Who is he?'

'Well,' I began, amazed that this young woman had never even heard of Bob Dylan, 'he's a singer and songwriter, probably the most famous popular musician to emerge in America since Elvis Presley. He's written some of the greatest and most famous songs of the last ten years and influenced just about everyone from The Beatles onwards. His lyrics are legendary...'

'Is he any good?' she interrupted.

Ignorance of Bob Dylan was not a crime in itself in those days, though it would certainly have counted against me when that same Ray Coleman had interviewed me for a job at the start of 1970. In any event Ray was telexing me – this was long before the fax, let alone e-mails – to ensure that I covered Dylan's Rolling Thunder Review, then about to begin up in New England, though unbeknownst to him I'd already made plans to head there with my pal Bob Gruen, New York's most streetwise rock photographer. (My recollections of one of the opening shows – at Springfield, Massachusetts on November 6 – can be found elsewhere in this book, as can my report of a Dylan show with The Band at New York's Madison Square Garden on January 30, 1974.)

Dylan was a favourite of all of us at *Melody Maker*. On my first day at the paper, in the first week of May, 1970, I sat at a desk in full sight of where Richard Williams, the assistant editor, had written out some Dylan lyrics and stuck them to the walls. Opposite me was a sign that read: 'You don't need a weatherman to know which way the wind blows' and to my right were the words, 'Don't follow leaders, watch the parking meters'. I well remember how, when Richard received an advance copy of George Harrison's triple *Concert For Bangla Desh* LP in December of the following year, the first thing he did was put on side five, very loud. When George announced, 'I'd like to bring on a friend of us all, Mister Bob Dylan,' all of us stopped what we were doing and gathered around the office record player. The delirious, ear-splitting ovation that preceded 'A Hard Rain's a-Gonna Fall' was a glorious, unqualified vindication of how we all felt about the direction our lives had taken.

More than the songs of any of his contemporaries, those of Bob Dylan – and the way he conducted his career – reflected the increasing maturity that popular music had discovered in the Sixties; that sense of endless possibility in which worldly insight, societal influence, and creative expression combined to elevate it way above the 'Moon in June' approach of the past. With the musicians who played on *Bringing It All Back Home*, *Highway 61 Revisited* and *Blonde on Blonde* and, later, the members of The Band, Dylan had discovered musical foils that framed his work in a perfect synthesis of poetry and rock 'n' roll. However, it was much more than mere instrumental virtuosity that we recognised, it was a journey into deeper realms of art, literacy, and culture that gave momentum to our mission to let the rest of the world know about it. Perhaps we were a bit idealistic or even naïve, but I like to think that all of us on the paper in those days felt we were part of something bigger than simply 'show biz' or 'entertainment', and that Dylan – along with Lennon, Townshend and Bowie – represented the best of the new world to which we were committed.

Unfortunately, it was the old world that greeted Bob Dylan when he made an early appearance at *Melody Maker's* offices in 1962. In November of that year, by an odd coincidence the same month that 'Love Me Do', The Beatles' first single, inched its way up to No 17 in the charts, 21-year-old Bob paid a visit to London, his first trip outside of the US, to appear in a radio play for the BBC. The play, the recording of which has long since been wiped, and the visit itself remain a footnote in Dylan's career, but while in London he visited and sang at various folk clubs, hung out at Dobells, the specialist record shop in Charing Cross Road, smoked plenty of dope and got drunk in Soho's pubs. He stayed for almost six weeks, initially at the posh Mayfair Hotel in Berkeley Square, where his smoking habits upset the management, subsequently moving to the more accommodating Cumberland, near Marble Arch. He befriended Martin Carthy, who encouraged his wayward, untutored genius, and may even have checked out Peter Cook's Establishment

Club on Greek Street, the cradle of the UK's satire movement that was lurking, ready to pounce on Harold Macmillan's complacent Tory government.

He also visited *Melody Maker's* offices, probably on the recommendation of US jazz critic Nat Hentoff, who wrote the sleeve notes for Dylan's second LP, *Freewheelin'*, and was an *MM* stringer. Hentoff was a pal of Max Jones, *MM*'s revered jazz writer, and it was Jones that Dylan sought out when he arrived at the offices at 161 Fleet Street. The doorman, concluding the scruffy-looking Dylan to be up to no good, denied him entry at first and it wasn't until Max was summoned that the issue was resolved. Max proceeded to interview the young Dylan, thus securing his first ever press coverage in the UK.

So, in closing, it gives me great pleasure to report that not only is Nobel Prize winner, Bob Dylan, a genius of enormous distinction in his chosen field, but that he never forgets a kindness, as I discovered for myself backstage at a Rolling Stones concert at Madison Square Garden in June of 1975. What I remember most about this concert is not Charlie's drumming, which as usual was exemplary, nor even the giant inflatable cock that appeared on stage and fomented so much distress in the God-fearing states down South, but being introduced to Bob, my only close encounter with the great man.

My friend Peter Rudge, then tour managing the Stones, had given me a couple of backstage passes and among those lingering in the corridor that led to the dressing rooms was Dylan himself, carrying a large pitcher of red wine from which he was drinking copiously. It was one of those big, round flagons with a ring on the neck through which you could insert a finger to raise it to your mouth, perfect for situations when glasses are unavailable. He looked much the same as he did on stage at the Rolling Thunder Review shows later that same year, without the white face make-up of course, his hair a mess of unkempt curls, in jeans and a black leather jacket, someone perhaps slightly dangerous to know. Most doormen, like the one in Fleet Street in 1962, would have thought twice about admitting him to whatever premises they were safeguarding.

Moments after clocking Bob I spotted Peter Rudge.

'Is that Bob Dylan?' I asked, unnecessarily.
'Yes.'
'Can you introduce me?'
Peter, whose staff I would join in 1977, gave me a wry look, then grinned.
'OK.'

We walked over to where Bob was standing and Peter tapped him on the shoulder, interrupting a conversation he was having with a pretty, dark-haired girl in a scarlet dress.
'Bob,' said Peter, 'this is Chris Charlesworth from *Melody Maker*.'
Bob looked at me and squinted. He did not offer a hand to shake. I was pretty sure he was drunk.
'*Melody Maker*,' he slurred. 'How's Max Jones?'
'Max is fine,' I replied. 'I'll tell him you asked after him.'
'You do that,' said Dylan. Then he turned away and resumed the conversation he was having before I intruded.
Come to think of it I'd have preferred to talk to the pretty girl in the scarlet dress too.

Chris Charlesworth, November 2017.

DULUTH ARMORY

31 JANUARY, 1959, DULUTH, IOWA

As a 17 year-old, Bobby Zimmerman saw Buddy Holly perform from the front row as part of the Winter Dance Party tour, at the Duluth Armory – an event that Dylan has mentioned many times throughout his career. Three days later on February 3, 1959, Buddy Holly along with Ritchie Valens, The Big Bopper, and pilot Roger Peterson all died in a plane crash near Clear Lake, Iowa.

What I got out of Buddy was that you can take influences from anywhere. Like his 'That'll Be The Day.' I read somewhere that it was a line he heard in a movie, and I started realising you can take things from everyday life that you hear people say. You can go anywhere in daily life and have your ears open and hear something, either something someone says to you or something you hear across the room. If it has resonance you can use it in a song.

BOB DYLAN

CRYSTAL BALLROOM
1959, FARGO, NORTH DAKOTA

I WAS THERE: BOB BECKER, GUITARIST, THE POOR BOYS

The Poor Boys had a great friend and follower named Ron Joelson. He was Jewish and when Bob Zimmerman came to Fargo, Ron's family befriended him and Bob lived with the family a few months. Ron mentioned that Bob played piano and said we should give him a try, so we did, but found Bob only played in the key of C and sometimes in the key of A.

We used him at the Crystal Ballroom in downtown Fargo one Saturday night. This ballroom was tops in Fargo, and if you worked for Doc Chinn, you were a top band! Doc was a big band man, and booked the big, popular, road band. He did not like Rock 'n' roll, but had to book some of us because big bands were slowly fading out and combos, etc., were becoming popular around the country. Anyway, Doc came to pay us and heard Bob sing a song and play piano, and was not impressed.

As I approached his office to get our money, he came out to meet me and said, 'That Guy's Gotta Go!' I nearly wet my pants for fear we were going to get fired! (I think Bob overheard it, as it echoed thru the ballroom.) But to not play at the Crystal Ballroom would have been a disaster for the Poor Boys, so I was forced to let him go. Bobby Vee hired Bob a couple weeks later, but also had to let him go! Bob was nice person, and it was hard for me to let him go.

I WAS THERE: JOHN BUCKLEN

Bob went off one summer (1959) for quite a while, and I knew he was spending some time in Fargo, North Dakota, playing with a group there called The Shadows – or so he said.

Now sometimes, as I said, he had this habit of putting people on, or making the truth a little different each time. So he came back one weekend and he was really telling me the ins and outs of show business, as far as making it is concerned – who you have to know, what you have to do. And I found this very fascinating because he seemed vastly knowledgeable. Anyway, a little while later, this record came out called 'Suzie Baby' by Bobby Vee, and I read of Bobby Vee being from Fargo, North Dakota and playing with this group called The Shadows. And so I sort of put one and a half and two together, and I came up with Bobby Zimmerman!

I was downtown one day and I saw Abe Zimmerman and I said, 'How's Bobby?' He said, 'Oh he's home now.' So I called, and I said, 'Whatcha been doin', Bob? Huh?' And he said, 'Well, I've been recording for this record label for a guy called Bobby Vee.' And I was really impressed, of course, because Bobby Vee was rather big in that particular area. Of course, we all know who Bobby Vee is now, but back then I just let it go at that. And by the time I got to know who Bobby Vee was, it didn't make much difference anyway.

I WAS THERE: BOBBY VEE

While The Shadows were on the road the summer of '59, we talked about how cool it would be to have a piano player in the band like Little Richard or Scotty What's-His-Name, with Gene Vincent. Not any old piano player, but someone who could put it down like Jerry Lee. But hey – the Fifties was about Fender guitars not pianos!

We couldn't find a rock 'n' roll piano player anywhere. Then one day my brother Bill came home and said he was talking with a guy at Sam's Record Land who claimed he played piano and had just come off of a tour with Conway Twitty. Bill made arrangements to audition him at the KFGO studio and said he was a funny, little, wiry kind of guy and he rocked pretty good. Wow! This must be the guy! He told Bill his name was 'Elston Gunnn' (with three Ns). Kind of weird, but let's try him out.

By now, we were making enough money to buy him a matching shirt and with that he was in The Shadows. His first dance with us was in Gwinner, North Dakota. All I remember is an old crusty piano that hadn't been tuned...ever! In the middle of 'Lotta Lovin'"' I heard the piano from hell go silent. The next thing I heard was the Gene Vincent handclaps, bap bap...bap...BAP BAP...BAP and heavy breathing next to my ear and I looked over to find Elston Gunnn dancing next to me as he broke into a background vocal part.

Obviously, he had also come to the conclusion that the piano wasn't working out. The next night was more of the same. He was good-spirited about the fact that none of us had the money to secure a piano for him, and there were no hard feelings on the part of anyone as he made his exit for the University of Minnesota. Bill was right. He sure had the spirit and he rocked out in the key of C. We felt bad that it didn't work out. Hey, he would have been great on the Floyd Cramer tunes.

That's basically the Bob Zimmerman story as it relates to The Shadows: Bob, aka Elston, aka Bob Dylan. It's been easy to chuckle and to minimise the story in view of Elston's amazing success. It was even suggested at one point that he had been fired. Not true. The truth is simple – it just didn't work out. What I remember most is his energy and spirit. Confident, direct and playful. A rock 'n' roll contender even then.

I WAS THERE: DERIK OLSON

At the young age of 12, David Hersk took an interest in the recording process after listening to a number of records that contained his Bar Mitzvah lessons. Hersk later started up a recording business and built a recording studio in his parents' basement in the mid-Fifties, and started the Gaity record label. David passed away July 19, 2016. I saw him about a month before at his home in Golden Valley. He was weak, but still smiling and talkative.

In 1958, David began to offer package deals to recording clients: for $495.00 individual artists or groups would get three hours of studio time and 1,000 45s pressed up on David's Gaity record label. Twenty-five of the 1,000 records were pressed on gold-coloured vinyl as promo copies, the rest were pressed on the standard black vinyl.

Many local acts recorded there: The String Kings; The Velquins; The Delricos; Jerry Robert and the Toppers; The Flames; The Wisdoms; Chuck Carson; Aldon and the ECs; Tommy Lee and the Orbits; Corvairs; Curtis and the Galaxies; Howie Butler and the Reflections; The Rhythm Rockers; Miller-Olsen Combo; Diane Edmond; and The Big M's.

David Hersk in his studio which was the home of Gaity Records

When I went to see him, I brought along my copy of The Blue Kats 45rpm disc, recorded for his Gaity record label, (they were the first group to record in his basement studio), which he inspected. He gave me some chocolate and other stuff that he couldn't eat due to the chemo treatments he was undergoing. I'm glad I went to visit him.

I have a story David never told publicly, but he shared with me at lunch one day:

In 1959, a group of folkies from Dinkytown came into his basement studio to record a few tracks. Among them was Bob Zimmerman. Bob sat down at the piano that David had in the studio. After banging away loudly for a few minutes, David asked him to stop, because he just wasn't making anything that sounded good to David's ears. David doesn't remember who the group was, or what they recorded. So that's the story of the almost first time Bob Dylan ever recorded in a studio. If that disc had been made, with Bob on it, it would be worth tens of thousands of dollars, I'm sure. David didn't want me to write about that story on my blog, for fear of backlash from Dylan. I assured him that I was sure he wouldn't care, or have any legal recourse even if he did. But David asked me to not share the story, so I didn't. Now that he is gone, I feel people should know about this little tidbit of Minnesota music history.

Though I only knew him the last two years of his life, I am richer for it.

GERDES FOLK CITY

GREENWICH VILLAGE, MANHATTAN, NEW YORK

I WAS THERE: MIKE PORCO

In 1952, my cousins bought a restaurant in The Village, an old place called Gerdes. One day, in late 1959, two guys walked in, Izzy Young and Tom Prendergast. They told me they were folk fans. I said, 'What's folk music?'

Izzy ran the Folklore Center and they kind of tried to explain to me the popularity of people like Pete Seeger, Joan Baez and Odetta. So, the folk tradition at Gerdes, which was renamed The Fifth Peg at Gerdes, began.

Gerdes Folk City was one of the most influential American music clubs located at 11 West 4th Street

Mondays were always slow nights on the New York club scene, so I wanted to try out the idea of an amateur talent night. I talked the idea over with Charlie Rothschild and Bob Shelton and they suggested I try a 'Hootenanny'. I figured it sounded better than 'amateur' nights, so Gerdes 'hoots' were born.

The 'hoots' went on all night and attracted many of the younger professionals who were still perfecting their craft: Judy Collins, Tom Paxton, Jack Elliott, Dave Van Ronk, even a very young Arlo Guthrie.

One day, this young boy came in asking to play. He said his name was Bob Dylan.

I WAS THERE: BARBARA SHUTNER

My husband, Logan English, and I met Bob Dylan at Bob and Sid Gleason's house. One night, we were all sitting around and Woody Guthrie said something like, 'Play something' to this kid sitting on the couch. The kid was Bob Dylan, and he sang and it was just beautiful. So Logan said, 'I'm working at Gerdes. I'm the MC. We'll get you to play there.' So that Monday night, Bob came in and did his first set.

I WAS THERE: TERRI THAL

We were active in left-wing organisations, and we talked politics. We talked theatre, art, and we brought the folk singers into that.

I WAS THERE: GEOFFREY STOKES

Bob Dylan, a woman known only as Fat Sybil, and I briefly, extremely briefly, formed a group called the White Horse Singers. We formed this group chiefly because I had my guitar with me and he didn't have his. We were truly terrible. We just played in Folk City's kitchen, totally one-shot.

I WAS THERE: CAROLYN HESTER, MUSICIAN

I was playing there for a week, I already had made two records, one for Coral, and the second for the Clancy Brothers label, Tradition, was just out, so I was a featured performer at Folk City, but I stopped by on hoot night, which was my night off to see what else was happening. And Bob was really startlingly different from almost everyone. He hadn't started writing an awful lot, but just as a performer he was so outstanding and magnetic. And afterwards we started talking. We talked about Buddy Holly and I told him that Buddy had actually helped me get recorded originally and he enjoyed that. But of course, I had no idea that Bob would be a rock 'n' roll musician eventually.

He surprised me by telling me that he had been to see Woody Guthrie, and I said, 'You've actually seen him? Isn't he very ill or something?' And he told me that he had gone to the hospital to see him, which was really surprising. I had never even thought of trying to do that myself. There were so many things about Bob that struck me. He was really different in every way.

I WAS THERE: ROGER MCGUINN, MUSICIAN

I first saw him at Gerdes Folk City. It was shortly after he moved to New York and he hadn't signed with Columbia Records yet. He was still just an itinerant folk singer.

He did a lot of Woody Guthrie stuff, covers, and kind of looked and sounded like Woody. But what was interesting about him was that most folk singers, like Cisco Houston, would get up and do a set and everybody would applaud.

But when Dylan played at Gerdes Folk City in the open-mic hootenannies, the girls would scream like he was a teen idol. That was different from what other folk singers evoked from an audience.

He wasn't doing a lot of original material, he wasn't doing his topical protest songs at that point. He was a good folk singer, he could carry a tune and he had the attitude and he was good at it. He knew his song well before he started singing.

When I first heard 'Mr. Tambourine Man' I was blown away by the imagery in it. We collected the verse about the boot heels because The Beatles wore those cool Cuban boots and it kind of reminded us of *On the Road* by Jack Kerouac, it had that kind of bohemian flavour to it.

But I think my favourite verse in 'Mr. Tambourine Man' is 'To dance beneath the diamond sky / With one hand waving free / Silhouetted by the sea / Circled by the circus sands /With all memory and fate / Driven deep beneath the waves / Let me forget about today until tomorrow.' That imagery is just incredible.

He was really a wonderful wordsmith. And his technique was great. He did inside rhymes, which was difficult. There'd be rhymes not just at the ends of sentences but inside the sentences. A sentence would have a rhyme in the middle of it that would rhyme with the middle of the next sentence. And then the ends would rhyme as well. So it's kind of doubling up on rhyming.

I WAS THERE: MARIA MULDAUR, SINGER, SONGWRITER

Johnny Herald from The Greenbriar Boys would keep saying to me, 'You've got to hear this guy Dylan. He's just fantastic. He's just amazing.' He dragged me to Gerdes to see Bob. Bob sang 'Talking Bear Mountain Picnic Blues,' and I wasn't that much impressed. It wasn't that musical.

A year passed, and one day Bob asked me if I wanted to hear a song he wrote, and he played 'Only a Pawn in Their Game.' The song just blew my mind. I suddenly understood what everybody was talking about. Instead of a lot of unmusical political complaining, which was how I perceived a lot of the protest-song style, this made sense.

Dylan's songs made me think. Instead of just reciting the obvious, he had a transcendent quality. It wasn't all black and white, and it wasn't so obvious who the villains were. Before this, it was just a lot of sloganeering going on.

The next time he played at Gerdes he sang 'Masters of War,' and that slayed me. That had me on the floor. Between the civil-rights movement and the whole Russian bomb scare and all that Cold War stuff that was going on, he started to really express it as an art form in a way that was multi-levelled and was very deep and went beyond any kind of party sloganeering. He completely raised my social consciousness.

I WAS THERE: PETER YARROW, SINGER, SONGWRITER

He was writing all the time, at night, sitting in the clubs. You'd see him reading a newspaper, and then the next day he wrote a song about what he had read. 'Blowin' in the Wind' was such a breakthrough, it was absolutely astonishing.

The 10 O'Clock Scholar was on the corner of 5th St and 14th Ave SE, and is where Dylan performed during his days as a fledgling Minneapolis folkie. The site is now a parking lot.

TEN O' CLOCK SCHOLAR

OCTOBER 1959, MINNEAPOLIS, MINNESOTA

I WAS THERE: ALLAN GARSKE

I was attending the University of Minnesota after I'd completed my military service. I was stationed at High Wycombe Air Force Base between 1955 – 1958 and when I got discharged I went back to college. Near the University was this small, commercial neighbourhood called Dinky Town and they had a coffee bar called the Ten O' Clock Scholar. It was a real tiny place where they would serve you coffee for 25 cents.

One day, when myself and my girlfriend (now my wife), Mary Phillips went into the bar, an eighteen-year-old Zimmerman was playing in the bar, just him and his guitar. There were about 10 other people in the room. At the time I was writing an entertainment column for the University of Minnesota paper. I wrote a review of seeing him perform, which was published either in the *Ivory Tower*, or *The Minnesota Daily* and was perhaps one of the first (if not the first) reviews of Dylan's music.

I didn't give him a good review because I thought he didn't sound like Burl Ives, who I liked at the time. Dylan, I thought had a real whiny voice and he was no Burl Ives as far as I was concerned!

After I'd given him the negative review, he did try to talk to me one day when we passed in the street but I had some of his fans screaming at me, so it never happened. I did see him playing again several times after that and I also saw him one night at a party, but I don't remember much about that night.

Some time after this, he decided to go to New York as there was a folk scene in Greenwich Village, which he plugged into.

Happy Traums' first appearance in a recording studio was at a historic session in 1963, when a group of young folk musicians, including Bob Dylan, Phil Ochs, Pete Seeger, Peter LaFarge and The Freedom Singers gathered in Folkways Records' studio for an album called Broadsides. Happy with his group, the New World Singers, cut the first recorded version of 'Blowin' in the Wind,' and Happy sang a duet with Dylan on his anti-war song 'Let Me Die in My Footsteps.'

I WAS THERE: HAPPY TRAUM, MUSICIAN

One of my happiest memories from that era was my first day as a teen-aged novice guitarist/folksinger, finding my way to Washington Square on a sunny Sunday afternoon and finding a park filled with like-minded players from all over the city, jamming on guitars, banjos, fiddles, mandolins and other acoustic instruments. They were playing bluegrass, folk songs, blues, ragtime, calypso, old-time and every other genre of 'folk music' you could think of. It was the start of many trips to the Village over the next decade.

Gil Turner and I began playing together, and I joined the New World Singers. We were the first to record 'Blowin' in the Wind' and 'Don't Think Twice It's All Right'. I first heard 'Blowin' in the Wind' in the so-called dressing room in the basement of Folk City.

Much later back in the late Sixties, Dylan said to me that Perry Como was the greatest living singer. I thought it was amusing at the time, but he was very serious and meant it.

1960

PIZZA VILLA

MARCH 1960, NEW YORK CITY, NEW YORK

I WAS THERE: BOB SCROGGINS

I was 21 years old and had known Bob Dylan for around two years.

I got to know Saint Paul, Minnesota and I got to know Bob Dylan because I got to know Bill Danielson. Bill owned the Pink Pizza Shack at Hiawatha and Lake in Minneapolis. In 1957, it was a hangout for me and my friends. Bill and his wife, MaryAnn, did pretty well there, but he wanted to be in Saint Paul, his hometown. He sold the Pizza Shack to brothers, Duane and Lonnie Anderson, who changed the name to Dulono's.

Bill then opened the Pizza Villa on West Seventh Street, about a mile from downtown. He was doing fairly well, but wanted to expand, so he leased a larger space near Hamline University and opened the Inn of the Purple Onion. I followed him from Minneapolis to West Seventh Street to the Purple Onion. I made pizza, waited on tables, washed dishes, and cleaned up after closing.

Bill wanted to attract the college crowd and hired young folk singers to come over when they weren't singing in Dinkytown. Performers included Spider John Koerner and Bob Dylan. Bill and I were impressed by Koerner's voice and style. But Dylan? I would tell my friends to come on the nights Koerner played. 'He might be famous someday. Bob Dylan is okay, but I don't like his voice and he's not great on guitar.' Even then, a teenager named Dave Ray was the best guitar player in that crowd.

There was an old upright piano at the Purple Onion. It was beat-up, but Bill had it tuned. Dylan would sometimes come over in the afternoon, looking for free pizza. He knew, as I did, Bill was a notorious soft touch. Dylan would play that old piano for groups of

Bob ran a bingo game with a traveling carnival during the summer of 1960, and below is Bob performing at a University of Minnesota student union show.

Hamline coeds. He would tell them he played piano for Bobby Vee, a pop singer of that time. Bill and I were sure he was lying. He wasn't that good at piano. Later I learned that he did play piano for Bobby Vee, but was fired. He really wasn't that good.

Bill and I doubted later Dylan stories. He said he met Pete Seeger in Chicago and played some of his own songs and Seeger said he would get him a gig in New York. We didn't believe him, but then it happened, and we know the rest.

Bill Danielson had a popular pizza place with great entertainment, and he was a really generous person – maybe too generous. Many Hamline students ran up tabs they never paid. He wouldn't even let me pay for my onion rings that last time I saw him at the State Fair, where the 'Danielson & Daughters' onion rings are now a tradition.

Working at the Purple Onion helped put me through college, and my first job after graduating was in Saint Paul. If I hadn't met Bill at the Pizza Shack in Minneapolis, I would have missed out on working near Hamline University, meeting Bob Dylan and Spider John, and eating those wonderful onion rings.

1961

CAFÉ WHA?

24 JANUARY, 1961, NEW YORK CITY, NEW YORK

I WAS THERE: JOHN BAULDIE

When Dylan first arrived in New York City on Tuesday, January 24, 1961, he caught a subway down to Greenwich Village and blew into the Café Wha? in a flurry of snowflakes. Dylan asked the owner, Manny Roth, if he could perform and he did, playing a short set of Woody Guthrie songs. In the following weeks, Dylan would appear occasionally at the coffeehouse, playing harmonica behind Mark Spoelstra and Fred Neil.

I WAS THERE: MARK SPOELSTRA

A friend of mine ran into me on the street one day and said there was a guy he thought I should meet. He was sitting alone in a joint, having just come to town. So I was one of the first acquaintances Bob Dylan met when he came to the big city. We hung out together a lot, because at the time we had a lot in common. One night we were playing at the Café Wha? and John Cohen, who was with the New Lost City Ramblers, came in and was blown away by my John Hurt style guitar and Bob's blues harp.

I WAS THERE: BOB NEUWIRTH

In those days, I was playing the banjo in folk clubs, thrashing away with a harmonica around my neck, and I saw this guy with a guitar who also had a harmonica around his neck and it was Bob Dylan. We all know these Hank Williams songs, and Jimmy Rodgers songs and Woody Guthrie songs and most folkies at the time weren't into that area. We met and we bonded and we became friends. This was way before he became famous.

Bob Dylan was like, damn, nobody could figure out what he was doing. It sort of sounded like you should understand it? And it had kinda country like to it, and a little folk here, and every now and then you would catch a 12 bar blues in there, but you just couldn't get your thumb on it. He inspired a lot of people. He inspired a lot of people that could write better. He inspired a lot of Nashville songwriters.

I WAS THERE: ALLEN GINSBERG

I first met Bob at a party at the Eighth Street Book Shop, and he invited me to go on tour with him. I ended up not going, but, boy, if I'd known then what I know now, I'd have gone like a flash. He'd probably have put me onstage with him.

CAFÉ WHA?

FEBRUARY 1961, NEW YORK CITY, NEW YORK

I WAS THERE: DAVID GEDALECIA

A bluegrass trio I was a part of, the Stony Island Boys (Mike Michaels, mandolin; Jon Aaron, guitar; me, banjo), were featured at the first University of Michigan Folk Festival in 1961. I think it must have taken place in the spring of that year at Hill Auditorium or Rackham Auditorium. Earlier, in February 1961, at the University of Chicago Folk Festival, our group was rehearsing and a raggedy guy came and listened to us for a half hour or so, bobbing up and down. When I asked who he was, after he left, Mike Michaels said that he was this guy called Bob Dylan who travelled around doing mostly Woody Guthrie songs. Since there were quite a few in the folk crowd doing that, my response was, 'well, that's cool,' and we continued the rehearsal. The next time I saw him, in the fall of 1961, at Gerdes Folk City in New York's Greenwich Village, he opened for the Greenbriar Boys, got rave reviews in the *New York Times*, and the rest is history.

I WAS THERE: BARRY KORNFELD, MUSICIAN

I first met Dylan in 1961, hanging out in the Village scene, and he of course was at that point the main Woody Guthrie disciple. At that time

Woody was in Brooklyn State Mental Hospital and I had a car! So Dylan came by and said let's go out and see Woody Guthrie, so we did and arrived there.

It was a depressing place; it was a little grey and seedy. Woody was in a bad place, the Huntington's Disease had advanced to the point where he really couldn't speak, and I certainty didn't understand what he said, but Bob did and what was interesting is that Woody would have Dylan sing Woody's songs because he couldn't do it himself. We spent quite a bit of time doing that. Dylan brought him a pack of cigarettes and the first thing Woody did was to tear open the pack and walk around the ward to all the other patients handing out the cigarettes, and to do this, because of the state he was in, Woody had to hang on the wall as he walked. It was typical of Woody Guthrie that he would have done that.

IDA NOYES HALL

SPRING 1961, CHICAGO, ILLINOIS

I WAS THERE: MIKE MICHAELS

A student named Mike Fleischer decided to start a folk festival to emulate the one at Newport, Rhode Island. It took a lot of moxie to do this, a quality not at all lacking in the character of this young man, and he pulled it off. The festival's opening reception took place on a Friday evening in Ida Noyes Hall and was filled with performers and students from the University and nearby colleges. It was the height of the folk boom, and having a guitar or banjo was almost as necessary as having a toothbrush – maybe more so.

So the instruments were out and the jams were on. I was standing there observing the scene when my roommate, Jon Aaron said, 'Mike, this is amazing. There's the Stanley Brothers, headlining bluegrass musicians Carter and Ralph Stanley, over in that room and a gang of musicians in the other, and over in that little alcove is this strange-looking guy with a funny hat and a harmonica rack playing his own songs with his guitar!' I looked over, and there he was – funny hat, pudgy face, harmonica in rack, and a guitar. A few minutes later, I had joined the jamming on my mandolin, with my bluegrass buddies, Jon on guitar and David Gedalecia on banjo.

Soon I noticed the guy with the funny hat right next to us, bobbing and bouncing to our music. Well, I figured if he liked us he must be OK, so I introduced myself. He told me that his name was Bob Dylan. It turned out that we both loved Woody Guthrie, and we spent a lot of time that weekend playing together in the dorm. Dylan said he was from New Mexico and that his parents were ranchers. I had no reason not to believe him.

On April 11, 1961, Bob Dylan played his first major gig in New York. It was the first night of a two-week run opening for the great bluesman John Lee Hooker at Gerdes Folk City in Greenwich Village.

GERDES FOLK CITY

11 APRIL, 1961, NEW YORK CITY, NEW YORK

I WAS THERE: TOM PAXTON, MUSICIAN

One night in Greenwich Village, Dave Van Ronk and I had already done our three songs apiece, and we were sitting there, drinking beer and this scruffy kid in a black corduroy cap, a harmonica rack, and I think a Gibson guitar got up and sang three Woody Guthrie songs. Both Dave and I, who were not easy said, yeah, not bad, this guy's all right. And then in next to no time, Bob Dylan was the most talked about and agued about artist in the Village. They were accusing him of being a Woody Guthrie clone, which was nonsense, he didn't sound like Woody Guthrie. Jack Elliot in his early days sounded much more like Woody than Bob ever did. But Bob had a tremendous repertoire of Woody Guthrie songs; he knew Guthrie songs that no one else knew.

I liked his writing right from the beginning. One night at The Gaslight, which was a place were most of us worked, (down in the cellar, about eight steps into the coffee house, no booths), it wasn't a large place at all. Upstairs on the first floor, at the back, there was a little apartment, which The Gaslight owned. It was like a storage room. We set up a table and had a poker game, which was continuous, and my roommate at the time was a guy called Hugh Romney, who later became known as Wavy Gravy. He was a Beat poet.

He had this portable typewriter, which he had left in this room. One night, I came in early for work and Bob was in there tap, tap, tapping away on this thing and had just finished a long poem and he said, 'What do you think of this?' I looked at this thing and I said, 'Well it's wild imagery. What are you going to do with it? Are you going to put music to it?' And he said, 'Well, do you think I should?' And I said, 'Yeah, otherwise its just going to go in some literary quarterly or something. This way you might get a song out of it.'

So the next night, Bob never worked at The Gaslight, but he was there a lot, and he would get up late at night and do a set. He got up and he sang this new song called 'A Hard Rain's a-Gonna Fall'.

Nowadays, when I hear him sing it, and he gets into what seems like the twentieth minute, I think, did I make the right decision in advising him to make it into a song?

I WAS THERE: BONNIE DOBSON, SINGER, SONGWRITER

I was booked for two weeks at Gerdes playing with Big Joe Williams. It was great fun and that's where I met Dylan and Robert Shelton. He was the New York Times critic who chronicled the folk revival.

Hoot nights at Gerdes were fabulous – just look at who got up to sing: Richie Havens, when no one knew who he was, Simon and Garfunkel, when they were still Tom and Jerry – I remember vividly standing at the bar and thinking: those guys are good. I saw Dylan there.

Dylan was always at the typewriter and I think that night he was writing 'Boots of Spanish Leather' because Suze Rotolo had gone off to Italy and I'd just broken up with the guy I was seeing, so I was also pretty miserable. Not a lot was said that night!

I WAS THERE: MARK JACOBSON

Staying at the $19-a-week Earle Hotel, Dylan had to walk across Washington Square Park to get to Gerdes on 4th Street, three blocks to the south. Not yet 20, he was just one more busker carrying his guitar and wearing a stupid corduroy cap.

Forty years later, fans can go to the Dylan websites and find the set list. Just five tunes, as many as any opening act got, especially when opening for John Lee Hooker: 'House of the Rising Sun,' 'Song to Woody,' 'Talkin' Hava Negeilah Blues,' and two others, identified only as 'unknown Woody Guthrie song' and 'a black blues.'

There were earlier nights, at Izzy Young's Folklore Center on MacDougal Street and out in East Orange (where Dylan played Jimmie Rodgers's 'Southern Cannonball'); later, there was Carnegie Hall, and the gone-electric boos at Forest Hills. But Gerdes was the official coming out, the start. Unlike most Dylan shows, no one recorded it, so we don't know if he did Rising Sun in the persona of a 90-year-old syphilitic whore, like on his first album, or how much Zimmerman showed through on Hava Negeilah. But this is good, this mystery, because with Bob, sometimes, not everything is revealed.

I WAS THERE: JOAN BAEZ, MUSICIAN

I think the first time I saw Bob was in Gerdes Folk City, he was just standing up there, a kid and singing things he wrote that I thought were phenomenal and I think the next time I saw him was in somebody's apartment and he was singing A Hard Rain, which he had just written. It's just hard to believe the words that he wrote, the stuff that came out, it just poured and poured and poured.

The music scene I was more involved in was in Cambridge, and I just sang Tuesdays and Fridays at a club in Harvard Square, and would go on little forays into New York City, because I was young and intimidated by all that. So I was at Gerdes maybe three or four times. I never did a gig there, officially. I sang with Bob a couple of times impromptu, and that's also where I met him and saw him for the first time. I went to the Café Wha? and a couple of other places.

But I didn't hang out a lot in New York City. I was very aware that that's where everything was happening.

After we became friends, we sang together a couple of times, in fact one night at Gerdes we were up on stage making up a song together, 'Troubled and I Don't Know Why.'

I remember leaving Gerdes Folk City, and I heard Bob do 'Blowin' in the Wind,' maybe not the first time, but he had just written it. And I got in a cab and I was so excited. Bob put me in the cab, actually, and I drove off and I wanted the world to know I'd been in on this phenomenal episode, this incredible new song. And I was telling the New York cab driver about it. I said, 'You wouldn't believe this guy. I mean, this is amazing. This is real poetry.' He said, 'Does it rhyme?' I said, 'Yeah.' He says, 'Okay.' He wasn't impressed. But something in me knew, probably, it was one of those songs that would last forever.

I WAS THERE: OSCAR BRAND

I went with Dave van Ronk to see Dylan's early performances at Folk City. I thought Bob was pretty crummy. He was a pale version of Woody, and I thought some of his songs were maladroit. Once in a while, he would hit the right element of poetry. He was like Woody, in that he wrote bad and he wrote good. When he wrote good, he was a genius. He was a performer of some considerable fire; and that makes you overlook a lot of things.

I WAS THERE: DAVID CROSBY, MUSICIAN

I was a young, not quite starving folkie in Greenwich Village, working in the basket houses. That's where you sing a set and then you pass a basket. If you did a really good job, you might be able to get that piece of pizza for dinner. Maybe. And you gotta be really good to get it. And it's humiliating and humbling to have to stand in front of people with a basket and say, 'Would you please give me a dollar?' It's a good lesson.

OK, so I hear about this guy Bob Dylan, gonna play at Gerdes Folk City. And everybody was talking about him. I didn't know why.

So I snuck in, got in close, and the first reaction I had was very egotistical: 'Well, shit, I can sing better than that!' And then I started listening to the words. And I nearly quit right then.

The guy's such a good poet. He's such a good poet, holy shit, is he a good poet. And I was pretty stunned.

I walked out of there very confused, because I knew I could sing better and I knew that I just had to up my game about words a thousand percent.

He was a terrific inspiration to me in the sense that I knew I had to become a much better poet. And so I tried my best to do that.

Between September 25 and October 8, 1961, Bob Dylan was the supporting act for The Greenbriar Boys at Gerdes Folk City. The Greenbriar Boys were a Northern bluegrass group who first got together in jam sessions in New York's Washington Square Park. Along with the New Lost City Ramblers, their urban traditional country sound inspired a generation of musicians and fans.

I WAS THERE: JOHN HERALD, THE GREENBRIAR BOYS

Dylan took us by storm when he opened for us that gig. He was getting a bigger hand than we were. We were supposed to be the main act, and he just won the place over.

I WAS THERE: LOUDON WAINWRIGHT III, SINGER, SONGWRITER

I heard Dylan maybe in 1961 or 1962. I heard his records, *The Freewheelin' Bob Dylan*, which was his second record, first. I kinda didn't like it that much. I remember a friend of mine was very excited about it and I was not enthralled. It sounded like an old black blues singer, it was somebody impersonating, those earlier records, to me.

Then I went to the Newport Folk Festival at some point in the early Sixties and I saw him play. And that was kind of a shattering experience because he was so charismatic and just this kind of scruffy, skinny guy.

Blonde on Blonde is a magical record, the songs are great, the lyrics are amazing. It's still kind of painful to listen to it – it's just so good. Even though it's a young man, probably on drugs, and the imagery is sometimes a little silly, but it's the power of the performance, the harmonica playing, the singing, and the production.

On September 29, 1961, Robert Shelton, a music critic at The *New York Times*, wrote a 400-word piece in the paper in which he welcomed 'a bright new face in folk music ... one of the most distinctive stylists to play a Manhattan cabaret in months.'

The next day, Columbia Records producer John Hammond, who had first heard Dylan two weeks earlier playing harmonica on a session for Carolyn Hester, invited him to his office and offered Dylan a recording contract.

I WAS THERE: JOHN HAMMOND

Here we have a guy, who in a way was a revolutionary, he was talking about race discrimination, which was a taboo subject, he was talking about war profiteers, he was talking about all the things that were no-no's, you couldn't talk about them in the pop music business, but he talked about them. He didn't like the people who controlled the industry in this country and he figured out that I was an honest man – so he signed with me.

As soon as I heard Dylan I knew that he needed a country background, he needed the kind of musicians we didn't have in New York, the kind of people who worked with Johnny Cash.

> Resembling a cross between a choir boy and a beatnik, Mr. Dylan has a cherubic look and a mop of tousled hair he partly covers up with a Huck Finn black corduroy cap. His clothes may need a bit of tailoring, but when he works his guitar, harmonica or piano and composes new songs faster than he can remember them, there is no doubt that he is bursting at the seams with talent.

ROBERT SHELTON
THE NEW YORK TIMES

Suze Rotolo was a 17-year-old art and poetry-loving Civil Rights activist from Queens when she met the 20-year-old folk singer from Minnesota at an all-day folk concert at Riverside Church in Manhattan in the summer of 1961. She became the girlfriend of Dylan from 1961 to 1964. Dylan later acknowledged her strong influence on his music and art during that period.

Rotolo was pictured walking arm-in-arm with Dylan down a partially snow-covered New York City street on the cover of his 1963 album *The Freewheelin' Bob Dylan*, a photograph taken by the Columbia Records studio photographer Don Hunstein.

I WAS THERE: SUZE ROTOLO

I was exposed to all different kinds of music from a very early age. When you grow up in that, you just assume everybody else knows this.

Bob was charismatic: he was a beacon, a lighthouse, he was also a black hole. He required committed backup and protection I was unable to provide consistently, probably because I needed them myself. I could no longer cope with all the pressure, gossip, truth and lies that living with Bob entailed. I was unable to find solid ground. I was on quicksand and very vulnerable.

Dylan made me think of Harpo Marx, impish and approachable, but there was something about him that broadcast an intensity that was not to be taken lightly.

People say I was an influence on him, but we influenced each other. His interests were filtered through me, and my interests, like the books I had, were filtered through him. It was always sincere on his part. The guy saw things. He had an incredible ability to see and sponge – there was a genius in that. The ability to create out of everything that's flying around. To synthesise it. To put it in words and music.

The Sixties were an era that spoke a language of inquiry and curiosity and rebelliousness against the stifling and repressive political and social culture of the decade that preceded it. The new generation causing all the fuss was not driven by the market: we had something to say, not something to sell.

For the photo he wore a very thin jacket, because image was all. Our apartment was always cold, so I had a sweater on, plus I borrowed one of his big, bulky sweaters. On top of that I put a coat. So I felt like an Italian sausage.

I've always been a shy person, so to have this relationship thrown right out there in public was very horrible. I see that that was just his way of working through it, making it part of his art, but at the time I just felt so exposed.

GERDES FOLK CITY

MAY 1961, NEW YORK CITY, NEW YORK

I WAS THERE: BONNIE BEECHER

He came to my apartment and said, 'It's an emergency! I need your help! I gotta go home an' see my mother!' He was talking in the strangest Woody Guthrie-Oklahoma accent. I don't know if she was sick, but it was an unexpected trip he had to make up to Hibbing and he wanted me to cut his hair. He kept saying, 'Shorter! Shorter! Get rid of the sideburns!' So I did my very best to do what he wanted and then in the door came Dave Morton, Johnny Koerner, and Harvey Abrams. They looked at him and said, 'Oh my God, you look terrible! What did you do?' And Dylan immediately said, 'She did it! I told her just to trim it up a little bit but she cut it all off. I wasn't looking in a mirror!' And then he went and wrote that song 'Bonnie, why'd you cut my hair? Now I can't go nowhere!'

He played it that night in a coffeehouse and somebody told me recently that they had been to Minnesota and somebody was still playing that song, 'Bonnie, Why'd You Cut My Hair?' It's like a Minnesota classic! And so I've gone down in history!

CAFFÈ LENA

JUNE 1961, SARATOGA SPRINGS, NEW YORK

I WAS THERE: ANTHONY SCADUTO

Dylan wasn't too well received at Caffè Lena. At one point it was so noisy in the place that Bill Spencer, (the owner), had to get on the stage and tell the audience to quiet down. He told the audience, 'You may not know what this kid is singing about and you may not care, but if you don't stop and listen you will be stupid all the rest of your lives. Listen to him, dammit.' His little speech didn't help much, Dylan's two-night stand was not an overwhelming success.

The Café Espresso opened its doors in 1962, ushering in a new music scene that would become famous worldwide. Folksingers came from all over to play here including Bob Dylan, Rambling Jack Elliot, Joan Baez and Peter of Peter, Paul and Mary. There is a room upstairs that Dylan retreated to when he needed a quiet place to work. The White Room with a view of Tinker Street is where it is said he wrote some of the songs to *Another Side of Bob Dylan*.

CAFÉ ESPRESSO

SUMMER 1961, WOODSTOCK, NEW YORK

I WAS THERE: HAPPY TRAUM, MUSICIAN

The first time I actually played in Woodstock was in 1962 in the dead of winter at the Café Espresso. The Café Espresso started out as a little coffee shop called The Nuck, and in 1962, Bernard Paturel moved in and took it over along with his wife Mary Lou, who was a wonderful cook, and they had a bunch of kids. They lived in the apartment above the cafe and very often, when visiting folk singers like myself would come to play there, we would stay upstairs with the

family and we would eat with them. It was a very warm scene.

The Café Espresso was kind of a gathering place; it was a cosy room with a wood-burning fireplace in the middle and folksingers would come up from various places, mostly New York City, and play for the locals. It was very informal, all the town characters would gather there and it was a very warm and welcoming atmosphere, which was one of the things that made me love coming to Woodstock to play. The food was good, the drinks were good, hospitality was excellent. It was just a fun place, but in a very small scale; it was it was a tiny place and maybe they could squeeze in 50 people. It was a very nice place to come to and experience as a musician.

I WAS THERE: MARLENA YANNETTI, AGE 22

I was around 22 at the time. I danced at the Robert Joffrey Studio. I knew Bob in New York primarily during the summer of 1962. We became friends. I was singing at a place called The Third Side. John Herald of the Greenbriar boys introduced me to Maria Muldaur and suggested we form a group, which we did with Artie Traum.

I believe it was the fall of 1962, and I had been singing with Maria Muldaur and Bob saw us sing and we had this conversation about music and what was happening in the city.

I was working in a restaurant called The In, which was upstairs from 'the out' on McDougall Street. Bob didn't have any money for dinner, so sometimes he would come in and I would share my dinner with him or I'd get some of the cooks to get him some food to eat.

The title we chose for our band was the Poolenoode Family, a nod to Charlie Poole and we sang at Gerdes Folk City and Bob was there. He was sitting with us at the table and he said, 'you've got to have a name for this group,' and he wrote down all of these possible names of groups for us. One of my favourites was Brute, The Deaf Mute, The Cockeyed Dude and the Lonesome Nude. I kept that, this piece of paper with all these titles for names for groups in Bob's handwriting.

Later that night, Bob asked me if I wanted to go to a party on Eighth St. The Clancy Brothers, who had been playing in New York City were going back to Ireland, so they were throwing a party. We arrived and it was very noisy, Bob and I were sitting on this couch and Liam Clancy picked up his guitar and walked over to us. He didn't look at us, but looked at the wall behind us, and he started singing 'Eileen Aroon'. At this party there were around 30 people in the room all talking and drinking and making a noise, and when he got to about half way through the song it all went quiet and you could hear a pin drop because he sang it so beautifully.

I hung out with Bob for the rest of the summer, we went to parties, we would go the The Gaslight and other places. There was so much great music and great performers hanging out at that time in all these great clubs. I eventually left the Village to go on tour with the National Company of 'How To Succeed In Business Without Really Trying'.

> There was a violent, angry emotion running through me then. I just played the guitar and harmonica and sang those songs and that was it. Mr. Hammond asked me if I wanted to sing any of them over again and I said no. I can't see myself singing the same song twice in a row. That's terrible.

BOB DYLAN
1962

The self-titled debut album to be released by Robert Allen Zimmerman (he did not legally change his name until August 1962) was released on March 19, 1962, on Columbia Records.

Recorded over two, three-hour sessions under the guidance of legendary CBS producer John Hammond, the album features 11 folk standards, plus two original compositions, 'Talkin' New York' and 'Song to Woody'.

His debut, which cost the princely sum of $402 to record, sold a paltry five thousand copies in its first year and earned Dylan the derisory title of Hammond's Folly by many who saw Hammond's belief in him misplaced.

FOLKLORE MUSIC FESTIVAL

21 APRIL, 1962, MICHIGAN

I WAS THERE: MARIE KIMMEY

I think we paid him 50 bucks. At that time he was still not known, and we actually had people complain, 'Who's this guy? What's he doing? He plays harmonica and talks. We want our money back!' But we were thrilled to be pulling this off – and for only 50 bucks. We knew he was going to go places, and he did, within a year or two.

He's about two years younger than me, and I thought he was pretty immature. I noticed that he usually had a pretty girl with him.

I really liked Dylan's talking blues stuff, which was pretty much what he was doing then. But in Ann Arbor at that time, the large majority of the students were of a preppy kind and not so much into what we were enjoying. I'm sure there were people who loved it. But a lot of the crowd didn't understand it.

I WAS THERE: HUGH 'JEEP' HOLLAND, MICHIGAN DAILY

As colourful as his red-checkered shirt, as lively as his skipping fingers, as dynamic as his wild harmonica, and as ethnic and varied as his audience, Bob Dylan proved his reputation as one of the most promising new stars in folk singing Sunday. While his guitar playing was intricate and strong, it was the combination of his frantic harmonica and his trance-like, searching voice that most enthralled the audience. Catching a note, Dylan would wrestle with it and squeeze every meaning and emotion from it, only to go after another and another.

Asked how he likes singing as a career, Bob Dylan answered that it was fine but that he'd rather be riding his motorcycle around the country. With his talent, and the hearty approval he receives wherever he performs, he's not likely to ride that cycle for a long, long time. Bob Dylan is bound for other roads right now.

UNION BALLROOM

22 APRIL, 1962, ANN ARBOR, MICHIGAN

I WAS THERE: JAY MARGULIES

I went to the hootenanny in April 1962. I was in my last term at the University, living on E Washington, just off State St. I wasn't planning to go, but while at a laundromat that evening, I saw the flyer. My memory is that I decided to walk two blocks to the Frieze Building and see the concert. I don't remember much of it – though I think it was the first time I'd seen any musician with headgear to support his harmonica – but I have a vivid memory of Bob Dylan at the party afterwards. For at least an hour, Dylan and a local musician I knew, Mike Scherker, sat opposite each other on beds, playing their guitars alternately and together. Mike was by far the more accomplished musician, but Dylan had a focus and intensity about his music that was memorable. Mike was playing for fun, Dylan to learn and improve.

On July 2, 1962, Dylan performed for the first time outside of the US on July 2, 1962 when he appeared at the Finjan Club, Montreal. July also saw more recording sessions for the Freewheelin' album and Dylan signing with the Witmark Music Publishing Company.

THE GASLIGHT CAFÉ

SEPTEMBER 1962, NEW YORK CITY, NEW YORK

I WAS THERE: AL ARONOWITZ

The Village Gaslight. That was the club's official name. Some people liked to call it the Gaslight Cafe. For 13 years, it had been one of America's leading folk music clubs, a Mecca for every kid who ever had picked up an acoustic guitar and tried to sing a Woody Guthrie tune.

The Gaslight was at 116 MacDougal Street, with its twin entrances at the bottom of a pair of deceptive stone stairways, located on either side of the flight of steps leading to the shops above. The past fades fast. Walk past that address today and there isn't a clue that 116 MacDougal Street was a landmark where music archaeologists ought to start digging.

John Mitchell was a celebrity on the MacDougal Street of the late Fifties. Greenwich Village already was long established as America's Left Bank, where the rents were still cheap enough for starving artists and runaway kids and where Italian bars and restaurants shared the street with silversmiths and sandal makers and dress designers. Picturesque MacDougal Street was turning into Boutique Row. It already had won fame as a hangout for America's avant-garde and its sidewalks were always full of suburban middle class hordes, arriving like sight-seeing tourists coming to behold the Grand Canyon. This was when the painters and poets and other arty types were still called Bohemians. This was when the Village became my beat for the *New York Post*.

The Village Gaslight started out as one of the first of the Village's basket houses, so-called because the entertainers got paid by passing a basket through the audience. The basket houses represented a new twist to the coffee house concept by offering poetry along with the pastry. This was in the Beat Generation days, predating the folkie tidal wave which later rolled in with Joan Baez and Bob Dylan riding its crest. This was in the Beat Generation days when Allen Ginsberg and Gregory Corso read their poetry at the Gaslight. Hugh Romney also read his poetry there and then reappeared as another persona, Wavy Gravy, the legendary clown, comedian, and founder of the communal Hog Farm. Len Chandler also started out as a poet at the Gaslight before he became the biggest folk music star MacDougal Street had ever seen until then. One of the

Gaslight's MCs was Noel Stookey, who later became the Paul of Peter, Paul and Mary. Paul's first gig was at the Gaslight. This was in the days when every truck driver would holler, 'Hey, beatnik!' at every man wearing a beard. This was when beer-drinkers from Jersey would look for Saturday night entertainment by driving into the Village to beat on beatniks. This was when MacDougal Street was still a Little Italy and the small kids, young hoods, and old toughs on the block would drop water bombs from their upper tenement windows onto the clogged sidewalk traffic below. The cops kept trying to close down the Gaslight. They wrote summonses because there was no soap in the bathroom or because there were no lids on the garbage pails. When the neighbours complained about the noise in the Gaslight, the audience was asked to applaud by snapping its fingers.

Music in the walls? It was such a dirty, crumbly, decaying place that at first Sam's image made me think of music infesting the walls of the old Gaslight like tuberculosis bacilli surviving in the walls of a slum tenement. But after a while, I began to like the romance of the phrase. Music in the walls? I began to think of music embedded in the walls the way music is embedded in a phonograph record. Were CDs invented at the time? How do you get to the music in the walls? How do you rediscover it? Do you dig like an archaeologist?

'I think Mississippi John Hurt put more music in the walls than anybody else,' Sam mused. 'I remember his second night in New York. He had just been rediscovered. He was right in the middle of a song and he walked off stage. The place was packed. I thought he was sick or something and I ran up to him. He said, 'I just had to take a pee!'

And there was Ramblin' Jack Elliott, and the night Johnny Cash stopped in to do a guest show, and Joan Baez singing along with a Doc Watson hymn and then, seven years later, singing along from the audience with Kris Kristofferson. There were a thousand things like that. And the nights when Bob Dylan would come in to work out a new song, to try it out in front of an audience. He did Hard Rain and 'Masters of War' for the first time in the Gaslight. Until 1965, whenever he got a new song worked out, he would stop into the Gaslight unannounced to try it out in front of an audience. I remember the night of the Cuban Missile Crisis. We closed early and sat around the big table: Dylan, Dave Van Ronk, Tom Paxton and Luke Faust. We said it was all over, the end of the world. Everybody just played music for themselves, with no audience. Those were the best nights.

I WAS THERE: RICHARD ALDERSON, SOUND ENGINEER

I recorded the Gaslight tapes in late 1962, although oddly the producers don't claim to have found any threads leading back to me, in spite of being told by the owner of The Gaslight (Sam Hood) that I was the engineer. I had made some improvements in the sound system at The Gaslight and I used my own microphones and a small 5 inch reel, 7.5 ips portable tape machine to record Dylan at these more or less 'invitation only' performances. I have some of these original tapes, and they are of higher quality than those issued. There are several living witnesses who can testify that I was the one who recorded these performances. In fact, at the time, I played these tapes for Dylan in my studio at Carnegie Hall and I also gave copies to his management.

I have never received any credit on the many issues on Sony/Columbia of these recordings either. It has always seemed odd to me that Dylan would not remember any of this. I have never sold, distributed, or given Dylan's (or other artists') audio material to anyone for the purpose of bootlegging or profit.

'Don't Think Twice, It's All Right' was written by Bob Dylan in 1962, and recorded on November 14 that year, and released on the 1963 album *The Freewheelin' Bob Dylan* and as a single.

I WAS THERE: BARRY KORNFELD

American folksinger Paul Clayton had a copyright on a song called 'Who's Gonna Buy Your Ribbons When I'm Gone.' The lyrics are 'Ain't no use to sit and sigh; ain't no use to sit and wonder why, tell me, who's gonna buy your ribbons when I'm gone.'

I was with Paul one day, and Bob Dylan wanders by and says, 'Hey, man, that's a great song. I'm going to use that song.' And he wrote a far better song, a much more interesting song, 'Don't Think Twice.'

When it became a legal question, the song was actually

traced down to a song that was exactly the same as Paul's called, 'Who's Gonna Buy Your Chickens When I'm Gone.' So, in effect, everything that Dylan took was actually public domain. They remained friends, but their publishing companies were suing each other, (they eventually settled out of court).

Paul was gay, which was something he could not live with. Paul had a tremendous crush on Dylan. I believe that 'It Ain't Me, Babe' was written for Paul Clayton.

On March 30, 1967, Clayton committed suicide by taking an electric heater into his bathtub with him. He is buried at Oak Grove Cemetery, New Bedford, Massachusetts. In 1970, Bob Dylan covered Clayton's song 'Gotta Travel On' as track 14 of his album *Self Portrait*.

❛Part of Dylan's magnetism lies in the fact that he is not the slightest bit afraid of falling flat on his face. If he gets an idea for a song or a story, he does it on the spot without worrying about whether it will come out exactly polished and right❜

SING OUT!
OCTOBER 1962

On December 14, 1962, Columbia Records released Bob Dylan's first single 'Mixed-Up Confushion'. The track was recorded with George Barnes on guitar, Bruce Langhorne on guitar, Dick Wellstood on piano, Gene Ramey on bass, and Herb Lovelle on drums on November 14, 1962, during the sessions for *The Freewheelin' Bob Dylan* but was not included on the album.

Bob Dylan first visited Britain to take part in a BBC play. It was

the coldest winter on record and the 21 year-old singer's first-ever trip outside America.

Dylan had seized an invitation from the UK and flew into London Airport. Dylan headed straight, not to the folk clubs of the capital, but to rehearsals for a BBC television play called *The Madhouse on Castle Street*, where Dylan was to take the lead role of Lennie, 'an anarchic young student who wrote songs'.

Dylan sang four songs in the production, including the first ever broadcast of 'Blowin' in the Wind'.

Screened on the BBC on January 13, 1963, five years later, in an act of possibly deliberate cultural vandalism, the corporation destroyed the tapes of the recording, and no copy of it has ever yet surfaced.

THE KING AND QUEEN

21 DECEMBER, 1962, LONDON

I WAS THERE: JIM McLEAN

I was there that night as my mate Nigel Denver was doing a spot, as were the Thames Side Four, and my future wife, Alison Chapman McLean, the photographer, was on the door. I didn't recognise Dylan, but when he came in with his guitar and I asked him if he wanted to sing, he declined and sat near the back.

I mentioned to Martin Carthy that an American kid with a guitar had come in and perhaps he should ask him to sing, which he did. Dylan and I had a chat in the interval, downstairs in the toilet, where I offered to share my half bottle of whisky with him and Nigel, but he declined.

We talked about a few things and he asked me if I was Hamish Henderson (Nigel had been singing some of my songs). I was hovering at the door that night as I was 'courting' and preferred my future wife's company to the singing, so I witnessed Bob coming in.

SINGERS CLUB, PRINCESS LOUSIE

22 DECEMBER, 1962, LONDON

I WAS THERE: PEGGY SEEGER, MUSICIAN

Somebody's whispered, 'Bob Dylan's here' and I said, 'Who is Bob Dylan?' I didn't really know who he was, but I do remember he was very withdrawn and when he stood up to sing he made literally no impression, because you couldn't hear him singing. But he did one song, and stepped down.

What might have puzzled Dylan was the non-nightclub atmosphere the folk clubs had. There were no lights, there were no microphones, there was no ritualised nightlife to it. It was a bunch of ordinary people coming to their pub.

THE KING AND QUEEN

23 DECEMBER, 1962, LONDON

I WAS THERE: MARTIN CARTHY, MUSICIAN

I saw his picture on the front of *Sing Out!*, whenever the hell that was. I suppose it was sometime in 1962 when they printed 'Song For Woody' and 'Blowin' in the Wind'. But there was also an interview with him and they were all very excited about him.

And just a few weeks later I saw him sitting in the audience in The King and Queen. There were very few clubs in London at that time and visiting Americans used to just make a bee-line for the few ones there were and, you know, anything that was loosely folky. And one of the clubs was a club I used. I used to be in a group called The Thameside Four – in the days when there were groups, not bands.

The Thameside Four ran a club at this pub called The King and Queen, behind Goodge Street Station, next to the Middlesex Hospital, and I saw this bloke sitting in the audience and I recognised him, and I went up to him in the interval and I said, 'Excuse me, your name is Bob Dylan isn't it?' He looked up and he said, 'Yes' and I said, 'Do you fancy singing?' and he said, 'No' and I said, 'Oh, all right' and he said, 'Well, maybe I will later on; ask me later.' So l said, 'OK.'

We got up in the second half and sang a few songs and I sang a couple of songs and I just looked across and nodded and he just nodded his head, and I called him up, gave him an introduction and said I'd seen a couple of his songs printed and they looked really nice songs and this was him and he stood up sang. As far as I know that was the first time he sang in England.

He asked about other places to go, and I told him there was The Troubadour on a Saturday and a Tuesday night. We were involved in both of those. At The Troubadour on a Saturday night, I was basically their resident singer at that time and The Thameside Four had a night at the Troubadour on Tuesday, and he came along to both of those. He also went to Bunjies, I think, and he went to the Singers' Club and sang there. I don't remember when it was, maybe the Saturday following that Friday when I saw him at The King and Queen or perhaps the following Saturday.

When he stood up and started to perform at The King and Queen, it was just... the audience knew they were watching something that was really good. Anybody who says anything different, that the audience didn't like him, is talking through their hat. The audience loved him. He did three songs and they demanded an encore. He was great, very funny, and very dry. He spoke a little to the audience, not a lot, just a little, but then he never did talk to the audience that much.

His coming to England had an enormous impact on his music, and yet nobody's ever said it properly. He came and he learned. When he sat in all those folk clubs in 1962, he was just soaking stuff up all the time. He heard Louis Killen, he heard Nigel Denver, he heard Bob Davenport, he heard me, he heard The Thameside Four, dozens of people. Anybody who came into The Troubadour, or came into The King and Queen, or the Singers' Club, and he listened and he just gobbled stuff up.

The first complete album he made after he first visited England was *The Times They Are a-Changin'*, and England is all over that album; it's all over *Another Side Of Bob Dylan* too and it's all over a large area of his work at that time. All those tunes he wrote sounded English, Irish, Scottish, you know, a particular kind of highly melodic tune. He stopped playing sort of raggy tunes, and blues – he went back to those later on, when he went back more into rock 'n' roll. But he was forever changing things around; he still is. He turns old songs upside down.

The Troubadour at 263–267 Old Brompton Road in Earls Court, was established in 1954, and is one of the last remaining coffee houses of its era in London. The clubroom in the cellar is famous as one of the primary venues of the British folk revival in the late Fifties and Sixties.

In the summer of 1961, Charlie Watts was 'found' by Alexis Korner playing drums in a Thelonious Monk-style jazz quartet and recruited to join Blues Incorporated. Bob Dylan performed there over Christmas 1962 under the name Blind Boy Grunt.

A key name in the history of the Troubadour is Anthea Joseph, who organised many of the folk events at the club and was often credited as 'the Manager' of the venue. It is widely reported that when Dylan arrived in London for the first time, he was given no instruction other than that of his mentor Pete Seeger to seek out 'Anthea at the Troubadour'.

THE TROUBADOUR

29 DECEMBER, 1962, LONDON

I WAS THERE: ANTHEA JOSEPH

Dylan didn't seem as interested in performing as he was in listening. I felt quite like a native in the presence of an anthropologist.

I WAS THERE: KARL DALLAS

The first time I heard Dylan perform, I thought he was awful. Everyone appeared to agree. He went to a great many of the clubs, and he learnt a great many songs, and he played some of his own, and he was greeted with derision wherever he went. He was also told to 'fuck off' from the Roundhouse, possibly after he was caught smoking pot there.

1963

JONES STREET

FEBRUARY 1963, NEW YORK CITY, NEW YORK

I WAS THERE: DEEANNE HUNSTEIN

The reason my husband Don was taking pictures at that time was because Columbia Records had already issued Bob Dylan's very first album and they knew he was on the road to being a popular artist and they had no pictures. So, they said to Don, who was on the staff there, go down and take some pictures of him.

Don went over to Dylan's apartment, where the singer was living with his then girlfriend Suze Rotolo. They were young, I think she was 18. They had a little apartment in a brownstone, up on the fifth floor walk-up. So, he took a bunch of pictures, then they went outside and it was a very cold and nasty day with a lot of snow in the street.

As they walked toward him, Don started shooting off pictures and because it was so cold out there they didn't want to do it for very long. So he did one roll of black and white and one roll of colour. He just did it in a very short time as it was a very cold day. It just so happened when he turned over what he thought were some of the best pictures with the art department, they really loved that picture of the two of them walking down the street. It became the cover for *The Freewheelin' Bob Dylan*.

An awful lot of people know that picture and didn't connect it with Don's name. I think that the album cover does give him credit but people never paid much attention to album cover photos or the photographers. That still remains one of the most popular pictures and a lot of people want it. A lot of people write the story, what that picture means to them. They say, yes, it brings back part of their youth. Even young people today, they look back, it says to them here are these young people walking in the middle of a harsh environment. It has become a kind of symbol of youth starting off in a harsh environment, but with hope for the future.

Bob and Suze in an outtake from Freewheelin'

FRETTED INSTRUMENTS

SPRING 1963, NEW YORK CITY, NEW YORK

I WAS THERE: MARC SILBER

I sold him a couple of guitars along the way during the Sixties. That 1930s Gibson Nick Lucas Special he played in *Dont Look Back* had belonged to my sister. It was in mint condition when I sold it to him, but it got a little wrecked. He had that guitar for a long time. Later, probably in the early Seventies, I drove up to Woodstock to sell him a really nice late Sixties Martin. He was a tough guy to do business with, though, because he didn't have any idea what the guitars were worth.

I WAS THERE: PAUL HOSTETTER

His guitar, serial number 87898, was sold to Bob Dylan by my friend Marc Silber at his shop, Fretted Instruments, in NYC sometime in 1963. It replaced Dylan's old Gibson J-50, which was, Dylan told me personally, lost in action. It's a 13-fret rosewood Nick Lucas that had been refinished blonde, and had had a Guild-type bridge and a Martin-type pickguard put on.

It had earlier belonged to Marc's sister Julie. Marc and Julie and their family are old friends of mine from Detroit, and I knew this guitar before Marc sold it to Bob Dylan. It was a lovely guitar in all ways, and kindled my enduring interest in the model, well before Bob Dylan ever laid eyes on it. The first time I saw Bob Dylan perform live, in Ann Arbor, before his first album was out, he was playing that old J-50, the one on the cover of his first album.

In January of 1964, I saw Dylan perform again in Denver, and he played this guitar. He stopped by the Folklore Center (where I worked then) after-hours the next day, and he told me that the J-50 had gone missing, but I never connected the fact that the new guitar, he'd played the night before was Julie's old Nick Lucas. It was a mongrel but it sounded great.

THE BEAR

25 APRIL, 1963, CHICAGO, ILLINOIS

I WAS THERE: MICHAEL BLOOMFIELD

When I first saw him he was playing in a night club. I had heard his first album, and Albert Grossman got Dylan to play in a club in Chicago called The Bear and I went down there to cut Bob, to take my guitar and cut him, burn him, and he was a great guy. We spent all day talking, and jamming, and hanging out and he was an incredibly appealing human being and any instincts I may have had in doing that was immediately stopped, and I was just charmed by the man.

That night, I saw him perform, and if I had been charmed by just meeting him, me and my old lady were just bowled over watching him perform. I don't know what it was – like this Little Richard song, 'I don't know what you got but it moves me,' man, he sang this song called 'Redwing' about a boys' prison and some funny talking blues about a picnic and he was fucking fantastic, not that it was the greatest playing or singing in the world, I don't know what he had, man, but I'm telling you I just loved it, I mean I could have watched it nonstop forever and ever.

In May 1963, Dylan was still just another aspiring singer, songwriter with a niche following but no national profile whatsoever. His second album, *The Freewheelin' Bob Dylan*, had not yet been released, but he had secured what would surely be his big break with an invitation to perform on *The Ed Sullivan Show*. That appearance never happened. On May 12, 1963, Bob Dylan walked off the set of the country's highest-rated variety show after network censors rejected the song he planned on performing.

The song that caused all the problems was 'Talkin' John Birch Paranoid Blues', a satirical talking-blues number skewering the ultra-conservative John Birch Society and its tendency to see covert members of an international Communist conspiracy behind every tree. Dylan had auditioned the song days earlier and had run through it for Ed Sullivan himself without any concern being raised. But during rehearsals on the day of the show, an executive from the CBS Standards and Practices Department informed the show's producers that they could not allow Dylan to perform John Birch.

While many of the song's lyrics about hunting down 'reds' were merely humorous, others equated the John Birch Society's views with those of Adolf Hitler and raised the fear of a defamation lawsuit in the minds of CBS's lawyers. Rather than choose a new number to perform or change his song's lyrics (as The Rolling Stones and the Doors would famously do in the years to come), Dylan stormed off the set in angry protest.

The story got widespread media attention in the days that followed helping to establish Dylan's public reputation as an uncompromising artist. The publicity Bob Dylan received from this event probably did more for his career than the actual *Ed Sullivan Show* performance would have.

FOLK CITY

SPRING, 1963, NEW YORK CITY, NEW YORK

I WAS THERE: RICHIE HAVENS, MUSICIAN

I remember going into Folk City and walking through the people peering over the partition at the performer on stage. It was Johnny Herald playing away – lots of fiddles and guitars. I usually didn't linger too long in the bar area, so I went down the stairs to the basement where we shared a common closet.

I took my guitar out of the large bath towel it lived in for protection and began tuning it. Casey Anderson stood outside in the cellar singing 'Lily of the West' and Tex Konig stood looming in the wings with his guitar dwarfed by his gentle giant size. I was on next and had to pass through the horde of folksingers and up the stairs to the dark corner to wait my turn.

This was only the second time I played the room and it was really exciting for me because I was actually being heard by people who liked my music... well, not really my music, because it was a Bob Dylan song I was singing when I hit the stage. I didn't even know it at the time – all I knew was that it was a great song and it truly expressed what I personally felt when I heard it (and I only sang songs that moved me personally).

And after singing a song that I learned from a friend (Gene Michaels) called 'A Hard Rain's a-Gonna Fall,' I remembered sitting in the living room of the dorm-like hotel suite he and I shared with a group of nuts from the Midwest (who were called the Tanners – a folk trio that turned me on to MC Escher).

Well, there I was in the living room trying to learn this new song, 'A Hard Rain's a-Gonna Fall'. It took me three days – the hardest song I ever learned. Images, lots of them, of a truth so subliminally obvious that you had to live the song to sing the song (as with all Dylan songs). So, when I finished the song and headed downstairs to the crowded telephone booth-sized dressing room, a guy stopped me on the stairs to tell me it was the best he'd ever heard the song sung. I said, 'Thanks', and continued on down.

Tex, or someone down there, asked me if I knew that the guy talking to me on the stairs was Bob Dylan, who wrote the song? Now it all came clear! I'd been singing the song for two years thinking that Gene Michaels wrote it! And, that's how I first met Bob Dylan, in 1963.

MASTERTONE RECORDING STUDIO

APRIL 1963, NEW YORK CITY, NEW YORK

I WAS THERE: JUDY COLLINS, SINGER, SONGWRITER

When I was working at the Gilded Garter – this was in Central City, Colorado and it was 1959 and it was my second professional gig, this guy used to come around and see me. He was homeless and he was badly dressed, even for the Sixties. He was trying to get a job, his name was Robert Zimmerman and he was sort of pathetic, you know? He was pathetic, there's no other word for it.

And that's where I met him. He would come in, sit down, and listen to all the songs. But then when I came to New York two years later for the first time, I was at Gerdes Folk City and he was singing these old Woody Guthrie blues and I dismissed him. He was like all these other raunchy boys with long hair and guitars. He wasn't terribly attractive and, you know, he was homeless. He was singing at the round robins and in the hootenannies. He still couldn't get a job.

I picked up a copy of our bible, which is a magazine called *Sing Out!* and I saw, with the music printed, this song called 'Blowin' in the Wind'. And I read it and I thought, 'Christ, that has to be…' He had changed his name to Bob Dylan. He explained to me who he was. He said, 'You remember me. I sat at your feet in Central City. My name was Robert Zimmerman. Now my name is Bob Dylan.'

I couldn't believe my eyes or my ears! I mean, this song was sophisticated, to say the least. It was unique – I'd never heard anything like it.

Albert Grossman called me one day, out of the blue, and he said, 'I'm gonna send you over a tape of this guy, Bob Dylan, I want to know what you think. I'm taking this tape around now to all the companies and I'm getting a lot of flak because they say he can't sing.' And I said, 'Albert, who cares? Who cares if he could sing? A lot of people can sing.' And of course, I love to hear him sing. I think those early records of him singing are just spectacular, singing his own songs. By the way, he was very clear, every single word was understandable. To me, that's the estimate of whether one is singing well. If you can understand the words, you're batting a million!

I thought he was the most brilliant thing I'd ever seen. I was just blown away, I was just totally – flabbergasted. I immediately started recording. I recorded 'Fare Thee Well' and 'Masters of War' and 'The Lonesome Death of Hattie Carroll.' I was swept off my feet, like everybody was. I mean, these poor guys in the Village, all these folk singers trying to get a job and write a song and get a record deal, and they just were flummoxed. All of them. No wonder.

From then on, it was a musical and lyrical revolution. Every moment of which was a surprise. I could have gone on recording nothing but Dylan for a long time.

THE ED SULLIVAN SHOW

12 MAY, 1963, NEW YORK CITY, NEW YORK

I WAS THERE: BOB PRECHT, PRODUCER

I explained the situation to Bob and asked him if he wanted to do something else, and Bob, quite appropriately said, 'No, this is what I want to do. If I can't play my song, I'd rather not appear on the show'.

The first Monterey Folk Festival took place over three days in Monterey, California. The festival featured Joan Baez, Bob Dylan and Peter Paul and Mary. Baez, who had a home in Carmel Highlands, was a huge star at the time, while Dylan was a still a newcomer making a name for himself.

Dylan was not treated kindly by the Monterey audience, who had come to see more traditional folks acts such as Peter, Paul and Mary, the Weavers, and the New Lost City Ramblers.

MONTEREY FOLK FESTIVAL

18 MAY, 1963, MONTEREY, CALIFORNIA

I WAS THERE: BARBARA DANE

He went down very badly. He didn't play for very long, and it felt like he was on for an hour. I think people were laughing. Even though he did three of his hardest-hitting protest songs, 'Talkin' John Birch Paranoid Blues,' 'A Hard Rain's a-Gonna Fall' and 'Masters of War,' the response was so bad it prompted Joan Baez to walk out unannounced and admonish the audience. She wanted everyone to know that this young man had something to say. He was singing about important issues, and he was speaking for her and everyone who wanted a better world. They should listen, she said – she ordered them. Listen! They performed Dylan's 'With God on Our Side' together, their voices an odd match, the tension between their styles made their presence together all the more compelling. They left the stage with people cheering.

I WAS THERE: JOAN BAEZ, MUSICIAN

I was getting audiences up to 10,000 at that point, and dragging my little vagabond out onto the stage was a grand experiment. The people who had not heard of Bob were often infuriated, and sometimes even booed him.

During the late Fifties, Barry Feinstein became a sought-after photographer in Hollywood, where he worked with Marlene Dietrich, Judy Garland, Charlton Heston, Jayne Mansfield, and Steve McQueen. His photos of celebrities and politicians such as John F. Kennedy and Richard Nixon, appeared in national publications, including *Time*, *Esquire*, and *Newsweek*. Feinstein photographed Bob Dylan over an 11-year period, starting with the 1963 cover photograph for *The Times They Are a-Changin'*. Feinstein was the official tour photographer on the European leg of Dylan's 1966 world tour (May 5-27).

BARRY FEINSTEIN

Bob and I were friends long before we worked together. We hung out and understood each other. When there was something to say we would talk, when there wasn't we were silent. We were similar in that way, no bullshit. That's the way it is in music. What often makes a piece of music great are the notes left out. And it's like that with photography; knowing when to take a shot and, more importantly, when not to. I wanted my pictures to say something. I don't really like stand-up portraits, there's nothing there, no life, no feeling. I was much more interested in capturing real moments.

The Freewheelin' Bob Dylan (provisionally entitled Bob Dylan's Blues) the second studio album by Dylan, was released on May 27, 1963. It showcased the 21-year-old's songwriting talent for the first time, propelling him to national and international fame, (the album was released three days after Dylan's twenty-second birthday).

Whereas his self-titled debut album, *Bob Dylan*, had contained only two original songs, *The Freewheelin' Bob Dylan* represented the beginning of Dylan's writing contemporary words to traditional melodies. 11 of the 13 songs on the album are Dylan's original compositions. The

...MANY ROADS
...T A MAN WALK DOWN...

...ylan has walked down many roads. For most of
... years he "rode freight trains for kicks and got
... for laughs, cut grass for quarters and sang
...es." And his songs today are the sounds he
... up all those years on the road—"the coyote's
...d the train whistle's moan, the ol' time pals an'
...n gals, the faces you can't find again."

...es what a true folk singer is supposed to do—
...out the important ideas and events of the times.
... does it better than anybody else. One Dylan
...an Baez, said, "I feel it, but Dylan can say it.
...henomenal."

...w best-selling album (the first was <u>Bob Dylan</u>)
... <u>Freewheelin' Bob Dylan</u>. It features ten of
...own compositions, including the sensational
...lowin' in the Wind." Also, songs on subjects
...g from love ("Girl From the North Country")
...nic fall-out ("A Hard Rain's A-Gonna Fall").
...t and you'll know why Bob Dylan is the
...of the times.

DYLAN ON COLUMBIA RECORDS

DON HUNSTEIN

album opens with 'Blowin' in the Wind', which became an anthem of the Sixties, and an international hit for folk trio Peter, Paul & Mary.

The album featured several other songs which came to be regarded as among Dylan's best compositions and classics of the Sixties folk scene: 'Girl from the North Country', 'Masters of War', 'A Hard Rain's a-Gonna Fall' and 'Don't Think Twice, It's All Right'.

Dylan's lyrics embraced news stories drawn from headlines about the Civil Rights Movement and he articulated anxieties about the fear of nuclear warfare. Balancing this political material were love songs, sometimes bitter and accusatory, and material that features surreal humour.

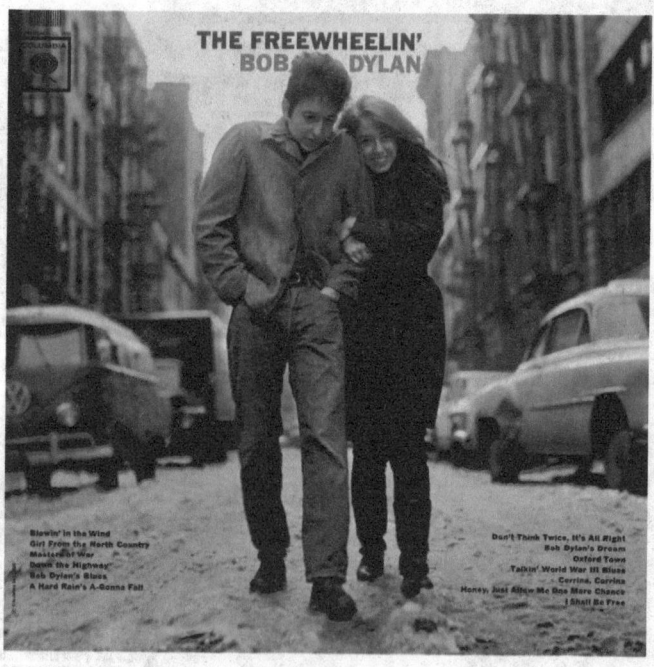

MONTEREY FOLK FESTIVAL

27 MAY, 1963, MONTEREY, CALIFORNIA

I WAS THERE: MANFRED MANN, MUSICIAN

I first heard Dylan in the very early Sixties. I liked the songs and also there was an element of social comment, but it was poetic rather than hectoring. I also like the fact that Dylan himself never really went for explanations; he just let the songs do the job.

I have gotten very tired of people who happen to be able to sing and write well, telling me what to think and what I should be concerned about. As far as I am aware, Dylan never did this.

The songs are able to be changed and interpreted in different ways; this would not be true of Elton John or other great writers. Also the songs are often quite simple pop songs, but when he does them they don't sound that way.

The Café Espresso was a hub of folk music and community gathering for the arts colony in the early Sixties. Folk artists like Joan Baez, Ramblin' Jack Elliot, and Bob Dylan would perform here when they traveled up from New York City. Bob Dylan wrote the bulk of *Another Side of Bob Dylan* in the White Room, an upstairs room that overlooked Tinker Street in the building.

CAFÉ EXPRESSO

WOODSTOCK, NEW YORK

I WAS THERE: MARY LOU PATUREL – CAFÉ OWNER

Back then the town had 3,000 people year-round and 20,000 in the summer. In the winter, it was very quiet and I think Dylan liked the quietness of the place. We never thought of him as somebody really special, he was just part of our lives. It's awesome when you think about it in retrospect, what he became. But back then, he was just Bob Dylan who stayed above the café. He was social, he was very open to people – as long as you didn't invade his life or his privacy.

Tom Wilson began producing Bob Dylan on the heels of his second album *The Freewheelin' Bob Dylan*, in 1963. Their first album together was Dylan's first LP of all-original compositions, *The Times They Are a-Changin'*. Wilson became Dylan's producer for the next three albums, producing the records that would shift Dylan's sound and image.

COLUMBIA STUDIO A

6 AUGUST, 1963, NEW YORK CITY, NEW YORK

I WAS THERE: TOM WILSON, PRODUCER

I was introduced by David Kapralik, at a time when I was not properly working for Columbia. I was being used by them, shall we say. He said, 'Why don't you guys stick around and do a couple of things?' I said, 'What do you mean? I don't even work for Columbia.' What's more, I didn't even particularly like folk music. I'd been recording Sun Ra and John Coltrane, and I thought folk music was for the dumb guys. This guy played like the dumb guys. But then these words came out. I was flabbergasted.

I said to Albert Grossman, who was there in the studio, I said, 'If you put some background to this you might have a white Ray Charles with a message.'

But it wasn't until a year later that everyone agreed that we should put a band behind him. I had to find a band. But it was a very gradual process.

YALE'S WOOLSEY HALL
OCTOBER 1963, NEW HAVEN, CONNECTICUT

I WAS THERE: JOHN RYAN

John Hammond, the great A&R head at Columbia Records took a small group, perhaps six or eight of Canterbury School students to listen to 'a new talent' opening for Dave Brubeck at Yale's Woolsey Hall. We ranged in ages from 13 to 17. I volunteered because I was a Paul Desmond fan but also interested in the growing area of folk music.

Later we answered questions about what we'd heard. Comments ranged from 'scratchy, whiney, hard to understand, and 'not Glenn Yarborough or Carolyn Hester' to 'very cool'. I later learned Bob Dylan was recording *The Times They Are a-Changin'*, I think his second album.

As a 'folky', I became a fan and remain a fan, even and perhaps more-so, after the electric controversy. Brubeck and Desmond were terrific.

The Times They Are a-Changin' the third studio album by Bob Dylan was released on January 13, 1964, with the title track becoming one of Dylan's most famous songs.

In January 1984, a young Steve Jobs recited the second verse of 'The Times They Are a-Changin'' in his opening of the 1984 Apple shareholders meeting, where he famously unveiled the Macintosh computer for the first time.

1964

In February 1964, Dylan embarked on a 20-day trip across the United States. Riding in a station wagon with a few friends (Paul Clayton, Victor Maymudes, and Pete Karman), Dylan began the trip in New York, taking numerous detours through many states before ending the trip in California.

It was during this trip that Dylan composed 'Chimes of Freedom', and 'Mr. Tambourine Man'.

The Times They Are a-Changin' was released as a single in the UK giving Dylan his first chart placing when the song peaked at No 9 in the British charts. Dylan is said to have written the song as a deliberate attempt to create an anthem of change for the time, influenced by Irish and Scottish ballads.

THE CAGE UMASS

26 APRIL, 1964, AMHERST, MASSACHUSETTS

I WAS THERE: JOHN BYRNE COOKE

We were kind of like his extended road crew – except we were not paid or anything! We had a least two cars, possibly three. I was in the same car as Bob. Paul Rothchild, way before he produced the Doors, was in another car. John Sebastian, just before he formed the Lovin' Spoonful, was there. At the time, we just knew him as this guy who played a mean blues harp.

After the gang arrived at Amherst, we met blues musician Taj Mahal for the first time. I know he was a student there, although he may have graduated by that time.

There was usually some Beaujolais around. It was just hanging out with a friend, and his road manager. Dylan could laugh, but he could also be cryptic and opaque – but he was not striking a pose.

At the time, to people like Pete Seeger and Alan Lomax, Dylan was the apotheosis; he was the new folk poet. They put their expectations on him.

This was not a daily topic (on the Amherst trip). It was not really brought up. What's interesting is that while people really know his protest songs – 'The Times, They Are a-Changin', 'Hattie Carroll'. The ones that lasted were the love songs. 'Don't Think Twice', 'It's All Over Baby Blue', and 'It Ain't Me, Babe' and 'Like a Rolling Stone', which are, I guess, the anti-love songs.

When it comes to Dylan, you have to be careful not to over-intellectualise. Dylan was writing the gospel truth. You can't listen to his songs and not think that he cared about what he was writing about. For people saying otherwise, it was just bullshit. I reject that. He put it all in the music – 'Hattie Carroll', 'Emmett Till'. He did not want to come out and say we needed civil rights. It was in the music.

It was a big room, a gymnasium. The stage was specifically constructed for the concert, and they brought in rows of folding chairs. It was in four sections, a pipe-constructed stage. There wasn't even a curtain. It was just one man and a guitar. The power of performing under one spotlight. It would mesmerise the audience.

CAFÉ ESPRESSO

JULY 1964, WOODSTOCK, NEW YORK

I WAS THERE: DOUGLAS R GILBERT

Photographer Douglas R Gilbert in the Look magazine offices.

As a young, new staff photographer for *Look Magazine*, I approached the editors in May 1964 proposing we do a story on a young, still not widely known, folk singer named Bob Dylan. They had never heard of him but were interested enough to explore it to assign me to do a photographic story on him.

In early July I found myself driving into the small town of Woodstock, New York where I was to meet up with Bob at the Café Espresso on Main Street. My interest was to photograph him primarily off stage, hanging out with friends, writing, and whatever else would happen. The plan was to finish the story later with his appearance at the Newport Folk Festival later in July.

The Café Espresso in Woodstock, NY turned out to be a kind of social centre for him and his friends to talk and catch up on news with one another. I asked Bob where he wrote and he took me upstairs over the cafe to a room with a small table containing a small manual typewriter, one or two ashtrays full of butts, a partly empty wine bottle, and a bulletin board on the wall. The owner of the cafe was a friend who made the room available to him at any time. As we talked, I told him of some situations where I would like to photograph him, adding, 'I want to take some photographs of situations, I have seen of him elsewhere and want to make them look real.' With that he stopped and looking me straight in the eye he said, 'Nothin's real, man'. I didn't raise the subject again.

Another day I got over to the cafe about mid-morning and found him in the back of the cafe with John Sebastian. Bob was playing an electric bass and John a lead guitar. Bob was watching John's fingers closely as he followed on the bass guitar. They jammed intently for quite a while before rejoining the group of friends around the table.

After lunch, Bob and John came to me and asked if I could drive then to a town about a half hour away. We got in my rental car, Bob in front, John in back with a guitar and started out. After some talking and joking John began picking out a tune I didn't recognise and then began to sing softly, 'Hey, Mr. Tambourine man play a song for me....' While Bob grinned, nodded his head and occasionally laughed. I thought little of it since they would occasionally sing songs by others. Only after the electric album as issued with all the accompanying variety of responses did I understand what was happening in the car. As we drove into the town they wanted, we came to a main intersection and started moving forward when Bob yelled, 'Stop!' I stopped and he jumped out to the street and ran to a newspaper box. He pulled out a paper, looked at it carefully, put in back and returned to the car. '*National Enquirer*,' said John. 'Must have a story about aliens.' We parked the car and went into a music store where Bob was looking for a particular record. As we waited, a salesgirl looked at him intently and said, 'Are you... aren't you...' Bob looked away and said, 'No,... No.' And with that we left the store, which did not have the music he was looking for.

At breakfast one morning in the house where Dylan was living, he was joined by Allen Ginsberg, recently back from India where he had acquired a harmonium. He didn't know how to play it, so he asked Dylan to help him. Bob took the instrument and began playing chords and then simple tunes as instruction. They both sang along, greatly enjoying the experience.

Later that month, I went of Newport, Rhode Island, to finish my project with Dylan photographing large public performances, as well as smaller afternoon venues called 'workshops'. A few days later, I met Dylan and Joan Baez at the *Look Magazine* building in New York City. The had just seen the proposed layout of the story as it was planned for the magazine layout. I asked Bob what he thought of the story and he grunted something not decipherable and shrugged.

Typical. At least he didn't reject it. But the editors did. Looking at the photographs they decided he was 'too scruffy' to appear in their family magazine. The story never ran.

In addition to its influence on music, 'Subterranean Homesick Blues' was used in one of the first 'modern' promotional film clips, the forerunner of what was later known as the music video. The original clip, which was shot in an alley close to the Savoy Hotel in London, was the opening segment of D. A. Pennebaker's film *Dont Look Back*, a documentary on Dylan's 1965 tour of England.

In the film, Dylan holds up cue cards with selected words and phrases from the lyrics while staring at the camera, and he flips the cards as the song plays. Dylan's cards align perfectly with his lyrics, but as he continues, he lags behind the beat and flashes intentional errors (the card for the line '11 dollar bills' reads '20,' others are scrawled 'pawking metaws' and 'sucksess').

SAVOY HOTEL

8 MAY, 1964, LONDON

I WAS THERE: D.A. PENNEBAKER

We arranged to meet in a bar down in the Village with Bobby Neuwirth, who was Dylan's road manager. We sat and talked, and then Bob said, 'I've got this idea for a film where I take a whole lot of sheets of paper and write lyrics for a song, and hold them up as the lyrics come up in the song and then I just toss them away.' And I said, 'That's a fantastic idea.' So we brought along about 50 shirt cardboards, and that's how we did the whole thing in the alleyway.

We first tried to do it in the garden of the hotel, and a cop came along and was grabbing me and telling me to stop. So we went into the alley, where there were no cops, and we did it just one time, and we just stuck a tape recorder in front of Bob and it played the song. We had done the signs the night before, and Donovan had helped – Donovan was a very good artist, it turns out – and Joan Baez. I think I'd even done some, but I can't remember which ones.

Five days before the Royal Festival Hall concert, Dylan headed up to Manchester to record three songs at Didsbury's ABC Studios, for later broadcast on ITV. The recording date was 14 May, and the three songs were 'Don't Think Twice', 'Blowin' in the Wind' and another first, the performance debut of 'Chimes of Freedom', five months before it appeared on *Another Side of Bob Dylan*. Tragically, this was somehow wiped from the tape, and only 'Don't Think Twice' still exists. Dylan and Grossman stayed at the Parr's Wood Hotel, opposite the studios, where legend has it Dylan drank two pints of Boddingtons Bitter and fell off his stool. CP Lee, author of *Just Like The Night* (an account of his attendance at the Judas concert two years later), wrote an article about Dylan's 1964 visit to Manchester in *Mojo* magazine several years ago.

ROYAL FESTIVAL HALL

17 MAY, 1964, LONDON

I WAS THERE: JOHN BUCKLEN, SCHOOL FRIEND

The place was all dark and Bob was doing a sound check when I walked in before the concert. He hugged me. It was a mind-blowing experience. I saw big, burly guys sobbing when he sang.

I WAS THERE: MARTIN CARTHY, MUSICIAN

I remember seeing him at the Royal Festival Hall when he did his solo concert there and he was astounding. He didn't talk at first, and then he started telling everybody... he told the audience the plot of the movie *Hootenanny* which is all about muscle men and bikini-clad young lasses all cavorting about singing folk, singing 'hootenanny' music.

SET LIST:

The Times They Are a-Changin
Girl From The North Country
Who Killed Davey Moore?
Talking John Birch Paranoid Blues
Ballad Of Hollis Brown
It Ain't Me, Babe
Walls Of Red Wing
Chimes Of Freedom
Mr. Tambourine Man
Eternal Circle
A Hard Rain's a-Gonna Fall
Talking World War III Blues
Don't Think Twice, It's All Right
Only A Pawn In Their Game
With God On Our Side
The Lonesome Death Of Hattie Carroll
Restless Farewell
When The Ship Comes In

Pink Floyd founder, Syd Barrett, and his then girlfriend, Libby Gausden, were in the audience and Barrett was inspired to write the song 'Bob Dylan Blues', which was one of his earliest songs, written before he even had a publishing deal. The song was largely forgotten about until Floyd guitarist David Gilmour unearthed the tape in his personal collection.

NEWPORT FOLK FESTIVAL

24 JULY, 1964, RHODE ISLAND

I WAS THERE: JOHN KAY, MUSICIAN

In 1964, before leaving Buffalo for good, a friend and I hitchhiked with our guitars down to Newport, Rhode Island for the folk festival and we saw Dylan there for the first time live. And at that point he was really into full-force writing; the Civil Rights movement still very much in the forefront of the folk community. Certainly the draft interested every young male who might be called up to join the Armed Forces, certainly made them interested in what was going on in Vietnam.

So it was a very heady time during which those such as Dylan, who were following in the footsteps of Woody Guthrie and writing about the here and now had a huge impact on our group of his contemporaries.

That was my first exposure to hearing him live. As it turned out a year later, I would be back for the Newport Folk Festival '65 and now of course was the time when he, together with some of the members of the Paul Butterfield Blues Band, started doing his electric work. Having been a rock 'n' roll junkie from early on, I was perfectly fine with it, but there were lots of people who were seeing their literary giant be somehow overcome by the less than desirable electric and rock elements.

Shortly after the '64 visit to the Newport Folk Festival, I migrated to the West Coast, getting my thing together as a journeyman folk acoustic blues solo performer, hanging out in places like the Troubadour.

In a club called the New Balladeer, where I would perform myself, I ran into people like David Crosby and the then still-named Jim McGuinn, who of course changed his name to Roger McGuinn and I basically witnessed the formation of the Byrds. Once they were formed and had an album out with 'Mr. Tambourine Man', a friend of mine, Morgan, who was the manager of the New Balladeer, he and I would go up to Sunset Strip to Ciro's. When the Byrds were formed, they played there for a week at a time, sometimes two weeks, several sets a night. So we would go because it was a very happening scene.

One night while we were there – well, lo and behold who walks out onto the stage with the Byrds – Dylan. And he started to play harmonica. Now I did not get to talk to him, it was just something that blindsided us. I said, 'God, there he is, playing harmonica.'

I, like so many others, stayed with him in terms of his musical progression through the various albums that followed the one that I had initially purchased, *The Freewheelin' Bob Dylan*. By the time he got into *Bringin' It All Back Home* and *Highway 61 Revisited* and then finally *Blonde on Blonde*, we were all really into those albums because it had tons and tons of really cool stuff to listen to.

I have a complete playlist on my iPod of nothing but my favourite Dylan songs. So he continues to be a musical touchstone and something that I have absorbed over time that I consider to be something I still value to this day.

WOODSTOCK

AUGUST 1964, NEW YORK STATE

I WAS THERE: JOAN BAEZ, MUSICIAN

Most of the month or so we were there, Bob stood at the typewriter in the corner of his room, drinking red wine and smoking and tapping away relentlessly for hours. And in the dead of night, he would wake up, grunt, grab a cigarette, and stumble over to the typewriter again.

Another Side of Bob Dylan, the fourth studio album by Bob Dylan, was released on August 8, 1964, by Columbia Records.

The album deviates from the more-socially conscious style, which Dylan had developed with his previous LP, *The Times They Are a-Changin'*. The change prompted criticism from some influential figures in the folk community – *Sing Out!* Editor Irwin Silber complained that Dylan had 'somehow lost touch with people' and was caught up in 'the paraphernalia of fame'.

Despite the album's thematic shift, Dylan performed the entirety of *Another Side of Bob Dylan* as he had previous records – solo. In addition to his usual acoustic guitar and harmonica, Dylan provides piano on one selection, 'Black Crow Blues'. *Another Side of Bob Dylan* reached No 43 in the US (although it eventually went gold), and peaked at No 8 on the UK charts in 1965.

After playing the first of two nights at Forest Hills Stadium on their first US concert tour, The Beatles met Dylan at The Delmonico Hotel at Park Avenue and 59th in New York City and his friend, a reporter named Al Aronowitz, who introduced the Liverpool band to marijuana.

Dylan had assumed The Beatles were well acquainted with the drug, after mishearing the lyrics to 'I Want To Hold Your Hand'.

Paul McCartney believed he'd attained true mental clarity for the first time in his life and instructed Beatles roadie Mal Evans to write down everything he said henceforth. Dylan, meanwhile, lost his cool and began answering the hotel phone by shouting, 'This is Beatlemania here!'

THE DELMONICO HOTEL

28 AUGUST, 1964, NEW YORK CITY, NEW YORK

I WAS THERE: PETER BROWN

Brian Epstein and The Beatles looked at each other apprehensively. 'We've never smoked marijuana before,' Brian finally admitted. Dylan looked disbelievingly from face to face. 'But what about your song?' he asked. 'The one about getting high?' The Beatles were stupefied. 'Which song?' John managed to ask. Dylan said, 'You know...' and then he sang, 'and when I touch you I get high, I get high...'

John flushed with embarrassment. 'Those aren't the words,' he admitted. 'The words are, 'I can't hide, I can't hide, I can't hide...'

I WAS THERE: JOHN LENNON

I don't remember much what we talked about. We were smoking dope, drinking wine and generally being rock 'n' rollers and having a laugh, you know, and surrealism. It was party time.

I WAS THERE: PAUL McCARTNEY

I remember asking Mal, our road manager, for what seemed like years and years, 'Have you got a pencil?' But of course everyone was so stoned they couldn't produce a pencil, let alone a combination of pencil and paper.

I'd been going through this thing of levels, during the evening. And at each level I'd meet all these people again. 'Hahaha! It's you!' And then I'd metamorphose on to another level. Anyway, Mal gave me this little slip of paper in the morning, and written on it was, 'There are seven levels!' Actually it wasn't bad. Not bad for an amateur. And we pissed ourselves laughing. I mean, 'What the fuck's that? What the fuck are the seven levels?' But looking back, it's actually a pretty succinct comment; it ties in with a lot of major religions but I didn't know that then.

We were kind of proud to have been introduced to pot by Dylan, that was rather a coup.

ANN ARBOR HIGH SCHOOL

19 SEPTEMBER, 1964, MICHIGAN

I WAS THERE: ED REYNOLDS

I made an unwise decision to get married in 1964, and the tickets were a wedding present, so it was worth the two-year marriage to get those tickets. That's the way I look at it. They were great tickets, right in the middle of the front row. You couldn't get any closer.

I had discovered Dylan about a year earlier, just after the release of *The Freewheelin' Bob Dylan*. I came as close as anybody could come to driving my mother to an asylum. The first time I heard the first cut, that was it. I was poleaxed. It's a wonder I didn't play it right through the grooves, over and over and over. It was the greatest thing I'd ever heard. I couldn't get enough of it.

He had on a suede jacket. The place was full. I don't remember how big the auditorium was at Ann Arbor High. But I remember thinking, I'll never see anything as great as this again in my life. It was absolutely unbelievable.

You've got to picture the whole experience. Here he is, the person who was folk music in 1964, in this auditorium, your typical American anywhere auditorium. The curtains are cheesy and motheaten, there's no set. You're in high school. You're in freaking high school. In the midst of all that ordinary stuff, which brings to mind things like lunch in the cafeteria in 10th grade, there's this person who's magic. The juxtaposition of all that made for a one-of-a-kind experience. I've never seen anything like it since. It was a thunderbolt to the brain.

I WAS THERE: BILL KIRCHEN, COMMANDER CODY

I'd been doing junior theatre and I knew my way around the auditorium. I crawled up in the light deck and I just sat up there, right above the stage, staring down at him.

I think if you don't know the first 10 Dylan albums, you don't know why he's an icon. You've got to go back to those to hear what he was up to. He was a great singer, a stunning songwriter.

I WAS THERE: DAVID GARELICK

Dylan was hard to listen to. He had a really edgy, gritty voice, and a gritty personality, and it was hard to like him. But it was a great show. He played 'Mr. Tambourine Man,' which hadn't been released yet. It was just incredible, and still is. I couldn't imagine that somebody from my generation was writing these kinds of songs – so rich, the imagery in that song.

I wanted to interview him for *The Michigan Daily;* I was an English major then. I wanted to ask him all these questions about his poetic imagery and how he wrote his songs and some of his influences, but he didn't want to talk to anybody.

The door was closed to the dressing room and I said to one guy, 'I'm from *The Michigan Daily* and I'd like to talk to Bob Dylan'. And he said, 'I'm his bodyguard and he doesn't want to talk to you.' The guy was just kind of a thug. I didn't have a press card or anything. If Dylan's agent had been pre-warned to it, maybe it would've made a difference. But I kind of doubt it.

I WAS THERE: JEAN CONLIN

I was driving into the parking lot with my friend, Kathy, when we saw Bob Dylan carrying two ice cream cones to a car at the other end of the lot. I parked and we jumped out, quite excited, and went up to the car window, which was open. There sat Bob Dylan, and in the back seat with him was Joan Baez!

I don't think he was used to young girls coming up to him, Kathy and I were pretty nervous. I asked him if he was Bob Dylan and he said, 'No'. I said, 'Well, I know you are and we wanted to tell you we're fans and we'll be going to your concert tonight'. He just nodded his head and gave a slight smile.

I was familiar with Dylan's music because of my boyfriend. He was the one that bought the tickets. When he played the harmonica and guitar at the same time, I remember thinking how odd that was. Kind of like a one-man band.

I WAS THERE: CAROL BISHOP

I was at the Michigan Union concert and remember it well. He was not known at that time, and it was a whole new experience, but as his fame grew, I remembered back to that solo concert many times. I live on the Monterey Peninsula in California and he and Joan Baez hung around here a lot when Joan lived here, and as both of them rose to fame and before the famous rift. His voice never really got better, but his persona did!

I WAS THERE: JANE KEON

I was 15 and my brother had just started his freshman year at Alma College, in our hometown. He called me in the afternoon and said he'd heard Bob Dylan would be giving a concert in Ann Arbor that night. My mom said I could go, and we jumped in the car and drove pell mell to get there on time. We were in time, but they were sold out! We waited around, and pretty soon the ticket person called us back and said he had one seat available centre front and one in a chair on stage. On stage? Sure enough, they had set up chairs on both sides of the stage, facing the performer, and I got to sit only a few feet away from Bob Dylan! What a night to remember!

A concert review from Woolsey Hall by John Rothchild appeared in the *Yale News* on November 17, 1964, where Rothchild interviewed Dylan after the show.

INDIAN NECK FOLK FESTIVAL

14 NOVEMBER, 1964, NEW HAVEN, CONNECTICUT

I WAS THERE: JOHN ROTHCHILD

Bright dress cuff links glittered ironically from the sleeves of his faded blue work shirt. He wore scuffed black boots, his hair was unkempt and sideburns grew wild down his face.

He spoke of the future, he leaned forward on a small wooden chair, and his volatile eyes seemed to ignite the room. 'What if, what if, what if everybody was a coward, then nobody would do a lot of things. What does anything mean? What does 'free' mean? I can't describe that in conversation.'

When he was finished, the man without meanings grabbed his unadorned guitar, picked up the harmonica 'with the least spit on it,' clumsily walked out onto the stage.

He was unprofessional and jerky as he switched from one microphone to another, but it was his lack of professionalism that made Dylan real. His individuality clashed with and nullified all the gilt and marble and extravagance that covered the walls behind him.

MEMORIAL GYMNASIUM

8 NOVEMBER, 1964, ORONO, MAINE

I WAS THERE: GUY MAINER

I was a freshman at University of Maine in Orono and this was the first concert I attended there. I lived in a dorm not far from the gym, so I would have walked there. The concert was promoted by a fraternity on campus, Sigma Nu, so there was probably a party there afterwards but I have no memory of it!

I've looked up the date and the internet tells me it was November 8 at the University of Maine in Orono. It was Bob Dylan by himself with a harmonica in a neck holder and an acoustic guitar. Everything else is pretty fuzzy.

WILSON HIGH SCHOOL

5 DECEMBER, 1964, LONG BEACH, CALIFORNIA

I WAS THERE: WALT QUINN, AGE 14

The Golden Bear were the promoters. I can remember his leather jacket and Beatle boots. He sang 'Gates of Eden', 'Mr. Tambourine Man', etc before *Bringing It All Back Home* was released.

I was in a recording studio and ran into Jeff from the Nitty Gritty Dirt Band. We realised we were at the same show and compared notes. He said Jackson Brown, his friend, was there too. I was 14. I lived in Riverside and he had played earlier that year in a small coffee shop at UCR. My dad wouldn't let me go because it was a Tuesday evening.

I WAS THERE: GHRAYDON WALLICK, AGE 17

I first saw Bob Dylan in 1964. He was playing the Wilson High School Gym in Long Beach. I should mention that the concert was not sold out.

Coincidently my mother's house was directly across the girls athletic field (100 yards) from the gym's entrance. An older friend of mine who had been to New York and saw Dylan in the coffee houses had an extra ticket; his date stood him up. I agreed to go but, was a little freaked out by the crowd of weirdos I saw waiting for the doors to open. I was a 17 year old high school junior and to say I was moved by the experience doesn't quite say it.

I was transformed by it; as the world would soon be too. One year later his songs were all over the LA radio waves and heading for the top of the charts. Dylan transformed my perspective and imagination in much the same way as Elvis Presley's first public appearance on the *Ed Sullivan Show*. I couldn't sleep at all that night and in a way Dylan woke me up for the rest of my life.

Before he went electric in 1965, Bob Dylan epitomised the hard-travelling folk troubadour, and he established this image largely on a vintage Gibson Nick Lucas model flat-top guitar. The young Dylan had played other Martin and Gibson models in the late Fifties and early Sixties, but in those final years of his acoustic era the Nick Lucas was his instrument of choice.

He played this guitar in the studio and on tour from 1963 to 1966, and used it for the legendary albums *Another Side of Bob Dylan* and *Bringing It All Back Home*. And, although it didn't appear on the covers of either of these, it is frequently seen in the many live performance tapes from the day, including broadcasts of the Newport Folk Festival in 1964 and 1965, and Dylan's famous appearances on BBC TV in England in 1965.

1965

Sixties-era folk musician and prolific session guitarist, Bruce Langhorne, was a mainstay of the folk scene in Greenwich Village in the early Sixties, playing or recording with Bob Dylan, Joan Baez, Odetta, Tom Rush, Richie Havens, and Richard and Mimi Farina.

It was Langhorne who Dylan said inspired him to write 'Mr. Tambourine Man'.

I WAS THERE: BRUCE LANGHORNE, GUITARIST

My professional career really started in Provincetown, where I used to like play music on the street. I used to work with this guy, this artist, and our street scam used to be, I would play music and get people to stop and listen, and he would sketch them, and then he would charge them for the sketch. And then they'd give me money, and then we could go and eat and drink. So that was how it started. And then when I was in Provincetown, I met a guy who used to sing and play guitar. And when I got back to New York, he introduced me to Brother John Sellers.

Brother John was emcee at Gerdes Folk City. And I started playing with him. And I started recording, because everyone who came into Gerdes Folk City heard me play, because I was there all the time. And a lot of people wanted me to sit in with them. And these same people started getting recording contracts, and they asked me to come and play. One of the people who was very instrumental for me in any contribution that I made to the electric end of this whole phenomenon was Sandy Bull.

He was a very sophisticated musician with really wide taste. I met Hamza El Din through him, and when I played the Dylan sessions, I borrowed Sandy's twin reverb amp to play. I had a pickup on my acoustic Martin, and Sandy introduced me to the work of Roebuck

Staples. And Roebuck Staples, I think, was one of the absolute masters of electric guitar. He was the first person I ever heard who used tremolo as a rhythm device. And he played this Fender through the tremolo, and he used the tremolo in time with the tunes that he was doing. And for me, he was about the most swinging player of the whole folk-gospel era. He had this inevitability of his tunes, based on this electronic rhythmic thing that he set up. So I have to credit Sandy with turning me on to what could be done in the medium.

I had been experimenting with just putting a pickup on my Martin for a while, before that. But not long, because my playing, it was just amplified and sustained acoustic playing, really. And I played the same sort of lines that I would play with somebody like Odetta, who would provide the same sort of thing that Dylan provided, or Dylan and the band, which was like a really inevitable rhythmic structure. I mean, I always thought that the people that I most enjoyed playing with were the people who had like an unstoppable thread to their music. And it couldn't be diverted easily. I mean, it was gonna be there, the root, the core was gonna be there. And my job was really, essentially, icing. I put icing on the cake. But in order for me to do my job, that basic thread had to be there.

I can't always remember what I did. Another thing that I was forced to do, though all this has been to my benefit – I was forced to play very much in the moment. Because I did not have a great deal of sophistication in classical or jazz technique. So what I had to do, was I had to rely on communication and empathy to get me to play the next note, the right note, the right phrase or something. Which I why I liked working with somebody like Dylan, who had an inevitability to their structure. Because they were able to, like, communicate what the next note or section was gonna be. And some of the Dylan tunes that were done on *Bringing It All Back Home* were done without rehearsal. They were just like everybody was able to tune into it what he was going to do next. Not that he was predictable, but he was inevitable.

I met Bob at Gerdes. And I think John Hammond set it up. And he probably set it up because I think I had recorded with Carolyn (Hester) before, who he was producing. And I think John called me, and said, 'Hey, how'd you like to come and play with Bob?' And I knew Bob. But I hadn't played his material. But I'd heard him. I think that's how that whole thing happened.

John Hammond was a very, very sophisticated producer. As you know he produced Billie Holiday, and he'd been producing jazz from the time Rover was a pup. And he probably gave Bob the advice to not alienate his old audience by doing something that was completely, that would turn a lot of people off. It did turn a lot of people off. A lot of people just hardly ever came around from Dylan as an acoustic musician, even though he's an icon now.

I was at a Newport Folk Festival, one year, and Alan Lomax and Al Grossman got into a fistfight. Here are two grown men, got into a fistfight. They were rolling around on the ground. Actually, Dick Fariña and I broke it up. But it was a real trip. I was not there at the start of the fight, but it's my projection that it was about that very thing. It was about aesthetics, and probably Alan Lomax, who tended to be kind of outspoken, probably said something that Albert, who was very loyal to Bob, extremely loyal to Bob, probably just didn't cotton to. So it was very interesting, and the feelings were very strong. Because there were a lot of people who were very heavily invested in the traditional folk music. And with the folk music revival, these were people who had been playing folk music for years and years and years in obscure venues, and suddenly they saw their time had come. And they probably saw electrification and rock 'n' rollation as co-option, total co-option.

COLUMBIA RECORDING STUDIOS

14 JANUARY, 1965, NEW YORK CITY, NEW YORK

I WAS THERE: KENNY RANKIN, GUITARIST

I was recording at Columbia at the time and so was Dylan. Tom Wilson, a buddy of mine, was producing Dylan and he asked me what I thought about the idea that Dylan wanted to record with an electric guitar. He asked me if I wanted to play on the session.

I said I'd just started to teach myself how to play guitar and I only know a few chords, but hey, Dylan only knows three or four himself! So I said, what's it pay, and he said something like 60 bucks a song or an hour, whichever was greater, so I said, 'OK, I'm there.'

I played on 'Maggie's Farm' and 'Subterranean Homesick Blues' and a couple of others. It was fun. I played rhythm. He had established himself as Bob Dylan, and we all loved what he did, so it was interesting. Of course, I didn't realise the enormity that it would bring.

I WAS THERE: DANIEL KRAMER, PHOTOGRAPHER

The musicians were enthusiastic. They conferred with one another to work out the problems as they arose. Dylan bounced around from one man to another, explaining what he wanted, often showing them on the piano what was needed until, like a giant puzzle, the pieces would fit and the picture emerged whole. Most of the songs went down easily and needed only three or four takes. In some cases, the first take sounded completely different from the final one because the material was played at a different tempo, perhaps, or a different chord was chosen, or solos may have been rearranged. His method of working, the certainty of what he wanted, kept things moving.

WHISKY A GO-GO

JANUARY 1965, LOS ANGELES, CALIFORNIA

I WAS THERE: MICKY JONES, DRUMMER

The first time I physically met Dylan, he came in the Whisky a Go-Go when I was playing with Johnny Rivers and called me over to his table on one of our breaks and said he really wanted to talk to me. He invited me up to a little party in the Hollywood Hills that night. So I went up there to hang out for a while. But I was ready to leave because there was all this Hollywood stuff around and I was just ready to go. I went over to say goodnight and he said, 'Wait, we have to talk.' So Bob, I, and Bob Neuwirth went back into the kitchen of this house and started just kinda chattin'. And that's when he told me that he wanted me to come and do some recording with him and I said, 'Yeah, I'd like to do that.' And that night, he said to me, 'You're my favourite rock 'n' roll drummer.' And then I ran into Bob about two or three times and he was like, 'I'm still gonna call you, man. Is your number still the same?' And I told him 'Yeah it is'.

I never heard from him – probably for about a year. And I thought well, this isn't going to happen. And when I got the call, it was from Albert Grossman. I didn't know who Albert Grossman was, and I didn't call him back because it was a long-distance call. I was working at a club in Detroit with Johnny Rivers at the time, and I didn't want to pay for a long-distance call to call somebody I didn't know. He called me probably half a dozen times. Finally, there was a message that said call back Operator 6 or something. So I called, and they said, 'My God, we've been looking for you for a couple of weeks'.

Albert said, 'Bob wants you to play with him.' And I said, 'Is this for an album, a recording, or what?' He said, 'No, no. He wants to put a group together, and he wants you for the drummer – nobody else.' I said, 'Well, what's the deal? What does this pay?' That's the first thing a good musician asks. And he said Bob would get back to me on that. So Bob called me two or three days later when I got back to LA, and we made a deal and I found out later on that I got a better deal than everybody else, because he was paying all my expenses – hotels, everything. And I think my meals too. And all the other guys were paying for their own hotels.

Dylan began writing and composing 'Mr. Tambourine Man' in February 1964, after attending Mardi Gras in New Orleans during a cross-country road trip with several friends, and completed it sometime between the middle of March and late April of that year after he had returned to New York. The song was first released on the 1965 album *Bringing It All Back Home*.

The Byrds recorded a version of the song that they released as their first single reaching No 1 on both the *Billboard* Hot 100 chart and the UK Singles Chart, as well as being the title track of their debut album, *Mr. Tambourine Man*. The single's success initiated the folk rock boom of 1965 and 1966, many acts imitating the band's hybrid of rock beat, jangly guitar, and poetic or socially conscious lyrics.

COLUMBIA STUDIOS

20 JANUARY, 1965, HOLLYWOOD, CALIFORNIA

I WAS THERE: ROGER McGUINN, MUSICIAN

I remember when I first heard the playback of 'Mr. Tambourine Man,' we were sitting on the floor of Studio A, Columbia Records on Sunset and Gower, and they had these big speakers that rolled around on wheels. Producer Terry Melcher pulled a couple of them up and he called for a playback of 'Mr. Tambourine Man' and I just was amazed at how good it sounded. Now I didn't know it was going to be a hit but I was surprised that we had accomplished that; even though it was the Wrecking Crew playing the band track, I was playing my Rickenbacker on it. It definitely sounded really good and I just didn't know the business well enough to know what would be a hit but it did become one.

I knew 'Turn! Turn! Turn!' was a really good song but we had internal struggles with that because Jim Dickson, who was our manager at the time, thought it was inappropriate because of its religious background, that it didn't fit with the rock 'n' roll audience; he wanted us to do another Dylan song. But Terry Melcher liked it so much that he went on a one-man campaign to get the song as the next single. And went to the extent of driving up and down the California coast to deejays and playing it for them so they would play it on the radio. It became a regional hit in San Francisco before it became a national hit.

I've never had a long conversation with Bob Dylan over anything. He's very cryptic when he speaks and sometimes speaks in a language that only he and maybe his friend Bobby Neuwirth understand. I remember when I first met them they were talking in some kind of poetic double-talk, it was hard to know exactly what they were saying. But generally speaking, Bob came to our rehearsals when we were learning 'Mr. Tambourine Man' and he and Neuwirth reacted positively to it. And in fact gave us permission to do it, to release it before Bob got it out. Albert Grossman tried to stop it but it was on its way up the charts. But Bob was friendly about it, he let us do it.

We never had a conversation about it, it was just sort of a nod, like, 'You can do that.' Neuwirth said you can dance to it and that appealed to the both of them.

I WAS THERE: RICHARD ALDERSON, SOUND ENGINEER

I was the live engineer for Dylan and The Band on the 1965-66 world tour, and most all of the concert tapes made from that tour were also feeds from my mixing board, but I never kept any copies of them.

I knew that Dylan had been performing electric, but I had no idea that the second half was going to be what it turned out to be. Everybody knew that they came to see the Bob Dylan that they were expecting – rock 'n' roll was something that no one expected. There was a lot of booing, it was practically everywhere we went, the audiences were hostile, and the band responded to the hostility by the audience by playing more aggressively. The audience reaction was mystifying to everybody, it was mystifying to me. I remember thinking why doesn't everybody think this stuff is as great as I do?

Bob was singing wonderfully, performing wonderfully, the songs were very exciting and I was wrapped up in that. You put good microphones up in front of good musicians and it sounds good! Obviously the musicians played their assess off, it wasn't even like the studio recordings, or like the performance at Newport because Micky Jones was a much louder and more aggressive drummer than anyone else who had played with him before and it drove the music harder. It made Robbie Robertson play some of the greatest stuff he ever played in his life.

It was kind of dismissed. The recordings weren't very important, it broke my heart, and Columbia just mis-handled it because they wanted to use their tapes. They sent expensive crews over and the fact that Bob wanted to use my recordings was not compatible with their desires. Grossman told me to take my tapes to Columbia and turn them over and that was it; I never saw them again.

I wanted the tapes to sound good and I didn't know until now that the 1966 Live Recordings would become anything and I'm glad they are getting appreciated after all this time.

CAPITOL THEATRE
21 MARCH, 1965, OTTAWA, ONTARIO, CANADA

I WAS THERE: BJORN AHLBLAD, AGE 19

I moved to Ottawa, Canada in 1964; I was 19. Ottawa is Canada's capital and a very beautiful city. We enjoyed the music of the time; Peter, Paul, and Mary, Kingston Trio, Joan Baez and others. I had been to two Pete Seeger performances in Montreal when I lived there.

I had a Joan Baez record, and was well familiar with her; and as Canadians we were also into Gordon Lightfoot, Joni Mitchell, Neil Young, Leonard Cohen and of course Ian and Sylvia.

One day a friend asked me to go with him to a Joan Baez concert – his brother had given him two tickets as he could not attend. These were expensive seats: C$4.50 apiece, or four trays of draft at the Ottawa House Tavern across the river in Hull, Quebec!

Joan Baez was set to perform on March 21, 1965, at the Capitol Theatre on Bank Street, a venue seating perhaps 2,500. Needless to say I was very excited at my good fortune.

Ottawa can be freezing cold even in late March; on that particular night it was 10 degrees F and we were glad to be in a heated theatre. We settled into our seats and gawked around balcony front row centre overlooking the stage – perfect – my friend's brother had great taste.

Soon enough Joan came on stage and everyone stood and applauded enthusiastically, a warm reception indeed. She probably did five or six numbers including 'The Unquiet Grave' which happened to be a favourite of mine and was on the record I had.

Then she announced she had a special treat for us and called up Bob Dylan – 'c'mon up Bobbie!' she enthused.

I did not quite know who that was, but since the audience went wild at the announcement I too got the fever! Joan and Bob had a special thing going at the time; I had no idea just how special and we were caught up in their magnetic performance. They laughed and joked; the audience loved every moment. Joan hilariously turned the knobs on Bob's guitar in mock tuning. I remember they sang 'Mama You Been on My Mind' with Joan helping Bob who forgot the words – it was tremendously entertaining and funny.

Joan and Bob seemed an odd mix. She the virtuoso singer and Bob the rag-a-muffin, the amazingly artistic and talented rag-a-muffin.

Then Joan sang a beautiful rendition of 'Silver Dagger' with Bob on harp and guitar; we were swept away.

I am sure they sang 'God On Our Side', perhaps one more, and maybe closed with 'Blowin' in the Wind' . Whatever it was, we all sang along.

Even though the two could once more mount that stage together, as they did in the mid Seventies and early Eighties, I for one would not want that – the memory of us all as young people lives on in my mind, unchanging and can't be erased.

Dylan's fifth studio album *Bringing It All Back Home* was released on March 22, 1965. The album is divided into an electric and an acoustic side, although the acoustic side included some tracks in which other instruments were backing up Dylan and his guitar, but no drums were used.

On side one of the original LP, Dylan is backed by an electric rock 'n' roll band, a move that further alienated him from some of his former peers in the folk music community. Likewise, on the acoustic second side of the album, he distanced himself from the protest songs with which he had become closely identified as his lyrics continued their trend towards the abstract and personal.

The album reached No 6 on *Billboard's* Pop Albums chart, the first of Dylan's LPs to break into the US Top 10. It also topped the UK charts later that spring. The first track, 'Subterranean Homesick Blues', became Dylan's first single to chart in the US, peaking just inside the Top 40 at No 39.

CIVIC AUDITORIUM

27 MARCH, 1965, SANTA MONICA, CALIFORNIA

I WAS THERE: GHRAYDON WALLICK

The second time I saw Dylan was in 1965 at the Santa Monica Civic Auditorium at the concert that became the pivotal event in his career. That concert thrust him into the mainstream popular culture as a star and icon. People just hung around waiting to be close to him and crowding his car in the parking lot when he tried to leave between shows.

LONDON

APRIL 1965

I WAS THERE: JOHN MAYALL, MUSICIAN

When he first came to London to do a tour, his whole entourage came and apparently the word got out that he wanted to meet me of all people, rather than more important people on the scene. I heard that he really like one of my records 'Crawling Up A Hill' and he wanted to meet me.

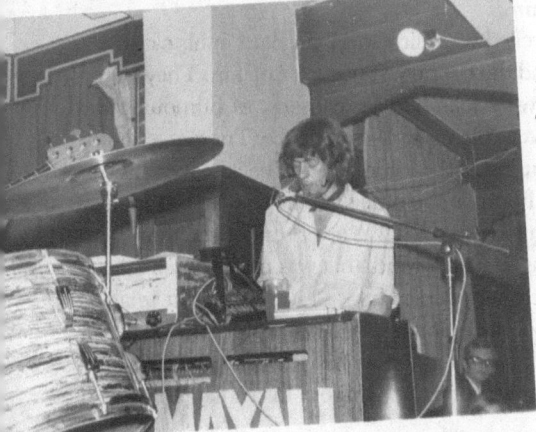

John Mayall on stage in the late Sixties

John Mayall thinks he has the answer to 3 across in the Melody Maker crossword

So, I was able to go over and meet him at the Savoy Hotel. He was a very nice guy, we got on very well. But what he was interested in was my single 'Crawling Up A Hill', and the story of how I got started on the London scene. He seemed to want to use me to get introduced to certain people, which was rather surprising in that why he picked me? He wanted to meet Marianne Faithfull and several other people so I was like the conduit and I have to say it was very nice hanging out with him.

I tagged along and travelled with him and Joan Baez in his car to a few of the concerts around the country. It was a lot of fun. They were great people to hang out with. Joan had a great sense of humour, it was very free and easy and a very pleasurable experience. There is a photo knocking around of me sitting in the middle of the back seat of his car with Joan on one side and Bob on the other. All the concerts, as far as I remember, he was very well received, it was a very successful tour.

Regarding the recording session we did, that was pretty much a disaster and it never came to anything. He was rather vague in what he wanted us to do, so as far as I remember Eric Clapton, myself, John McVie, and Hughie Flint all went to the studio. We were at a total loss as to what he was up to. We were all set up with our instruments and ready to play but he just didn't seem to know what he wanted from us. And he didn't seem to know what he wanted to play. We just waited for some ideas that we could get our teeth into. We were mystified in why we were there, we'd been chosen to come and play with Dylan, but we weren't doing anything!

Tom Wilson was the producer as such, but we just diddled around and we were just waiting for something to happen. If he'd just given us some guidelines as what he wanted us to do. I think he just wanted us to play with him as his backing group, but who knows what he wanted, but we were summoned.

THE OVAL

30 APRIL, 1965, CITY HALL, SHEFFIELD

REVIEW FROM THE SHEFFIELD UNIVERSITY PAPER

His dark-circled eyes seemed to peer above the conglomeration surrounding him (two microphones, a table with two glasses of much-needed water and a harmonica cradle round his polo-sweatered neck), while his penetrating songs convinced even the most cynical that Bob Dylan is worthy of the mound of superlatives which has been heaped upon him and under which his earlier followers feared he might suffocate.

An essential part of the popular image is the loneliness of Bob Dylan. He sings about it, in haunting symbols. He sings too about bitterness, of 'The flesh-coloured Christ's that glow in the dark'. Make no mistakes though – Dylan can write in glowing images about war and violence but he can write with equal insight, and strictly for laughs, about the things that are reality to a greater part of his audience, like the boy trying to persuade his girl to stay for the night.

Dylan has been set up as everything from a blue-denim god to a guitar-playing Socrates, corrupting youth by opening the door on hooliganism, warning the universal parent: 'Your sons and your daughters are beyond your command'. It was for this reason that we approached him with some trepidation (and considerable difficulty, owing to positive festoons of red tape). We anticipated meeting the 'sullen, bored Mr. Dylan' about whom so much has been written in the Press lately – and found instead an individual who was very tired but very willing to talk. He answered our questions in his room at the Grand Hotel, perched on the edge of a couch, a cup of black coffee in one hand, a cigarette (Player's, untipped) in the other. Around him his entourage: a tough, voluble manager with flowing grey hair; a hip-talking young man with glasses and [a lovely?] jacket; a tall negro with an engaging chin; a dark, chatty girl hitching a plastic iris.

THE ODEON, LIVERPOOL

1 MAY, 1965, LIVERPOOL

I WAS THERE: JOHN SHARPLES, AGE 16

I went to the 1965 gig in Liverpool, it was the day Liverpool Football Club won the FA Cup!

At the end of the concert I went round to the stage door and met a guy called Pennenbaker, he was with a blonde girl and they were making a film about Bob's UK tour. I asked them if they'd seen The Cavern, the Pier Head, the Liver Buildings etc and they said no. So I took them on a tour on foot of the 'must see' sites around the city.

The Georges Plateau was full of Liverpool Football Club fans celebrating their win, much to my disgust as I'm a Blue, (I support the other team from Liverpool – Everton).

John Sharples (center) takes some mature Dylan fans on a trip around Liverpool

I was asked if this was a typical Saturday night in the city and had to explain why it was like this.

I took them to see Matthew Street were The Cavern Club was and the Iron Door where The Beatles also played, the Pier Head, Liver Buildings, the India Buildings and the famous Dicky Lewis statue.

They asked me if I would like to meet Bob Dylan and on the following day, (Sunday) at 12.30 I turned up at the Adelphi Hotel where Pennenbaker waved me through the police cordon and I was introduced to Bob sitting in the back of his limo. I had a Dylan hat on and he said, 'I've got one of those' and put my hat on. I found him to be a quiet – shy young man. These are days I will never forget.

I WAS THERE: COLIN EATON, AGE 14

I was at both of the concerts in the Sixties (and the 'comeback' at the Isle of Wight' in 1969). I was 14 years old in 1965 and a huge fan of Bob Dylan. I remember that the day got off to a great start as Liverpool FC won the FA Cup for the first time in their history that afternoon. I watched the game at my relatives' flat in Birkenhead, after which my uncle 'taxied' me and my cousin to Liverpool through the Mersey Tunnel dropping us off in Lime Street, just round the corner from the Odeon . Our seats were in the circle and gave us an excellent view.

Colin Eaton was lucky enough to get a signed photo of Dylan in Liverpool

I was expecting Dylan to perform his most popular songs but my memory of the gig was being stunned to hear one brand new song after another, most of which formed *Bringing It All Back Home*. Happily some of that tour was captured on film in *Dont Look Back*.

In the Sixties, my cousin Pat (Patricia) was head of the record department at Boots the Chemist when it was situated on the corner of Church St and Hanover St in Liverpool. She frequently received promotional material from the big record companies, which were displayed in her department. In 1966 they where given large black and white cardboard-backed photos of Dylan (the one on back of the *Highway 61 Revisited* cover) by CBS records and told her that she could, if she wished, meet Dylan at his suite at the Adelphi hotel on the day of the concert.

At that time, a colleague of Pat's was keener on Dylan so she passed the invitation on to the young lady (who's name I have long forgotten). Pat gave her colleague one of the photos and asked her to ask Dylan to sign it for me. She returned to work on Monday with the photo signed 'Hi Bob Dylan' in black ink. She met him very briefly and said that he stood when they were introduced – a gentleman!

1966 was a very different experience. Dylan seemed to race through the acoustic songs but the audience were happy. When he resumed with The Hawks (then unknown to most people in the audience including me) the atmosphere rapidly changed. They opened with 'Tell Me Mama' which I thought was fantastic. Unfortunately many others were not impressed and made their feelings known. The booing soon started and Dylan responded by boosting the volume to almost painful levels. My cousin and I were in the stalls close to the stage this time and I remember turning in my seat and yelling at the barrackers to SHUT UP!

After 50+ years I struggle to remember any more details. I do know for certain that I was thrilled to be at both gigs and still have the Official Programme and ticket stubs from 1966 (£1 admission!).

I WAS THERE: SPENCER LEIGH

I saw the ad in the *NME* that Bob Dylan was undertaking a concert tour in the UK and the second date would be at the Odeon Cinema in Liverpool City centre on Saturday, May 1, Cup Final day, as it happens. The Odeon, around the corner from the Empire, showed films but there was the occasional stage show and I saw Brook Benton and Dion there in October 1963.

Only a few weeks earlier, I had gone to a poorly attended Tamla-Motown package at the Empire Theatre with Stevie Wonder, the Supremes, and Martha and the Vandellas, so within a month, I saw Stevie Wonder, Diana Ross and Bob Dylan. I had no trouble in purchasing Dylan tickets – the *NME* said when tickets would be on sale and I simply walked across town to the Odeon in my lunch-hour: there wasn't a queue. Couldn't have been easier: I don't even think tickets cost more than £1.

The day before I saw Bob Dylan, I got a letter from Frankie Vaughan's musical director, Basil Tait. I had heard a record 'I Keep Forgettin'' by Chuck Jackson that I thought might be suitable for Frankie. I told Mr Tait about it and he sent me a letter to say, 'No, it wasn't suitable but I've recorded it with Ray Cousins and here's a copy.' I didn't know who he was but he sounded okay. It was the first time I'd ever had any influence on anything on vinyl, so I felt a little proud. I hoped it would crash into the Top 10 but it meant nothing.

I bought two tickets, one for myself and one for my girlfriend, Diana. I wasn't sure that Diana would like it. She'd heard me play Bob Dylan's albums, especially *The Times They Are a-Changin'*, and she didn't care for him. She hated his voice, his songs, his stark instrumentation – in fact, the whole enchilada. I told her that he would be quite different in person and she would love him. I realise how naive and stupid I was – you don't browbeat your tastes onto other people. Mind you, I play records I like on local radio each week so maybe I haven't changed much.

We went into Liverpool on the bus, got off at the terminus and walked down Lime Street towards London Street. As we turned the corner we saw the lettering above the entrance: 'The Sound of Music, 2.30' on the top line and 'Bob Dylan, 7.30' on the bottom. The cinema's plush curtains were shut and in front of them on a small stage, a platform really, were two microphones, one head-high, one waist-high, a stool and a table which contained harmonicas, a carafe and a glass; minimalism, but strangely exciting. If the show had been at the Empire, the curtains would have covered the stage, but this was great – the anticipation of knowing that my hero was about to appear, stand there and play his songs. If there was a programme, I wouldn't have bought one – in my arrogance, I would have told Diana that I knew it all already: I was insufferable and I'm embarrassed to write this but it's true.

The place was full and Dylan did two sets, but everything didn't go to plan. Dylan started with 'The Times They Are a-Changin'', or at least I think he did, as his vocal mic wasn't working. A technician came on stage to sort it out and Dylan just hung around. Surely the man who was so good with words could have said something to us through the good mic. As it turned out, he didn't say one word to us all night. When the techno got it working, there was a huge cheer from us all, and Dylan started on his rallying song, opening with a quick burst on his harmonica. It was followed by the beautifully sensitive 'To Ramona'. He was singing his lyrics much clearer than on record as if he wanted to get every word across to a UK audience.

The lengthy and complex 'Gates of Eden' was next but he lightened the mood with the humorous 'If You Gotta Go, Go Now', which we'd never heard before. He played up the absurdity in 'It's Alright, Mama (I'm Only Bleeding)' but I'd noticed Diana had stopped clapping – did she ever start? The wonderfully lyrical 'Love Minus Zero/No Limit' was next and he closed the first half with 'Mr. Tambourine Man'. 'Don't worry,' I told Diana, 'the second half will be better.' I don't remember anything else about the interval except that it was awkward.

The funniest moment of the night occurred in the opening song from the second set, 'Talkin' World War III Blues'. He changed a line so that when he turned on the radio, it was no longer Rock-a-day Johnny but 'Donovan (pause, laughter from audience), whoever Donovan is (more laughter).' He changed the line, 'I think Abraham

Lincoln said that' to 'I think Robert Frost said that'. A friend told me that he said, 'I think TS Eliot said that' in Newcastle so he was testing variations.

'With God On Our Side' was chilling and I still think that the line about Judas Iscariot is the most surprising, the most thoughtful, the most provocative line ever written in a popular song. It was followed by the cheerful mysteriousness of 'She Belongs to Me' and the bitterness of 'It Ain't Me, Babe'. I had a friend with an active sex life and we had written a new version for him, 'It Ain't My Babe', and the alternative and much feebler words were going round in my head. Sorry, Bob.

Then there was the tragedy of 'The Lonesome Death Of Hattie Carroll', one of the few protest songs in which he named names. Dylan had a coughing fit when he started 'All I Really Want To Do' and after drinking water, he started again, almost yodelling the title line. Everything about Dylan was anti-showbiz so why did he close with 'It's All Over Now, Baby Blue'? But it was all over now, baby blue, as there was no encore. You knew an artist wasn't coming back when the National Anthem started. I'd been hoping for 'Subterranean Homesick Blues' as it was in the Top 20 and even though he had recorded it with rock musicians, surely he had composed it on an acoustic guitar. Not to worry, the concert had been great, superlative even.

I was on my feet applauding as were most of the audience. As we were going out, somebody said, 'I don't how he remembers all those words' to which the reply was 'I don't know how he wrote them.' Amen to that.

There was a wonderful feeling on Lime Street as Liverpool had beaten Leeds at Wembley and had therefore won both the League and the Cup. The supporters who were coming off the London trains or out of the pubs were as happy as we were. Did Bob Dylan think Liverpool was always as happy as this? Did he appreciate that Liverpool had won the Cup?

I'd love to add that Diana was converted but she complained that I had wasted two hours of her life. She finished with me there and then. We did get back together and in 1966 we were again having a threesome with Bob Dylan.

DE MONTFORT HALL

2 MAY, 1965, LEICESTER

I WAS THERE: ANGIE HIRST, AGE 16

The first time I saw Dylan was at the De Montfort Hall, Leicester in 1965. My friend and I were 16. De Montfort Hall is surrounded by a park. We arrived early and saw Joan Baez sitting on the grass, reading a book. Considering we spent most evenings after school trying to emulate her 'Death of Queen Jane' and 'Silver Dagger' we couldn't believe our eyes, no idea she was even in the UK. We plucked up courage to speak to her, upon which she gathered her belongings to head inside. But we did ask her if she was going to sing with Dylan, and she said she was! She didn't of course, and thereby hangs a whole other tale.

Second time was same place 1966, two days before Manchester I believe, but the mass walkouts were well documented before then. First set was acoustic of course. We were standing room only, but so many people walked out after the interval that we helped ourselves to front row seats. I still have the programme.

CITY HALL

6 MAY, 1965, NEWCASTLE UPON TYNE

I WAS THERE: BRIAN SWALES

My friends and I first became interested in Bob Dylan in 1964 after hearing the Animals version of 'House Of The Rising Sun'. When we heard that Bob Dylan was to tour the UK in 1965 we just had to get tickets. In those days you could apply by post for tickets to a music shop in Newcastle, the cost of the tickets was £1.10s (£1.50). May 6 was the day and we travelled to Newcastle by train, really looking forward to seeing the concert. We had been to several pop shows at the City Hall previously and generally the stage was full of guitars on stands, drum kits, amplifiers, and microphones, etc. But when we got into the City Hall, the stage was empty apart from one microphone and a stool with a glass of water on it. Eventually the lights dimmed and we waited with bated breath for the concert to start.

I seem to remember (but I could be wrong) but I don't think he was actually announced he just ambled on the stage from the right to tumultuous applause. He stood there for a few moments and eventually started to sing his opening number, which I think was 'The Times They Are a-Changin''. Then the PA system failed and nobody could hear him! While the PA system was being fixed, he just chatted to the audience, unfortunately our seats were several rows back and we couldn't hear what he was saying but I remember hearing people laughing nearer the front. As it turned out this was his last ever solo acoustic tour, two months later he was booed at the Newport Folk Festival for going electric.

The UK tour was documented by film maker Donn Pennebaker, who used footage of the tour in his documentary *Dont Look Back*.

FREE TRADE HALL

7 MAY, 1965, MANCHESTER

I WAS THERE: ALAN H FRASER

I was introduced to folk music, believe it or not, in my days in the Scouts in the late Fifties and early Sixties. We Scouts went camping regularly in the spring and summer months, and one of the things I liked most about Scout camps was sitting round the campfire in the evening (we had dry summer evenings then), singing rousing songs, many peculiar to the Scout movement, many just stupid or in bad taste, but also many from the British and American folk music traditions.

Therefore, when I left home in October 1963, to attend the

Alan H Fraser studies his record collection at Hulme Hall, Manchester

Manchester University Institute of Science and Technology, I left my Scouting days behind, but one of the undergraduate groups I joined was the Folk Club. We had meetings at people's homes where those who could, played, those who couldn't, sang, and those like me who couldn't do either, just listened and enjoyed. We also played the records of our favourites, sometimes went to local clubs, and also to concerts at venues like the Free Trade Hall. We even, on fine weekend days, went on rambles in the nearby Peak District stopping at country pubs for lunch and singing as we rambled – especially after lunch! I continued to enjoy with friends the music I was familiar with, such as that sung by the Spinners (who I saw at the Free Trade Hall), Ewan MacColl and Peggy Seeger, Martin Carthy, and Alex Campbell, to name but a few. I was also introduced by the more adventurous to a completely new type of folk music. This was the new American folk scene – artists like Joan Baez, Judy Collins, Pete Seeger, Phil Ochs, Tom Paxton, and eventually Bob Dylan.

Peter, Paul and Mary's version of 'Blowin' in the Wind' was popular, so I bought and loved it. I decided to check out the song's author, one Bob Dylan – no-one I knew actually had one of his records at that time. He had no singles out that I could trace, so off I went to the record shop and bought his current LP, *The Freewheelin' Bob Dylan* (at £1/12/6, or about $6.50 at the then exchange rate, a major investment in those days). First track was 'Blowin' in the Wind'. I took it out of the sleeve, put it on my record player, and dropped the arm down. What a shock! No vocal harmonies by PPM here, just that harsh solo voice and guitar. I didn't like it at first, but I listened to the whole album anyway, after all, it had just cost me good money that could have gone on beer. I eventually decided that the guy had something, even if it wasn't conventionally appealing, and kept listening. When *The Times They Are a-Changin'* came out, I bought it straight away, and went through three copies of that LP. *Another Side Of Bob Dylan* – completely unaware of the controversy in the Village, we loved that album too.

In May ,1965, a group of us went to the Manchester Free Trade Hall to see Bob Dylan for his all-acoustic solo show; a little skinny guy with a guitar and a table of harmonicas filling the hall with his music. What an event! Everyone enjoyed it very much indeed – a classic concert with plenty of songs that we'd never heard before – 'Mr. Tambourine Man', 'It's All Over Now, Baby Blue', and the song I remember as a tour-de-force – 'It's All Right Ma (I'm Only Bleeding)'. Wonderful stuff! After the show I bought Bob's new album *Bringing It All Back Home*. It was the second great surprise of my Bob fandom to set the needle down and hear the first electric song, with electricity continuing for the rest of side one. All unfamiliar songs in an unfamiliar style. No-one was impressed. Side two was a different matter, of course. Here were all but one of the new songs that we had enjoyed at the concert. We all agreed that one of the new songs on side one should have been dropped to accommodate the song we'd guffawed at the Free Trade Hall – 'If

Alan H Fraser (jacket on the left) meets other folk music fans outside a public house in Derbyshire

You Gotta Go, Go Now'. The obvious one was 'Maggie's Farm', that was rubbish. However, I lent the album to Tony Morriss, a guy who lived in the same house who was definitely not a Dylan fan. He thought that side two of the album was boring, but that side one was amazing – he especially raved about 'Maggie's Farm'! So, a new perspective on Dylan was emerging, a new group of fans who had no interest in his old stuff. I, probably alone amongst my folkie friends, played side one secretly, and started to get into it...

In May, 1966, Bob was coming back to the Free Trade Hall, but rumours came along that this time he was playing a dual format show, his acoustic songs solo in the first half and his electric songs with a band after the interval. There was no formal decision not to go, and certainly no idea of going and booing in the second half. We just didn't go. Also, it was right in the middle of my final exams – under the circumstances I didn't feel like going on my own. (I'm sure I had an important exam that I hadn't prepared well enough for on Wednesday, May 18!) That's how on one of the most momentous nights in the history of rock music, I wasn't at the Free Trade Hall, even though I was there in the city, and only a couple of miles away from the event.

One day in 1966, I left my classes in Central Manchester to get the bus back to Rusholme where I was living (Rusholme is now known as the 'Curry Mile', but there was not one Indian restaurant there then). On the way to the bus stop, I passed a record shop (more than likely Johnny Roadhouse's on Oxford Road) and saw in the window a new album from Bob Dylan, *Blonde on Blonde*. I checked my pocket – I had enough to buy an album with some left over, so I went in to buy it. To my great surprise, the assistant handed me a double album, the first I'd ever seen. And it was £1 more than the regular price. I checked my pocket again – I had just enough to buy it, but not enough to buy the album and get the bus home. My choice was simple, buy the album and walk home, or leave it for another day and get the bus. I looked at the album again, I folded out the amazing gatefold sleeve with the full-length sideways picture of Bob... I walked home.

I WAS THERE: JOHN KAPPES

I first saw Bob Dylan in 1965 at the Free Trade Hall in Manchester UK, my ticket was in the stalls HH21.

John Kappes (in white t-shirt) joins in a sing song with his multi-instrumentalist friend

I first became a fan maybe a couple of years earlier at school – a friend of mine came into class asking if anybody had any Bob Dylan LPs, as his older brother wanted to listen. Someone brought two in the next day to school – *Bob Dylan* and *The Freewheelin' Bob Dylan*, the only two LPs so far. On the way home we played these on my record player – 'House of The Rising Sun' was first – what was this? We thought as it was not what we were used to hearing on the radio in those days – the more we played the more we liked.

My friends brother was at Salford University and one day I was asked if I would like to see Bob Dylan at the Free Trade Hall in Manchester, tickets were 20 shillings plus a 1 shilling booking fee. Somehow my Dad bought one for me – a lot of money in those days, my friend's brother was able to get to the ticket sellers early because of his proximity to Manchester town centre.

Eventually the day arrived and off we went in a grey Ford Anglia van with me rolling around in the empty space in the back, into the Free Trade Hall we went, and on Bob came strumming the chords to 'The Times They Are a-Changin'' from halfway across the stage. Needless to say he was brilliant. I remember people sitting on the stage behind him and a camera pointing through the curtains at the side – *Dont Look Back* no doubt. Well, the recording is available so I cannot add much more, memories of the Donovan quip and a really captivating performance – I have never seen anyone so good since – Jimi Hendrix was great too!

A 23-year-old Bob Dylan made his first appearances at the Royal Albert Hall on May 9 and 10, 1965, soon after the release of his fifth studio album *Bringing It All Back Home*. The concerts were the final dates of Dylan's England Tour 1965 – noted as being his last ever solo acoustic tour. A selection of songs from these performances can be seen in DA Pennebaker's documentary film *Dont Look Back*.

ROYAL ALBERT HALL

9-10 MAY, 1965, LONDON

I WAS THERE: PATRICE HAMILTON

Patrice Hilton who later in life spent an afternoon with Dylan drinking wine

I first heard about this new 'folksinger' in 1963 when I was only thirteen years old, but because I mixed with an older crowd at Croydon Art College, I'd been introduced to Blues and Folk music at an early age. There was a thriving coffee bar scene in Croydon at the time and people like John Mayall and the Bluesbreakers, Long John Baldry, Alexis Korner and Bert Jansch regularly played in venues around the town. The first Dylan LP I ordered was *The Freewheelin' Bob Dylan* – record shops in those days were really only electrical appliance shops with a couple of peg board booths upstairs where you could listen to new releases. When it rained we'd stay up there all afternoon listening to all sorts of stuff that we never bought because we couldn't afford records back then. It took six weeks for my precious Bob Dylan LP to arrive and once I'd put it on my record player it blew me away and I've never looked back!

Back in the early Sixties there weren't a lot of music magazines around, *Melody Maker* and *New Musical Express* were the main ones and *Pop Weekly* was a small semi-glossy magazine that I collected at the time. So hearing about gigs was difficult to say the least, very different times from now where everything is global and at your fingertips, musical news of any kind didn't seem to reach the suburbs much. Also there were no pop music radio stations, just *Family Favourites* on a Sunday with the likes of Bing Crosby and Rosemary Clooney!

In 1965, I heard from one of my Beatnik mates that Bob Dylan was coming to the Royal Albert Hall. What a bit of luck! My dad worked at the *Daily Express* in Fleet Street so was in London most days. He

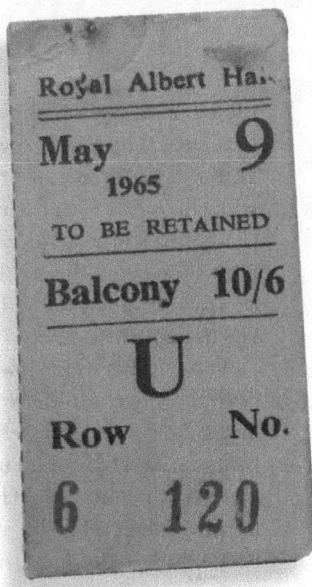

Patrice still has her ticket to this day

managed to get tickets for me and my four friends, so I didn't even have to go up to London to queue! The editor on the *Sunday Express*, who I will always be grateful to, secured the tickets and my dad went over to the Royal Albert Hall to collect them and said that the queue went round the building twice! We were so lucky to get them, they were 10/6d which was a fair bit to a schoolgirl at that time. I didn't care if I was sitting on the floor as long as I was going to be there.

I couldn't really believe that Bob Dylan was actually going to be there in person on stage. I'd seen Billy Fury at the ABC in Croydon back in 1962, The Rolling Stones at the Fairfield Halls in 1964, and a handful of musicians in smaller venues, but my concert going was in its infancy and this was BOB DYLAN!!

My friends and I met on May 9, 1965, outside the venue. I'd spent a long time deciding what to wear and had finally settled on a cream crocheted top, black velvet jacket, a black and white pinstriped mini skirt, cream lace tights and black bar shoes with wine coloured satin ribbons to add a bit of colour. I'd put my hair up to look older and was made up to the nines with false eyelashes and lipstick to match the ribbons on my shoes, I thought I looked the bees knees!

Going into the Albert Hall was like entering a Victorian Cathedral, the buzz of excitement was all around us as we made our way to our seats. The Beatnik brigade in their duffle coats, arty beards, long hair and Campaign for Nuclear Disarmament (CND) badges mixing with the mods with their cropped hair and sharp suits, with girls with bouffants, stiffly lacquered, and then the forerunners of the hippies in their flowing clothes and sandals, everyone was there! (In 1966, it was mostly the suited lot with their girlfriends who booed and hated the electric concert.)

As the lights went down this lone figure in a single spotlight came onto the stage and there he was – the beginning of something amazing. He was dressed in a black leather jacket, blue shirt, black trousers, and black cuban heeled boots, carrying his guitar and a clutch of harmonicas. He looked so small, I had no idea how tiny he was. I'd seen lots of publicity shots of him but somehow I didn't realise he was so slight, but my God what a powerhouse! He held the audience in the palm of his hand and after the initial polite applause you could have heard a pin drop. Crazy as it sounds I had the idea that I would try and write down the song titles in the dark, needless to say that didn't work, but I did manage to jot down a few notes which have come in handy for writing this piece. I was so captivated by his incredible performance that I couldn't concentrate on writing much, I didn't want to miss anything. We really didn't know if we would ever hear some of these songs again, we didn't have pocket recorders or sophisticated video equipment, I hadn't actually managed to get hold of a copy of *Bringing It All Back Home* at this point so I suppose that's what made it all the more magical, we had to soak it up and hope sometime these amazing songs would break into our world again.

Everyone applauded and then fell silent throughout each song. He spoke to the audience like a shy, excited, and giggly teenager; he sounded nervous but at the same time in total control. At some time during the concert he asked if anyone in the audience had a harmonica in a particular key and I think someone close to the stage actually gave him one! He changed his harmonicas quite a bit, slotting them into a metal holder around his neck, something I'd never seen any other performer use. He had a high stool on stage and a glass of water (I'm assuming it was water) which he occasionally sipped.

The first two songs, 'The Times They Are a-Changin'' and 'To Ramona' were sung in pretty much the same way that he'd sung them on his LPs but when he got to his third song, the masterpiece 'Gates of Eden', I was spellbound by his artistry. How could someone so young write such a magnificent song? Nobody else was writing or singing anything like this, of course at the time none of us realised the significance of what we were seeing – musical history being made. Who would have imagined that over 50 years later people would still hold this concert in such high esteem.

The next, 'If You Gotta Go, Go Now' was a light-hearted, comical song. Dylan giggled a lot introducing it and while he was singing it, it obviously reminded him of an event that almost certainly happened to him. The audience could relate to it and enjoyed it enormously, they laughed especially at the lines

> It ain't that I'm wantin'
> Anything you never gave before.
> It's just that I'll be sleepin' soon,
> It'll be too dark for you to find the door.

I hadn't heard this song before and nor had I heard 'It's Alright, Ma (I'm Only Bleeding)' to which he added 'Ho Ho Ho' to the title which again, amused the audience no end. Yet another phenomenal song, where were they coming from? He closed the first half of the show with a hauntingly beautiful 'Love Minus Zero No Limit' and the now legendary 'Mr. Tambourine Man', which I was hearing for the very first time. It was all too much to take in!

In the second half of the performance, Bob opened with 'Talking World War III Blues' which I'd heard before on Freewheelin' but he was in a very playful mood and changed some of the words around including saying that he 'looked in the closet and there was Donovan' this got a big laugh from the audience. There had been a lot in the press about Donovan, some said he was the 'English Dylan', he wishes, and they had tried to hype up that there was some kind of competitive feud going on between them, which really wasn't true at all. Later on when the film *Dont Look Back* came out, it was pretty obvious to all who saw it just who reigned supreme and who was in awe!

One of the many drawings of Dylan by artist Patrice Hamilton

A classic, 'Don't think Twice, It's All right' and 'With God On Our Side' came next, followed by a mix of older stuff and brand new, 'She Belongs to Me' and finishing with 'It's All Over Now, Baby Blue', his fifteenth song of the evening. These were magical new songs to my ears, but it had all gone too quickly. I was already wondering if I would be able to come here again next year. Well, I did and what a difference a year makes!

I WAS THERE: DAVID ROSE

The Beatles saw the evening performance by Bob Dylan at London's Royal Albert Hall.

After the show they visited Dylan at his suite at the Savoy Hotel, also present, as Dylan's guest, was beat poet Allen Ginsberg.

The atmosphere was tense at first, until Ginsberg fell into John Lennon's lap from the arm of a sofa. Asked by Ginsberg if he knew William Blake, Lennon replied that he'd never heard of him. His wife Cynthia said: 'Oh John, you liar, of course you have!' The exchange broke the ice.

After the Savoy meeting, Dylan suggested that John and Paul went to John Mayall's house in South East London to an impromptu party. Also present were Peter and Gordon, Donovan (who had also been at the Savoy), Alexis Corner, Eric Clapton, John McVie, (Fleetwood Mac), Hughie Flint, Manfred Mann (who lived a few doors down from John Mayall) and me! (Why I was there is a long and different story.) Much jamming went on that night! Dylan recorded with the Bluesbreakers a few days later at Levy's Recording Studio, London where they recorded (an unreleased version) of 'If You Gotta Go, Go Now', which Dylan had yet to record. You can hear a Bluesbreakers influence in Dylan's version – and this is where Manfred first heard the song, which they turned into a hit later that year.

COLUMBIA STUDIO A

15 JUNE, 1965, NEW YORK CITY, NEW YORK

I WAS THERE: MIKE BLOOMFIELD, GUITARIST

There was no concept. No one knew what they wanted to play, no one knew what the music what supposed to sound like other than Bob who had the chords, the words, and the melody. But as far as saying we're going to make folk rock records, no one had any idea what to do. They had the best studio drummer, they had a bass player – a guy called Russ Savakus (it was his first day playing electric bass); no one understood anything. The producer was non-producer, a guy named Tom Wilson; he didn't know what was happening, man. I think they wanted to rock 'n' roll, we did a least 20 takes of every song and it got ridiculous because they were long songs and poor Dylan, who was cranking out these 14 minute long songs, doing it three times. I finally said, 'Do you guys realise this is a 10 minute song?' It was never like, OK, here's one of the tunes, now let's learn it, work out the arrangement, it was just never done. Things just sort of fell together in this haphazard half-arsed way.

I WAS THERE: MIKE MICHAELS

On June 16 to be exact, the Paul Butterfield Blues Band was playing a regular gig at a Greenwich Village nightclub called the Café Au Go Go. I was hanging around backstage, a large cellar-like room with folding chairs scattered around and a small curtained-off section with a spinet piano. Bloomfield, popping in a few minutes before the first set, said in his Chicago accent, 'Hey man, I was just recording with Dylan and played on this really neat song.' He sat down at the piano and started playing a chord sequence: C, D minor, E minor, F, G7. That day Dylan, Bloomfield, and keyboard player Al Kooper had shown up at Columbia Record's New York studios and virtually on the spot put together 'Like a Rolling Stone,' with Bloomfield's lead guitar sparking and defining the swirling sound of the recording and thereby creating folk rock. Within a few months you could not turn on the radio without hearing 'Like a Rolling Stone,' with the same chord changes and the soaring lead lines by the guitarist on the session, Michael Bloomfield

WOODSTOCK

JUNE 1965, NEW YORK STATE

I WAS THERE: JOHN HERALD, MUSICIAN

He had just gotten an acetate of 'Like a Rolling Stone', and he was so excited he wanted everyone to hear it. Anybody he knew who would pass by the Café Espresso, he would run out and say, 'I've got this great new song, it's going to be really big, you've got to hear it.' Then he would take them inside and play it for them.

I WAS THERE: LEVON HELM, DRUMMER

We had never heard of Bob Dylan, but he had heard of us. He said, 'You wanna play Hollywood Bowl?' So we asked him who else was gonna be on the show. 'Just us' he said.

When Bob Dylan's 'Like a Rolling Stone' was released, on July 20, 1965, copies serviced to US radio stations cut the song in half and spread it over both sides of a red vinyl 45, giving them the option of airing only the first three minutes, thus preserving their normal song-to-commercial ratios. Dylan demanded that 'Like a Rolling Stone' play through, and soon a new pressing replaced the first. When the word spread stations were inundated by callers demanding the full six minutes of the song.

> **When I heard 'Like a Rolling Stone' in 1965 I wanted to quit the music business because I felt: If this wins and it does what it's supposed to do, I don't need to do anything else**
>
> **FRANK ZAPPA**

NEWPORT FOLK FESTIVAL

25 JULY, 1965, RHODE ISLAND

I WAS THERE: BRUCE LANGHORNE, GUITARIST

I saw part of the performance. I didn't see the whole performance, 'cause I think I came in in the middle of it. But I did catch half of it. I liked it. I thought it was excellent.

Some people were going, 'What the hell's that?' And some people were going, 'Oh wow!' But my overall impression was that more people were offended than were enchanted. That was my overall impression.

I WAS THERE: BOB LOVE

The folk community, the folk artists, the folk appreciators thought that rock 'n' roll music was beneath them, that it was pop music for teenage angst. And they thought that Dylan was trying to sell out. And it was shocking from top to bottom. He was dressed like a bluesman, like a rhythm & blues artist. He was not dressed like the proletariat ragamuffin that he presented himself as to the world for years. These folks, the elders of the folk community, had embraced Dylan as their own.

But somebody forgot to ask Dylan. And he had a different point of view about that. He didn't belong to anybody. He didn't belong to any movement. He didn't want to stay that way forever. He was doing what a true artist does, which was following his muse and his inner voice, which told him to go in this direction. He wasn't waiting for the approval of the audience. He wasn't seeking the approval of the audience and he hasn't many other times in his career; he was behaving the way an artist behaves.

I WAS THERE: JOE BOYD

I think there were a lot of people who were upset about the rock band, but I think it was pretty split. I think probably more people liked it than didn't. But there was certainly a lot of shouting and a lot of arguing, and a sound, which you can hear in a lot of ballparks. You used to get this confusion when Bill Skowron used to come up

The back cover of Like A Rolling Stone single released by CBS

to the plate for the Yankees, 'cause his nickname was Moose. And everybody used to go, 'MOOSE!' And it sounded like they were booing him. Because you don't get the articulation of the consonant, so that a crowd shouting 'more, more, more' at the end of Dylan's three songs sounded very much like booing. I've heard recently a recording of that night, and it doesn't sound to me like booing so much as a roar, just a kind of general hubbub between songs, and during Yarrow's attempt to get Dylan back on stage… I really wouldn't be prepared to say it was 50–50, or two-thirds/one-third, or whatever. But I think that there was a segment of the audience, somewhere between a quarter and a half, that was dismayed or horrified or varying degrees of unhappy about what he was doing.

I WAS THERE: AL KOOPER, MUSICIAN

The reason they booed is because he only played for fifteen minutes, when everybody else played for forty-five minutes or an hour. They were feeling ripped off. Wouldn't you? They didn't give a shit about us being electric. They just wanted more.

I WAS THERE: MURRAY LERNER

There's been a lot of debate over the years as to who exactly was doing the booing and who were they booing? Dylan? The organisers? The shortness of the set?

It's a good question. When we showed the film at The New York Film Festival in October 2007 one kid gets up and says, 'About this booing... I was sitting right in front of the stage, there was no booing in the audience whatsoever'. There was booing from the performers. Then another kid gets up and says, 'I was a little further back and it was the press section that was booing, not the audience'. A third guy gets up and says, 'I was there, and there was no question, it was the audience that was booing and there was no booing from the stage'.

People remember hearing what they thought they should hear. I think they were definitely booing Dylan and a little bit Pete Yarrow because he was so flustered. He was not expecting that audience's reaction and he was concerned about Bob's image, since they were part of the same family of artists through Al Grossman. But I absolutely think that they were booing Dylan going electric.

I WAS THERE: PETE SEEGER, MUSICIAN

Howlin' Wolf was using electric instruments at Newport the day before Dylan played his set. But I was furious that the sound was so distorted you could not understand a word that he was singing. He was singing a great song, 'Maggie's Farm', but you couldn't understand it. I ran over to the sound man and said, 'Fix the sound so you can understand him'. And they shouted back, 'No! This is the way they want it.' I don't know who 'they' was, but I was so mad, if I'd had an axe I would have cut the cable right there.

But I wasn't against Bob going electric, matter of fact; some of Bob's songs are still my favourites, what an artist he is. I would say maybe he and Woody, Buffy Saint Marie, Joni Mitchell and Malvina Reynolds are the greatest songwriters of the twentieth Century. Even though Irving Berlin made the most money, they wrote songs that tried to help us understand where we are and what we've got to do.

FOREST HILLS STADIUM

28 AUGUST, 1965, QUEENS, NEW YORK

I WAS THERE: DANIEL KRAMER

Dylan held a conference with the musicians who were going to accompany him in the second half of the concert. He told them that they should expect anything to happen, he probably was remembering what occurred at Newport. He told them that the audience might yell and boo, and that they should not be bothered by it. Their job was to make the best music they were capable of, and let whatever happened happen.

I WAS THERE: TONY GLOVER, MUSICIAN AND MUSIC CRITIC

Bob Dylan split 15,000 of his fans down the middle at Forest Hills Tennis Stadium. The most influential writer-performer on the pop music scene during the past decade, Dylan has apparently evolved too fast for some of his young followers, who are ready for radical changes in practically everything else... repeating the same scene that occurred during his performance at the Newport Folk Festival, Dylan delivered a round of folk-rock songs but had to pound his material against a hostile wall of anti-claqueurs, some of whom berated him for betraying the cause of folk music.

I WAS THERE: MICKEY JONES, DRUMMER

The Hawks never re-arranged anything with regard to Bob's songs. They were Bob's songs. Bob put them in the order that he wanted to do them and the arrangements were Bob's as well. We only played what Bob wanted. Bob did ask me to do a couple of eighth note build-ups and that is what I did. The rest of everything, I played the way I though was the best for the song.

Once we got together for rehearsals with Bob, we blocked everything else out. I tried to play straight ahead and kick Bob's music the way I saw fit. Bob liked everything I did but he did want those eighth note build-ups.

I had my style of playing. I had a heavy right foot and Bob loved that. Bob was pretty much bored with the first half of the night with his acoustic guitar. He could not wait to strap on that black Fender Telecaster and get out there and rock 'n' roll. There was no trick to that. He just wanted to rock.

We rehearsed for a couple of weeks before we started the tour but you have to remember, we were all pros at what we were doing. It didn't take much to make it happen. Once the tour started, it was the usual routine. We would travel to the next gig. Once there, we would do a sound check in the afternoon. That was not to rehearse but to check the acoustics of the room and to balance the sound system. Back to the hotel for a bite to eat and a change of clothes and then on to the hall for the concert. After the concert, we would all get together in someone's room and talk about the night's performance and listen to a tape of the evening's show. I think that is when I really realised that there was some booing.

Many nights Bob and I would talk until all hours of the morning. One night, in particular, I remember Bob and I being hungry and riding around in the Rolls Royce looking for a hot dog stand. It was pretty funny, Bob and I standing at the counter having a hot dog at four in the morning with no one around to see Bob having a hot dog.

I WAS THERE: SCOTT ROSS, RADIO AND TV DJ

It's difficult for me to comprehend, not just then, but even now, at so many different other levels. It's amazing the things that people deem important. Who cares, honestly, who cares? The guy plays music. If he wants to change his sound, who is he playing for? If you look at it as an artist, as a person, if you write certain kinds of music or use styles, lyrical content, rhythms, or whatever, it's an extension of who you are. That's how it was for Bob. And if any real artist, whether it's a painter or a writer or author, that's who they are, that's what they do. Critics and the public ... you know Scripture says, 'When all men speak well of you, beware.' I see all that fandom and I've seen a lot of it, been around a lot of it. It's next to irrelevant. It doesn't matter. I'm speaking for myself, and I don't want to project anything on to Bob, but you write out of who you are. If people like it, fine. If they don't like it, fine. It doesn't really matter. I saw all that criticism as a lot of foolishness, and I still do.

I WAS THERE: BRUCE SPRINGSTEEN

The first time that I heard Bob Dylan, I was in the car with my mother, and we were listening to, I think, WMCA, and on came that snare shot that sounded like somebody kicked open the door to your mind, from 'Like a Rolling Stone.' And my mother, who was no stiff with rock 'n' roll, she said, 'That guy can't sing.' But I knew she was wrong. I sat there, I didn't say nothin', but I knew that I was listening to the toughest voice that I had ever heard. It was lean, and it sounded somehow simultaneously young and adult, and I ran out and I bought the single. I played it, then I went out and I got *Highway 61*, and it was all I played for weeks. Bob's voice somehow thrilled and scared me. It made me feel kind of irresponsibly innocent. And it still does. But it reached down and touched what little worldliness a 15-year-old kid in New Jersey had in him at the time.

Dylan was a revolutionary – the way that Elvis freed your body, Bob freed your mind. He showed us that just because the music was innately physical, it did not mean that it was anti-intellect. He broke through the limitations of what a recording artist could achieve. Without Bob, The Beatles wouldn't have made Sgt. Pepper, maybe The Beach Boys wouldn't have made *Pet Sounds*, the Sex Pistols wouldn't have made 'God Save the Queen', U2 wouldn't have done 'Pride (In the Name of Love),' Marvin Gaye wouldn't have done 'What's Going On,' Grandmaster Flash might not have done 'The Message,' and the Count Five could not have done 'Psychotic Reaction'. And there never would have been a group named the Electric Prunes, that's for sure.

Highway 61 Revisited, the sixth studio album by Dylan, was released on August 30, 1965. Having until then recorded mostly acoustic music, Dylan used rock musicians as his backing band on every track of the album, except for the closing 11-minute ballad, 'Desolation Row'. He named the album after the major American highway which connected his birthplace, Duluth, Minnesota, to Southern cities famed for their musical heritage, including St. Louis, Memphis, New Orleans, and the Delta blues area of Mississippi.

Leading with the hit single 'Like a Rolling Stone', the album features songs that Dylan has continued to perform live over his long career, including 'Ballad of a Thin Man' and 'Highway 61 Revisited'.

'Like a Rolling Stone' was a Top 10 hit in several countries, and was listed at No 1 on *Rolling Stone's* 500 Greatest Songs of All Time list.

I WAS THERE: PHIL OCHS, MUSICIAN

It's the kind of music that plants a seed in your mind and then you have to hear it several times. And as you go over it you start to hear more and more things. He's done something that's left the whole field ridiculously in the back of him.

I WAS THERE: HARVEY BROOKS, BASSIST

I get a call from Al Kooper who said, 'I'm doing a session, some good players. Can you make it over? We need a bass player.' I said, 'Sure, I can be there.' So I went over to Columbia Studio B, on 799 Seventh Avenue, Victoria Hotel. I go in the elevator, I think it was the seventh floor, and I walk into the studio and the first thing I see is Albert Grossman. At the time, I'm not a longhaired guy, just a regular shorthaired guy, and I see this late fifty-year-old guy. I think that in that time, anyone over 40 was an old guy. I know better now. I see this guy listening to the playback, skinny kind of guy with folky looking clothes and it's Dylan.

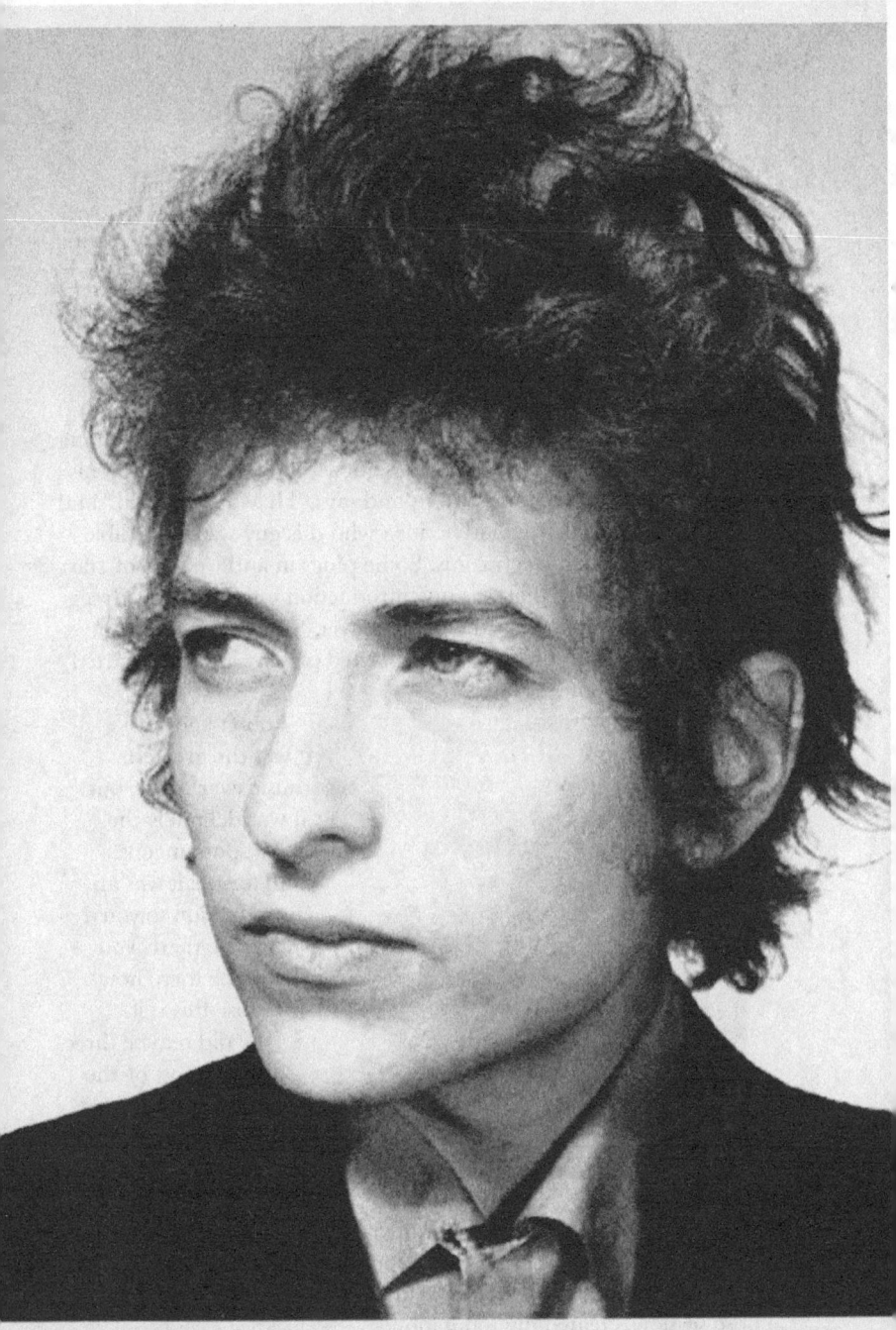

So we listen to the playback, they all sort of ignore me, and I didn't realise that that was how the lay of the land was and you are ignored until your presence is acknowledged. So I sit down and nothing's really happening for me, I then get up walk into the studio, I look around and see a bass amp and I think well this must be my point of contact. So I plug in and started playing a little bit and as I suspected, Dylan came out and said, 'How are you doing' man?' He introduced himself and we started talking and as I'm talking to Dylan the door in the studio bursts open and this guy comes running in with like wild electric hair and he's got a Fender Telecaster on his shoulder, no case. He runs up to us and says, 'Hi Man, Hi Man,' and it was Mike Bloomfield. I had no idea who this guy was, incredible guy, right off the bat, electric guy. So he plugs in and we kind of start noodling around and that was my introduction into it. Bobby Gregg the drummer, Paul Griffins the piano player, Kooper is on Organ. Dylan did a sort of nod and we just started playing and they started recording, it was almost surreal.

I don't know if it was the greatest music ever made, but it was definitely the most spontaneous, and for me it was an introduction to you'd better be there, you know, be there now, because this is it.

We did maybe three takes of most of the stuff; they were short sessions, maybe three to four hour sessions. The arrangements were basically just chord charts, I had to make my own, I would listen to the song and write them down as fast as I could and we just went. No arrangements, it was just as it was. Those sessions created my reputation.

HOLLYWOOD BOWL

3 SEPTEMBER, 1965, LOS ANGELES, CALIFORNIA

I WAS THERE: GARY 'DR BOOM' BAKER

Gary bought tickets to see Bob Dylan whilst in a queue to buy Beach Boys tickets.

'It's All Over Now Baby Blue…strike another match… go start anew…'

I didn't enter the Hollywood Bowl on the evening of September 3, 1965, as an angry young man. I walked to my seat as a naive, small town boy and left with my eyes wide-open. It was more like 'Take me on a trip upon your magic swirlin' ship. My senses have been stripped, my hands can't feel to grip. My toes too numb to step. Wait only for my boot heels to be wanderin'. I'm ready to go anywhere, I'm ready for to fade. Into my own parade, cast your dancing spell my way. I promise to go under it.'

The first time I heard 'Like a Rolling Stone' on the radio I was blown away – as Bruce Springsteen would later say about first hearing 'Like a Rolling Stone' he was in the car with his mother and heard that snare drum shot that sounded like someone kicked open the door to your mind, believe me that is exactly the way I felt hearing it for the first time the summer of 1965.

My world was rapidly changing the summer of '65 as I moved from a rural town of 10,000 to Los Angeles with more than three million. I was a small town boy who had found a whole new world in the city. After arriving in Los Angeles, I got to see my first live performances with The Rolling Stones, then The Beach Boys, followed by The Beatles, and at the end of that summer I saw my favourite songwriter – Bob Dylan.

When I was in line at the Hollywood Bowl box office to get The Beach Boys Summer Spectacular tickets earlier that summer, word spread threw the crowd that the Bob Dylan tickets had just gone on sale. When I got to the ticket window I asked for two Dylan tickets after purchasing The Beach Boys tickets. I scored third row box seats, little did I know what a life changing experience I would have in just four weeks.

Let me set the stage – there was something happening and it was in the air – new sounds coming out of the radio – a new attitude about life and what was important was sweeping the country. We were questioning what kind of life we wanted and how to create a culture of tolerance and understanding. Dylan was becoming the spokesperson for a generation, yet he never intended for that to be his calling.

Dylan's early 1965 album *Bringing It All Back Home* was released March 22, 1965, and was the precursor to *Highway 61 Revisited*. Dylan said The Beatles had an influence on the music he was creating at the time. Because The Beatles chord changes and harmonies were according to Dylan outrageous, he realised that you could only do what they were doing if he had other musicians playing with him. Also when Dylan first heard The Animal's version of 'The House of the Rising Sun' with Eric Burdon, a song he had covered on his first album, he made a decision to change the direction of his music he would now include rock musicians. The first seven tracks of *Bringing It All Back Home* had rock musicians accompanying him and the last four tracks mainly with acoustic guitar. Clinton Heylin would write; '*Bringing It All Back Home* was possibly the most influential album of its era'. Although I wasn't hooked on the electric change right away. I was mesmerised by the lyrics especially 'Gates of Eden', 'It's Alright Ma (I'm Only Bleeding)' and 'It's All Over Now, Baby Blue'. The last lines of Baby Blue was a clue of what was to come. 'Leave your stepping stones behind, something calls for you, forget the dead you've left, they will not follow you, the vagabond who's rapping at your door is standing in the clothes that you once wore, strike another match, go start anew, and it's all over now, baby blue.'

The night of the concert at the Hollywood Bowl, I drove from my apartment in North Hollywood to pick up my date who was a radiology student at The California Hospital on Hope Street in downtown Los Angeles. I got lost trying to find her dorm but eventually we made it to the parking lot of the Hollywood Bowl. It was a beautiful evening with a late summer fragrance floating in the air that was intoxicating as we walked in the promenade entrance between the garden boxes and the terrace boxes, the top of the garden boxes began with the ninth row and we walked down to our box seats in row three. I suddenly realised I had walked into another dimension of space and time. I had never seen so many freaks (a term at the time for counterculture folks that would soon be labeled hippies). I looked at my date in wonderment with her turquoise summer dress with spaghetti straps with full petticoats that caused her dress to flair out. I had on slacks, button down collared shirt, with a sport coat and realised we were the ones dressed differently than most of the crowd. Remember, these were the days when you put on a coat and tie when you got on a plane to say the least – we had stepped out of our past and into our future that night. We were a sight to behold – we were throwback before it was popular.

The show opened with Dylan solo-playing acoustic guitar accompanying himself with harmonica – this was the Dylan that most of the folkies came to see. He walks on to the stage without introduction and appeared somewhat vulnerable standing all alone with just his guitar and harmonica – he opened with 'She Belongs to Me'. Next up was 'Gates of Eden', I was really hearing this song for first time – not the first time I actually heard the song – but the first time I was affected by the lyrics, as I said the night air was intoxicating and the words were mesmerising .

The motorcycle black madonna
Two-wheeled gypsy queen
And her silver-studded phantom cause
The gray flannel dwarf to scream
As he weeps to wicked birds of prey
Who pick up on his bread crumb sins
And there are no sins inside the Gates of Eden

Next was the song that gave us the clue to what direction Dylan was headed, 'It's All Over Now, Baby Blue' is still one of my favourite Dylan tunes.

Another hypnotic song that evening was 'Desolation Row'.

> They're selling postcards of the hanging
> They're painting the passports brown
> The beauty parlor is filled with sailors
> The circus is in town
> Here comes the blind commissioner
> They've got him in a trance
> One hand is tied to the tight-rope walker
> The other is in his pants
> And the riot squad they're restless
> They need somewhere to go
> As Lady and I look out tonight
> From Desolation Row...

This song had just been released a few days earlier and the lyrics cause me to take inventory of how I had perceived my world up to this night and how my world would expand as Dylan took me on his magic carpet ride.

After a 50 minute acoustic set, he took a short break and came back with his band that included Robbie Robertson on guitar (replacing Mike Bloomfield who played the first electric show at the Newport Folk Festival and Dylan's show at Forest Hills, New York), Levon Helm on drums, Harvey Brooks on bass, and Al Kooper on organ.

The electric set started with a few boos from the crowd, but they soon subsided once everyone got into the amped up sound Dylan and the band were generating. I can't emphasise how affected I was by Dylan as a performer and songwriter – it would later be one of my musical highlights in the pantheon of artists and performers I would see over the next 50 plus years. He opened the electric set with 'Tombstone Blues', 'I Don't Believe You', 'From A Buick Six', 'Just Like Tom Thumb's Blues', 'Maggie's Farm', 'It Ain't Me, Babe', 'Ballad of a Thin Man', and he closed with the No 1 hit of the summer 'Like a Rolling Stone'.

Photo by Elliott Landy

Here are some of the highlights of the evening:

At the end of 'To Ramona' Dylan hears some guy in the audience blowing a horn and says, 'What is that thing out there, what are you trying to say?' That's all it took for the horn to silence and the songs proceeded without interruption from the audience.

Al Kooper, who was on organ, his playing was prominent and above the other instruments during the Bowl show. His organ playing on the 'Highway 61 Revisited' was phenomenal. He appeared on the album only because he showed up to the recording session at the invitation of the producer, Tom Wilson. Kooper brought his guitar and once he heard Mike Bloomfield play he packed up his guitar and went into the control booth, and when keyboardist Paul Griffin moved from organ to piano, Kooper snuck back into the studio and took up a position at the organ. Producer Wilson saw Kooper on organ but dismissed it because they could take the organ out of the final mix. After everyone went back into the control room to listen to the playback and after 30 seconds into the second verse of the playback, Dylan asked Tom Wilson to turn up the organ. Wilson responded 'That cat's not an organ player' but Dylan wasn't having any of it, 'Hey don't tell me who's an organ player and who's not. Just turn the organ up.' That's the moment Kooper said I became an organ player.

Since Robbie Robertson and Levon Helm were not Dylan's backing band yet, I wasn't familiar with them but I do remember Helm and bassist Harvey Brooks laid down a great bottom-end for the electric set.

The band was tuning for their last song and Dylan needed a 'C' harmonica and asked if anyone had one. Harmonicas started sailing towards the stage and Dylan had to step back to keep from being pelted with the flying harps.

Dylan and I had similar small town experiences growing up listening to late night radio stations broadcasting hundreds of miles away, circus shows and the midway barkers that brought some colourful characters to town once a year, along with the desire to explore more of the world than what we had known up to this point.

After this night, I would put albums on the turntable and really listen to the words to the songs looking for a deeper meaning especially the forthcoming Dylan albums.

Others attending that night were Johnny Cash, Peter Fonda, Mel Brooks, and Gregory Peck sitting near my seat.

Dylan would later become one of the most influential songwriters in America – I am forever thankful that I was able to experience this life changing concert. Dylan took 'me disappearin' through the smoke rings of my mind. Down the foggy ruins of time, far past the frozen leaves. The haunted, frightened trees, out to the windy beach. Far from the twisted reach of crazy sorrow. Yes, to dance beneath the diamond sky with one hand waving free silhouetted by the sea, circled by the circus sands. With all memory and fate driven deep beneath the waves.'

I WAS THERE: ROBERT ORLANDO, AGE 20

This was not only my first concert; it was my first Dylan concert. I went to the show with my 16 year-old brother and a couple friends from the city college I was attending at the time. My brother is also an avid fan.

I'd been a fan for some time before the show and had taken a lot of heat for it. 'How can you listen to this Dylan guy?' – they pronounced it Die-lan – 'He can't even sing?'
To me the Bowl show was spectacular. Both sets. Funny, I don't remember any booing if there was any. I was seated way in the back of the arena, Dylan looked tiny, but came across as a giant to me.

I was a fan before that, but that night pushed me over the edge. I was a 20-year old California transplant from rural Pennsylvania and that night I became a fan for life.

Songs that stood out: 'Desolation Row', 'Love Minus Zero/No Limit', 'Ballad of a Thin Man', 'Like a Rolling Stone' and 'Just Like Tom Thumb's Blues.'

Since then I've been to somewhere in the neighbourhood of 150 shows. I've stopped counting. LA, Hollywood, San Francisco, San Diego, Los Vegas, Santa Barbara, Sacramento, Visalia, Bakersfield, Anaheim – can't remember where else. And in all those times, I've never really seen the same Bob twice. That's what I love about him.

It was at Columbia's Studio A, on 52nd Street in New York City, that Dylan began working on the follow-up to *Highway 61* in October and November of 1965. On hand to provide the backing were the Hawks in the form of guitarist Robbie Robertson, bassist/violinist Rick Danko, keyboardist/saxophonist Garth Hudson and drummer Bobby Gregg. Also present were Al Kooper, guitarist Bruce Langhorne and keyboard player Paul Griffin.

COLUMBIA STUDIO A

OCTOBER 1965, NEW YORK CITY, NEW YORK

I WAS THERE: BOB JOHNSTON

When I walked in and I said, 'Bob, I'm Bob Johnston,' he said, 'Well, I'm Bob Dylan,' and he stood up and smiled the sweetest smile, and I said, 'Is that the way it's gonna be?' He said, 'Why not?' And I said, 'Great. What's this piece of paper?' It was a notebook and it had 22 takes of a song in it. I said, 'What's this 22 here?' He said, 'That's what we did.' I said, 'I just wondered why did you do 22 takes?' He said, 'The musicians all say we've got to do this and that.' I said, 'I thought your name was Dylan. I thought you cleared your mind to get other stuff in and once is enough. You don't have to entertain that bunch of goddamn people.' I turned around and walked off and he said, 'Let's do it.' They did a song. We finished and Al Kooper said, '10 or 15 more of those and it'll be great.' Dylan said, 'That's it.' He never did another song twice for me. He blew my mind. He went into the studio about 9 in the morning, and he never came out until about 3 o'clock in the afternoon.

Those musicians worked in their own way, and they knew what they did and didn't want to do. However, I told them that if they quit during a take, they could collect their coats on the way out the door. I didn't want the bass waiting for the guitar to come in before the pianist did his thing – play all the way through. If you've got a band, it's gonna be good; if you don't have a band, it'll sound like shit. So, that's what they did.

I WAS THERE: KRIS KRISTOFFERSON

I was a studio setup man, it was sort of like a janitor, at Columbia Records. They had people like George Jones and Carl Perkins and I got to know Johnny Cash. I also got to see Bob Dylan recording *Blonde on Blonde*. I never said a word to him – I didn't dare – but I spoke to his wife and son. In Nashville at the time, if you didn't cut three songs in three hours, you were being extravagant and wasteful. He just went in there and sat down at the piano, all by himself, and wrote all night long. The band were playing ping-pong and waiting for him. I'd never seen anything like it.

VETERANS MEMORIAL AUDITORIUM

19 NOVEMBER, 1965, COLUMBUS, OHIO

I WAS THERE: RICKI CACCHIONE

November was a pretty big month for me and rock 'n' roll shows at the now, sadly demolished Veteran's Memorial Auditorium. I saw Dylan there on November 19, 1965, The Doors there on November 2, 1968, and The Who touring *Tommy* for the first time.

I was in eighth grade when this show took place. I was smart and I read a lot of books but I was also so shy, so socially backward, that some of my classmates regarded me as mentally retarded. I think Dad brought me to those shows just because he was gratified that I took an interest in anything that happened outside of books or outside of our home. The only two songs I knew by Bob Dylan at that moment were 'Like a Rolling Stone' and 'Positively 4th Street.' As such, I was totally unprepared for and mystified by the solo acoustic opening half of the show that Dylan performed. At that point I didn't even know Dylan ever was a folksinger. Plus I could not for the life of me figure out why I couldn't understand anything that Dylan was singing about. From later record-buying research I know that he performed 'Gates of Eden' and 'Desolation Row' that night. I could clearly understand every word being sung, but I couldn't parse what any of the songs were about. At that point I had my little Dave Clark 5 and my Lovin' Spoonful singles: I knew what those guys were singing about, but what was this?

By time he finished with 'Mr. Tambourine Man' (which I at least recognised from The Byrds' version, but where did all those extra verses come from?) I was actually frozen in my seat, physically afraid of what had just transpired. Plus the people sitting all around me were not the usual teenage fans of rock 'n' roll shows, they were the wispily bearded college boys and girls with long, straight, ironed hair: the proto-hippies whose ranks I would join much later in the Sixties. That night – to my eighth-grade self – they were just alien, scary and weird. Dad would usually come to check on me at the intermission of shows. That night – as he related to me later – I wouldn't even look at him when he came to say hello. 'Are you okay?' he said after I stared straight ahead through his greeting and attempts at simple communication. 'Yes!' I said, a little too loudly and quickly for the question. 'Is something wrong?' Dad continued, genuinely concerned about my obviously nerved-out state of being. 'No, everything's fine,' I insisted, even though it was painfully obvious it wasn't. 'Do you want to leave?' Dad asked. 'No,' I said quietly, finally looking up at him, 'the show's not over yet.'

Dylan and The Hawks started the second half of the show blaring, it was completely epic and totally deafening, (I didn't see a show that loud again until The Who in 1969, and I haven't heard a show as loud as those two right up to this day). They opened – again in hindsight, I couldn't possibly have known it then – with 'Tell Me, Momma' and it was the greatest fucking thing I had ever heard. Finally, this is what I had come here for, this was the rock 'n' roll. So imagine my further confusion when people in the audience started yelling and throwing things at the stage and walking out in droves. And I'm serious about droves, it wasn't one or two people walking out, I would say I saw at least two dozen people leave and I was in the thirteenth or fourteenth row. I have no idea how many people from the balcony left. Here's another thing I should mention at this juncture: Veteran's Memorial Auditorium held 3,174 people at that point in its history. Of all the shows I've mentioned – The Doors,

Hendrix, Cream – not one of those shows sold out Vet's Memorial. If the show sold out, Dad couldn't pull me a ticket. At that point in the Sixties there just simply were not 3,000 rock 'n' roll fans in Columbus, Ohio. Of course after Woodstock in 1969, every show sold out because people came just to get high and/or make the scene. Before that August, only people who were interested in the actual music attended shows.

There was no functioning rock press in November 1965, to clue me in that fans of Dylan's earlier topical folk-song period were upset that he 'had gone electric' and – in their folky-cataracted eyes – 'had sold out.' For the moment I just had to remain perplexed that anyone could walk out on this sacred din. Things I remember like it was yesterday: during Robbie Robertson's solos, he and Dylan would stand practically nose to nose while Robertson snaked, snarled and slashed out those spark-spitting lead breaks that unfortunately he would never touch on again in the later days of the ever-so-much-more polite The Band. Also, on the subject of those leads, to this day I believe Dylan stood like that because he wanted the audience to think he was playing lead guitar. Even at 13 I had been studying John Lennon and George Harrison's hands long enough to know who was playing rhythm and who was playing lead.

Further great memories: Drummer Levon Helm (or was it Bobby Gregg that November evening, different Dylan tomes tell me conflicting stories) bashing away so hard on his high-hat cymbal that it kept sliding away from him all through the show and he would have to reach out and yank it back mid-tune; Dylan having a nicotine-inflicted coughing fit between tunes and informing the audience that he was 'just getting over a slight case of leprosy', having no earthly idea what it meant when Dylan sang, 'Baby, let me follow you down,' with The Hawks pounding out rock 'n' roll behind him, but simultaneously knowing, as the good little eighth-grade Catholic boy that I was at that moment, that whatever it was, it was totally wrong and evil, almost assuredly a mortal sin, and that I wanted to do it, too. Someday, when I was older, so much older than that day.

Bob Dylan married Sara Lownds on November 22, 1965, at a judge's office on Long Island, New York. The only guests were Albert Grossman and a maid of honour for Sara.

BURLINGTON

23 NOVEMBER, 1965, VERMONT

I WAS THERE: ROGER LATHBURY

There were perhaps 2,500 people there. I was already something of a fan after I'd first heard him. Tickets were $3.50 or $4.50; I bought my ticket at the window of the venue. Dylan was late coming on stage. When he did appear, he was surrounded by six burly bodyguards. They left and he launched into the first segment of his show, the acoustic half. Dylan himself was pale and extremely thin; he looked frail, vulnerable. He wore a light grey suit. The spotlight was bright white, just him on the bare stage. However, in contrast to the waif-like Dylan, the musical was strong, a striking contrast. I specifically remember 'Don't Think Twice It's All Right,' 'It Ain't Me, Babe' and 'Mr. Tambourine Man'.

What sticks even more in my head from this half is his harmonica. The solos were loud and piercing and could run as long as the singing. Sitting on a bleacher high above, I noted how many good songs he had, unlike other

Roger Lathbury with his guitar in his basement studio

singers with which I was familiar. People clapped for the harmonica solos; Dylan continued playing through the applause. There was no talk between the songs.

There was an intermission, after which the lights dimmed and the curtain rose on Dylan and his band. By this point the idea of reserved seating was abandoned, and the audience, I among them, with some of my peers, including a girl with whom I was in love, from Middlebury College, from which we had driven, crowded around the stage. At this time *Highway 61 Revisited* was the last Dylan album out, and from this album I recall hearing 'Tombstone Blues'. He sat at the piano for 'Ballad of a Thin Man'. My memory of the playlist is less clear because I was less aware of the songs. At one point, Dylan made some kind of remark, intended to be humorous, about Chicago, but I didn't hear it clearly. The whole show lasted about the same amount of time as the first half, with the same harmonica solos but because there were other musicians present, I don't remember which ones were played except that he ended, perhaps predictably, with 'Like a Rolling Stone'.

I was struck in this half as I was in the acoustic section, by how very close the performance was to the records. It could almost be that he was imitating his own sound, but the urgency and drive, evident in both halves, projected forcefully, so that the overwhelming impression of genuineness, rare enough in any show business performance or in life in general, came through. It is one of the qualities, to my mind, that separated Dylan from slicker, commercial singers or groups.

After this superb concert – whose greatness I came to see more clearly in retrospect – I and others felt satisfied. I could do this again, and again, and I tried. In the spring of 1966, a return engagement in Vermont was announced for Norwich. However, driving back from Massachusetts in late July of 1966, I heard that Dylan had been in a motorcycle accident,

Roger Lathbury still has Dylan's autograph from the Burlington show

and there was a notice in a newspaper that I saw when I returned to Middlebury, that that concert had been cancelled or postponed.

I also saw Dylan once on Macdougal Street in Greenwich Village. I was looking for a place to park. There he was, outside a bar, talking to a man I didn't recognise. His profile was unmistakable.

ARIE CROWN THEATER

27 NOVEMBER, 1965, CHICAGO, ILLINOIS

I WAS THERE: BOB CONDREN, AGE 10

I saw Bob Dylan at the Arie Crown Theater in Chicago right after Thanksgiving. I was all of 10 years old at the time. I became interested in Bob Dylan, I think, after hearing 'Subterranean Homesick Blues' on the radio. Or, it could have been that I had heard his name mentioned in some of the teen magazine interviews with The Beatles. But, at this young age, I became somewhat obsessed with Dylan's music.

So when it was announced that he was coming to town my mother, who was not a fan but had taken my sister and me to several British invasion concerts (her favourite music at the time), in a sense of fairness, I think she felt she owed it to me to get the Dylan tickets.

Now my memories are clouded by more than 50 years and the haze of preadolescence. But I do recall that like most shows from the '65 and '66 tours, it began with an acoustic set and was followed by the electric set with the Hawks.

I'm not sure if I was at the November 26 or 27 show. I have seen set lists for the November 26 show but not the November 27 show. However, I recall him playing 'Visions of Johanna' and that is not listed on the November 26 set list. If I am correct, and it was played, I think it may have been the first time it was performed publicly and it would've been in the opening acoustic set. The first documented version of it being played live is at the Berkeley Community Theater, on December 4, 1965. Unfortunately, I cannot find any set lists from the November 27 concert to verify this.

The biggest contrast from the British Invasion shows that my sister and I went to around that time, was that at the Herman's Hermits and The Beatles' shows, the music was drowned out by screaming. But with Dylan, especially during the acoustic set, every word, including the between songs banter could be heard. The crowd, that included many bearded 20 somethings, laughed appreciatively to the banter. I remember looking at the crowd in their jeans and longer hair and feeling pretty uncool in my blazer and turtleneck sweater! The songs were intensively performed by Dylan and they made quite an impact on me.

The electric set was great too, of course. What I do remember was that the keys on Garth Hudson's keyboard seem to be constantly changing colour as he played. Whether the keys were actually changing colour or there were some overhead lights making it appear that way I am not sure. And, at my naive young age, this was not due to any mind altering substances! Once again, I have tried to research this but have not come up with anything. As for any booing, when he came out with the Hawks, there may have been some boos but it was definitely not overwhelming.

I do wish I could be more specific about my recollections but at this time it's more of a general memory than a specific one. It was quite a thing for a 10-year-old kid to see and I am eternally grateful to my mother for her selflessly taking my sister and me to the show.

One note of trivia, the show was at the original Arie Crown Theater, at Chicago's McCormick Place. Unfortunately, it burned down in 1967 and was reopened in 1971. Bob returned to the rebuilt venue on October 31, 1989.

KQED

3 DECEMBER, 1965, BERKELEY, CALIFORNIA

I WAS THERE: RALPH GLEASON

When Bob Dylan's five concerts in the San Francisco Bay Area were scheduled in December 1965, the idea was proposed that he held a press conference in the studios of KQED, the educational television station. Dylan accepted and flew out a day early to make it. He arrived early for the press conference accompanied by Robbie Robertson and several other members of his band, drank tea in the KQED office and insisted that he was ready to talk about 'anything you want to talk about.' His only request was that he be able to leave at 3.00pm so that he could rehearse in the Berkeley Community Theater where he was to sing that night.

At the conclusion of the press conference, he chatted with friends for a while, jumped into a car and went back to Berkeley for the rehearsal. He cut the rehearsal off early to go to the hotel and watch the TV programme, which was shown that night and repeated the following week.

CIVIC CENTER

12 DECEMBER, 1965, SAN JOSE, CALIFORNIA

I WAS THERE: GHRAYDON WALLICK, AGE 19

In 1965 I saw Bob Dylan once more. Earlier in the day I had run away from an angry Marine Sergeant who was lying and trying to shanghai me into the Vietnam War. So it was a day of contrasts for sure.

I arrived at the Civic a couple of hours early because I had painted a portrait of Dylan (from a photo on one of his early album covers) and I wanted to give it to him. In those innocent times, crowd security had a softer face and this one was attached to a kindly old man.

Without so much as a metal detector wand or weapons pat down, he said, 'follow me', then dutifully led me from the ticket window, through the front doors, down the centre isle of the auditorium, up the steps to the stage, across the stage, down the steps to the back stage, to a back stage door. He pointed with his thumb and said, 'I think he's in there'. Then he walked away leaving me, a 19-year old kid on the opposite side of the door from my hero.

I was kind of confused but thought, 'What the Hell'. I knocked on the door. A very nervous (paranoid actually) voice said, 'Who's there? What do you want?' I replied 'My name is Grady and I have something for Bob Dylan.' He shot back,

'Slide it under the door man'. 'It's a painting in a frame. It won't go under the door,' I informed him. 'OK, OK, hold on a minute man,' sounds of many anxious feet shuffling away at speed. In those times even a stray marijuana seed in your pocket could land in you in prison.

A few moments later, the door opens a crack and a paranoid young man grabs the painting from my outstretched and hand and quickly slams the door shut. His 'thank you' was nearly clipped in two between the door's edge and frame. My, 'You're welcome' hit the door and bounced back at me sticking to the fresh barbs of my burr cut hairdo.

I was alone back stage so... I walked back across the stage and took a seat in the front row and centre and waited for the show to start. A few minutes later Dylan and the Band walked on stage and did sound checks and rehearsals. I was the only person in the huge auditorium and they were playing just for me. They did this for about ten minutes, then walked back off stage leaving me along with my grin aching from strain.

As the theatre eventually filled up I took my assigned seat further back from the stage. A young girl eventually came and sat down in her seat next to me. I couldn't help myself, I had to tell somebody. I told her what had just happened. She said, 'That's Amazing!' Then she informed me that it was her job to get the band sodas at the break and deliver them backstage for the band. Then she asked me if I wanted to help her. Out of the thousands of people who filled that auditorium that night I was sitting next to the one!

Of course I helped her and backstage I saw the same paranoid dude that took my painting. He looked at me and said, 'Who are you?' I said, 'My name is Grady, I brought the painting for Dylan'. He said, 'Oh, the painting, he loves it man! He's in his dressing room looking at it right now!'

I didn't ever get to meet him but I saw my painting on top of the grand piano waiting for the roadies to pack it up. I left on a high. It's lasted for many decades.

1966

WBAI FM

27 JANUARY, 1966, NEW YORK CITY, NEW YORK

I WAS THERE: PETER BROWN

It was sometime after midnight in the early hours of January 26, 1966, when I fell asleep, as I usually did on week nights: listening to a show on New York's WBAI FM called *Radio Unnameable*, hosted by Bob Fass. I woke up an hour or two later and, in the first few seconds of consciousness, realised that Bob Dylan was on the air, in the studio, and taking phone calls. Let's just say I woke up really fast, and found myself with a quick decision to make: whether or not to wake up my older brother who was sleeping in the next room.

I was 14 years old and in ninth grade. It was the worst possible night for this to happen – right in the middle of a weeklong nightmare known as midyear exams, and I was supposed to take a math exam (the worst) only a few hours later. I decided that exams come and go, but Bob Dylan at the height of his rock and roll stardom taking phone calls on the air was a one-time-only event. So I ran into my brother's room and said, 'Get up! Dylan's on BAI.'

Bob Fass was a sometime actor and *Radio Unnameable* was one of the first freeform radio shows. The show ran on weeknights, according to the WBAI programme guide, from midnight to exhaustion. Anything could – and did – happen on the show. It was underground radio for the city that never sleeps. I consider Bob Fass to be a radio genius. He rarely announced records, and often mixed all kinds of music together – comedy records, poetry records and sound collages – just to make a point. For instance, a Lyndon Johnson speech about the Vietnam War would be accompanied by the sound of bombs dropping and Stormtroopers marching. Yet, even though Fass rarely announced the songs he played, you somehow always found out what they were.

For the next hour or so, we listened as Bob Dylan joked around and parried with callers. Dylan was accompanied by a few friends who you could hear laughing in the background, all using aliases, but it's a good bet that Al Kooper and Robbie Robertson were among them since they had come to the show straight from the recording studio, where Dylan had been working on a new single, 'One Of Us Must Know (Sooner Or Later)'.

THE GASLIGHT

1966, NEW YORK CITY, NEW YORK

I WAS THERE: RICHARD ALDERSON, SOUND ENGINEER

I lived in a fifth floor walk-up on Bleecker Street right across the street from where the Village Gate was, and I just hung out in the village and I met Bob for the first time when he was just playing folk music and hanging out. My friend introduced me to the new owners of The Gaslight, they had me put in a sound system and then somebody said Dylan was going to premier a bunch of songs after hours and you should come and tape it.

The atmosphere was so wonderful at The Gaslight, it had a special quality that studio recording could never have. It was just overwhelming. I had seen all kinds of people perform and nobody gave me chills like that, nothing even came close to it.

I'd done a lot of live work sound for Albert Grossman and when it came time for Dylan to go on tour Grossman asked me to build the sound system, and I said yes. I fit perfectly into that situation because I was really a kind of Hi-Fi purest as far as sound is concerned. I had no rehearsals with Dylan, as I was busy getting the gear together and setting it up. I had to build the sound system, I had to make up the cables, I had to connect everything and put it into the road cases and get it on the plane where it was shipped to Honolulu, Hawaii.

The first time I used the whole sound system was on the stage at Honolulu and I was still soldering wires on the stage in Stockholm, Sweden. I remember that very well.

I barely had time to get everything set up at every venue. I knew that he'd been performing electric, but I had no idea that the second half was going to be what it turned out to be.

Everybody knew that they came to see the Bob Dylan that they were expecting; rock 'n' roll was something that no one expected. There was a lot of booing, it was everywhere we went, the audiences were hostile and the band responded to the hostility from the audience by playing more aggressively.

The audience reaction was mystifying to everybody, I remember thinking why doesn't everybody think this stuff is as great as I do?

I was always about the music; I was never about the mechanics of being a sound man. So if the music was good, I was happy.

THE KETTLE OF FISH

GREENWICH VILLAGE, NEW YORK

I WAS THERE: JIMI HENDRIX

I saw him one time, but both of us were stoned out of our minds. I remember it vaguely. It was at this place called The Kettle of Fish in the Village. We were both stoned there, and we just hung around laughing – yeah, we just laughed. People have always got to put him down. I really dig him, though. I like that *Highway 61 Revisited* album and especially 'Just Like Tom Thumb's Blues'!

He doesn't inspire me actually, because I could never write the kind of words he does. But he's helped me out in trying to write about two or three words 'cause I got a thousand songs that will never be finished. I just lie around and write about two or three words, but now I have a little more confidence in trying to finish one. When I was down in the Village, Dylan was starving down there. I hear he used to have a pad with him all the time to put down what he sees around him. But he doesn't have to be stoned when he writes, although he probably is a cat like that – he just doesn't have to be.

> Dylan really turned me on. Not the words or his guitar, but as a way to get myself together

JIMI HENDRIX
MARCH 1968

Bob Dylan kicked off his 1966 World Tour on February 4, 1966. Notable as the first tour where Dylan employed an electric band backing him, following his 'going electric' at the 1965 Newport Folk Festival. The musicians Dylan employed as his backing band were known as The Hawks, who subsequently became famous as The Band.

The touring musicians consisted of: Bob Dylan, harp, guitar, vocal, Robbie Robertson, guitar, Richard Manuel, guitar, Garth Hudson, organ, Rick Danko, bass and stand-up bass and Mickey Jones, drums.

SHRINE MOSQUE
6 FEBRUARY, 1966, RICHMOND, VIRGINIA

I WAS THERE: TOM MEAD

I went to this concert with my girlfriend (now my wife). The most popular groups around at the time were The Beatles, The Beach Boys and The Supremes and most of our college classmates regarded Bob Dylan fans as weird. This concert took place just as Dylan was transitioning from folk music to rock and performed the first half of the concert acoustic – vintage Dylan with his harmonica and guitar. When he came on stage for the second half, he was carrying a Fender electric guitar. When he started playing, somewhere between a third of the audience (the venue held around 3,000), walked out in protest of his 'betrayal' of the folk tradition. We stayed and enjoyed the rest of the concert. I was blown away by Robbie Robertson and others in the back up band that became The Band.

The poster advertising this concert is worth in the neighbourhood of $5,000 now. I got mine for free from a neighbourhood restaurant that was using the back of the poster as a sign giving its hours of operation!

February, 14, 1966, was the date of Dylan's first session at Columbia's Studio A in Nashville. The large live area that had recently been converted from seven small booths featured the man himself placed centrally inside a glass booth, while the other musicians milled around him.

COLUMBIA STUDIO A
14 FEBRUARY, 1966, NASHVILLE, TENNESSEE

I WAS THERE: BOB JOHNSTON, PRODUCER

I was standing there with Dylan, his manager Albert Grossman, Clive Davis, and the President of Columbia Records, Bill Gallagher, (in late summer 1965) and I said, 'Dylan, you've gotta go down to Nashville sometime. They've got the studio straightened out down there – I made sure they got rid of all the little rooms with a saw and a sledgehammer so that it's one big room. The musicians are great there, and you can do anything you want to, all in the room together.' He said, 'Hmm.' He would never answer you, but, just like Jack Benny, he'd put his thumb up to his chin and think about what you'd said, and in this case he then walked out and Grossman, Davis, and Gallagher came over to me and basically said, if you ever mention Nashville to Bob Dylan again, you're fired. When I said, 'Why?' I was told, 'Because we don't want him working with a bunch of goddamn stupid people down there. You've got him going good here, and it looks like we're going to have a great record. So keep it that way and just remember what we told you.' I said, 'Yes, sir, you're the boss.'

They could all play and watch each other. The room was so large, it looked like a football field, and the drums were in the middle, up against the back wall. Then, in the centre of the room, I had this glass booth built for Dylan, and he was in there with a table and chair – it was like his study. He'd sit in there, stand up, turn around and do whatever he wanted to do, and I usually had three mics in there so that if he turned his head to the left or right, I wouldn't miss anything.

Al Kooper was great, man, as were all of those people, but he was worried about the country guys not liking him. When he got there, he had on high-heeled boots, a big hat, and a black cape that made him look like an undertaker. Well, he went to Ernest Tubb's Record Shop on Broadway, some guys chased after him and they cornered him in a phone booth outside. They were trying to get the door open, and he called Elvis Presley's buddy, Lamar Fike, who came and picked him up in his Cadillac convertible. It was hilarious. However, nobody knew Dylan. He could walk down the street and no one would bother him

Written in the CBS recording studio in Nashville over the space of eight hours on the night of February 15-16, 'Sad Eyed Lady of the Lowlands' eventually occupied the whole of side four of *Blonde on Blonde*.

I WAS THERE: KENNY BUTTRY, DRUMMER

He ran down a verse and a chorus, and he just quit and said, 'We'll do a verse and then a chorus, and then I'll play my harmonica thing. Then we'll do another verse and chorus, and we'll play some more harmonica and see how it goes from there.' Not knowing how long this thing was going to be, we were preparing ourselves dramatically for a basic two-to-three minute record, because records just didn't go over three minutes. If you notice that record, that thing after like the second chorus starts building and building like crazy, and everybody's just peaking it up 'cause we thought, 'Man this is it. This is going to be the last chorus and we've got to put everything into it we can.' After about 10 minutes of this thing, we're cracking up at each other, at what we were doing. I mean, we peaked five minutes ago. Where do we go from here?

I WAS THERE: CHARLIE MCCOY, MUSICIAN

We sat there from 2pm till 4am the next morning and we never played a note. This was unheard of, everybody was on the clock. We couldn't believe it. You're figuring out ways to stay awake because he might decide at any minute that he wanted to record and we wanted to be ready for him.

I don't know how many games of ping pong we must have played. Then at 4am he came up with 'Sad-Eyed Lady of the Lowlands', an 11-minute ballad. And everybody's sitting there saying, 'Please don't let me make a mistake.' He just started playing it and kind of left it up to us to decide what to do. Every recording, there was no conversation.'

I'd say, 'Bob, what would you think if we did this or that?' And his answer would always be, 'I don't know, man, what do you think?'

So I finally went over to the producer and I said, 'You know what, I've got to quit asking because he's not answering. If we do something he don't like, maybe he'll say something.' And the producer said, 'That works for me, so go ahead.' So that's the way that it went.

I WAS THERE: HARGUS 'PIG' ROBBINS, KEYBOARDIST

I'm primarily a country player. Back in the mid Sixties, country songs were two minutes and 30 seconds long, if you had a song that was over three minutes – that was a long song. When Dylan came into the studio with a seven or twelve minute song – it completely blew my mind.

The studio would book sessions for him for 6 pm and 10 pm at night. Back then, there were four studio sessions that you would work on any day. Usually you'd go in at 10 am and work till 1pm, then take a break, then go from 2 pm – 5 pm, 6 pm to 9 pm, and then 10 pm to 1 am. We were all used to being there on time and you'd show up and you'd get started. Any of the country boys that would come in would be ready to start recording, but with Dylan he would come in at 10 pm, and say, 'Alright boys I need to finish this song, or I need to start writing this song tonight.' So, instead of playing we'd end up walking around the hallway of the studio or we'd play a game of cards until Dylan was ready to record.

HERALD STATESMAN, YONKERS, N.Y., MONDAY, FEBRUARY 7, 1966

DYLAN COMES TO 4TH ST.

Fans Cool It With The FreeWheelin' Prophet At County Center

By ED KRITZLER

The young audience wanted to scream when he came on. They didn't. This was a Bob Dylan concert and you cool it with applause.

The County Center in White Plains was packed Saturday night when Dylan walked in from the wings. He is short and thin and pale. His brown hair sprouts f r o m his head like the stalks of a turnip. He was dressed in a brown and black checkered suit—the checks were four inch squares.

He stood straight in his black suede boots, two inches taller because of the heels. Around his neck hung a harmonica holder. This was Bob Dylan. He looked more like the Mad Hatter from Alice in Wonderland.

After strumming a few cords on his guitar, he sang. Introductory words would have been extraneous. To today's youth Dylan is a guitar wielding Buddha a James Joyce of song, a Holden Caulfield of the '60s.

One g i r l said: "He seems to know the few essentials worth knowing, and he goofs so beautifully on the rest."

When the 24-year old Dylan first came e a s t in 1961 he was compared with folk hall of famers—Leadbelly, Guthrie, Seeger. Apparently he wasn't listening. "Times are a Changing," he sang, and he changed with them. His audience grew. Comparisons are made only on the way up—Bob Dylan is on top.

HOW DOES it feel? "Open, very open," he said with deliberation, during intermission.

"No l o n g e r does he stand straight and give voice to the emotional causes of our time. His words are now more personal. He sings of alienation, absurdity and unselfrightous honesty.

"You mob the Beatles; you sling the works at the Rolling Stones. When Dylan sings you listen silently and inwardly. Saturday's audience was no different. One long-haired youth in light jeans, boots and brown suede vest, sat sucking his thumb. Another put his head back, eyes closed. Some rolled softly with the beat. All listened.

It has been said the real Dylan fan n e v e r attends his concerts. Dylan's words are his essence. They can be better absorbed in the solitude of one's room.

HIS FANS include primarily intellectual rebels of the late fifties and early sixties, young villiage hippies in their polo shirts and pea jackets and English mods who are into everything British.

They were all well represented at the County Center. They filled the balcony and the rows of portable twin chairs that covered the main floor. And they all heard Dylan as he whistled with sardonic bitterness: "You know something is happening, but you don't know what it is — Do you Mr. Jones?"

A policeman stood below center stage, his legs spread, arms extended and hands curled over a night stick. He stared down at his h a n d s. He typified Mr. Jones.

"Am T h e r e or am I alone," Dylan sang giving voice to the outsider. But Dylan was also describing today's adults, and more than likely, his fans.

The policeman had no trouble. When a Jackie Wilson performs, girls surge forward to tear clothing. When Bob Dylan performs, the only girls advancing cradle cameras.

They slithered self-consciously down the aisle one at a time. They walked shall. Cameras clicked and they scooted off like startled fawns. This scene was repeated every few seconds during the entire concert.

BOB DYLAN took his second

BOB DYLAN
"Very Open"

slug of water from a plain glass resting nearby at 9:13 p.m. Then, while returning his guitar, he spoke his first words. "This song is called Freeze Out," he said. He came to sing, not talk.

He began each number by strumming a few introductory cords. It became a statue race to see who in the audience would applaud first, signifying recognition.

Lee Lamb, a friend of Dylan's for years, said backstage during intermission. "Bob always knew he had it, and he has been able to remain aloof from the adulation. But he can't goof on it any longer — it's too big."

"Before a concert, Bob tells me 'I gotta go to work,'" just like some cat going down to the piers to load trucks."

The white spot light on Dylan made him appear paler than he actually is. It lent a reflected rainbow off the unhooked amplifiers behind him. Their surfaces shone like tinsel on a Christmas tree. They looked out of place, for an early Dylan was in his pure folk bag: plain guitar and soulful harmonica.

At last summer's Newport Folk Music Festival he discarded that image and came on with a rocking electric guitar. He was booed off the stage. He came back. The purists protested but the wedding of folk to rock took hold.

NOW THE backdrop of amplifiers and the naked set of drums stood out, picking the purists, reminding them where Dylan's preference lay.

Twaaaaaang! Dylan's electric. The soft - spoken brown guitar was gone, replaced by a plastic coated one, colored black-dash - white. A rubber coated umbilical cord connected it to the amplifier which blasted forth the metalic sound. A five-man combo joined him: two more galvanic strummers, two piano players and a head shaking drummer.

The pace picked up. The thumb sucker switched to biting his nails and the head shakers davined to the beat. Some yelling is sanctioned when Dylan turns electric, but a cool should still be maintained. One kid, who ran into the aisle jumping and moaning with his hands to his head, blew his cool. "The uncomfortable cop was gone. A uniformed usher took his place. His look of contempt for the whole scene was belied by the beat he tapped out on his leg with his flashlight.

DYLAN HAD thawed. The pulsating sounds broke his earlier freeze. He roamed the stage s w a p p i n g onboard words with his men. He leaned into the mike like a penguin catching fish. His return was a backward sway from the waist, legs somewhat bowed.

A few in the audience even had the temerity to hurl requests. He was warm and few intimidating. He began to goof. He took off on a few simple harmonica riffs and held them a long time. The crowd thought it was something special. They applauded. Dylan smiled.

With the last garbled words of "Like A Rolling Stone," the concert was over. There were no encores, no second bows. He nodded twice and split.

Pop artist Andy Warhol, king of underground movies, finished off the Ring - Ding he was munching. He shook the crumbs from his lap and left. With him was the poet Gerard Malanca and others of the In Crowd. They went unnoticed.

The talk was of Dylan. "Dylan doesn't build walls, he builds bridges," said 15-year-old Chris McDonald of Mahopac. She swept her long blonde hair back and added, "Dylan is today. He is the oneness of existence."

Abbie Slocum of White Plains clipped in: "It's simple. Dylan is the only person who knows where it's at."

This is the image Dylan conveys. His words have become more obscure, his images more abstract, but his message is clear: Don't get hung up; no total commitment, not even to self.

Ashley Pendalton of the Bronx said: "If he lives by this, one day Dylan might drop out of sight like a firefly on a summer night."

Handshake Can Please Or Irritate

By EMILY POST

A handshake may create a 'made briefly, but there should be a feeling of strength and clasp than she does to a mere gives a much firmer, warmer

A column in the local newspaper about Dylan coming to town.

OTTAWA AUDITORIUM

19 FEBRUARY, 1966, ONTARIO, CANADA

I WAS THERE: ROGER HACKER

I saw him at the old Auditorium in Ottawa, Canada, it was the tour where he did an acoustic set followed by a plugged in one with what became The Band. Both performances were different to anything that was being offered as music at that time, very refreshing and cutting edge. But the audience was very green. After his last planned song he and The Band left the instruments on the stage expecting to return for an encore, but the majority of the audience simply got up and left. Also later it was rumoured that he referred to Ottawa as the 'very cold asshole of the world'.

'Rainy Day Women #12 & 35', is a track that the Nashville players remember best – not only because of the apparent drug reference in the song's double-entendre chorus 'Everybody must get stoned,' but also because of the circumstances surrounding the session.

Dylan said he wanted the song to have the loose sound of a Salvation Army Band – not an easy task for some of the best musicians on the planet.

COLUMBIA STUDIO A

10 MARCH, 1966, NASHVILLE

I WAS THERE: WAYNE MOSS, MUSICIAN

At that time I didn't know much about him. I only knew that he was the guy who wrote 'Blowin' in the Wind'. I had a saxophone player friend of mine that had known him a bit and he told me that Dylan was into motorcycles and that he was originally from Minnesota. I once went through Dylan's home town in Minnesota and at the city limits there is a sign that reads 'Home of the World's first Strip-Mine'. You'll think that they'd have something up about Dylan there?

Dylan was really a treat to play with in the studio though. As a guitarist there isn't much outstanding work on *Blonde on Blonde* except, maybe on 'I Want You.' I also played on 'Sad-Eyed Lady of the Lowlands' and 'Stuck Inside A Mobile With the Memphis Blues Again' as well. The recording of 'Sad-Eyed Lady' went from 2 o'clock in the afternoon until 8.30 the next morning. We only did two takes of it, and they ended up using the first on the album.

His way of working wasn't what any of us studio guys were used to. We were used to recording four sides in a single session. That would be over three hours and then we'd leave the studio. When Dylan came and recorded *Blonde on Blonde* it opened the doors and things changed. Artists would come in and they would take their time recording. After Dylan came everyone started to come: Joan Baez, Simon & Garfunkel, Charlie Daniels.

BOB DYLAN

ISLAND GARDEN
Hempstead Turnpike · W. Hempstead

SATURDAY FEBRUARY 26 at 8:30 P.M.

Tickets: $4.50, 3.50, 2.50
On Sale Island Garden Box Office — phone: IVanhoe 3-3000
Mail Order remittance to Concerts, 330 E. 48th St. New York 17, N.Y.
Enclose stamped, self-addressed envelope

We'd ask him: 'What do you want me to play on this?' He'd respond with, 'I don't know. What do you think?' It didn't take too long for us to realise that we could just do what we wanted. He respected us and allowed us to shine.

We all got inebriated on Dylan's request. He didn't want to sing a song with the lyrics: 'Everybody must get stoned....' with a bunch of straight people. He sent out for some spirits. Our bass player Henry Strzelecki got so drunk that he couldn't play – so I played bass on the recording. He was so drunk that he was rolling around on the floor playing the bass pedals of an organ with his hands. We had a good time with it. When we all left the studio that night none of us remembered to sign our time cards.

I WAS THERE: HARGUS 'PIG' ROBBINS, KEYBOARDIST

That's the only song I can remember recording in detail with Dylan! I remember it because it was a commercial hit on the radio. Dylan had wanted the sound to be similar to that of a Salvation Army Band on that. I can't even remember all of the musicians that played on that with us now. Dylan had instructed us to start to hooting and hollering during the recording as well. None of us on that were used to doing that sort of thing in the studio. It was really fun.

KIEL OPERA HOUSE

11 MARCH, 1966, ST. LOUIS, MISSOURI

I WAS THERE: MIKE BEGLEY

Kiel Opera House, Missouri, I think it was 1966? The first half of the concert was Bob Dylan solo acoustic songs and then after intermission he was full electric with The Band. It was a great concert but my memories are somewhat clouded...

QUEEN ELIZABETH THEATRE

26 MARCH, 1966, VANCOUVER, CANADA

I WAS THERE: BONNIE ELENDIUK

I saw Dylan at the Queen Elizabeth Theatre in Vancouver in 1966. After the show, we went to an after show party at the house of a jazz pianist by name of Al Neil. I was surprised that Dylan wasn't wearing his denims as he did at the concert (very acoustic and folky, he was) but at the party he was all dressed in black and I thought, 'This guy is a street hipster, not a hippie!'

RIVERSIDE COLLEGE

APRIL 1966, ORANGE COUNTY, CALIFORNIA

I WAS THERE: SANDI BACHOM

We were total Dylan freaks. We were folkies, and just starting to get into the protest thing. I just remember it was a huge theatre. It was fancy. The first half was 'Mr. Tambourine Man' and all that and then he came out with The Band. It was like the scene from (the Mel Brooks' movie) *The Producers*, the audience's jaws dropped. I remember that pretty well. They played 'Like a Rolling Stone'.

I'm pretty sure our friend Jackson Browne was with us but I'm not sure, hey, it was the Sixties after all! Jackson and I were friends in California, so we probably went to the show. He was so influenced by Dylan. He idolised him. I have a picture he signed some place, he wrote on the back, he signed it 'Jack.' We called him 'Jackie' in those days.

There was a party after the concert. It was a big deal. Donovan was there, and Dylan. They spent a lot of time in another room, probably getting high and playing guitars.

THE WHISKY A GO GO

8 APRIL, 1966, LOS ANGELES, CALIFORNIA

I WAS THERE: DONN PENNEBAKER, FILM DIRECTOR

Bob Dylan and I once went to see Otis Redding at the Whisky a Go Go in LA. Otis wanted to get Dylan, and Jimi Hendrix was the same way. Dylan was the magic thing and anything that connected with Dylan they would have done at the drop of a hat.

Australia was the first major stop (outside the US) for Dylan's legendary World Tour in 1966. By the time he arrived in Australia, just prior to his 25th birthday, Dylan was at the height of his fame and was now, along with The Beatles, one of the most famous and popular performers in the world.

Audience reaction to the tour was very mixed; many were excited by the new direction, but older fans objected vehemently to Dylan's new style, and expressed their displeasure loudly. Volume was a critical issue: Dylan and his musicians were using the best amplification available, and by 1966 standards they played very loudly indeed. Used to the moderate sound levels at folk concerts, many fans were taken aback by the unprecedented volume, causing further negative reaction.

The site of Sydney Stadium and its revolving stage

SYDNEY STADIUM

13 APRIL, 1966, SYDNEY, AUSTRALIA

I WAS THERE: DAVID N PEPPERELL

We were so excited at the prospect of finally seeing and hearing Bob Dylan in Australia that we didn't notice he was on the stage until the first few strums of his acoustic guitar, apparently loaned from a Sydney musician after Bob's own guitar was damaged in transit, rang out through the old Sydney Stadium, more used to wrestling and boxing than musical genius.

He cut an amazing figure on that stage, dressed in an orange and brown hounds-tooth suit, floral shirt and cuban heel boots whilst his hair was teased out in an afro reminiscent of the corona of the sun. At certain times when the light struck his hair, you could see right through it and it resembled a halo.

Beginning with 'She Belongs to Me', which brought a gasp of recognition from the crowd, he followed up with two new songs which we guessed were from his new album as yet unreleased. '4th Time Around' was so obviously a send-up of 'Norwegian Wood' that everyone laughed, especially at the way Dylan sang it with heavy inflections on certain words like 'drum' and 'crutch'. Next was the masterpiece of 'Visions of Johanna' a song that seemed endless and to have endless interpretations and ramifications. It quite stunned us all and the applause was rhapsodic at its end.

'It's All Over Now, Baby Blue' put us back in familiar territory again and we started to notice that he sang slower and more intensely live than he did on his records and each word that he uttered seem to drip with meaning. Harmonica breaks came often amongst these songs and reminded of a keening bird in the ether, something otherworldly and almost eldritch. Skeleton keys in the rain indeed.

We were marvelling at how he could remember all those words during 'Desolation Row' yet he did and he made no mistakes at all despite the extreme length of that apocalyptic ballad. When he came to the final verse he was snarling the words and he made that song the great judgment on humanity that we finally saw that it was.

'Just Like a Woman' was a break from that intensity but was by no means less intense. Again new to us all it seemed to be almost the ultimate love/hate song speaking of some love affair that never came to pass.

I should mention here that the stage at the Sydney Stadium sits in the middle of the room – well it is for boxing and wrestling – with the audience all around it. So that everyone got a fair view of Dylan singing it rotated 45 degrees after each song! Bob looked very surprised after the first number but seemed to get used to the rotation after a while. He did have a highly bemused look on his face though while it was turning.

From the opening strummed chords of 'Mr. Tambourine Man' the whole room was hanging on every word. What was interesting was that despite everyone in the audience knowing the words no one sang along, the song was accepted with deference and awe. Still the applause was deafening as Bob left the stage for the interval. After the interval things got dark.

After we got back to our seats, after smokes and cokes, he walked back on to the stage, again with no introduction, a Fender Stratocaster electric guitar hanging around his shoulder and accompanied by five musicians playing piano, organ, guitar, bass and drums. This event provoked a furious response from a section of the crowd who began catcalling and booing. Dylan ignored them and started the electric half with 'Tell Me, Momma' another new tune. However it wasn't the tune that was so surprising but the volume of his backing band who played louder than I had ever heard a band play, including The Rolling Stones and The Kinks. It was wonderful music though that swept you up in it and it was obvious Bob loved playing like this as he was dancing around, sometimes raising one arm up in the air in a kind of mad joy. I looked at the people with me and they reacted the same was as I did, enraptured by the best music we had ever heard.

At the end of that song the noise was horrific. Again booing, shouts of 'traitor,' 'what happened to Bob the folky' and a slow handclap, although I could see that this response came from one section of the audience who seemed to be organised in some way. Dylan's response was to look more bemused as the stage rotated and go into a rocked-up version of another oldie, 'I Don't Believe You' which again seemed to gain so much from the electric backing compared to the rather spare version on *Another Side of Bob Dylan*. 'Baby Let Me Follow You Down' was rocked up next – well, why not, when The Animals had already had a hit with it as a rock tune two years before – and Bob had me and practically everybody else in his sway, except of course the yahoos. This was amazing, inspiring music played brilliantly and sung by a singer whose ability was only half shown by his records. Dylan sang and whooped and hollered and hit notes right off the scale. My heart was beating so loud I felt it could almost be heard above the tornado of Bob and The Band's music.

A totally glorious version of 'Just Like Tom Thumb's Blues' ensued with the same latin, south-of-the-Border feel that it had on *Highway 61 Revisited*. He began it so slowly, dragging out every word and it was revealed as a comic song when he said, ' ... and your gravity fails and negativity won't pull you through' making nearly everyone burst out laughing.

Regrettably the detractors, many of whom had symbolically walked out, yelling epithets and insults, were still booing and slow clapping after every song – the band was far too loud to hear them during songs which was a blessing. It seemed obvious they were some kind of folk purists/leftie dogmatists who had decided that Dylan was a fake and a sellout – I heard these words often used – and they were determined to disrupt and destroy his performance. How they were unaware of Bob's two most recent, electric albums I couldn't work out. They failed in their intent anyway as the bulk of the audience was totally enraptured with the music and only wanted to hear more, so there then began screaming matches between the pro - and anti-Dylan forces in the audience which didn't make being there any easier.

Undeterred the group and Bob continued with a comic 'Leopard-Skin Pill-Box Hat' which really drove the 'folkies' into a frenzy followed by a beautiful re-arrangement of 'One Too Many Mornings'. The harmony on the last line of the verses sung by Bob and the groups bass player was just gorgeous.

On 'Ballad of a Thin Man' Dylan crossed to the piano and, seemingly annoyed at the nay-sayers response, really spat the words 'but something is happening here but you don't know what it is' in the direction of the section of the crowd still cat-calling. They couldn't wreck the show – it was far too good for that – but they were so annoying you just wished they would either stop or get out.

Those elements must have got under the Bob's skin because instead of ending the show with 'Like a Rolling Stone', as we all had expected, he finished with a vicious 'Positively 4th Street', again aimed at the goon squad, then stormed off the stage despite the tumultuous applause from most of the people there. It was a sad end to a magnificent show but it could not spoil it for me – I was just dazzled by Dylan's performance. I had never heard musicianship like that, had never heard such a cavalcade of extraordinary songs and could not remember ever hearing a greater singer.

After we left the show to walk and to our car, my four friends and I did not say anything for about half an hour.

What we had experienced was really beyond words.

> **❛**...the stage at the Sydney Stadium sits in the middle of the room with the audience all around it. So that everyone got a fair view of Dylan singing it rotated 45 degrees after each song! He did have a highly bemused look on his face though while it was turning.**❜**

I WAS THERE: MARSHA ROWE

Sir Robert Menzies who'd been prime minister of Australia since I was six years old, resigned. In his place Harold Holt. Holt trebled the number of Australian troops going to Vietnam by adding 500 of the conscripts from the birthday lottery in April. It was the month of Bob Dylan's concert in the Sydney Stadium.

With its revolving podium, built to stage boxing matches, under a tin roof, this was the only big-capacity venue in the city. I sat with my boyfriend, Michael, and three friends in cheap seats high on the perimeter, single benches held up by tall metal stanchions. 'Drop your lighter down there, Marsha, and you'd never get it back,' said Michael. I tried to avoid looking down between the gaps in the walkway boards.

Dylan was a small figure far below us wearing what looked-like a green checked suit, which seemed incongruous, his hair a fine nimbus in the lights. At first there was the familiar voice and his harmonica, and then came the electrically charged instrumentation of the second half. The music powered up the huge space of the stadium. The connecting of the songs to a plug-in energy felt dangerously exciting, as if something authentically individual was vanishing, as if control was going over to who knows where. We were carried with it, our ears absorbing every pulse, but tiers began to empty. About a third of the audience were disturbed enough to walk out.

We stayed and afterwards we streamed up the hill with the rest of the crowd, thrilled to the bone, jangling with the echoes of songs that touched on our world, took us into an expanding space and reinforced our own sense of youthful power. We were, for sure, in a world where barriers were coming down.

PALAIS THEATRE

22 APRIL, 1966, ADELAIDE, AUSTRALIA

I WAS THERE: GUS HOWARD

Dylan appeared in Adelaide on April 22, 1966, on the electric outing world tour. The venue was better and more stylish – a vast, dusty old ballroom with a sprung floor and a proscenium stage called The Palais. Dylan played the same acoustic-electric set with the Hawks/Band all over the world, which included the infamous Manchester 'Judas' show, but they were in Australia about a month earlier. Even though electric rock music was well established and I had played myself, and had seen all the international acts that framed the music scene of the time, including The Who and their Marshall stacks, nothing prepared me for the perverse sound of Richard Manuel hitting single piano notes through a very loud and edgily distorted PA for The Band's on-stage tune up, followed by my first experience of hearing a miked-up snare drum being hit as hard it could be. After that the music started. Bam! I went with a guy who was young jingle writer, and who later made a fortune with a studio and an advertising agency. He was never the same again either. After the show we looked at each other and sort of knew what we had to do.

I WAS THERE: TONY BABONY, AGE 15

I was at the Adelaide concert, aged 15, attending with my friends despite, in my case, my parents' veto. We are already pretty huge Dylan fans on the basis of the albums up to *Highway 61 Revisited*, so anticipation is high.

The lights go down and Dylan, as we referred to him in those days, appears on stage to a quite warm welcome. Fiddles with the tuning on his guitar a bit, launches into 'She Belongs to Me'. The sheer sound of the guitar and voice is beyond what anyone there has heard. For a start, it's stupefyingly loud and clear. The Yardbirds (with Beck and Page!) have by this time played in Adelaide, so people are becoming aware of big, sophisticated amplification, but this is a whole other level. The thin, penetrating voice we have heard on Dylan's records, here becomes a rich velvety roar, and the harmonica bursts are ear-splittingly powerful.

The next songs are '4th Time Around' and 'Visions of Johanna', never heard before in Australia because *Blonde on Blonde* hasn't yet been released. The audience laughs at lines like 'Your words aren't clear, you better spit out your gum', and 'I covered her up and then thought I'd go look through her drawers'. What we made of 'Visions of Johanna', on that night, is kind of lost in time and obscured by hindsight, but I imagine most of us there were impressed. The other song in the acoustic set from the future *Blonde on Blonde*, 'Just Like a Woman', is familiar to us from Jonathan King's cover, played on radio in Adelaide. King's version is, of course, kicked out the door of history, through the cat flap, by Bob's performance. The harmonica on this song, and 'It's All Over Now, Baby Blue' and 'Mr. Tambourine Man', flies out to poetic reaches beyond the understanding of my 15-year-old self – it takes years, a lifetime, for these wonders to be taken in.

Somewhat shell-shocked after the first half, we anticipate the arrival of 'the band', later The Band. In Adelaide the second half begins not with 'Tell Me, Mama' but with 'Leopard-Skin Pill-Box Hat'. And now the impact of the sound system is really felt – it's fucking loud, as all the world now knows. Despite the volume, every word is crystal clear and lines like 'I saw you making love with him, You forgot to close the garage door' get laughs from me and the people around me. But the mood is turning in some parts of the audience. After 'Leopard-Skin Pill-Box Hat' there are walkouts – I swear to God, I hear a woman say, 'And he calls himself a folk singer!' as she harrumphs out of the building. A voice from the front rows is heard, 'Hey Bob! Tell your lead guitarist to TURN DOWN!' Bob comes back with, 'I'm the lead guitarist.' And then, 'This next song is called 'I Don't Believe You'. It used to be like that, now it goes like this...' and another sonic onslaught is launched.

The last number is 'Like a Rolling Stone,' played disturbingly slowly compared with the single version, and presumably intended to blindside the audience in case we were thinking we knew what was happening. Bob snarls it out with a nightmare intensity that lacerates mind and soul, it ends, applause from most, shocked silence. Bob looks around at the enormous tin shed in which this concert has been playing, and deadpans, 'Thank you for having me in your airplane hangar...' and they're gone.

And that was my first rock concert, and no one was ever in Kansas any more.

I don't know if there is a recording of this concert, but presumably it would be similar to the two Melbourne performances on April 19 and 20, 1966, which are partly documented from a televised performance. That's right, mind-blowingly, part of the concerts were shown on *Australian Bandstand* on primetime commercial television. The broadcast was, I believe, interrupted by news dispatches from the Vietnam War – 'interesting' times, I guess. I couldn't watch it anyway, what with Auntie Joan's birthday party. 'But Mum, Bob Dylan's on Bandstand...' 'Will you just get in the car, you're coming to this damn party!'

After the final concert in Perth, Dylan and his band were forced to stay in the city for a further three days after the Australian government commandeered commercial aircraft for the shipping of troops to Vietnam and no other flights were available.

On April 28, 1966, Bob Dylan arrived in Stockholm, Sweden for the first show of his European tour. Dylan met with journalist Klas Burling in a Stockholm hotel room. Burling later said of the interview, 'He was totally out of it. When he took his shades off, his eyes were like raisins. It was the worst interview of my life.'

Klas Burling: What would you call yourself, a poet or a singer, or do you think that you write poems and then you put music to it?

Dylan: No ... I don't know ... It's so silly! I mean you can't ... You wouldn't ask those questions of a carpenter, would you? Or a plumber?

Klas Burling: It would not interesting in the same way, would it?

Dylan: I guess it would be. I mean if it's interesting to me, it should be just as interesting to you.

Klas Burling: Well, not as being a disc-jockey anyhow.

Dylan: What do you think Mozart would say to you if you ever come up to him and ask him the questions that you've been asking? What kind of questions would you ask him, you know, 'Tell me, Mr Mozart ...'

Klas Burling: Well, first of all I wouldn't do it.

Dylan: Well, how come you do it to me?

Klas Burling: Well, because I'm interested in your records and I think the Swedish audiences are as well.

Dylan: Well, I'm interested in the Swedish audiences too and Swedish people and all that kind of stuff, but I'm sure they don't wanna know all these dumb things, you know.

Klas Burling: No, well they've read a lot of dumb things about you in the papers I suppose, but I thought you could straighten them out yourself.

Dylan: I can't straighten them out. I don't think they have to be straightened out. I know ... I believe that they know. They know. Don't you know the Swedish people? I mean, they don't have to be told, they don't have to be explained to. I mean, you should know that. I mean Swedish people just don't have to be explained to. You can't tell Swedish people something which is self-explanatory. Swedish people are smarter than that.

Klas Burling: Do you think so?

Dylan: Oh, of course.

Klas Burling: Do you know any Swedes?

Dylan: I know plenty. I happen to be a Swede myself.

ADELPHI CINEMA

5 MAY, 1966, DUBLIN, IRELAND

I WAS THERE: JAMES DOHERTY, AGE 19

On Thursday morning, May 5, I met up with two close friends, John Doherty (no relation) and Pat Glenn, to make the long journey south to Dublin to see Bob Dylan's first concert in Ireland. A friend of Pat's, called Tony McLaughlin, also travelled with us. Pat 'borrowed' his older brother's car, a blue Austin 40 Farina, for our road trip. Pat was still not 17 so he had no driving license and very limited driving experience. He had never driven the car outside the narrow streets of the Bogside, Derry where we all lived. A few years later John's house would become famous worldwide when the British Home Secretary James Callaghan addressed a huge crowd from an upstairs bedroom window with a loudhailer. Derry in 1966 was a great

1966

place to live and there was no real sign of the political unrest that was unleashed a few years later.

Earlier in the year when the Dylan concerts were announced we snapped up two tickets quickly. When we arrived in Dublin late afternoon we read that Dylan and his entourage were staying in the famous Gresham Hotel in O'Connell Street where Elizabeth Taylor and Richard Burton had previously stayed. As we had a couple of hours to spare on this warm May afternoon, we decided to stake out the Gresham in the faint hope of seeing Dylan or possibly getting his autograph. Eventually, as we were passing the Gresham for the umpteenth time we spotted a guy with shades, long hair and Beatle boots reading the *Melody Maker* sitting on a bench in the outside covered porch area of the hotel. We approached him and asked him was Bob Dylan still in the hotel. He said in a strong American accent that if we waited a few minutes he would be leaving the hotel to go to the concert venue. We didn't know it at the time but the 'American guy' reading the *Melody Maker* was Robbie Robertson from Dylan's band. Sure enough, within a couple of minutes Dylan came out of the main hotel entrance surrounded by his entourage. I quickly approached him as he was being ushered towards a waiting limo and asked for his autograph. I can still remember distinctly standing beside Dylan and thinking to myself that this is the demi-god who recorded 'Like a Rolling Stone'. This was surreal, a truly once in a lifetime experience for me personally. As Dylan got into the back of the limo I followed him and again for a brief few moments exchanged a few words. He then scrawled his autograph on a piece of paper for me before I was quickly and unceremoniously turfed out of the car. A young guy from Dublin who was also looking for his autograph jumped on his bike and told us to follow him as he knew a short cut to the venue. So a group of us ran after the boy on the bicycle and sure enough we got there in time to see Dylan get

James Doherty and girlfriend

out of the limo at the back of the theatre. I tried unsuccessfully to get a second autograph as Dylan with a tall long haired girl walked past quickly into the back entrance of the theatre.

The atmosphere inside the foyer just before the concert was crackling with expectancy, with hundreds of fans pouring in to the theatre to get their seats before Dylan appeared on stage. I noticed there were a good number of students male and female from University College Dublin in the audience as you could tell by their distinctive college scarfs. As we scanned around the audience from our fifth row seats we noticed Keith Moon walking through the crowd carrying several ice creams. Then the other members of The Who took their seats about three rows in front of us(The Who were in Ireland to play four concerts).

At around 8pm the lights dimmed and Dylan appeared on centre stage with acoustic guitar and harmonica holder around his neck and was quickly into his first song 'She Belongs to Me' from *Bringing It All Back Home*. You would literally hear a pin drop throughout this mesmerising performance. During this acoustic set Dylan played three new songs from *Blonde on Blonde* which had not been yet released including 'Visions of Johanna' and 'Just Like A Woman' both sounding mysterious, almost spiritual on the dramatically darkened stage. The set included a magnificent 'Desolation Row' and ended with a beautiful version of 'Mr. Tambourine Man'.

Rapturous applause followed and I would have gone home then very happy and totally in awe of Dylan's performance. However, although there was great anticipation for the 'electric' half of the show no one could have been prepared for what followed next.

Starting his 'electric set' with 'Tell Me Mamma' and finishing with 'Like a Rolling Stone' this was jet-powered, pulsating rock music which has never been bettered. Dylan spitting out the lyrics and the band with Robbie Robertson's searing guitar and Garth Hudson's swirling organ provided the most exquisite sounds, which filled every corner of the theatre and could probably be heard in Dublin City centre 500 yards away. As I was transfixed on what was happening on stage I do not remember seeing anyone walk out or hear anyone booing. That is not to say that it did not happen. It has always intrigued me as to why anyone walked out because he 'went electric'. *Highway 61 Revisited* had already been in the shops for several months and you would assume that anyone attending the

concerts must have heard this album which heavily featured the late Michael Bloomfield's wonderful rock and blues guitar on Dylan's ground breaking first rock album. What did they expect? After all, he also performed a truly amazing acoustic first half set at these concerts to please everybody with three new songs.

After the concert, we headed to the nearest pub still on a high and with the music still ringing in our ears. A truly unforgettable and historic night at the Adelphi, which will live forever in my memory.

ABC

6 MAY, 1966, BELFAST, NORTHERN IRELAND

I WAS THERE: JIM MULLIGAN

I still have vivid flashbacks of this concert. I was five rows from the stage. I sat beside a girl who I thought looked a bit like Cher (yes, Cher has been around that long!). We chatted a bit and I borrowed her programme. When Dylan walked on stage, bang on 8 o'clock, she uttered a stifled scream and buried her face in her hands in embarrassment. Dylan, smallish, slightly built but well put together, had an aureole of fair, gingerish curly hair and looked very strung out. Very intense. He spent a long time tuning his guitar, shifting his balance foot to foot, head and shoulders jerking in quick, bird-like movements. He wore that brownish, beige large-check suit with, if I remember correctly, a sartorially clashing black and white check shirt. His face was deathly pale. Strange face: not the face of a rock singer. A face from who knows where? He never smiled once in all the two hours plus that he was on stage.

First number, 'She Belongs to Me'. His voice is the killer. It's not the voice of the folksinger or even searing-soaring voice from *Highway 61 Revisited*. It's a haunted and haunting mysterious stranger, prodigal son voice. *Blonde on Blonde* has not yet been released so none of us has heard this Dylan.

'Visions of Johanna' stands out from the acoustic set – of course I'd never heard it before, and this is the only experience in my life to which the appalling cliché 'spine-chilling' could be applied and justified. '4th Time Around' – the audience laughs at the line 'You better spit out your gum.'

During the interval, I made a visit to the toilets. At the urinal, a hard case with a Falls Road accent, acne, and scimitar sideburns says to me out of the corner of his mouth, 'Isn't he fucking great?'

The electric set: Bob Dylan and The Hawks. Never going to forget this. They began with 'Tell Me, Momma' and ended with 'Like a Rolling Stone'

Maybe the greatest rock music ever played. I thought about that show almost hourly for months afterwards. The applause was rapturous at the end. He stood alone on the stage after The Hawks had left and acknowledged the cheers with a slight bow and a bemused expression.

This must have been one of the very few places on the 1966 tour where Dylan and the Hawks were not booed.

I feel so lucky to have witnessed a moment out of time.

I WAS THERE: JAMES DOHERTY, AGE 19

Before we left for Dublin I also secured a ticket for Dylan's concert in Belfast the next night at the ABC cinema. I would be going to this on my own. On our way to Belfast the next day, we were overtaken by two, large blue Vauxhall Estate cars with members of The Who aboard. However I had a major problem to overcome to get there. At that time I was a 19-year old full time professional footballer with my home town team Derry City and we had just reached the final of the Top Four inaugural cup. We would be playing Linfield in the final at Solitude, which was Cliftonvilles stadium also in Belfast. The game was scheduled to be played that same Friday evening at 6.:30 pm.

We won the game 2-1 and l left right after the game without taking a shower or waiting for the trophy and medal presentations. When I got to the venue there was a crowd outside listening to the concert inside. When I eventually took my seat, the acoustic set was over but the second half of the concert was just as powerful and exhilarating as the Dublin show 24 hours before. I often wonder did anyone else attend both these incredible Irish concerts? I consider myself both privileged and lucky to have witnessed these truly historical shows.

COLSTON HALL

10 MAY, 1966, BRISTOL

I WAS THERE: CHRIS JAMES

We weren't prepared for the electric side of it. When he brought the band on a few people heckled and a few people walked out, but I thoroughly enjoyed the concert.

I WAS THERE: RICHARD EVANS

I saw Dylan there as part of his Judas tour and the change from acoustic to electric. It was very similar to the Manchester Free Trade Hall gig, where some wag called out 'Judas' during the electric set. The first half show was all acoustic and included some early songs and wonderful tracks from *Bringing It All Back Home* including 'Mr. Tambourine Man' and 'It's Alright, Ma (I'm Only Bleeding)'. In the second half Bob brought on the Hawks (later The Band) and proceeded to shred the air with 'Subterranean Homesick Blues', 'Maggie's Farm' etc. However, the folk purists booed and some left. I was still at school. Great memory, 52 years ago.

I WAS THERE: ROBBIE ROBERTSON, MUSICIAN

At the time, people were pissed off because they had this purist attitude about Dylan. We did not see what was wrong musically. We were treating the songs with great respect.

SET LIST:

She Belongs to Me
4th Time Around
Visions of Johanna
It's All Over Now, Baby Blue
Desolation Row
Just Like a Woman
Mr. Tambourine Man
Tell Me, Momma
I Don't Believe You (She Acts Like We Never Have Met)
Baby, Let Me Follow You Down
Just Like Tom Thumb's Blues
Leopard-Skin Pill-Box Hat
One Too Many Mornings
Ballad of a Thin Man
Like a Rolling Stone

When the tour hit Cardiff, Wales, Dylan met up with Johnny Cash backstage at The Capitol Theatre. The country legend was at the height of his well-documented pill addiction and was swallowing Dexedrine and Equanil like candy. Film director Pennebaker shot Dylan and Cash playing some Hank Williams classics.

CAPITOL THEATRE

11 MAY, 1966, CARDIFF, WALES

I WAS THERE: BARRY FRINSTEIN

It was the British weather that made him look so gloomy. It was a really long tour and everyone was just worn out.

I WAS THERE: BREN THOMPSON

I don't remember the date, but I saw Bob Dylan in the Capitol in Cardiff. May 1966 sounds about right. I was a medical student and a fan of the American Folk Revival but had never seen any of the big names performing live. I remember the performance well.

He looked stoned and did not engage with the audience, which disappointed me. He shuffled on to the stage and stood in the spotlight and looked bewildered. I remember thinking that he probably did not know where he was. He had an acoustic guitar and a mouth organ on a holder around his neck. He said very little and I think he began his performance without any introduction and went from song to song with just a few mumbled words.

In one way I was disappointed, because he was so shambolic, but in another way he was living up to his hippy, rebel image so I felt he was the real deal.

When he gave up his acoustic guitar I could not understand what all the fuss was about – he sounded better to me. He had a raw passion in his early years when he was a one-man band but 'the times they were a changing' and he had to change too.

To me, he remains one of the great songwriters of the Sixties and I am glad I saw him, even if he was semi-catatonic!

I WAS THERE: GRAHAM BRACE, AGE 16

I was lucky enough to be there and remember it very well. It was three days short of my seventeenth birthday and a close friend of mine studying at Cardiff College of Art managed to get tickets for myself and a half a dozen school friends. We hitch-hiked up

Graham Brace draws a crowd at an outdoor concert in Cardiff

to Cardiff from 'the sticks' of Milford Haven in Pembrokeshire, highly excited at the prospect of actually seeing Bob Dylan in the flesh – a figure who was close to achieving legendary status and who represented the voice of protest for a generation of young people who were becoming increasingly aware of the wrongs and political follies of the world that we were growing up in. It seemed too good to be true!

Anyway, we had great seats in the front row of the balcony and sat mesmerised during the first half as he stood waif-like with his mop of tousled hair, centre-stage, in black, illuminated by a spotlight and sang a host of great songs with which we had all become familiar, accompanied simply by his guitar and harmonica.

When he appeared with The Band and an electric guitar in the second half we were all shocked and, I suppose, a bit disappointed to see this sudden transformation from plaintive folk singer to loud pop singer. Furthermore, I recall that it wasn't a particularly polished performance, musically speaking.

Of course, we all soon came to love 'Like a Rolling Stone', 'Lay, Lady Lay', 'Subterranean Homesick Blues' and other non-acoustic renderings. Sadly, my interest in Bob Dylan waned as we got older and as he changed dramatically over time. I have seen him twice since and on each occasion been extremely disappointed.

However, there is no doubt that his uniquely poetic style of songwriting and the relatively simple instrumental technique with which he presented it at the time had a huge influence on the music of our generation.

I count myself very lucky to have seen him on that controversial 1966 tour and at the age of 68 and having been to hundreds of live gigs representing all types of music in my lifetime, that concert at the Capitol Theatre in Cardiff in 1966 is still one of the stand-out musical events of my life.

ODEON THEATRE

12 MAY, 1966, BIRMINGHAM

I WAS THERE: MUFF WINWOOD, MUSICIAN

Dylan was playing in Birmingham with The Band on the famous face-slapping tour. I was in the Spencer Davis Group then, and he'd heard our records and when he came to Birmingham he wanted to meet us. We were going to the concert anyway, so we just met him backstage before the show.

Anyway, while we were backstage, he was telling us how he was really into ghosts and he loved Britain because of the history and everything and he thought there'd be some wonderful ghosts around. And we knew of a very old massive house in Worcestershire, near Kidderminster I think, that apart from a gatehouse, which was occupied by a caretaker, was left abandoned. It had been burnt and left with all the rafters blackened. And we told him how the guy that had lived in the house had died with his dog, and how if you went there you could see him walking around with the dog. And he was absolutely fascinated with this story and he said, listen, after the gig you've got to take me to this place! There was just me and my brother Steve, and I thought, bloody hell!

After the gig they'd got the limos ready and so we just jumped into these limos – there we were in four bloody stretch Princess limos all driving out to Worcestershire at 12 o'clock at night!

Well, we got to the place, so I jumped out and flagged all the limos down and I said, look, there's somebody living in the gatehouse, so we'd better turn all the lights off and go in very quietly. So one by one, all these limos turned their lights off and drove carefully through the gates and up the long, long drive to where the house was. We got all the limos up there without anybody in the gatehouse knowing.

And out poured Dylan and the band and girlfriends and hangers on and we started wandering around. The house looked absolutely magnificent – it was a clear night with a great moon and everything, and Dylan was just absolutely knocked sideways by it, just enraptured by it. And of course the classic happened...

We said, Let's be very quiet, let's see what we can hear. And in the mists there were these old statues in the garden that had got ivy growing all over them and they looked really eerie... and somewhere a dog barked!

Now this is likely to happen in the countryside in Worcestershire at gone midnight, but Dylan is convinced that he's heard the ghost of the dog! He was like a kid! He amazed me because I looked up to this great man, but he'd just keep running up to you grabbing you by the arm, saying, this is unbelievable! This is fantastic! Really child-like enjoyment of the whole thing. It was great fun...

I WAS THERE: KEVYN GAMMOND

I was in a group called The Shakedown, and Dave Mason and the gang used to come and jam at a club called The Elbow Room until about three in the morning. I think it was about the time of the first tour Dylan came over, in the mid Sixties.

We were 17 or 18 and he was in his 20s and he was a good pal of Steve Winwood. He turned up at the Elbow Room and we'd all been jamming – Dylan didn't actually join in – and when we'd finished playing we all headed off to Witley Court to go ghost hunting.

From what I can remember he looked a bit like he did on that first album – the corduroy cap, sheepskin coat. He always had a kind of cherubic look.

I WAS THERE: MERYL EDWARDS, AGE 16

I was a big Dylan fan and remember getting a friend to get up really early to walk to the city to buy tickets. I was 16 in 1966 and had just left school when I saw him. I'm sure I was wearing my duffle coat! He'd got the big hair and the only thing he said was 'there's some dirt on the stage'! Odeon Birmingham used to be a good concert venue but now it's solely a cinema.

I WAS THERE: MICHAEL DANGERFIELD, AGE 18

I cannot remember that much about 1966, other than I was there. The tide was turning, and we, the baby boomers, were surfing upon the great wave of change. Once upon a time, there were Pearl Carr and Teddy Johnson, crooning along on the sedate airwaves, as men cycled to work on sensible bicycles, and women stayed at home to raise the next generation, and then there were The Beatles, and nothing would ever be the same again.

It is hard to describe how much of a seismic shift it was, as if the old familiar world had shed a skin, and a beautiful new butterfly had emerged. It was not all dreams and play, we still had to go to work/college, but we were young and immortal, and the candle was lit at both ends and burning furiously.

Looking through a stack of LPs at a local shop, I picked up *Bringing It All Back Home*, and anxiously counted the cash in my wallet, 32/6 out of my meagre wages was an awful lot of money, but it jumped out of the box, and was carried home under my arm, so that everyone could see how hip I had become. To say it was played incessantly is something of an understatement, and I will be eternally grateful to my confused parents as the music, and, particularly the lyrics, became enshrined in some part of my inner being that was just awakening to the brave new age.

Birmingham Town Hall was a great small/medium venue with wonderful acoustics, and it was there in 1966 that I saw an advert for a concert by a group of artists known collectively as The Festival of American Folk and Country Music. Ordinarily, I would have had little interest in this music, but I did note that anyone attending this concert, was guaranteed a ticket for The Messiah's upcoming concert at The Odeon in May. After a quick chat with two other disciples, tickets were purchased, and the diary duly noted. Somewhat surprisingly, the concert at the town hall was quite enjoyable, sowing the seeds of a love of the music that is now called Americana which continues to this day.

On Thursday, May 12, 1966, a bright and sunny day, at 18-00, John, Ian and myself travelled to Birmingham in Ian's A35 van. From what I can recall we were in good spirits, and after a pre-concert drink, took our seats, slightly to the right of the stage with a clear unobstructed view. As at most of the concerts that year, the acoustic set was treated with reverence, total silence during the songs, followed by thunderous tension breaking applause at the end of each song. The set list was the same for each concert, the only exception being a solitary performance of 'Positively 4th Street' in Australia, so there no surprises, and the only words I can remember Dylan speaking were when he dropped a harmonica, and mumbled something about a dusty floor. That long forgotten memory was triggered on February 11, 1993, when Roddy Frame, formerly of Aztec Camera, made a similar comment as the floor was swept prior to his set. For me, this was a Proustian moment, and the contrast between the Ghost of Electricity in 1966, and the shambling tramp of 1993 was truly shocking.

When the curtains parted, both literally and metaphorically, the air was prickly with tension generated by the men in cardigans preparing to condemn heresy, manifest in the form of an electric guitar. One of the more remarkable things about that iconic tour, and there were many, is how clear and balanced the sound was, considering the technology available at the time, with clear and distinct separation of instruments, and vocals sharp and bright, and, in spite of the hostility, utter commitment to the cause.

Even now, 51 years later, the tapping the heel, counting in the band, followed by the swirl of Garth Hudson's mighty Hammond never fails to set the senses tingling and the evidence is there for all to hear, not at all distorted by rose coloured memories, it really happened that way. There were boos, somewhat hesitant and perfunctory at first, but building to a climax as the cardigans began to spontaneously combust. I do remember wondering what I could do to counter such shocking ignorance and bigotry in the face of musical history being made before our very eyes, so I began to clap louder pre-dating Dylan's command to 'Play Fucking Loud' prior to the final apocalyptic 'Like a Rolling Stone' at the Albert Hall.

Barry Feinstein, a photographer who accompanied Dylan during his world tour didn't like performance pictures and would take Dylan out to shoot on location. On the afternoon of May 13, 1966, Feinstein took pictures of Dylan on Dublin Street, close to Liverpool's Dock Road with a group of children who were out playing in the street. Liverpool football team Everton were completing one of the greatest FA Cup Final comebacks against Sheffield Wednesday that afternoon at Wembley.

I WAS THERE: BARRY FEINSTEIN

We were down in this area and all these kids were around. I said to Bob 'Let's have a picture of them'. The kids all sort of gathered around him and filled in the spaces. He was just sitting there. I think he was enjoying it. He likes kids.

ODEON THEATRE, LIVERPOOL

14 MAY, 1966, LIVERPOOL

I WAS THERE: SPENCER LEIGH

Although Bob Dylan's first tour had been a runaway success, I don't recall it being any harder to obtain tickets. As before, I had bought my tickets from the Odeon Cinema in Liverpool during my lunch-break and I had bought two, taking along my hapless girlfriend, Diana, who so loathed him the first time round. Maybe I genuinely believed it would be different: maybe I was being pig-headed, but I did know from the music press that Dylan had been performing with a rock band and that the fans hadn't liked it. 'Probably folkies,' I thought and because I liked rock bands more than acoustic folksingers, I knew that I'd be happy.

It was again Cup Final day and again a Lancashire v Yorkshire match, in this case, Everton v Sheffield Wednesday. Unlike most people in Liverpool, I didn't support Liverpool or Everton. I supported both local teams as I felt that if either did well, it was good for the city.

That evening I told Diana that I had a surprise for her in Liverpool. I took her to Reece's Bar and Grill: I didn't do much eating out back then – we relied on our parents to feed us – so maybe I was serious. More likely, I was sweetening the pill for what was to follow.

Again we turned the corner into London Road and again she saw 'Bob Dylan' on the marquee. 'Oh no,' she moaned, 'not him!' 'Don't worry,' I replied, 'he's changed – he's got a rock band with him. You're going to love him.'

As we went into the auditorium, we could see the instruments on stage and at the front, those two microphones, and a table for harmonicas and water. Resting on the floor on either side of the stage were two large speakers, much larger than the ones used for rock 'n' roll concerts. For the first set, it was Bob Dylan on his own. And he was stoned. Really stoned.

Spencer Leigh still has his Liverpool tickets and programme

Dylan sang, spoke, and played his opening song, 'She Belongs to Me', which was taken very slowly and deliberately. He had that measured phrasing so loved by his imitators. Indeed, it is ironic that such a serious performer has, unknowingly, prompted so much laughter. I've never heard Dylan comment on his impersonators and I'd love to know what he thinks of them. In 1966, nobody else was singing like that.

'4th Time Around' was even slower. *Blonde on Blonde* had not yet been issued and so this was a new song. Again it was incredibly slow and we wondered what it was about – was his girlfriend in a wheelchair – and what was that tune? Wasn't it 'Norwegian Wood'? Most of us would have been confused, but not Diana who felt she was on the road to hell.

In a rambling introduction, Dylan criticised the music press for saying he wrote drug songs: 'I wouldn't know how to write a drugs song. This is not a drugs song. It is vulgar to think so.' He was talking about 'Visions of Johanna' which he sang with nearly every syllable emphasised. It was brilliant but I was thinking, 'Oh please sing something that Diana will even half like.'

No chance. The 10 minute 'Desolation Row' put paid to that. He sang another new song, 'Just Like A Woman', but what was that about? 'She breaks just like a little girl' sounded dodgy to me. He closed the first set with an acoustic 'Mr. Tambourine Man' although by now, it had been a transatlantic No 1 for the Byrds. Dylan still chose to perform it acoustically. There had been no protest songs and his delivery had been strange, but by and large the folkies approved and he left the stage to warm applause. However, those instruments were on stage, so what was coming next?

No one in the audience really knew what would happen. The 1960s weren't like the 2010s where ardent fans follow their heroes on tour. I didn't know anyone who went to more than one venue. I knew a girl who went to both houses of a Cliff Richard show in Liverpool, sitting in the front row each time. She took a change of clothing just in case Cliff recognised her and thought she might be a stalker.

The tension was high as the band – or perhaps The Band – came on stage with Bob Dylan for the second half. The volume was up as they launched into a new Dylan song, the bluesy 'Tell Me Mama'. I assume the loudness was deliberate; Dylan had thought that if he was going to wind up his audience, he might well go the whole hog. Whereas the audience had been as one 20 minutes earlier, there was now a marked division. An older, definitely male contingent was jeering. Some would leave noisily, banging their seats, shaking their fists at the stage and even throwing their programmes away. The diehards went across the road to the Washhouse Folk Club which met in Samson and Barlow's restaurant building. Pete McGovern ran the club and he had written the singalong favourite, 'In My Liverpool Home', for the Spinners. Just like Robert Johnson at the crossroads, you had the old music on one side of the road and the new on the other.

The famed criticism of 'Judas'!' was at Manchester three days later, but Liverpool was up there too. When Dylan said, 'You don't have to be like this', a guy close to me shouted, 'Nor do you!' Before 'Ballad of a Thin Man', he said, 'There's a feller up there looking for the Saviour. The Saviour's backstage, we have a picture of him.'

The Liverpool concert was recorded by Columbia but the only song released at the time was a live version of 'Just Like Tom Thumb's Blues', a brilliant set of lyrics with a blistering accompaniment.

It was not a long set, perhaps 45 minutes, and it included 'I Don't Believe You', 'Baby, Let Me Follow You Down' and 'One Too Many Mornings', all of which he had recorded acoustically. The final number, 'Like a Rolling Stone' already had the status of a rock anthem and it became the one constant in Bob Dylan's tours.

Diana thought, 'God Save The Queen' the most musical moment of the evening. By this time, there were many empty seats – a third of the audience had left early, a third was clapping politely and a third was on its feet, applauding loudly. I was on my feet but I knew that my time with Diana was well and truly over. I couldn't come back from this, couldn't even try. I hardly saw her again and I wonder if she appreciates that she saw a genius musician at the height of his powers or if it is still a nightmare. When we meet again, introduced by friends...

After we left the Odeon, there was again euphoria on Lime Street as this time Everton had claimed the FA Cup.

A passing word about Mr Dylan's appearance – he was broomstick thin, dressed in a black suit and a black-and-white polka dot shirt with a wide collar and cuffs – maybe the cufflinks were a present from Joan Baez. Everybody talks about the many recorded tributes but they overlook the biggest tribute of them all – the man who copied his 1966 look and still does – the Salford poet, John Cooper Clarke. Dylan looked fantastic on this tour and he was surprisingly animated in the second half, waving his arms like Mick Jagger as he pranced around to 'Leopard-Skin Pill-Box Hat'. He dedicated the song to all the people who read *Time* magazine, but none of them would be in a Liverpool audience.

Around this time, I was promoting a young folksinger from Formby, Stephen Murray, then known as Timon and later Tymon Dogg. I was greatly impressed by Bob Dylan doing a whole concert of his own songs and I thought Timon should do the same. Timon was writing new songs every day and we did a few shows around Liverpool, mostly his own material but also with a full version of 'Desolation Row' and I doubt if anyone else in the UK was doing that. He was good too – he recorded for Apple, cut singles for Pye and Threshold and played for years with Joe Strummer. Great guy and still going today.

Looking back to 1966, that show seems even more remarkable with hindsight, easily the most extraordinary night I have spent in a theatre. Since that first appearance with a band at Newport, Bob Dylan knew that many were coming to boo him but he took no prisoners and made no compromises. Those audience members were the losers as they had paid for their seats and Bob Dylan wasn't giving refunds.

DE MONFORT HALL

15 MAY, 1966, LEICESTER

I WAS THERE: GREIL MARCUS

In Leicester, Dylan began 'Mr. Tambourine Man', and it would take him nine perfect minutes to find an ending in the song he could accept. As he sings, his words are clipped, his diction almost effete, as if each word can and must be presented as if it means exactly what it says. But very quickly, his odd speech becomes its own kind of rhythm, and paradoxically it releases the burden Dylan has seemingly placed on each word, and each word along with every other, and the song becomes a dream of peace of mind. You cease to hear the words. For nine minutes, what you hear are two long harmonica solos, each pressing well past two minutes – solos that sway, back and forth, back and forth, a cradle rocking in their rhythm, until without warning, the sound rises up like a water spout, hundreds of feet in the air, the cradle now rocking at its top, then down again, safe in the arms of the melody.

I WAS THERE: GEOFF TOVELL

Geoff Tovell (front row, first on the left) and friends at North Staffordshire College of Technology

In 1966 I was a student at the North Staffordshire College of Technology in Stoke on Trent. I used to return home for weekends to the family address in Coalville. (Still my home.)

I had already started to collect Dylan's albums. I vaguely remember some friends going to see Dylan at De Mont', (that must have been 1965) but somehow I missed it. The following year I was there. I think it may have been my very first visit to De Montfort Hall.

In the first half, Dylan stood alone with just his guitar and harmonica. He sang many of the old favourites including 'Desolation Row', (the first time I ever heard it), and I seem to remember that he ended the half with 'Mr. Tambourine Man'.

In the second half, The Band came on and Dylan went electric. This received a mixed response from the audience. Some found it OK, but for many the shock was too great and they voted with their feet. Quite a lot left, I would guess at least a third of the audience. I continued to collect the albums for several years and have altogether the complete sequence from *Bob Dylan* up to *John Wesley Harding* (With the exception of the *Greatest Hits* album.)
After that my interest in Dylan rather faded but I still have the albums and from time to time I refer to a book of his lyrics.
In 2000 I was tempted to go to see Bob again at the NEC in

PROGRAMME

It is not possible to print a list of songs Bob Dylan is to perform as he invariably makes up his programme shortly before the performance, sometimes during the course of it. This space has therefore been left to enable the programme holder to list the songs Bob Dylan sings.

Geoff Tovell and his hand written notes from the 1966 De Monfort Hall concert

Birmingham. I'm glad that I went but I have to say that I really preferred the first version.

Just one more follow up experience. Just a few years ago I went with my wife to Birmingham Symphony Hall for a classical concert (The City of Birmingham Symphony Orchestra playing Schubert's Great C Major Symphony.). Pre concert we went for a meal in Bank restaurant. On the next table were a bunch of younger folks who were obviously Dylan Fans. They all had Dylan t-shirts and Bob was appearing at the National Indoor Arena that night.

As we got up to leave I went over to the 'youngsters', leant over their table and said, 'Have a wonderful evening gentlemen, I was there in 1966.' They stared at me in awe. And it felt great to me that we had something in common, but that my experience went back to before they were born.

The trip from Leicester to Sheffield took Dylan via Nottingham, where he was photographed by Barry Feinstein outside 18 Castle Boulevard, a betting shop bearing the letters 'LSD' (pounds, shillings and pence).

I WAS THERE: RICHARD EVANS

Bob Dylan definitely visited Nottingham in 1966 because I saw him and his entourage there at the gatehouse of the Castle. I, and a

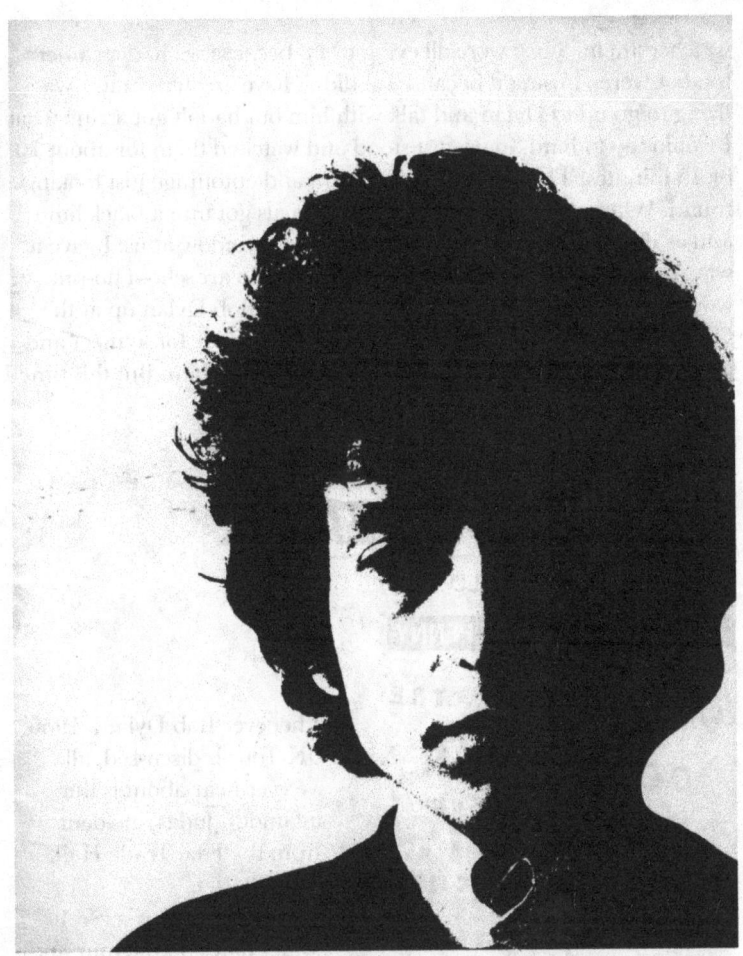

friend had taken the afternoon off from Nottingham School of Art where we were both students. We had borrowed the photography department's Bolex cine camera as we were planning on making a short film. We went up to the Castle for a scout around for ideas and when we walked into the grounds there was a group of about eight people standing round. One had a movie camera and there was a sound man with a mic on a boom. We stood and watched them and I realised that one of the people was Dylan with his curly hair and skinny clothes. We couldn't believe it was him so we just stood and watched them. They were all eying us up because we had a camera too but weren't using it because we didn't have any film in it. I was dying to go up to Dylan and talk with him but hadn't got a clue what I would say to him! So we just stood and watched them for about 10 or 15 minutes. They were filming Dylan and entourage just looking round. When they finally left, Dylan and pals got into a black limo and as they drove off he looked out the back window at us. I gave a wave and he waved back. When we got back to art school no-one would believe us when we said we'd just seen Bob Dylan up at the Castle. Fifty years later I was backstage at Wembley for a 'meet and greet' with Bob Dylan and was still awe-struck by him. But this time I shook his hand and did speak with him!

GAUMONT THEATRE

16 MAY, 1966, SHEFFIELD

I WAS THERE: STUART PENNY

Whenever Bob Dylan's 1966 UK Tour is discussed, all we ever hear about is the infamous 'Judas' incident from the Free Trade Hall, Manchester.

But there were several other dates on the tour and on May 16 (just one day before the Manchester show) Dylan played a concert 30-odd miles away across the Pennines in Sheffield and I was there.

My story begins some weeks earlier when I was dispatched to the Gaumont Cinema in the heart of Sheffield to secure tickets for a group of school friends. This was not as straightforward as it sounds. Ticket buying back then was a much more labour intensive affair than it is now and often required a morning off work/school. Telephone booking was still many years away (as, indeed, were telephones themselves for many British households) and getting concert tickets involved fronting-up in person at the box office on the specified date and conducting an uncomfortable cash-only transaction with the grim-faced matron behind the glass.

In those pre-multiplex days of course, the Sheffield Gaumont was still a busy full-time cinema, featuring live music only a handful of times a year (it had played host to The Beatles just six months previously) and buying concert tickets involved a curious double queuing method out on the street alongside (but separate from) those who were waiting to see *Alfie* or *The Good, The Bad and The Ugly* or whatever the latest flick was.

The task of policing the twin queues was entrusted to an old school commissionaire of the type still seen outside swanky hotels and restaurants in London but hardly anywhere else these days. This bloke was probably a retired war veteran and he certainly had a military bearing with his peaked cap, white gloves, and burgundy greatcoat which almost brushed the ground as he walked. The ensemble was completed by twin rows of brass buttons and, to borrow an Ivor Cutler line, gold epaulettes like bath brushes.

The Gaumont, Sheffield. It's gone now, of course, demolished to be replaced by a nightclub and department store. Bob Dylan, The Beatles and many other great names played here in the Fifties and Sixties. It became a multiplex in 1969, which spelled the end of its days as a rock venue and it finally closed as a cinema in 1985.

Bespectacled and self-important in the style of Captain Mainwaring, the commissionaire strutted up and down outside the Gaumont intoning the same line over and over: 'Queue this side for the film, queue this side for tickets for, er, Bob Die-Lon' he indicated with a wave of his immaculately gloved hand. He was clearly having trouble getting to grips with the name and those of us wanting to see 'Bob Die-Lon' sniggered at his mispronunciation. Eventually he gave up and changed his mantra to 'This side for the film and this side for the, er, folk singer' which only made us giggle even more. Incidentally, the tickets cost 10 shillings and sixpence each. For younger readers that translates to $52\frac{1}{2}$ of the Queen's new pence folks – outrageous, I know.

Finally the big day came and I arrived at the Gaumont to take my seat in the circle alongside John Tams, then just a school friend, but later to become properly famous in the folk music world as a member of The Albion Band and part of the cast of the TV series *Sharpe*, for which he also wrote and performed some of the music.

Old beyond his years, Tams cut a kind of benevolent Flashman figure and carried himself with a casual self-confidence the rest of us were sadly lacking. He dressed in the latest boho chic, sported an impressive Brian Jones haircut and most galling of all, he had a desperately attractive girlfriend. Even at school Tams was a passable guitarist and while we were still struggling with the basic chords to Dylan and The Beatles he had many of the Bert Jansch tunes down and knew loads of traditional material besides. At 17 he was already the complete package and his opinion of the concert would be sought many times in the coming weeks.

I don't remember if there was an introduction, but the heavy velvet cinema curtains creaked open and Dylan appeared in the spotlight. Pipe cleaner thin and looking like the coolest man on Earth with that iconic haircut, he teetered across the stage in Cuban heels and the now-familiar tight houndstooth check suit and polka dot shirt. People have based entire careers on Bob Dylan's '66 look and I'm not just talking about John Cooper Clarke. Marc Bolan was clearly influenced by Bob's wild curls and even Hendrix was inspired to grow his own Afro to impressive proportions after seeing Dylan during this tour. We were witnessing one of the truly defining looks of rock and roll.

Save for a few stray details which refuse to budge, the nuts and bolts of the show itself have long since faded from the memory. The first half consisted of a folkie-appeasing acoustic set which was much more edgy than the previous year's solo shows had been. Whatever chemicals Bob was using gave the performance a mesmeric intensity and his harmonica playing in particular was quite bizarre. Onstage he had a stool and a pint glass of water in which lived four or five assorted harps. He would select one, shake the water out of it and painstakingly install it in his Heath Robinson-style neck harness. This curious ritual would then be repeated for almost every song. But instead of playing the harmonica fills as we knew them from the records he simply went up and down the entire instrument randomly, blowing and sucking furiously on every available note over and over again. It sounded just fine but it was certainly a little surreal to witness.

As the curtains re-opened for the second half the stage lights remained dimmed. In the gloom we could clearly see the red stand-by lights of the guitar amplifiers as several shadowy figures shuffled on and plugged in. The Hawks! A spotlight found Dylan and I had just a second to register that the acoustic guitar had been replaced by a Fender Telecaster before all hell broke loose and a glorious cacophony filled the hall. It was louder than anything I'd ever experienced before and the sound was massively distorted. But it was also unbelievably exciting.

The staging of rock concerts was still in its infancy in 1966 and cinemas in particular weren't geared-up to handle this kind of thing, anymore than they had been three years earlier when the beat group package tours arrived. I'm not even sure if there was a proper PA system or if Dylan was singing through the Gaumont's own set-up. Compared to a modern rock show the presentation was not that slick and there were long delays between songs as Bob mumbled incoherently into the microphone and fiddled with his guitar and harmonica harness. He seemed to take forever to start each number and that's when the booing started in earnest. The murmurings of dissent had begun about three songs into the second half, reached a climax as Dylan sat down at the piano for 'Ballad of a Thin Man' and continued on and off until the very end.

Anyone familiar with the unreleased (but much bootlegged) DA Pennebaker movie *Eat The Document* will have seen the disgruntled fans interviewed in the foyer of a north of England venue (possibly Sheffield). 'I've heard pop groups produce better rubbish than that!' opines one red-faced farm boy with vowels flatter than a dead hedgehog. 'It were a bloody disgrace. He wants shooting! He's a traitor!' he adds with perhaps a touch of hyperbole.

We'd read about the booing, of course. Sheffield was the sixth date on the 1966 UK tour and news of unrest from the fans had already started to filter through. Let's be honest though, it was basically just a copycat protest. After all, what were they expecting? *Blonde on Blonde* was still a month or two away, but Dylan had already released a couple of full-on electric albums in the shape of *Bringing It All Back Home* and *Highway 61 Revisited*. As if that weren't enough of an indication, the trio of loud and nasty singles 'Like a Rolling Stone,' 'Positively 4th Street,' and 'Can You Please Crawl Out Your Window' had been all over the radio and the charts like a rash for almost a year, so the blueprint of Bob's new direction was right there for all to see.

They'd no doubt read that a few folkies were protesting in America and felt they should follow suit. But who in Britain, other than perhaps stuffy old Ewan MacColl and his traditionalist ilk, really cared about that stuff? Did we boo? Of course we fucking didn't. The short-haired squares could complain all they liked, this was Bob Dylan at his absolute creative peak and we had just seen the future of rock and roll.

Walking home afterwards we were on a real high. Someone produced a harmonica (John Tams, probably) and we sang Dylan songs on the platform of Sheffield Midland station, wishing the night would never end.

A day later in Manchester Dylan would be denounced as a 'Judas' and soon the entire world would sit up and take notice. But that was yet to happen and for just a few hours more he still belonged to us.

I WAS THERE: ARTHUR DEAKIN, AGE 17

It is always said that, 'you always remember the first time' and this certainly rings true with me in regard of the 100+ live Dylan concerts I have attended. May 16, 1966, Gaumont Theatre, Barker's Pool, Sheffield was an event which in a small way really did change my life.

I had been into Dylan's records, especially his words and delivery, for a while and as a 'Maths/Physics/Chemistry' A-level student I was a bit of a 'funny-ossity', in matching my scientific 'spanner man' background with a deep love of Shakespeare, medieval English History and Poetry and, er.... rugby. Why is it that Science students who are into the Arts are more common than Arts students into science? So as a 17-year old sixth form student with aspirations for University – at a time when this was hard – I snapped off the hand of someone at school who I really cannot remember who sourced Dylan tickets and arranged a minibus to transport us to Sheffield for the concert. I think the ticket was 7 shillings and six pence (37.5 p) but I cannot really verify this.

When we arrived at the 2,500-seater theatre (a cinema really) I remember walking up the steps to be greeted by loads of cine photographers, where the audience were asked for their views of Dylan – presumably for *Eat the Document*? I didn't get interviewed, but it did set the stage for 'something happening here' – especially given the recent musical press coverage of mass walk outs at Dylan concerts prompted by Bob 'selling out' and going electric/commercial farrago. So, on we rocked up to the 850-seater balcony – if memory serves, we were centre stage about 1/3 back, with a superb view of the stage.

The house lights did dim, maybe 20 minutes late and there was himself, alone and acoustic striding into 'She Belongs to Me' – you could hear a pin drop in the theatre as he performed. Next up came '4th Time Around' – I hadn't heard this before and was taken with a middle-aged guy on the front of the balcony who, to my 17-year old pretentious brain, was dressed like a University don, who laughed out loud on the line 'you'd better spit out your gum'! 'Visions of Johanna' followed – which was stunning, lyrical poetry. 'Desolation Row' was, well, epic – I loved the reference to TS Elliott, having just got to grips with *The Wasteland*. 'Just Like a Woman' was new to me, and somewhat erotic/risqué I thought. Then the highlight of the concert, 'Mr. Tambourine Man', with eerie, haunting harmonica that seemed to go one for eons – the best harp I have heard from Bob in all the concerts I have attended.

Then the break, followed by the loudest music every heard in Sheffield as Bob and The Hawks launched into 'Tell Me, Momma' – with a vengeance 'how long is it going to take you to jump off the edge' – indeed. Later we had Bobby kicking into his story about the painter's (paaaaynterrr in stoned American drawl) blue period, before launching into a blistering 'It's All Over Now Baby Blue'. By now I thought I would be seeing lots of people leaving, but this really didn't happen, a few maybe but by no means an exodus. Later we had 'Ballad of a Thin Man' with Bob on grand piano – I was impressed by his playing and the song – with lines very prescient about mobile phones. Between songs we had bouts of Bob going into his '… a moon, a spoon, a June' spiel, ending with 'remember I was a baby once' and also at one time 'If you just wouldn't clap so hard' – I think this was Sheffield, but I've listened to so many bootlegs over the years I may well be miss-remembering. I also recall the intro to 'I Don't Believe You' – 'It used to go like that, but now it goes like this'. I do recall a deal of booing at this stage in the concert.

The climax of the show, just as the Judas concert at The Manchester Free Trade Hall on the following night was undoubtedly 'Like a Rolling Stone' – delivered in a full-throated, joyful, loud, ecstatic, 'stoned' voice. On reflection, it has always seemed to me that a line from the stage play of *Amadeus* by Peter Shaffer said of Mozart always seems apt – the song seemed to be coming through him, rather than from him – as though he had a direct line to The Almighty. Something I really would not see again until the Born Again 1979-1981 period, recently captured wonderfully well in the *Trouble No More* – deluxe edition (2017) – a musical film. After LARS we had the National Anthem – a mighty strange juxtaposition, and then we ambled off home, dodging the cinema-verite interviewers on the theatre steps. It took me more than a few days to 'process' what I had seen and heard and for the loudness of the music and 'ear-worms' to subside – but having done that I determined that I was right to defend and attend Bob as often as possible for the rest of my life. In terms of my musical taste I became somewhat monotheistic.

My next Bob experience, having got my Chemistry degree, was The Isle of Wight – we did do our best to sink it – and the 'new voice' was a revelation. Then came 1978, and the birth of my first son – Robert of course it could have been Richard, after Richard III, another of my passions, but a nephew was born a month before and my brother nabbed the Richard first name. Incidentally I joined the national Richard III Society at University and so was extremely fortunate to attend the Richard III re-interment events in Leicester in 2015, and do illustrated talks on Richard for charity. I am currently working in a Dylan related talk!

Anyway, all was well in the new life my wife and I had with Rob, until a clash appeared with his christening and the sale of Dylan tickets for Earls Court. To cut a long story short I finished up sleeping all night on the pavement – perversely on Barker's Pool in Sheffield – to get said tickets – only to panic three hours before the start of the christening event and asking the person behind me in the queue to get me the tickets because of the circumstances: I did not know this person from Adam, despite, as it were, having slept with him. I got back home in the nick of time, the Christening went well, despite shall I say, my wife being somewhat less than happy with me! The good soul in the queue I had trusted and given my money to, came up trumps, I got a phone call later in the day and tickets through the post from him in due course – great bloke! The Earls Court show was great, and recall 'One Of Us Must Know', and 'Senior' as highlights.

So, there we are, my first, second and third shows. I then caught Bob as often as I could, in all four nations of the UK, Ireland and occasionally in France. After my second son, Phil, arrived and he and Rob became teenagers they often accompanied me to concerts, willingly or not. They both developed an acute awareness of Dylan quotes to suit every mood and emotion. With Phil, arguably, having an even greater mastery of obscure Dylan lyrics than his older brother!

Then came the Never-ending tour, and through John Baldwin's good offices at Desolation Row, this has allowed me to attend at an accelerating rate. This year I attended eight UK shows in 10 nights, making the score well over 100. I'm still not sure about Bob Sinatra though, nor about the rip off price of *Official Bootlegs* to complement my unofficial collection.

In conclusion, I have to pay tribute to my long-suffering wife, who does not share my Dylan-philia but who has supported me all the way with it, including commissioning two original Dylan paintings for my sixtieth birthday. Kate readily appreciates his artistry/poetry/lyricism but cannot stand his voice, so whilst she applauded the well-deserved Nobel prize, she had more than enough with ½ a concert in incredibly cramped London Palladium balcony seats earlier this year.

However, a couple of months ago, we both attended *Girl From The North Country* at the Old Vic which she declared the best piece of musical theatre she has ever seen – and in fairness she has seen a lot, as she has a very catholic appreciation of all genres of music. The upshot of this is that we now happily play the CD of the original cast of *Girl From The North Country* at some volume as we drive up and down the country to Whitby where we are living for six months. Happy days!

FREE TRADE HALL

17 MAY, 1966, MANCHESTER

I WAS THERE: JOHN CORDWELL

I think most of all I was angry that Dylan... not that he'd played electric, but that he'd played electric with a really poor sound system. It was not like it is on the record. It was a wall of mush. That, and it seemed like a cavalier performance, a throwaway performance compared with the intensity of the acoustic set earlier on.

There were rumblings all around me and the people I was with were making noises and looking at each other. It was a build-up. I'd heard Dylan was playing electrically, but my preconceptions of that were of something a little more restrained, perhaps a couple of guitarists sitting in with him, not a large-scale electric invasion.

Maybe I was just living in the past. And I couldn't hear the lyrics in the second half of the concert. I think that's what angered me. I thought, 'The man is throwing away the good part of what he does.'

I think I was probably being egged on. I certainly got a lot of positive encouragement as soon as I'd done it. I sat down and there were a lot of people around me who turned round and were saying, 'That was great, wish we'd have said that' – those sort of things. And at that point I began to feel embarrassed really, but not that embarrassed. I was quite glad I'd done it.

I don't regret doing it because I think I did it for the right sorts of reasons. I felt betrayed by someone who'd formed a very big part of my life for two or three years. But, y'know, with the benefit of hindsight, I don't think I would do it now.

The view from the stage looking up into the audience seating at the Free Trade Hall in Manchester

I WAS THERE: KEITH BUTLER

We were just really disappointed. That wasn't the Bob Dylan we'd been used to listening to. The Dylan we were used to was *The Freewheelin' Bob Dylan*. Can you imagine what it's like as a 20-year-old kid? You were just crushed. I was there with another guy, and that's when we decided to leave.

I WAS THERE: MICKEY JONES, DRUMMER

It was just a gig. I don't think anybody feels like they are creating history when they do something. We certainly didn't. It was a gig, we were having fun. We knew that we were giving them good music, even though we got booed everywhere we went.

I've had people ask, 'Is that you?' No, it wasn't me. 'Is it Bob?' I tell them no, it wasn't Bob. I don't know who it is who said, 'play loud,' but all I can tell you is it's a British accent. It's somebody yelling loud, and they're off mic. We had six British roadies all over the stage. I believe it was one of our roadies sticking up for us in the moment. It just wasn't in Bob's nature. And why yell if he's that close to Robbie's ear? I was five feet from Bob. If he'd said it, I would've known it.

I WAS THERE: MARK MAKIN

The gig had two halves: the first saw Dylan taking the stage alone and acoustic, while in the second, he played with the backing of his band, The Hawks. Everybody was whisper quiet. These days, everyone roars with the recognition of the first line. It never happened then. You didn't dare miss a second of it. I suppose there was an expectation that he might not play electric, he just might carry on – because we had such a good first half, he might just do more of the same.

When he came on, he'd got a smirk on his face, because he knew what was going to happen. He'd had this elsewhere in the months prior to this and he had it completely under control and was not going to be dissuaded by anybody.

He piled in with 'Tell Me, Momma', and it hit like a freight train, because it was a real rocker and screamer. People sat there stunned.

I think the problem was the Free Trade Hall's total lack of musicality – it was a square-sided building and when the sound was projected from a PA like that, it hit the wall at the back and came straight back at you with an echo and a reverb. All you could hear was this mush of sound. I think that was what hurt people.
It wasn't that we didn't expect him to be electric, but if he had just come in at three quarters of the decibels, it might have worked.

I WAS THERE: SUSAN GREY

The first time I saw Dylan was in 1965, when I was 14. The second was in 1966.

If I had to pick one thing it would be the words. But I think it was much more complicated than that. I remember hearing the buzz about a Pete Seeger concert that some friends of my elder brother had been to. Some of them played the guitar, banjo, or harmonica and they started up an evening folk club at school, so I used to go to that. They played a mixture of traditional folk and the newer Pete Seeger style of songs. But there was one boy who used to turn up and do Bob Dylan songs. I liked pop and rock music – I'd spent years listening to Radio Luxembourg and Radio Caroline. When folk came along it was an introduction to a whole new genre – especially the political and protest songs. 'Little Boxes', or 'We Shall Overcome', for example, challenged the accepted order of things and couldn't have been more different from what was usually in the charts. Dylan had that folk sound, but was a bit different – sometimes bluesy, poetic and often rather mysterious. Songs like 'Masters of War' were incredibly powerful and like nothing else I'd heard before.

I think the context was important. As children in the Fifties we'd heard a lot about world war – supposedly as a thing of the past. But now we were seeing very shocking images of the Vietnam War on television night after night – we forget that in those days media coverage wasn't managed the way it is now. Not long before we'd had the Missile Crisis and extremely alarming talk of World War III. Protest movements were gathering momentum, not just about the war, but also about civil rights, apartheid, nuclear weapons , etc. Young people were questioning the establishment. There was also beat poetry, pot and jazz and I was on the threshold of all that. So for me I think the folk revival in general and Dylan in particular represented an entry into something very exciting and grown-up, both musically and in terms of involvement with bigger issues.

My parents didn't think much of him – especially his singing voice. But they were pretty tolerant and didn't stop me monopolising the family record player.

I wasn't aware of what he'd been doing over the year between 1965 and 1966. In 1965, at 14, I was absolutely enthralled. I'd never experienced anything like this before. He came on stage and stood in the spotlight – just a slight figure with guitar and harmonica. He said very little, just worked his way through all these wonderful songs. Everybody loved it. Afterwards my friend and I went round to the stage door with a dozen or so other people in the hope of seeing him and getting his autograph. Of course he didn't appear, so eventually we had to accept that the evening was over and get the train home.

In 1966 I suppose we expected more of the same – and this time I knew more of the music. The first half was fine then the second half was a real surprise. I didn't know what to make of it. It wasn't just that he'd added the band and an electric sound, the arrangements were different as well.

Part of me felt cheated that he'd changed his style and we weren't hearing what we expected to hear, but I was intrigued too. I didn't want Dylan to give up what I thought were his principles, but also I didn't want to give up on him. It didn't take me long to get on board and I bought the single 'Like Rolling Stone' as well as the album, *Bringing It All Back Home*.

The electric set was noisily dramatic. Very loud in comparison with the acoustic set – and the words were hard to follow, as much as anything because we couldn't hear them properly. I can't say I particularly enjoyed the electric numbers – but it was still Dylan and, after all, you had to work at it a bit with some of his acoustic songs too. So for me it was a case of waiting to see what happened next.

I thought did he really say Judas? By that time there'd already been plenty of noises from the audience – slow, hand clapping and so on – so it was clear not everyone was happy. Dylan was clearly not happy. After 'Judas', he said, 'I don't believe you, you're a liar.' There were some other comments at various points but they were difficult to hear.

This individual hostile exchange was quite dramatic. Obviously I was aware of the fuss in the press afterwards, but I don't remember that particular incident being singled out until the official album came out years later and Andy Kershaw wrote about it, and interviewed the chap who shouted 'Judas'. I remember thinking, 'Ooh I was there!' But looking back it was only one of many turning points for him. He turned out to be even more versatile and extraordinary than he seemed in the Sixties.

I think some people in the audience felt that we might have lost a hero for no good reason – other than his own wilfulness and I could relate to that. In retrospect, it's clear there were a lot of unwarranted assumptions being made about his interests and motivation. But at the time we were at a loss as to how it would all pan out – would he continue to be interesting and sing songs with a message, or would he become just like any other rock 'n' roll band?

After the concert a small crowd of people sat down on the floor in the foyer in protest. My friend and I hung around for a bit to see what would happen, but nothing much did. We knew by now that stage door appearances were not Dylan's style, so we headed off for the train. Such antagonism between a performer and the audience was all very strange. But it was exciting to be there when things were happening that people cared about. Sit-down strikes and protests were like a new language for young people, so it seemed like a natural way to react.

I didn't see the film until many years later. I think it pretty much showed how Dylan and others in that scene behaved at that time. I'd followed all the coverage of Dylan's tours in the newspapers, so I knew he liked to be challenging or contrary with interviewers. I'd like to have felt I knew more about him, but that didn't make me any the less fascinated.

It was good that it wasn't a very big venue, so you could always see. By today's standards it was quite intimate and they even had seats on the stage behind the performer. As far as I can remember the tickets were reasonably priced. I don't count them as a gigs, but I'd been there a couple of times as a much younger child with my family to see our next-door neighbours' Scottish Country Dancing Nights, so it was familiar.

The venue was near to Oxford Road Station and concerts always ended in time for the train back to the nearest station in Cheadle Hulme. If my parents had any concerns about me going to a gig in town at 14, they didn't say so.

Over a few years following the first Dylan gig, I saw acts like Simon and Garfunkel, Julie Felix, Incredible String Band, and Donovan. One gig had a young David Bowie doing a mime act supporting Tyrannosaurus Rex. Then there were acts like Manitas De Plata with his flamenco guitar group. I collected a few autographs as some of them were stage door friendly and didn't mind chatting with a few of us who stayed behind after the show. The Free Trade Hall was also home to the Halle orchestra – where I saw Daniel Barenboim, Vladimir Ashkenasky and Jaqueline Du Pre. There were a couple of other gigs I went to during those years – The Beatles at ABC Ardwick, and I think Charles Aznavour was at The Palace, but those venues didn't have the intimacy of the Free Trade Hall.

I remember feeling dismayed by a newspaper story that the Free

Trade Hall might be demolished or developed in some way. So, although I knew the battle had already been lost, when I was visiting Manchester a few years ago I felt compelled to go into what's left of the building to have a look. I stood in the foyer and felt quite bereft. I had to go over to the receptionist and tell her how sad it was and how much those concerts meant to me growing up. She was very nice and friendly and said they understood. In fact they'd tried to acknowledge these events by naming rooms after some of the artists.

> **...a young woman walked down the centre aisle right up to the stage. Dylan and the band are watching her and she handed Dylan a folded up piece of paper. Dylan took the piece of paper, unfolded it, read it and folded it up, put it back in his pocket and blew the girl a kiss. I actually met the woman and asked what the note had said and she was really embarrassed and said, 'it said, 'Send the band home.'**

I WAS THERE: CHRIS LEE

I was born in 1950, which puts me in a very good vantage point for the second half of the twentieth century. Dylan entered my consciousness about 1964. We went to a very interesting school called the High School of Art. It took artistically inclined kids and gave them an extra boost in that direction. So, particularly in sixth form and whatnot, there were people who were very trendy. They were ace faces at the Twisted Wheel, they were into the folk movement, they were into CND. They were into all these things. And being slightly younger I'd be looking up to them.

During lunch breaks you'd hear records being played in the common room. Folk was very, very, popular and Dylan, of course, was a major part of that. At 14 I started going to folk clubs as well, sneaking in wearing a trilby trying to look a lot older.

I nipped out of the queue for tickets to see The Rolling Stones at the Palace Theatre in Manchester to go and buy Dylan's new album when it came out. I did that because you could actually get the album whereas a lot of this was very mythical.

With Dylan, there was this direct voice speaking. 'The Times They Are a-Changin'' resonated with all the things that were happening on the TV news. You'd see black civil rights activists in America being teargassed and hosed and having dogs set on them. And so it was part of that. Something like 'Masters of War' appealed directly to that CND-element side of me.

It was couched in a language that was biblical in its splendour. It was like a singing King James Bible. Not that I was in any way religious, but it was couched in a poetical style that appealed directly to me.

I didn't go to the 1965 show at the Free Trade Hall because I couldn't afford it. Buying a ticket was a significant investment and I'd probably blown it on Who records or something. But I was there in '66, a nice Tuesday evening in a town called Malice.

The Free Trade Hall was a mid-Victorian civic hall built by public subscription to remember the dead of the pro democracy movement slaughtered at Peterloo in 1819. It's despicable that it's now an upmarket hotel. It was given to the people of Manchester in perpetuity on condition that it was not sold or used for any commercial gain. In 1996, the council sold it to become a hotel, thereby betraying the principles of democracy and socialism; but that's Britain for you.

I went with a mate from school, Mike King, but we were sat in different parts of the hall. I was at the back of the stalls on the right and I think he was midway up on the left. So I was separated from him once we got there. I'd been there loads of times before, to school speech days and things like that. This was the first proper concert that I'd ever been to.

It was packed. Sold out. In those days, there were seats on the stage. If you look at photographs of that night you can see the audience sat behind Dylan and the band as they're playing. It was just bizarre but very standard to sell more seats in those days. I saw various people – the Incredible String Band, Joan Baez, Phil Ochs – and it was always like that.

There was an enormous amount of anticipation before he came on. People talking in the foyer, people talking around me as we were sat in our seats, wondering what he was going to do. Because vague stories had filtered through organs like *Melody Maker* where they'd reported that he'd been booed in Dublin and we just didn't know what to expect.

Now you could see there were amplifiers and a drum kit on stage and the red lights on so it was obvious that something was afoot. But then the lights went out and Dylan came on – this tiny, tiny little figure – solo, and there was almost a sigh of relief went through the audience. 'Oh all right, nothing bad's going to happen.'

He then proceeded to do 45 minutes of absolutely enchanting music and there was this desperate scrabble to find bits of paper, to write down lyrics as you heard them, because so many of the songs – you had no idea what they were and you never knew if you'd hear them again. So to hear something like 'Just Like a Woman' or 'Visions of Johanna'? We'd never heard them before. And '4th Time Around' was quite astonishing so – I loved it, and everybody else did as well.

Then the intermission comes and there's a bit of a wander round and people talking again. I overheard somebody say, 'oh he saw sense. He decided not to use the band'. So then, when the bell rang for the second half to begin we went back in, all sat down and then you suddenly heard Garth Hudson playing 'In an English Country Garden' on the organ and we knew that something else was afoot.

And then Dylan comes back on with his Fender. The band are all there, looking a bit cheesy really, in different coloured velvet suits. Which was rubbish as far as we were concerned now, because the Stones broke that mould in '65 and things were getting a bit more bohemian with British rock bands, particularly in 1966. so this was odd that they were wearing suits.

And then – crash – into 'Tell Me, Momma' which did physically blast me back into my seat. I imagine now things would be a lot louder but then it was unprecedented. I'd seen The Who in beat clubs, I'd seen the Small Faces. That was loud but this was something else altogether. It was not helped by the fact it was a Victorian hall because the sound boomed out and then boomed right back again so it was a giant hodgepodge; a bit unnerving.

And the shock reaction in the audience, because they'd never heard 'Tell Me, Momma'. I had no idea what it was about. It was a beat song and there was Dylan cavorting like a miniature Mick Jagger. That seemed to get up people's noses more than the songs, because he'd be striking poses, putting his arm in the air and stamping his foot and what not.

But then the set proceeded and I think the second number saw dumb insolence on the part of the audience and a continuation of the shock reaction: 'He's playing this stuff!' It was completely divisive. By the third number you start getting the slow handclaps and the animosity began to rise from a group of maybe 100 people out of 2,000. There were enough of them to make their presence felt. A lot of people were non-committal, they were waiting to see what it was going to be like, and a lot of people were very partisan in Dylan's favour. So a lot of the argy-bargy is in fact people shouting down people who were heckling.

But there is a momentous bit, which happened before 'Leopard-Skin Pill-Box Hat', where a young woman walked down the centre aisle at the Free Trade Hall, right up to the stage. Dylan and the band are watching her and she handed Dylan a folded up piece of paper. Dylan took the piece of paper, unfolded it, read it and folded it up, put it back in his pocket and blew the girl a kiss. She walked back and then they went into 'Leopard-Skin Pill-Box Hat'. Years later, I actually met the woman and asked what the note had said and she was really embarrassed and said, 'it said, 'Send the band home'.'

He had another trick as well, which was that he'd mumble. It's an old carnival barker trick, where you just keep a load of gibberish going and every now and again you put a recognisable word in and then eventually people who are slow hand clapping or heckling will go quiet to listen and then he always finished it off with 'I was just a baby once myself'.

Then everybody's listening again. So he was pulling out old carnie tricks, doing this, that and the other. Then there was the penultimate song, 'Ballad of a Thin Man', which is followed by the 'Judas!' shout, which I didn't hear. I heard somebody shout but I didn't hear what they said because I was underneath the balcony that the person was sat on.

The reaction from Dylan was 'I don't believe you' and then he went into an absolutely stunning version of 'Like a Rolling Stone' which I recall, some people around me cheering because this was the song that had been a bit hit the year before. Then he mumbled 'thank you' and left.

Then we get the national anthem which was the signal that it all had ended. But there were a lot of us hoping that there was going to be an encore. And also a lot of people had walked out.

That was the way of it in 1966. I saw a handful of people walk out from the ground floor over the course of the second half, probably no more than two dozen. It was a trickle in between numbers and they were very ostentatious to be doing it, making a big show of marching out. Manchester University Folk Society had had a meeting about what to do about 'The Dylan Problem' and they'd actually voted not to go so they missed a chance to protest at the gig. Apparently in Glasgow, the Young Communist League also had a meeting about what to do and they voted at which point the signal would be given, and then they'd all walk out.

So the end of it was just chilling. There was a frosty atmosphere and lots of antagonism between the different factions of the audience as they were leaving. There was no actual pushing or shoving but I remember some people being absolutely knocked out by it and some people claiming to be very, very disappointed and betrayed. 'Betrayed' was the big word. Dylan had betrayed something precious. And sold out. 'He's gone commercial.' That was the other big complaint.

How that squares up nowadays it's hard to say. It's hard to imagine anyone getting a reaction like it nowadays. I know Miles Davis did in some respects. But nowadays we can loot the cultural supermarket in all respects and pick and choose what we like and what we don't like. And often we can like all things from different aisles.

Since that night I've talked to people who booed but who, six months on, had bought *Blonde on Blonde* and absolutely loved it. So not exactly Damascene conversions but pretty close to it.

I was surprised at their naivety because 'Subterranean Homesick Blues', had come out in the previous March, well over a year before. 'Like a Rolling Stone' was a hit in September of 1965. And there was 'Positively 4th Street'. So he'd had a whole succession of electric singles and at least one and a half electric albums.

But not a lot of people had the albums. It was a big thing to get an album in those days. And I knew one guy who was there that night who had the album but didn't have a record player. So he hadn't actually heard it. This is a very different country – or planet – than the one we're on now, where people had very little really compared to what we have now. And what we did have was precious. To go to a concert and spend 17/6 or maybe even £1, when people were only earning about six or seven quid a week, was a mighty investment. So I suppose in a way you would want them to dance like a monkey and do the tricks that they were supposed to do. And there was Dylan confounding them. He's second-footed people throughout his entire career.

SET LIST:

ACOUSTIC:
She Belongs to Me
4th Time Around
Visions of Johanna
It's All Over Now, Baby Blue
Desolation Row
Just Like a Woman
Mr. Tambourine Man

ELECTRIC:
Tell Me, Momma
I Don't Believe You (She Acts Like We Never Have Met)
Baby, Let Me Follow You Down
Just Like Tom Thumb's Blues
Leopard-Skin Pill-Box Hat
One Too Many Mornings
Ballad of a Thin Man
Like a Rolling Stone

> So the knockers are all stations go again. I am referring to the fantastic performance given by Bob Dylan at the Free Trade Hall last Tuesday night. I think Bob put his feelings over to the knockers just great. When someone shouted out to him 'Judas!', he just calmly went to the microphone and quietly drawled 'Ya liar'

OLDHAM EVENING CHRONICLE
MAY 1966

GLASGOW ODEON

19 MAY, 1966, GLASGOW, SCOTLAND

I WAS THERE: MATT WILSON

The headline on the front page of the *Evening Times* declared, 'Dylan Blows In!' They were actually giving copies of this special edition away for free, but nobody took one. This was 1966, the only thing to be seen carrying in public was the mono LP *Highway 61 Revisited*.

I had been totally hooked on Dylan since watching the two BBC TV 1965 concerts as a 14-year-old whose musical education had been limited to my big sister's singles collection, Cliff Richard, and the smooth haircut brigade. It wasn't the musical content of his performances that hit me; it was the huge spectrum of his subject matter wrought into breathtaking lyrics.

From then on it was a rollercoaster of discovery, borrowing or buying the LPs and playing this wonderful music over and over. Not surprisingly, the whole Dylan experience led me down some marvellous side roads to poetry, art, photography and the obvious guitar bashing.

So, there I was, taking my seat in the Odeon Theatre to actually see and hear the music for myself. Much had been reported about the booing and heckling at previous concerts, so this Glasgow audience was not going to be outdone. As the euphoria from the acoustic first half performance wore off, we cleared our throats in readiness for a heckle-fest. As I mentioned earlier, my sister was my musical mentor until 1965. She dragged me to concerts by the Searchers, Freddy and the Dreamers, the whole package tour adventure. This had not prepared me for Dylan and Co unleashing their electric storm. We were all thrown back in our seats as they let us hear some good old American music.

Of course we shouted abuse between songs, this was audience participation included in the ticket price. Song after song, each one better than the last right up to 'Like a Rolling Stone'. What a way to go!

Looking back on this great landmark night, I feel that we weren't really ready enough for this experience to do it justice. Personally I peaked too early musically because of this. 15-years-old, going home on the bus with two hours of Bob Dylan ringing in my ears. What chance did I have? Nothing can match that.

As news travelled of his current shows, some members of the audience at Dylan's May 20, 1966, concert at the ABC, Edinburgh, Scotland brought along harmonicas along and tried to drown Dylan out.

HOTEL GEORGE V
23 MAY, 1966, PARIS, FRANCE

On Monday, May 23, 1966, Bob Dylan faced the media during a press conference at the Hotel George V. He brought with him a puppet named Monsieur Finian which he had bought from a Paris flea market. Every time one of the journalists asked him a question, he put his ear to the puppet's mouth and pretended to listen to the answer. Then he would tell the press. It drove them nuts. They didn't understand him.

Reporter: What did you think of your first night in Paris?
Dylan: It was very dull.

Reporter: Why is the puppet here?
Dylan: It followed me.

Reporter: Is it a mascot?
Dylan: No, it's a religious symbol.

Reporter: What religion?
Dylan: It's a symbol of the religion of tears.

Reporter: How much are you getting paid for your concert in Paris?
Dylan: 350 million dollars.

Reporter: Tomorrow is your birthday – how do you feel about that?
Dylan: It's a crime to talk about it.

Reporter: Why do you sing?
Dylan: Because I like to sing.

Reporter: Do you want to express something with your singing?
Dylan: No.

Reporter: What do you think about death?

Dylan: Very exciting.

Reporter: Which song will you open with tomorrow night?
Dylan: 'Hello Dolly.'

Reporter: What did you think of the American intervention in the war in Europe in 1944?
Dylan: Do you think that's an easy question?

Reporter: Yes.
Dylan: Well, I don't answer easy questions.

Reporter: What do you enjoy doing?
Dylan: Smoking and eating.

Reporter: What interests you in life?
Dylan: Nothing.

Reporter: What makes you happy?
Dylan: A bowl of soup. Being kicked in the ribs by a friend.

Reporter: Are you happy?
Dylan: Yes. As an ashtray maybe.

L'OLYMPIA

24 MAY, 1966, PARIS, FRANCE

I WAS THERE: RICHARD ALDERSON, SOUND ENGINEER

The Paris show was problematic for any number of reasons. Bob took forever tuning his acoustic guitar – I think just to irritate everybody, he took like 20 minutes to tune his guitar. The audience was hostile from the get-go. They had an attitude about America already, that we were a bunch of fascists warmongers.

They opened the second half with the biggest American flag that Bob could find in Paris and the audience didn't get the joke at all.

> **There was a marked and disturbing contrast between the two parts of the concert given by Bob Dylan, the American folk singer, at the Albert Hall last night. In the first, and infinitely better, half of the evening, Mr Dylan gave an agreeable solo rendering of some of the songs for which he is best known: in the second half he was accompanied by the thunderous quintet who made it virtually impossible to distinguish a single line of the lyrics.**
>
> **THE TIMES**
> **27 MAY 1966**

ROYAL ALBERT HALL

26 MAY, 1966, LONDON

I WAS THERE: HELEN LOCK, AGE 14

It was my first concert and I was pretty far from the stage, but it was still an amazing experience. I was 14-years-old at the time. I was in the 'gallery promenade,' which is an area in the top level of the Albert Hall that doesn't (or didn't, don't know about now) have seats, unlike the rest of the venue, AKA 'the gods,'

AKA 'the nosebleeds.' This was the cheapest ticket available, it cost three shillings and sixpence (in pre-decimal currency). I received sixpence a week pocket money (allowance), and so this represented seven weeks' savings, in a jam jar with a slot punched in the lid. I also saved to buy a programme. Tickets sold out really quickly, and they put in a second night. I made a calendar chart on which I could cross off the days.

On the appointed day, my Dad drove me to London (about an hour away) for the show, and I believe went to the movies while I was in the theatre. The poor man had a long wait, because the show started an hour late for some reason. I'd never been to the Albert Hall before, and I remember it was both exciting and confusing finding my way up to the top of the building, then seeing all these people standing at the rail at the top, and panicking thinking I wouldn't be able to see. Most of the people up there seemed to be college students, plus some folks who looked like leftovers from the beatnik era. Fortunately one young couple spotted me, and took pity on this little girl (I'm five feet tall), inviting me to stand in front of them so I could see. (In fact I attracted some attention being so young and generally outside the audience demographic).

I could hardly believe I was seeing Dylan in real life, in the same room (more or less). I memorised everything he was wearing and everything he sang or said, so that I could write it all down as soon as I got home. ('He wore a green striped suit and in the light his hair looked grey!') The whole show had the feeling of an event, not just a concert – I knew, for example, that members of The Rolling

Stones were there somewhere, and possibly a Beatle or two. In particular, there was a sort of frisson in the air, a feeling that there might be trouble.

In the first half of the show he played songs I knew and loved, and he got a reverential response from the audience. Audio of the show is now widely available as *The Real Albert Hall 1966 Concert* and all the songs familiar, but at the time one of the only songs I knew that he played in the second half was 'Like a Rolling Stone', the closer. I later wrote things like 'There was one song about 'she makes love like a woman but she plays [sic] like a little girl' that I liked a lot.' Hard to believe now that there was a time when I hadn't heard all the songs on *Bringing It All Back Home* and *Blonde on Blonde*. It was of course during the second half that the 'trouble' occurred and people started heckling and walking out. Only a few people, it must be said, and even at the time I felt they were just attention-seekers, since it was known that Dylan would have the electric band in the second half, so those who objected could have just left. (Hard to believe there was a time when I wasn't familiar with The Band, too, who weren't even called that at this point.) Most of the audience, certainly where I was, were on Dylan's side, and were irritated by the interruptions. I understood that some people felt Dylan had somehow betrayed them, but even so I remember thinking the protesters were incredibly rude. At the same time, though, it made the whole event feel more memorable and somehow special. Not just a run of the mill show by your average artist.

My last notation was that after 'Like a Rolling Stone', 'his group went off and the spotlight was just on him and then he walked off and waved in our [ie, my] direction.' I remember the feeling of my hero having very vaguely acknowledged my presence. Then I guess I went outside and found faithful Dad in the crowd.

I WAS THERE: MIKE PETTY

I remember being surprised (and relieved) at how he seized the Hall with such authority, right from the first song. It's a big place, and not particularly friendly to one bloke with a guitar singing 'Visions of Johanna' or 'Desolation Row'.

I remember the walkouts of course, and booing and counter-booing.

The electric half was the loudest thing I'd ever heard in my life. I can still conjure up how Robbie Robertson's stinging guitar made my ears ring on 'Leopard-Skin Pill-box Hat'.

'Like a Rolling Stone' was just awesome. I was on a cloud of joy all the way home.

I WAS THERE: CHRIS WHITHOUSE AGE 15

Chris Whithouse poses in his garden in his best 'going out' gear

I was 15 going on 16 years old when I saw my first Bob Dylan concert over 50 years ago. I'd certainly been aware of Dylan since 'The Times They Are a-Changin'' had been released as a single, but I still have an embarrassing memory – probably from late 1964 – of mispronouncing his surname in the playground and quickly being corrected by a boy from the year above me.

Anyhow, I was still at school in Sussex at the time and must have applied for tickets by post, I really don't remember now. As things turned out the schoolfriend who had wanted to go with me couldn't make it so I ended up going up to London with another friend from my class, Jeff Reynolds.

It was May 26, 1966. *Blonde on Blonde* had only been released 10 days earlier.

We arrived at the Royal Albert Hall early. The doors hadn't opened yet so we made our way towards the one that we needed to enter by, door No 3. The reason that I still remember the number is that we'd only just positioned ourselves outside it when who should walk out past us but Brian Jones and Anita Pallenberg. Just at that moment a passing car hooted at them and someone looking very like Bill Wyman raised an arm towards them in greeting as he drove past.

Our seats were reasonably good ones. Row 23 in the arena and priced at 15/-, which I would have had to get up early and do my morning paper round for about a week and a half to pay for.

The first acoustic half of the show was nothing short of majestic. The sound seemed to resonate throughout the hall as Dylan, in what I later learned he called his hound's-tooth 'rabbit' suit, delivered a series of classics (including three less familiar songs from the new album) to a respectful, awestruck audience. Unfortunately, the mood of the audience was to change dramatically as a defiant Dylan delivered the electric set that followed.

The acoustics in the hall were dreadful. It was virtually impossible to identify most of the songs that he was singing. His voice struggled to be heard from behind a wall of sound and I still believe that this was probably the main reason that the electric sets were received with such hostility during this period. Most of the audience knew that the second set would be electric but hadn't realised that the old cinemas and small halls that Dylan was playing in just couldn't balance or cope with this level of sound. A situation that wasn't helped by the fact that Dylan chose to open the electric set with an unrecorded song that was totally unknown to the audience.

There was a certain amount of heckling but Dylan was obviously used to handling this by now and adept at putting it down, either by mumbling some incoherent nonsense that would quieten the detractors down while everyone tried to decipher what he was saying or, as at this show, with a disparaging retort. His response to slow hand clapping after 'Baby, Let Me Follow You Down' was to explain that, 'These are all protest songs. Now, come on. This is not British music, it's American music.' However, Dylan never lost control of the audience and by the time that he had led them back into more familiar territory with 'Ballad of a Thin Man' and 'Like a Rolling Stone' (bizarrely dedicated to the Taj Mahal) he seemed to have won everyone round again.

Despite his ultimate triumph against seemingly insurmountable odds at times I still left the hall feeling exhausted but exhilarated and with a feeling that I'd just been escaped from some kind of riot. Strangely, though I wouldn't be aware of it until several years later, two days earlier my future wife Sheena had seen Dylan deliver a similar show in front of a huge American flag in Paris.

The Rolling Stones shared a box at Dylan's concert at the Royal Albert Hall. Earlier that evening they were seen performing their new single, 'Paint it Black', on *Top of the Pops*, which went out on BBC at seven in the evening.

Following the show, Brian Jones and Keith Richards went to Blaise's nightclub, a few hundred yards away in nearby Queensgate, where Dylan later arrived. Nervously, Keith had approached him. With a sardonic sneer, Dylan looked straight through him and said: 'I could write 'Satisfaction' but you couldn't write 'Mr. Tambourine Man'. Richards took a swing at Dylan, and a short melee ensued.

ROYAL ALBERT HALL

27 MAY, 1966, LONDON

I WAS THERE: PATRICE HAMILTON, AGE 15

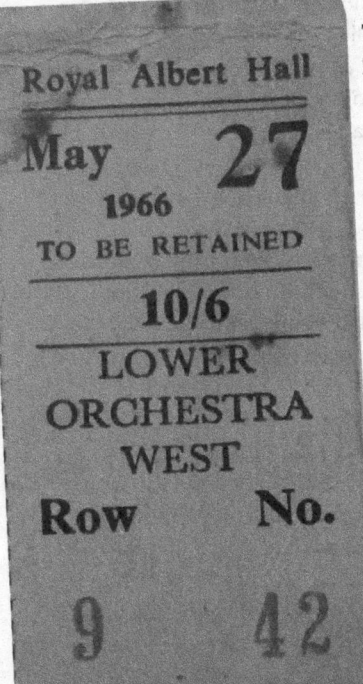

The concert that took place on May 27, 1966, was a completely different experience from that of the concert that I had been to the year before. It was later claimed to have had the noisiest audience and the highest proportion of walk-outs of all the European concerts!

Once again my dad had used the same method to get tickets for me and my four friends, the Editor of the *Sunday Express* had kindly secured tickets for Dad to pick up. This time I had my long, blonde hair loose, curtain style as was the fashion in '66 and wore a wine velvet mini dress with cream lace tights and the same bar shoes as before with the wine coloured ribbons. Fashion in the

Sixties was at its height and we all wanted to look really 'groovy'.

I'd previously heard 'Subterranean Homesick Blues' on the radio and thought it was fantastic, very different from his Folk stuff but very exciting just the same, even though some of the words were difficult to decipher. However, I hadn't heard the *Blonde on Blonde* LP which I'm not sure was even released by the time I went to the concert, so I, like most other fans at the time, was expecting a similar concert to 1965. Oh boy, what a surprise was in store for us all.

When Dylan wandered onto the stage he looked like a very skinny elf, with the wildest tangle of hair I'd ever seen, he was dressed in a dark green, houndstooth check suit, which clung to him making him look even more waif like. His movements were quite jerky and deliberate, a bit like a puppet and his face was very white and angular with half closed eyes as if he'd had a few heavy nights. He seemed extremely nervy and uncoordinated but then he knew what was coming later – we didn't!

The first seven songs were spellbinding, reminiscent of the previous year's acoustic set, but sung in a more exaggerated way, including an amazing rendition of 'Visions of Johanna' and a magnificent 'Desolation Row' then ending the first half of the show with a splendid 'Mr. Tambourine Man'. The audience were very appreciative and clapped politely after each song, falling into reverential silence when he sang and hanging on his every word. The echoes in the Albert Hall were eery, quite haunting and Dylan was mesmerising, he looked so fragile in the spotlight as if he could be snapped in half.

By the time The Hawks joined Bob on stage, he was buzzing with nervous energy, his limbs seemed almost out of control, he kept plucking at the electric guitar he now had strung across his slight frame as he kept up an almost conspiratorial conversation with the band. Something was happening!

Before they even started there were already catcalls from the audience proclaiming that Dylan didn't need the band and they should go home. Bob was oblivious to everything beyond the stage and carried on engaging in conversation with his fellow musicians, the tension in the air was palpable. Then as they struck up with 'Tell Me, Momma' it felt as if an earthquake had hit and the roof had been blown off! The booming vibration on my seat shook me to bits.

Wow, I'd never heard anything like it as Dylan whined and strangled every word against an enormous wall of sound. It was unbelievable. The rumbling of the crowd was instantly drowned out by the extraordinary music coming from the stage, you couldn't tell whether they were loving it or hating it until the first song of the second half dramatically ended, leaving Bob rubbing his hands through his hair and looking totally on his own planet!

The crowd were very definitely upset now. They were whistling, shouting, stamping their feet, slow hand clapping and very loud booing seemed to be rising all over the hall and echoing round the walls, it was like a scene from *Bedlam*! Seemingly completely undeterred, Dylan and the band launched into the next song, a fantastic version of 'I Don't Believe You' and once again the sound was enough to make your ears bleed. I was ecstatic, it certainly wasn't what I'd expected but I thought it was the most exciting thing I'd ever seen and heard in my life (and probably since)!

Bob seemed to be drawing out starting the next song each time and tuning his guitar, whether this was in the hope that the audience would quieten down, I really don't know but he continued to be quite animated and still seemed a bit unsteady on his feet, I don't know if I dreamt it but I seem to have a memory of him dropping some harmonicas on the floor and him scrabbling around on all fours giggling as he tried to pick them up, it was probably a good thing that he appeared to be off with the pixies!

A non plussed Dylan and now a band beginning to look somewhat apprehensive, carried on regardless, steam rolled through the next few songs to ever increasing shouts of abuse and constant slow hand clapping. At one point somebody shouted out 'Woody Guthrie'd turn over in his grave!' which was odd because in 1966 Woody Guthrie wasn't dead! There were also more insistent calls for the band to go home, 'You don't need them, Bob'. Whole droves of people were up out of their seats, fists were being waved and it looked as if a riot might break out. They never did this at a Billy Fury concert! Hoards of people were streaming out of every exit, I couldn't believe what I was seeing, fans in the upper tiers were stamping so hard it made the seats shake, it was like a thunderous roar that made me think the whole building might collapse!

I was even more worried that the concert wouldn't continue, I thought maybe Bob and the band would leave the stage in fear or disgust and we'd be left sitting in an empty hall! Besides I'd spent 10/6d on a ticket, I wasn't going anywhere. I couldn't really understand why people were so upset, yes this was different stuff but why were they so angry? I was just grateful Bob had turned up and I'd got a seat!

Bob made several attempts to talk into the microphone to try and quell the chanting and general mayhem but he couldn't be heard above the din and I think he was probably burbling a stream of nonsense just to try to attract their attention, although most of what he said was inaudible, I did manage to hear him say something along the lines of 'I won't be coming back' which filled me with despair. As Bob moved over to the piano and started playing the opening bars of 'Ballad of a Thin Man', things seemed to temporarily quieten down a bit and he managed to do a cracking version of this song with relatively no interruptions. I remember thinking how delicate he looked as he sat at the piano and attacked it with his long white fingers, his beautiful face, shining like white glass in the spotlight.

Then it was time for the final song, Bob and the band launched into 'Like a Rolling Stone' what an anthem to end on and I swear the sound had gone up a few more notches, it was sensational, even his harmonica seemed to be screaming, what a phenomenal sound!

As it came to an end Bob looked absolutely exhausted and was almost held up by his band members to get him off stage. Meanwhile the chaos and booing continued, becoming more of a subdued rumble as people seemingly couldn't wait to get out, get together with their mates and orally take the concert apart. I sat rooted to the spot for quite a while, for one thing I was totally blown away by being at this concert and secondly I was a bit apprehensive about getting in amongst so many angry people! I was only 15 and felt quite intimidated. Fortunately my friends had enjoyed it as much as I had, so we gradually eased our way out into the night air, bombarded with the sound of complaining punters.

Groups of angry fans were huddled together outside, mostly made up of school kids and teenagers in suits with their hair lacquered girlfriends, still shouting the odds and being challenged by people who'd enjoyed the concert and were of the opinion that Bob could do what he liked! Posters were being sold along the pavement and I saw one group of people actually set light to a poster...reminiscent of Nazi Germany? We couldn't get out of there fast enough.

My ears were ringing and continued to do so for several days but in the words of Bob after the 1965 concert, 'I felt like I'd been through some kind of thing!'

I WAS THERE: JACKIE PARSONS

I went with my friend Pamela, we had tickets in row E, well done us, we did some serious early morning queueing. The first half Bob does alone with guitar and harmonica and very nice it was too. He comes back for the second half with an electric band, The Hawks (essentially The Band without Levon Helm), we loved it, others seemingly didn't. Much shouting and booing from diehard folkies, The Beatles were in the audience to see this farrago. I wonder what they thought?

I WAS THERE: CHRIS GARDINER, AGE 16

Chris Gardiner spent his first working wage buying a copy of the Bob Dylan album

I was 16 and had been living and breathing Dylan since early '65, unknown to me he'd entered my DNA via *The Madhouse on Castle Street* which I'd watched with my parents who were horrified at the singing, it sounded good to me and if your parents don't like it...well what better excuse. I filed that away and about that time my elder brother began a subscription to *Billboard* magazine, in which started to appear large advertisements for *The Freewheelin' Bob Dylan*, I still didn't make the connection between the two. My favourite band in '64 were The Animals and Eric Burdon started to namedrop Dylan in interviews and songs, finally it all came together and I was smitten.

In '65 I started work and spent my first weekly wage on the *Bob Dylan* LP. I then bought each album in order of release as I could afford them. I made no attempt to see him at the Royal Albert Hall (RAH) in '65, in fact I have no recollection of the gig being advertised or even taking place until reading the reviews. But in '66 I was ready!

Living in Surrey I was only an hour's journey to London, so I got on a train and bought a ticket from the RAH box office, it cost £1 and was the top price, the man in the booth told me that, 'it was a good ticket'. He was right it was a stalls seat, for those of you who don't know the RAH, the stalls are the slightly raised area encircling the arena the area in front of the stage which traditionally would be called the stalls in any conventional theatre. My seat was at about the 2 o'clock position and had great sight lines.

There is no curtain in front of the stage at the RAH so you could clearly see the amps and drum riser even for the acoustic part of the show, so even if you hadn't read any of the press reports you knew that something was about to happen.

The lights dimmed and a spotlight hit the stage, Dylan entered stage right wearing the houndstooth suit (which I would refer to as Rupert Bear check for many years after!), my side, clutching a handful of harmonicas making his way to the stool positioned at the microphone. His hair was amazing and where was the leather sports jacket that I'd lusted after and finally found a version of.

All goes very well until the start of a new song,'Visions of Johanna' where we got the 'this is not a drug song' rap, someone shouts 'we're with you Bob' from way up above me, in fact you can just hear this on the Gelston acetate recording, after which our hero answers 'yes all right.'

He drops a harmonica before one of the songs and does a funny Chaplinesque stoop down to pick it up, the audience laugh at which Dylan says, 'Don't do that, that's terrible.' again, clearly audible on the Gelston recording.

The harmonica solo in 'It's All Over Now, Baby Blue' is spellbinding. It floats around that huge hall, which in those days had quite an echo depending upon where you sat, long before the saucer structures were hung from the ceiling in an attempt to 'cure' this. The security in those days consisted of elderly gentlemen in slightly military uniforms and hats, the one at the door nearest to me looked totally mesmerised by this song. Then it was 'Mr. Tambourine Man', lots of applause, and intermission.

Now remember that the amps and drums have been visible throughout. When Dylan and The Hawks hit the stage (Robbie in the white striped suit) there is mixed applause and derision, the atmosphere has changed, Dylan has changed, he's pumped up now in complete contrast to the quiet reservation of the first half. It's loud, but no problem to me as I've been going to rock gigs since I was 13 years old, Little Richard at Kingston Granada anyone, and been fed a diet of Chuck Berry and Muddy Waters by my brother.

When they do 'One Too Many Mornings' and 'I Don't Believe You' I start to get a bit agitated, I didn't see why he had to amp up what I perceived to be 'folk songs' that I'd been besotted with for a year or more, yes I wasn't totally ready for the electrification, I loved the already familiar new rock songs though.

Dylan is very animated he keeps throwing his arms around Robbie's neck, which for a Surrey boy of 16 is quite shocking!

Someone struts forward at each chorus to share the microphone in 'One Too Many Mornings', with hindsight probably Rick Danko.

There is a lot of booing and shouting and people do leave. I'm totally shocked that people could buy a ticket to someone they wanted to see and then boo.

Two girls next to me are worried that, 'he'll walk off in a minute', it was clear to me that he wouldn't, he seemed to be almost enjoying it and was in a way in control. Now of course with the knowledge of the Pennebaker footage in *No Direction Home* we can assume that he was part elated at the thought of it being the last gig and he was going home.

'Like a Rolling Stone' is long and then it's all over, it all passed very quickly. I wish I could remember more.

I do remember walking along Exhibition Road (I may have levitated) back to the tube station that I really didn't know if I loved or hated the man. It was that good. I dreamt in colour that night, something I rarely ever did or do.

In 1970, a good friend of mine, Jeff Thomas, sadly no longer with us, called me up and played me a tape down the phone, it was he said Dylan at RAH the electric half, it was amazing. Well, I knew it wasn't the May 27 set but it could have been the night before, it was of course the Manchester gig. It was long before any bootlegs of this existed, and as far as I'm aware was one of only a few copies in the country at that time.

A few years ago I was invited to a friend's dinner party and a friend told the story of how he went to see Peter, Paul and Mary at the Royal Festival Hall in 1964. After the show he and his friends went for a drink at a pub near the venue only to find that Peter Yarrow was also having a drink there. They told him how much they had enjoyed the gig and he remarked that if they'd enjoyed that, then they must go and see 'a friend of his called Bob Dylan' who was going to perform there in a few weeks time, 'he's sensational' he told them. Dennis went and was totally underwhelmed, apparently Dylan didn't speak at all between songs, but he did remember that he sang 'Mr. Tambourine Man'. At that dinner party you had three people who had seen Dylan in '64, '65 (the host) and myself '66, there can't be many instances of that surely.

I WAS THERE: JACKY PALMAN

I first saw Dylan in 1966 at the Albert Hall in London (I still have the programme and the play list). I was probably one of the youngest there, and had already been a fan since *The Times They Are a-Changin'* album. I was wearing a borrowed coat that was far too big for me. We sat in the circle, but had a good view. In my diary I wrote, 'lots of slow hand-claps and cat-calls', but I was mesmerised throughout, especially by the electric stuff. He was wearing a brown suit and looked very thin, and really st-r-etched out the words and twisted his body as he sang. To quote from a friend's poem that was published later that week in *Melody Maker*: 'his unique voice – a sort of drawl; the movement of his head; the twitching mouth, the burning eyes – I'll remember till I'm dead.' That sums it up.

I saw him next at the Isle of Wight in '69, then Earls Court in '76 and at other times in other countries over the years – finally in Glasgow in 2016; but the Albert Hall concert was the life-changer.

Two months after the last concert of the World Tour, Dylan was involved in a motorcycle accident late on Friday afternoon, July 29, 1966. Subsequent to Dylan's withdrawal to Woodstock, he refrained from undertaking a major tour until 1974.

Dylan's seventh studio album *Blonde on Blonde* was released in the summer of 1966 and completed the trilogy of rock albums that Dylan recorded in 1965 and 1966, starting with *Bringing It All Back Home* and *Highway 61 Revisited*.

Recording sessions began in New York in October 1965 with numerous backing musicians, including members of Dylan's live backing band, The Hawks. Though sessions continued until January 1966, they yielded only one track that made it onto the final album 'One of Us Must Know (Sooner or Later)'.

At producer Bob Johnston's suggestion, Dylan, keyboardist Al Kooper, and guitarist Robbie Robertson moved to the CBS studios in Nashville, Tennessee. These sessions, augmented by some of Nashville's top session musicians were more fruitful, and in February and March all the remaining songs for the album were recorded.

The cover shows Dylan in front of a brick building, wearing a suede jacket and a black and white checkered scarf. The jacket is the same one he wore on his next two albums, *John Wesley Harding* and *Nashville Skyline*.

375 WEST STREET

NEW YORK CITY, NEW YORK

I WAS THERE: JERRY SCHATZBERG, PHOTOGRAPHER

I wanted to find an interesting location outside of the studio. We went to the west side, where the Chelsea art galleries are now. At the time it was the meat packing district of New York and I liked the look of it. It was freezing and we were very cold. The frame he chose for the cover is blurred and out of focus. Of course everyone was trying to interpret the meaning, saying it must represent getting high on an LSD trip. It was none of the above; we were just cold and the two of us were shivering. There were other images that were sharp and in focus but to his credit, Dylan liked that photograph.

Bob Dylan's new smash single, **'I Want You'** from his deluxe two-record set...

Blonde on Blonde
including the hit, 'Rainy Day Women #12 & 35'
Where the action is.
On COLUMBIA RECORDS

1967

Bob Dylan's Greatest Hits, the first compilation album by Dylan, was released on March 27, 1967, on Columbia Records. It contains every Top 40 single Dylan enjoyed through 1967. It peaked at No 10 on the US album chart and No 3 in the United Kingdom. Certified five times platinum, *Bob Dylan's Greatest Hits* is his best-selling album in the US.

After his *Blonde on Blonde* double-LP of May 1966 and his motorcycle accident of that summer, with no activity by Dylan since the end of his recent world tour, and no new recordings on the immediate horizon (the sessions that would in part be later released as *The Basement Tapes* were still months away), Columbia Records needed new product to continue to capitalise on Dylan's commercial appeal. Hence the appearance of this package, the label's first Dylan compilation and its first LP release with a $5.98 list price, one dollar more than that of standard releases.

The cover photograph used on the cover was taken by Rowland Scherman at Dylan's November 28, 1965, concert in Washington, DC. Bob Cato was the designer of the album cover, which won the 1967 *Grammy* award for 'Best Album Cover, Photography.' The original album package also included Milton Glaser's now-familiar 'psychedelic' poster depicting Dylan.

I WAS THERE: MILTON GLASER

I liked Dylan very much. I knew him. He was represented by Albert Grossman, who was a good friend of mine. And I would see him occasionally, actually I haven't seen him since I did that poster which is a very long time ago, (the poster that came with *Bob Dylan's Greatest Hits*). He was just one of the true poets and artists around who's work moved you in a way that went beyond entertainment.

He was very famous and he hated the album that was produced, which was the last album he did for Columbia. They did all the editing and assembly of that album. He had nothing to do with it and he had already broken his contract. So he tended to hate everything in it, and although he's never told me that he never liked the poster, in fact we've never discussed it at all – it will probably remain the most iconic representation because its been reproduced so many times.

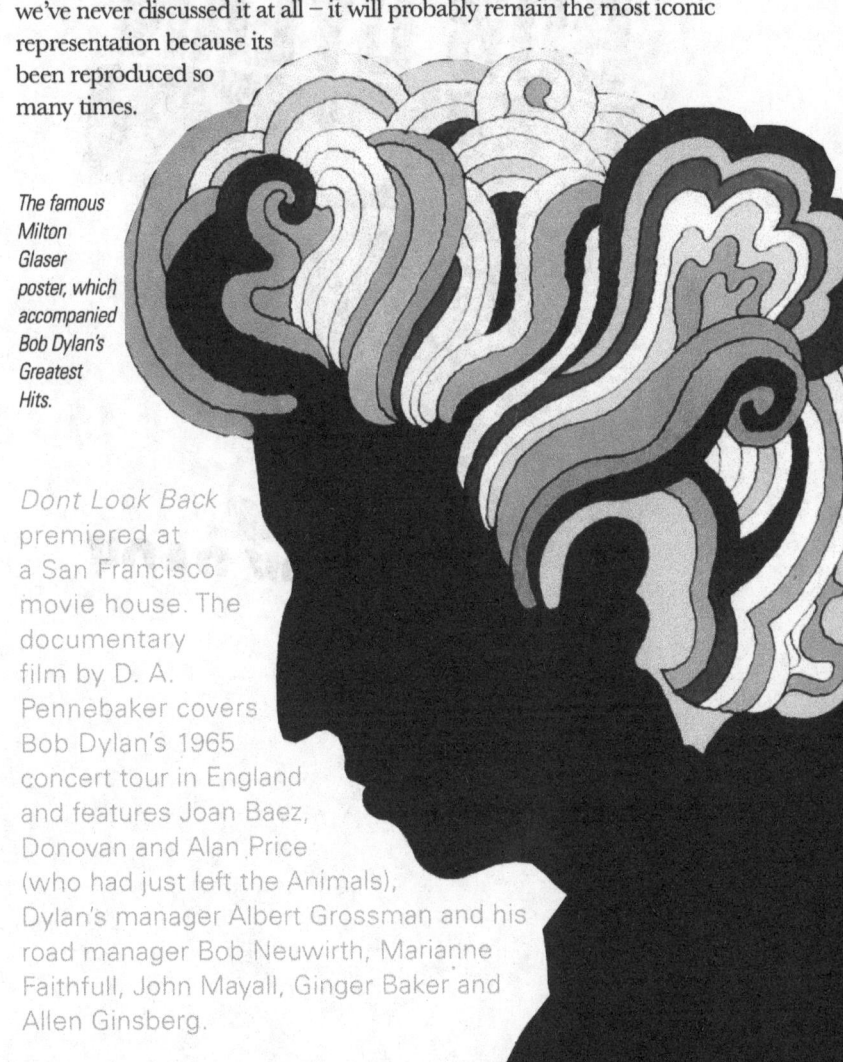

The famous Milton Glaser poster, which accompanied Bob Dylan's Greatest Hits.

Dont Look Back premiered at a San Francisco movie house. The documentary film by D. A. Pennebaker covers Bob Dylan's 1965 concert tour in England and features Joan Baez, Donovan and Alan Price (who had just left the Animals), Dylan's manager Albert Grossman and his road manager Bob Neuwirth, Marianne Faithfull, John Mayall, Ginger Baker and Allen Ginsberg.

The opening scene of the film also served as a promotional film clip (the forerunner of what was later known as the music video), for Dylan's song 'Subterranean Homesick Blues', in which the singer displays and discards a series of cue cards bearing selected words and phrases from the lyrics (including intentional misspellings and puns). Allen Ginsberg makes a cameo appearance during this episode.

THE PRESIDIO THEATER

17 MAY, 1967, SAN FRANCISCO, CALIFORNIA

I WAS THERE: D.A. PENNEBAKER

I didn't know his music at all when we started. I had heard maybe one song on the radio. Albert Grossman came to me and asked me if I wanted to go on the tour, and I assumed he wanted to put on film promotional material to further what Dylan was doing. I thought I'd just be filming music, so I only took one person with me. After about two or three days in London, I got kind of interested in Dylan as a person. The way he talked. I decided not to make just a music film. No one had told me what I could or couldn't do. So I assumed I could make a film any way I wanted.

When I finished it, he saw it out in Hollywood at a dreadful screening. Afterwards, he said, 'We'll have another screening and I'll write down all of the things we have to change.' Of course, that made me a little gloomy. The next night, we assembled again and he sat in the front with this yellow pad. At the end of film, he held up the pad and there was nothing on it. He said, 'That's it.'

I put that in a porn house on Manhattan's Lower East Side. It was the only Theatre I could get. It ran for a year. People would come. In fact, the same people would come every Friday and they'd all be smoking grass in the johns. The guy who ran the theatre was so happy. He was making money left and right. He didn't want it to ever stop.

I WAS THERE: PATTI SMITH, MUSICIAN

It was just such a pivotal moment for me because it encompassed everything for me. It encompassed our poetry, the perfect sunglasses, everything, the way he walked. I love everything in it and I saw it after that so many times – I knew all the words, you know like you'd know all the words to a rock 'n' roll song or the first page of *Little Women*, I knew all the dialogue of *Dont Look Back*. I just saw all the ways in which I connected with myself, how I walked, how I phrased things. The way I reacted to it wasn't in an intellectual way, it was like, yes, I can do that.

If anyone doubts the roots even going from Mozart to the Beats, to Bob Dylan to punk rock – he is in this continuing stream. You look at him talking to reporters and he was nobody's Patsy, that's for sure. This is a badass guy you know.

BIG PINK
JUNE 1967, WOODSTOCK, NEW YORK

I WAS THERE: ROBBIE ROBERTSON, MUSICIAN

In his approach, the poetry aspect of it, poetic license in songwriting; it's a culmination of a whole bunch of things but because we were working with Bob it was really obvious. I didn't pay attention to a lot of the things that he wrote, though. It was too talky for me. It was just like I was getting lost and this was like reading subtitles to a song. I was saying if this thing could be more soulful and simplified. Later on things like 'Just Like a Woman' came, things that I thought were really touching.

When we would play with Bob he would do this acoustic set and then the electric set. In the acoustic set it was just blah, blah, blah, blah all the way through. Not that he wasn't saying amazing things, it was just too much. I didn't want to listen to that many words from anybody – anybody! That was just somebody that talked too much. It was brilliantly done.

But, from my background, I came in on a rock 'n' roll train, blues and country music mixed together where the music played a part of it. There was a sound, there was an effect to this whole thing and it all added up. That's what made rock 'n' roll to me. You mix this and you mix that and a little bit of this and a little bit of that and you get something and God knows what it is. It's just magical when you put it all together. I wasn't getting that out of Dylan's music.

Between all our influences, my influences, Bob's opening up this door, it was like a calling. It was like adding up these pieces together where you actually are going to hear the humour of

Little Willie John's 'All Around The World' and you're going to hear these voices doing Staple Singers stuff, and a high singer like Smokey Robinson, but with these kind of lyrics, the Hank Williams-influenced things. All of these things add up – you mix them all in a big pot and you stir them with a spoon and you get the *Music From Big Pink* and The Band albums.

Dylan's eighth studio album *John Wesley Harding* was released on December 27, 1967, by Columbia Records, (the album is named after Texas outlaw John Wesley Hardin, whose name was misspelled).

Following the motorcycle accident in July 1966, Dylan

spent the next 18 months recuperating at his home in Woodstock and writing songs. All the tracks for *John Wesley Harding* were written and recorded during a six-week period at the end of 1967.

With one child born in early 1966 and another in mid-1967, Dylan had settled into family life.

The album marked Dylan's return to acoustic music and traditional roots, after three albums of electric rock music. Although the lyrics are somewhat enigmatic, the music is simple, direct, and melodic, providing a touchstone for the country-rock revolution that swept through rock in the late Sixties. 'All Along the Watchtower' became one of his most popular songs after it was recorded by Jimi Hendrix the following year.

The Jimi Hendrix Experience began to record their version of Dylan's 'All Along the Watchtower' on January 21, 1968, at Olympic Studios in London. Hendrix had been given a tape of Dylan's recording by publicist Michael Goldstein, who worked for Dylan's manager Albert Grossman.

Hendrix only met Dylan once – a fleeting encounter at the Kettle of Fish in Greenwich Village, New York City.

❝We met at the Kettle of Fish on MacDougal Street. That was before I went to England. I think both of us were pretty drunk at the time. I like his Blonde on Blonde and Highway 61 Revisited. His country stuff is nice too.❞

JIMI HENDRIX

❝I liked Jimi Hendrix's record of this [All Along the Watchtower] and ever since he died I've been doing it that way. Strange how when I sing it, I always feel it's a tribute to him in some kind of way.❞

BOB DYLAN

1969

COLUMBIA STUDIO A

14 FEBRUARY, 1969, NASHVILLE, TENNESSEE

I WAS THERE: BOB JOHNSTON, PRODUCER

I told Kenny Buttrey to get the cowbell. He said, 'Cowbell is ass. What do you want a cowbell for?' I said, 'You're gonna hit it against your head. It's a perfect sound.' He said, 'I'm not hitting that against my head.' I said, 'Use your stick.' He got a stick and put the cowbell on and Bob goes, 'I thought that was crazy when you said that, but it all worked out.' I'm not a damn genius – I didn't know whether that would work or not. I might have said, 'Get that cowbell out of there.' That's my whole life, just listening at the spur of the moment. I wanted everything to be better than everything else was with everybody on all they did.

Highway 61 Revisited took about two weeks or a week and a half. *Blonde on Blonde* took about two weeks. I got Al Kooper, Rick Danko and Robbie Robertson down there. They said, 'We can't play with those Nashville people.' I said, 'Well, go back to Canada.' They said, 'We'll play with them,' and they did and they all fell in love with each other.

Dylan was like an eternal spring. He would have 20 songs and be writing and performing. It got to be real quick with him because of the way we did it. He came to Nashville and did *Nashville Skyline*, which was a huge album. I got all the papers and put them out on the floor in the control room. He said, 'What do you think about doing bass, drums and guitar?' I said, 'That's great, but there ought to be a steel too.' I got Pete Drake, who's about the best steel player, and we started in. About midnight Dylan said, 'Let's do another one.' I said, 'You're finished.' He said, 'You're kidding!' And I said, 'No.' We did it in one day, *Nashville Skyline*.

I WAS THERE: JOHNNY CASH

I was deeply into folk music in the early Sixties, both the authentic songs from various periods and areas of American life and the new 'folk revival' songs of the time, so I took note of Bob Dylan as soon as the *Bob Dylan* album came out in early 1962 and listened almost constantly to *The Freewheelin' Bob Dylan* in 1963. I had a portable record player I'd take along on the road, and I'd put on Freewheelin' backstage, then go out and do my show, then listen again as soon as I came off.

He and I were writing each other letters before we ever met. I got a letter from him saying like he was from Hibbing, Minnesota and there was nobody else out there like me and Hank Williams and he was glad to hear about the part of the world that was out there.

The first time I met him was at the Newport Folk Festival in 1963, I was on the show with Bob, Joan Baez and Rambling Jack Elliot. Then Bob Johnston brought him to Nashville to do his *Nashville Skyline* album. Bob and his wife and children stayed at my house while he was doing the album and he asked me to be a guest on it. And as it turned out we were in the studio and they turned on the recorders for about two hours and just recorded us.

I WAS THERE: CHARLIE DANIELS, MUSICIAN

I was brought in by Bob Johnston who asked me to come to the studio and fill in for a guitarist who couldn't make the session. There were 15 sessions booked and I was only supposed to play on one. And, of course, I played with all my heart and soul as much as I possibly could.

When we had finished the session, I was packing my gear up to leave and Dylan asked Johnston, 'Where's he going?' He said, 'He's leaving. I got another guitar player coming in.' And Dylan said, 'I don't want another guitar player. I want him.' They were the greatest words I've ever heard spoken in my life! Its things like that, that encourage you to go on, and get back out on the street and look for that record contract and to stick with it and to write those songs and stay with it no matter what.

Something that always sticks in my mind from working on *Nashville Skyline* is that when Bob started doing 'Country Pie' and I had my Telecaster and Bob was on the piano, and he started playing those chords – that is my favourite piano part that he ever did. And I came in on my Telecaster and that was the spirit of things, we were having fun! We had 15 sessions booked and I think we did nine, it was done, it was over with.

I found him to be totally and completely different from what I read in the press. He was friendly. He was conversational. He had a sense of humour. He was having fun in the studio. And that album went like clockwork. Everybody was so into it. All the players and Dylan, it just happened. It was so relaxed. Dylan's doesn't like to spend a whole lot of time on a song. If the first take is good, it's the first take.

If you listen to every other album he made before then and then go back and listen to *Nashville Skyline*, it is a totally different album. His vocal sounds, the material he did, the way he approached it, all of the arrangements – everything – the total thing was kind of a departure for him.

COLUMBIA STUDIO A

15 FEBRUARY, 1969, NASHVILLE, TENNESSEE

I WAS THERE: BOB JOHNSTON, PRODUCER

They've got 32 songs with Dylan and Cash laughing. The band had left for lunch, Dylan was in the studio and Cash came by. Dylan said, 'What are you doing here?' Cash said, 'I'm going to record here next.' Dylan said, 'I just finished.' Cash said, 'Let's go to dinner. Come on, Bob.' I said, 'No, I want to stay here.' While they were gone I built a bar and had their microphones and guitars out. They got back and looked around and saw their guitars and a bar. They didn't say a word, got their guitars, started playing and singing together and we started requesting songs. About two hours later Dylan said, 'We're finished.'

Bob Dylan graces the cover of British rock music magazine Zig Zag

Dylan's ninth studio album *Nashville Skyline* was released on April 9, 1969, by Columbia Records as an LP record, reel to reel tape and audio cassette. The album reached No 3 in the US and gave Dylan his fourth UK No 1 album.

RYMAN AUDITORIUM
1 MAY, 1969, NASHVILLE, TENNESSEE

The Johnny Cash Show, a summer replacement for ABC's *Hollywood Palace* variety program, got off to an impressive start on June 7, 1969, with performances by Bob Dylan and Joni Mitchell.

A few weeks after the release of *Nashville Skyline*, Dylan and Johnny Cash performed 'Girl From the North Country' on *The Johnny Cash Show*. It was taped on May 1, 1969, at the Ryman Auditorium in downtown Nashville. Despite Dylan's reported nervousness, the performance was well received. 'I didn't feel anything about it,' Cash said later. 'But everybody said it was the most magnetic, powerful thing they ever heard in their life. They were just raving about electricity and magnetism. And all I did was just sit there hitting G chords.'

Joni Mitchell first met Bob Dylan in May, 1969 in Nashville, while she was taping an appearance on the Johnny Cash television program and he was in town to record for the *Nashville Skyline* album. One particular evening during that time has gone down in musical legend as the visiting and local talent gathered at Cash's home.

I WAS THERE: JOHNNY CASH

That night in my house was the first time these songs were heard. Joni Mitchell sang 'Both Sides Now,' Graham Nash sang 'Marrakesh Express,' Shel Silverstein sang 'A Boy Named Sue,' Bob Dylan sang 'Lay Lady Lay,' and Kris Kristofferson sang 'Me and Bobby McGee.' That was the first time any of those songs were heard.

WOODSIDE BAY

29-31 AUGUST, 1969, WOOTTON, ISLE OF WIGHT

Dylan was initially reluctant to perform his comeback show at the Isle of Wight Festival. After weeks of negotiations, the promoters of the festival showed him a short film of the island's cultural and literary heritage; this appealed to Dylan's artistic sensibilities, as he was enthusiastic about combining a family holiday with a live performance.

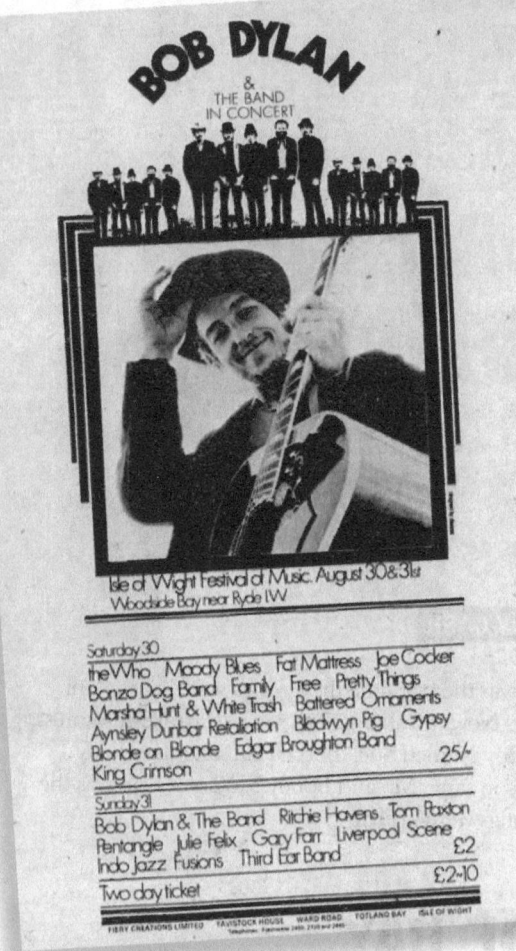

Bob Dylan makes a special appearance at the Isle of Wight Festival of Music, accompanied by other well recognised names such as the Who, Moody Blues, Joe Cocker, Free, Bonzo Dog Band and others

The family was scheduled to travel to Britain by sea on the Queen Elizabeth 2 (QE2) and nearly missed the gig completely when Dylan's son Jesse was hit by a cabin door and was taken to hospital. Dylan instead travelled by plane at the last minute.

Around 150,000 people saw Dylan's performance. As well as three of The Beatles, (John Lennon, George Harrison and Ringo Starr), Keith Richards, Bill Wyman, Syd Barrett, Eric Clapton, Elton John, Françoise Hardy and Jane Fonda.

DYLAN'S SETLIST:

She Belongs to Me
I Threw It All Away
Maggie's Farm
Wild Mountain Thyme
It Ain't Me, Babe
To Ramona
Mr. Tambourine Man
I Dreamed I Saw St. Augustine
Lay, Lady, Lay
Highway 61 Revisited
One Too Many Mornings
I Pity the Poor Immigrant
Like a Rolling Stone
I'll Be Your Baby Tonight
The Mighty Quinn (Quinn the Eskimo)
Minstrel Boy
Rainy Day Women #12 & 35

I WAS THERE: RAY FOULK

The Isle of Wight Festival 'mark one' had seemed makeshift in many ways. We definitely wanted to make our festival-goers more welcome and comfortable – to go bigger and better in every way. It was important that we found a decent grassy site with proper facilities. Probably the biggest difference was that we styled it a 'Camping festival', which was unusual at this time. Because we were on an island we wanted people to have enough time to travel. Trench type toilets were replaced by cubicles and we appointed staff, often friends, to different departments overseeing every aspect of festival necessities. Everything was more designed from the tickets, to the programmes, posters, etc., to the stage. We tried to address everything with excellence.

It was obvious that we needed the biggest names to draw people across the water. Dylan really was the holy grail in 1969, he had acquired a god-like status due to his influence upon a whole generation. He was more than an ordinary musician, whether he liked it or not.

I don't think we set out believing that we had a chance to get Dylan. The fact that Dylan's management didn't dismiss us out of hand was a green light to us. We resorted to scheming over what might make the difference, bearing in mind that we had very few resources at all.

We had less dealings with Al Grossman than with Bert Block, owing to the demise of the Dylan-Grossman contract. Dylan was in the process of distancing himself from Grossman. During my visit to New York for the signing, when I dined with Grossman and the lawyers almost immediately at a Chinese restaurant (something I'd never experienced before), and after the signing when we visit Grossman's flat at Gramercy Park, it was there that Al skinned up a joint to celebrate the deal (to my alarm). Al was like a presence but not so much involved. He came to the festival with Michael Lang and seemed more interested in seeing the Who than Dylan.

I mostly dealt with Grossman's partner, Bert Block. We developed a good rapport, over the phone initially. Sometimes Bert wrong-footed me. When he said. 'bring the dollars' (in preparation for my trip to meet Dylan) I really had to think about what he meant. I looked after him whenever he visited the Island. I made it my mission to make sure Bert was okay and therefore Dylan was okay. Bert seemed a really good old timer, kind of avuncular, though he probably wasn't that old in reality. I recall I scared Bert a couple of times with my driving, but he always had faith in our abilities as promoters. As for the process of dealing with Block and Grossman it was pretty smooth, apart from Rikki Farr's little indiscretion. They were decent, friendly and business-like. We knew we had to present ourselves in a business-like way at all times, especially in order to surmount our youthfulness and it paid off. I had too much to think about to be too overawed by their stature as managers.

Travelling to New York was a lot of fun. I hadn't been abroad before of course. Once I had my passport, visa, and the guarantees for at least most of the performance fees I could almost sit back and enjoy the ride.

Securing Dylan was unbelievable but the time period – five weeks between him signing and the festival itself, was so short that there was really no time to do anything but get organised as rapidly as possible. Ticket sales were the priority. We had to raise enough cash to meet the contracts and build a city. But it wasn't like a relief it was more euphoric than that.

Dylan was a way bigger draw than the Stones or Hendrix at this point. The Beatles would have measured up to Dylan but they were in the process of their break up and hadn't played live in eons. Elvis's name even came up, but we couldn't imagine him playing in a field. We were after one of the big three. Dylan was the only viable option. It's easy to underestimate how big Dylan was at this time.

Crowds sit down to enjoy the 2nd Isle Of Wight Festival of Music

In some ways, organising the massive Dylan festival was easier than it might be nowadays. We had less technology available, but those were the days when the fixed line telephone really worked. People tended to answer reliably and it was easier to make contact even with celebrities. In the case of going above people's head a person-to-person call would often do the trick. Social media nowadays can take up a lot of time and work. Being restricted to largely paper publications, telephone, radio and television for advertising actually meant concentrating on the job would have been easier in some ways. We employed messengers to deal with some of tasks now taken care of by email and text. Conditions at Mother's house were hardly consistent with a world-class rock festival but we did make use of a suite of rooms on the upper floor, which became workable office space. Of course dining tables doubled as desks , etc., as far as furniture was concerned. Mother was fairly self-contained in a separate wing of the house, but would help on occasion by answering international phone calls in the middle of the night, or providing voluminous quantities of good home cooked food for whoever might be staying.

Raising funds was always the most problematic planning issue from the moment that Dylan agreed to sign especially in the early stages when potential backers just really wouldn't believe that an event headed up by Dylan would happen. Without funds nothing could happen smoothly, but once Dylan had signed of course tickets were selling like lightning, which freed us up to concentrate on other vital matters like building the arena and finding Dylan and co. places to stay. One of the hairiest moments was when Dylan disembarked from the QE2 following his son's accident onboard. Everything was riding on Dylan's appearance. We suddenly realised how vulnerable we were.

It was quite surreal meeting famous people like The Beatles and other rock titans but to be honest I wasn't interested in hanging around such people too much. There were plenty of others ready to do that. We were so consumed by the operation at hand that you could only take it in your stride. We were there to do a job and we had to concentrate hard on the necessities of keeping the thing together.

My first impression of Dylan was that he was quite shy, probably shyer than me even. He was very ordinary, a regular down to earth kind of guy, polite and well spoken. He was dressed in jeans and a leather jacket and I suppose he appeared smaller than I expected, not that he is especially small but anyone with that big a name you kind of imagine to be larger.

George Harrison had all eyes for Dylan and clearly set about resuming the relationship he had been building with him after he had visited the Dylan's home some months before. I enjoyed very much standing there and listening to them harmonising beautifully to some Everly Brothers hits. That was a truly special moment, like a private concert.

The Beatles were very charming and seemed relaxed either hanging out at the farmhouse or backstage. They were keen on talking between themselves and were apologetic, saying that they didn't get much chance to talk shop. John and Yoko were quite clingy as I remember.

I enjoyed Dylan's set immensely. Sure he was different. He sounded for the first time like he could really sing well. It was a well-constructed set, The Band were perfect in sync with what he was doing. There were quiet moments and raucous moments. It was great music. The digital release of recent times bears out the quality of the gig and it is a joy to hear it in its remastered form. The audience listened attentively rather than reacted in raptures and calls for encores continued for 20 minutes. There is no doubt that he was well received. For all those expecting the wired rock poet of 1966 they would have been disappointed. Dylan had leapt ahead in with his stage persona. Many were left behind wondering where the old Dylan was.

After the festival and the initial exhaustion, we felt elated combined with a huge sense of relief for having pulled it off. We were astonished at how well it had gone really. We were completely inspired to repeat the event, if not to surpass it.

I WAS THERE: MALCOLM COLTON

I went down to the Isle of Wight with my workmate Pete (who is featured in the foreground of one of the crowd pics) from Chesterfield where we both lived at the time.

The abiding memory of the festival was that everyone in the crowd was so quiet and respectful and were not used to such a strange concert gathering, as this was one of the first. I think there had been a festival there the previous year, but on a much smaller scale.

The Who were the stars on the first day. Dylan came on at the end of the second day after hours of delays. By the time he appeared it was very late and some had already left the festival to be sure of getting home.

Malcolm Colton's workmate Pete in his festival gear sits amongst the thousands of fans at the IOW festival

We left at the end of the set not expecting to find thousands of people waiting in crushing crowds at the Ryde Ferry Terminal. We did eventually get on a ferry after several hours waiting, being forced to stand in the crush constantly through the night, but it was worth it just to say we saw Dylan.

I think it was his first appearance following years of absence from the stage.

I remember the promotional posters saying, 'Help Bob Dylan sink the Isle of Wight!' in the *Melody Maker*, etc. Sadly we were right at the back of the huge crowd when Dylan was on and so photography was all but impossible even with my telephoto lens.

He and The Band did two sets I think, the first in his new (to us) *Nashville Skyline* voice, which many didn't expect and yet he did include some solo acoustic. He was dressed in a white suit that the critics later said used to belong to Johnny Cash – a bit harsh!

He did a good set and having seen him twice since then, I have always found him to be totally professional on stage and he works extremely hard to give the audience a good concert experience. I am still a huge admirer and a fan.

I WAS THERE: PER BERGLUND, AGED 16

I got my first Dylan album (*Greatest Hits*) at Christmas 1967. Then in February 1968, (in Sweden anyway) there was *John Wesley Harding*. I got that one too and played it, and played it, and played it. I have loved it so much over the years that I even hunted down a copy of the recalled *Biography* box just to get the extra seven seconds of 'I'll Be Your Baby Tonight'.

Then I met a guy who had all of Bob's albums. I borrowed them and taped them on a reel-to-reel tape recorder. Little did I know that tape was going to consume a fair amount of my free time in a not so distant future.

I knew Bob had had a motorcycle accident and live shows were not on the menu. So I was quite surprised when the news came: Bob will play a show in Europe! But seriously – what were the chances of a boy at 15 making a pilgrimage to the Isle of Wight (IOW). You could just as well take a trip to the moon. But hey! Didn't somebody do that? Just a couple of days ago? The next day I sent for a ticket.

That summer I worked hard to get enough money for a festival ticket and the trip via Hamburg – Hoek van Holland – London – IOW. My parents did not like the idea at all. I was 15 years old but I would not take no for an answer. But the world was different then and in the wee hours of Thursday 28 August I set out on my journey. By Friday night I was at the IOW, enjoying some of the best British bands. I turned 16 years old that Friday, and I had the Nice and Bonzo Dog Band playing at my party!

Saturday brought more interesting performers. As the audience grew we listened to The Who, Fat Mattress and Edgar Broughton Band.

Sunday came and I tried to get as close as possible to the stage. This was not easy and I had to settle for a spot comparable to the last row in a mid sized arena. Like, say the Hammersmith Odeon.

As the sun was sinking after appearances of Pentangle, Tom Paxton and Richie Havens you could feel there was something in the air. And that something didn't go away until The Band came on stage after they had kept us waiting for at least two hours. They played a fantastic but rather short set of their own. I can't believe there is no official live album from that show.

After another pause, (who knows how long), Bob and The Band came on. He opened with one of my favourites: 'She Belongs to Me'. Well, wait a minute. I must find my binoculars! Did he wear a suit? Was it white? Was that a small beard? Yes. He looked confident, at ease, really enjoying himself. Now and then a tiny trace of nervousness could be heard but his voice was in great shape and the phrasing as good as it gets. You could say it was mellow, very much like his voice on the *Nashville Skyline* album. Quite a few songs were being performed for the first time: 'Mighty Quinn', 'Minstrel Boy', and more. The sound was really good, you could hear him perfectly even at a distance. A fantastic evening, the only thing you could complain about was the 'old suitcase' sound coming from Levon Helms drum kit.

The arrangements were great. Take for instance 'Like a Rolling Stone' – a few years prior this was a majestic but violent song. It was less singing and more of spiting it out. Here it was mellow, subdued. And 'She Belongs to Me' – on the record sweet, caring, here rough and randy. Seventeen songs, about an hour of music. I wouldn't have said no to more songs, for me coming so far I would gladly have listened all night. It was a perfect ending of a perfect weekend. Bob playing on top of his form is indeed a show to remember, a concert of a lifetime

Although we were many who went to the IOW, I have yet to meet a fellow festival goer.

I did not see Bob again until 1978. And now 104 shows later, (and counting) I still cherish the moment when I saw Bob with 200,000 of my closest friends.

I WAS THERE: JACKY BEVAN

Jacky Bevan discovers that a dog has left an unwanted mess on her sleeping bag

My memories of the IOW are a bit vague, because, 'ahem,' times had changed. The camping area was liberally spread with straw, which looked sparkly in my condition. The groups of tents had names to help recognition – we were near Desolation Row. The speakers played 'Amazing Grace' by The Great Awakening quite a lot, and I still love it. I played pinball a lot. Lots of people went down to the sea in various stages of undress. A dog pissed on my sleeping bag. My diary just says, 'Dylan played the old songs in a new way,' but there are recordings anyway.

Evening Standard
SOUVENIR EDITION

DYLAN IS BACK

He stars in pop festival after years in isolation

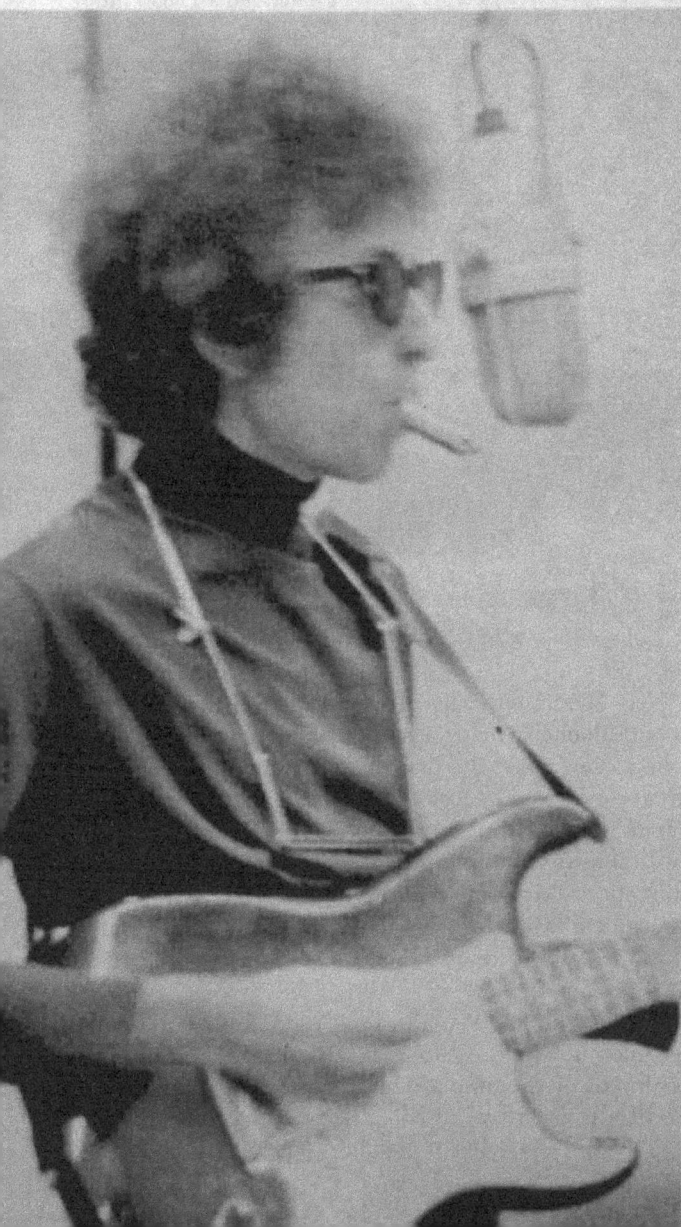

On Sunday night Bob Dylan will be back on stage at Woodside Bay, Ryde, at the Isle of Wight Festival of Music.

It will be his first appearance in Britain since 1966, and as far as Dylan is concerned it will be his come-back show following the three years seclusion which he chose to live.

It should be a night to remember—one of the great nights in the history of pop music.

A few days ago Dylan had this to say: "I'm very anxious to get back on stage. Singing and playing my music is just what I like to do.

"When I come back I'll be with The Band, of course, but I'll be doing some of those old songs with just the guitar and the harmonica too.

"Really I hope to be able to sing just about whatever the people want to hear, including some songs from my four new albums."

Toured

Since he last toured Britain in May 1966, he has lived in some degree of confinement at his Woodstock, New York estate.

Serious injuries in a motorcycle accident were one of the reasons for his retirement, but he now admits that it was not some good came out of the crash.

"It really slowed me down," he says. "Touring had become such a grind to keep up. And was getting into a rut."

He is determined that won't happen this time. In Woodstock he has grown used to the normal family life of a place man with his very young children, and the contentment of the last few years seems...

I WAS THERE: NIGEL TANT, AGE 19

Nigel Tant shows off his long sleeved t-shirt from C&A

I had been a Dylan fan from, I guess, around 1965. The first album I owned was *Bringing It All Back Home*, which to this day is probably my favourite Dylan record. I had been aware of him and his songs before this mainly via covers by other artists – Manfred Mann had sung 'With God On Our Side' on *Ready, Steady Go!*, The Byrds' 'Mr. Tambourine Man' and Peter, Paul and Mary's version of 'Blowin' in the Wind' were always on the radio, and he was being name checked by people like The Beatles.

'The Times They Are a-Changin'' had been an unlikely hit but I think like many of us, it took me a while to acquire a liking for his singing voice. But that album was funny, challenging, and had great tunes, and I loved the electric Dylan. I could never understand at the time why the folkies had an issue with all this, but I then was coming to him via rock rather than from the other direction. Friends had other albums – *The Freewheelin' Bob Dylan* became a favourite from the early years, and I think I got the *Greatest Hits* set next, and then the underrated *John Wesley Harding*.

My first live gig was The Who, in June 1966, but I don't recall another live gig much before 1968 when we started seeing some of the blues bands of the time around the pubs and clubs in London, and I was at Cream's final concert in September of that year. Of course Dylan stopped playing live in 1966 and the very real thought was that he might never play again, so it was a huge deal when it was announced that he would play something called the Isle Of Wight Festival in August 1969.

By this time I was working part time so could afford the ticket price of £2/10s (£2.50 in today's money) for the weekend, and I had a tent!

I think I bought the tickets from Harlequin Records in Oxford Street – I was working at C&A Marble Arch at the time. I remember The Rolling Stones being in Hyde Park that summer too, a...ahem...stone's throw from the shop, but I was working!

I went with a friend called John Barker and we hitch-hiked down on Friday, August 29, and I remember we arrived in time to see the Nice after a bus and a walk to the site.

Dylan was obviously the main attraction, but the bill for that weekend was awesome, including The Who performing *Tommy*, The Moody Blues and so many others. The Festival was crude by today's standards – I remember some very basic catering and there were some stalls selling souvenirs. The Sunday bill was very acoustic with people like Pentangle, Julie Felix and Tom Paxton preceding The Band and Bob Dylan. I didn't really know much of The Band at this time, but I'd heard Dylan's *Nashville Skyline* and hated it. Would he revert to the old Dylan? As we now know and appreciate, he had moved on and I remember walking around with people having signs like Desolation Row on their tents and wondering if they were going to be disappointed!

My main memory of the Sunday evening was the interminable wait for Dylan to come on. Then The Band did a set and we had to wait even longer. It had been a long weekend and I distinctly remember we just wanted to get this thing done and go home! In those days there was no concept of timekeeping and we put up with an awful lot that today's audience just wouldn't countenance. When Dylan eventually came on it was more a relief than anything else. It soon became clear this was not the Dylan we remembered. As I had feared, the voice had changed and he was dressed in what looked like a white suit! There were no big screens of course, and we must have been 100 yards or so back. My abiding memory is one of being disappointed – as I suspected, this wasn't the Dylan of the imperial 1965/66 period, and he would embark on a bumpy period with the likes of *Self Portrait* being released which have reinforced my memory of this time. The set is now well documented and even officially available via the *Bootleg* series, but I don't think I've ever listened to it, and I certainly don't own it, which is very strange as I am still a huge fan and love so much of his music from both before and after this period.

I WAS THERE: PENNY WARDER

My boyfriend of the time had long holidays from art-college and was working at the festival, doing artwork for the signs on the front of the stage, and helping with security and management. As a result, he had a VIP pass and, being his partner, I got one, too. Otherwise it was £2 for a ticket. Ringo Starr, George Harrison, John Lennon and Yoko Ono were sitting behind us. The talk of the festival was that they might join Dylan on stage. It never happened. I was a huge Beatles fan, but had not seen them live; I kept turning round to look at them. We were about three rows from the front and could smell the hash that someone was smoking behind us.

When Dylan finally came on, he was barely 10 feet away from me. It was so exciting. He played for only an hour, for which he got some stick in the press, but it was incredibly exhilarating. He did two encores.

After he finished, I went back to my parents' house on the island, where I grew up. Even though I had been away at college for two years, there was no way they would allow me to stay out all night. I remember it was a real struggle trying to find a lift, because we didn't have cars and couldn't afford taxis.

This was my first festival. I went to the Isle of Wight the following year, when Jimi Hendrix played shortly before his death. I've been to others since, but nothing will match those two experiences.

I WAS THERE: PETE MILLER, AGE 16

Pete Miller became a Dylan fan at just 12 years old

I suppose the seed was planted around 1965. My parents owned a Milk Bar (a coffee shop/café) which housed a large jukebox which boomed all the top Sixties hits and I recall being blown upside down by 'Like a Rolling Stone'. I was around 12 years old at the time. I must have had a hip ear for music because I remember hearing The Beatles do 'Love Me Do' on their first TV appearance in 1962 and thought they were fab and I was only nine years old.

When I began working in 1968 I had money to buy my own albums, *The Freewheelin' Bob Dylan* was the first and from then on I have been a disciple. I still am at 65-years-old, with one hand wavin' free!

I was just 16 and Bob Dylan was (is) my messiah. When it was announced that he was to play the Isle of Wight festival in 1969 I had to get tickets to see him, especially having missed his '66 tour of the UK. I even talked a couple of work mates to also get tickets and drive me down to the south of England. After '66 and then the motorcycle accident there were all kinds of rumours about what was going to happen. What would he play? What would he sound like? Would the vibes of 200,000 fans cause the island to float?

I loved the 'hippiedom' of the festival. I lost contact with my friends, but alone, by the Sunday night, I made my way to be at the very front of the crowd, just behind the VIP area that included The Beatles. After great sets from Richie Havens and The Band, the evening was getting late by the time Bob came on stage. Not the top hat and shades. In a white shirt with short hair and a voice up an octave came Hank Williams!

After some technical delays, Bob came on stage around 11pm and performed songs from my favourite period at the time, *Bringing It All Back Home* and *Highway 61 Revisited*. I don't know what the sound was like half a mile away, but from my place at the front I thought it was great. 'She Belongs to Me', 'Maggie's Farm', 'To Ramona', 'Like a Rolling Stone', 'Mr. Tambourine Man'. I particularly remember his 'Wild Mountain Thyme' which of course was new to me. Also only available on bootleg recordings at the time was 'The Mighty Quinn'.

Of course after the one hour set and a very short encore, I wanted more! Dylan was only contracted to one hour, which I didn't know about at the time. I wanted another hour to include such gems as 'Desolation Row' 'Visions of Johanna' or 'Tombstone Blues'. But at least I had witnessed Dylan 'live' at the UK's very own Woodstock.

I WAS THERE: DR MIKE HOWARTH

I was at Portsmouth Polytechnic and went to the Isle of Wight with my friend looking for yacht crew opportunities at Cowes, which fell through, so we ended up dishwashing at a holiday camp along the coast. On our day off we went for a walk. As we wandered up a narrow lane there was a silhouette of a bloke with a cowboy hat (this must have been Rikki Farr) who, as we walked past said, 'Do you want a job?' Well, anything was better than the camp kitchen and as we both played guitar, this seemed too good an opportunity to miss.

I don't actually remember doing any real work. I suppose I was helping put up the boards round the site and painting them. I think there was some digging pits for the loos. There were a few people all sleeping together in a tent provided. I do remember someone being run over by a lorry in the night as he slept outside in the grass.

Perhaps we were there for a week, then rapidly the empty site filled up with stalls at the far end of the enclosure and behind the stage. We stood on the stage at some point and played our guitars when the sound system was put up.

There was a point when the arena was cleared, because the bands were practicing. Ignorant of the fact, for the two of us were focused on inhaling illicit substances under the stage – me for the first time. A group started up above and stopped suddenly as furious, full volume expletives were let rip on someone unfortunate who had strayed in, ignoring a complete ban on watchers. Mmm, so it was just us two and The Band! Not that I really knew who they were, but the sheer power of the sound and the excellent musicianship about three feet overhead was not to be forgotten since. This was the first inkling that something quite big was happening.

Then thousands of people began to arrive. To my horror someone told me to stand by the white picket fence of the VIP enclosure – about knee high – and stop people coming in! I found a short piece of wood to protect myself because I could see that I wasn't going to last long as I faced the sea of humanity rapidly growing behind me. Fortunately, I had no need to worry as everyone was most polite and nobody ever stepped over the fence all the days I was there.

Meanwhile the VIP area was nearly filled up and, compelled to make myself useful, I tried to stop a line of people squeezing their way in. There was big guy with a beard and then I noticed behind him was Ringo Starr. Mmm, not a good idea. The big guy I learnt later was Al Grossman. I quietly retreated to my place and sat down to find that, I am sure it was Marianne Faithfull, or was it Patti Boyd was just in front of me, and I had stood on her hat. A withering look confirmed I was just not cut out to be a bouncer.

The ringside seat was just amazing, and as I had nothing to do, I just enjoyed the show as it went on and on. After a bit I wandered about and started taking pictures right up at the stage. There were perhaps five people taking stills. One guy opened up a huge plastic bag and gave me a few extra rolls. I would have an excellent set, but a very nice guy dressed as a vicar took most of them to be processed with my money, and that is the last I saw of them. How naïve! So I have only a few left; Marsha Hunt, The Who arriving by helicopter.

But the close up shots in my mind's eye remain. Bob Dylan about five feet away. They booed when he played electric guitar? I can't remember, but with The Band it was just fantastic. Nice: seeing how the knives got into the Hammond and how rocking it affected the echo plates. Tom Paxton, his shirt stuffed with money refusing to go back and play some more. Richie Havens as it went dark. Such quality playing – Joe Cocker was amazing. A lot of drink, but no violence, except I did see a guy climbing over the backstage fence being smashed on the head with a beer bottle. There were naked women wrestling in mud and gladiatorial contest with two decorated VWs.

I used the money I was paid to make a demo record, and my band made backing tracks for a climber and photographer called Denis Kemp, for his climbing lecturers with Joe Brown and Chris Bonnington. As soon as I saw all the recording gear and cameras I got really keen, and three years later I was a producer making BBC radio children's programmes.

It must have been 15 years on, I was looking in a window in Portland Place and a Dutch guy came up to me as said, 'I have seen you before. Were you at the Isle of Wight? You are in an exhibition in Holland standing up amongst thousands of people.'

Perhaps it was all that creativity and energy I saw so close up that made me want a slice of the action for myself. I do think that three day event helped kick start me on a very interesting and enjoyable career.

The Who live on stage at the IOW festival

I WAS THERE: RAY CONNOLLY

Bob Dylan was getting angry. The trailer he'd been given as a changing room didn't have a loo. His pregnant wife, Sara, had mentioned it first, and now, as he waited a two full hours while a problem with the sound on stage was fixed, pre-show nerves were making him uncomfortable. He now needed the bathroom.

Outside 200,000 fans, who'd trekked from all over Britain to witness the Second Coming of the songwriter they then saw as the coolest man on the planet were also getting fractious. This, therefore, was not the time for Dylan to be told that the only loo for artists was somewhere out in the dark across the field. In his newly pressed, crisp white stage suit he didn't like the sound of that.

Ray Connolly was one of many who witnessed Dylan's show at the IOW festival

In the end, he couldn't wait any longer. Getting up, he relieved himself out of the window of the trailer, and then triumphantly took the stage at the Isle of White Festival of Music.

That night, August 31, 1969, is now remembered on nerdy lists as one of the most epoch making rock music nights ever. Was it? Well, I was there, and in some ways it was. But not because of the 17 songs Dylan sang. The fact that he was there at all, resurrected, as it were, from his three years of self-imposed isolation following a motorcycle accident, was what made it special, and what had acted as a magnet, not only to his fans, but also to British rock aristocracy.

There they all were paying homage just below the stage: a couple of Rolling Stones, two Pink Floyds, Eric Clapton, Elton John, Stevie Winwood, three Beatles and their wives – along with Elizabeth Taylor, Jane Fonda, Roger Vadim, Lionel Bart and other assorted celebs of the time. Some of them had blankets wrapped around them, which was understandable because it was freezing cold.

Today, when we think of rock festivals, we envisage hi-tech, digitised Glastonbury events, where everything is televised, where thousands of mobile phones twinkle in the blackness, and where the stars are cosseted in state-of-the-art, en-suite trailers.

But, back then, rock festivals were in their infancy, and the midwives to this one were two young brothers on the Isle Of Wight called Foulk who'd had a crazy idea.

Which was: why don't we invite the biggest singer-songwriter in the world, the man most difficult to reach, to be the headline act at a rock festival on an island off the South coast of England of which he's probably never heard? The fact that they did invite him, and that he came, is what made that moment in August 1969, special.

It really was a mad idea. Why would any New York manager even bother replying to the organisers, two young brothers in their early twenties, whose experience of business was, at best, limited? How could these boys ever get such a vast undertaking together? And whoever heard of anything big, new or exciting happening on the sleepy, genteel little Isle of Wight?

The Foulk brothers themselves, Ronnie, 24, and Ray Foulk, 23, didn't know the answers to any of these questions, nor dozens more they asked themselves daily – not least, where, exactly, they were going to find the money to even begin their venture? But, with the innocence of youth, they pursued their dream, discovered the name and address of Dylan's manager in an underground newspaper, and wrote their pitch. They may not have been sharp-elbowed music businessmen, but they had one great thing going for them. Timing.

It was the end of the Sixties, and they were both imbued with the boundless, youthful optimism of that time which said that anything was possible for those who tried – even if you lived in the back of beyond. The story of how they achieved their dream has now been told by Ray Foulk in a memoir of sheer get-up-and go enterprise. Whatever the Foulk brothers lacked in experience, they made up for in energy – and maybe a little cheek, too.

Having both left their fee-paying boarding school in 1961 without an O-level between them, and been put to work, Ronnie in an estate agency, and Ray as an apprentice printer, six years later Ray had his own little print and design firm, a wife and twin daughters. And, as both chairman and secretary of the West Wight CND since his teens, he knew all about organising events – albeit only jumble sales and dances. Nevertheless, it had been useful experience, and by 1968 he and his brother were ready for bigger things. Neither of them knew much about pop music, but slowly the idea of organising a little pop happening began to take shape.

So, persuading a farmer to mow a field of barley, the remaining stubble of which would prove painful to the bottoms of the festival goers, and them rent them the space, by August 1968, they'd put together their first trial run of a festival. With Jefferson Airplane, Fairport Convention and the Crazy World of Arthur Brown on the bill it attracted 10,000 fans, which was pretty impressive for what turned out to be a rehearsal – even though, as some ticket agencies didn't pay them, it lost money.

Dylan, a year later, would be the real thing. Hardly expecting a response from his management they were astonished when they weren't rejected out of hand. Call us in another month, they were told. They did. This time offering the great man an all expenses paid voyage on the maiden voyage of the QE2, a limousine, a manor house to stay in, a chauffeur, a cook and a governess for the Dylan children.

Bob wants to know more, came the reply. So, fibbing about their youth by adding two years each to their ages, they printed a whole brochure, displaying the delights of visits to the home of Alfred Lord Tennyson and Queen Victoria's Osborne House, and mentioning some of the British groups who had already agreed to be at the festival – The Who, Joe Cocker, the Moody Blues.

Finally came the crunch. Money. Bob would come, but he wanted his musicians, The Band, to be with him, as well as singer-guitarist Richie Havens. In all, with expenses, that would cost $87,000 dollars, which, in today's money would be around £470,000. Furthermore Bob wanted to meet Ray Foulk in New York – with his American lawyer.

Foulk didn't even have an English lawyer, not one who knew the vagaries of showbiz, anyway. But even worse than that. He didn't have a passport either. He'd never been abroad. Yet, somehow, by working the phones and his friends, he got both within three days, the local bobby countersigning his photograph to take to the Passport Office in London. As for Dylan, he was as pleasant and quiet at the meeting as could be imagined. The only nervous moment came when Dylan's manager suggested to Foulk that it was 'time for a little pot' and offered him a joint.

Ray Foulk may have been about to put on Britain's biggest rock festival ever, and he may have been 23 years old in 1969, but he was from the Isle of Wight, and he had never encountered drugs before in his entire life. He said, 'no thank you.' They'd already rented the site of the festival near Wootton Bridge, so, now, back on the island, all Ray and Ronnie Foulk had to do was to find the money to pay for it all, to arrange the building of the stage, the hiring of the sound system, the fencing around the arena, the lights, the phone wires, the buses to ferry the fans to and from Ryde, the lavatories, the food concessions, the security, the insurance, the St Johns Ambulance people, and a hundred other things.

The design of the tickets and the advertising they left to their younger brother Bill Foulk and his enthusiastic friends from the Royal College of Art. Throwing themselves into the spirit of the project, the students came up with a motif of a King Kong gorilla with fairy wings on what looked like a psychedelic juke box with female bosoms on the front. Well, it was the Sixties! They knew that ticket sales would pay for Dylan and the other acts, but until the ticket agencies paid up, investment had to be found to cover the guarantees. They got it, of course, when the company hired to print the programmes decided to invest as did the printer's rich next door neighbour, their mother, and some friends.

Hairdressers on the Isle of Wight had been kept busy leading up to the 1969 festival

With the first man landing on the moon in July, and the murders of Sharon Tate and company in Hollywood in mid-August, the summer of 1969 was quite an incident filled time. But the Foulks could have been forgiven if the only news story that was gathering their full attention was the US rock festival at Woodstock (not far from where Dylan lived) which occurred just two weeks before their own extravaganza was launched.

The Woodstock organisers had secretly hoped that Dylan would suddenly turn up there. The Brothers Foulk had feared it. But by ignoring Woodstock in favour of Wootton Bridge, Dylan did what he most liked to do – the unpredictable. It also meant he didn't get wet, Woodstock being famously remembered for days of torrential rain and mud. Although it was a bit nippy on the Isle of Wight, the rain kept off.

Not everything went according to plan, of course. The Dylans missed the maiden voyage of the QE2 and had to fly from New York, the grand house they'd been promised during their stay became unavailable so they stayed at a more modest but homely cottage-type farmhouse. Nor did a top chef materialise for them, so they were fed on porridge, pies and plum crumbles.

They didn't complain. On the contrary they seemed very happy there, with Dylan and John Lennon taking on George Harrison and Ringo Starr in a game of tennis – a sport none of them knew much about. And Dylan and George Harrison cementing their friendship by playing and singing the old Everly Brothers hit 'All I Have To Do Is Dream'. Meanwhile all roads led to Wootton Bridge as the Isle of Wight ferries and hovercrafts disgorged thousands upon thousands of fans, their sleeping bags and tents on their backs, some with bands around their heads, as they'd seen in the TV news from Woodstock.

Ever since then we've become accustomed to seeing the English lanes filled with festival pilgrims, all blushing with youth. But in 1969 the sheer numbers of them, with their jeans and hair, so much long hair, was new, and somehow exhilarating. It was all so harmless. In those days before there were huge screens at festivals, most fans would have been too distant to see anything more than a tiny spec of a guy in a white suit on a stage a hundred yards away. And the songs the minstrel sang almost certainly sounded better on the records they had at home.

But that wasn't the point. What was important was that they were there with their friends on the night Bob Dylan made his comeback on the Isle of Wight. The show ended at just after eleven. And, as Dylan left the stage, outer fences were suddenly pulled down and free souvenir festival copies of the *Evening Standard*, which I'd written earlier that week, were used as kindling paper as little bonfires were lit, around which satisfied fans huddled to keep warm.

The Foulk brothers didn't get rich out of their 1969 festival, although this time they didn't lose money either. They did something better than that. They had the craziest dream and they made it come true.

I WAS THERE: ROB HUMPHREYS

I was there, travelled down from London for the day only and remember the long wait for Dylan to come on stage. Such a thrill to see him at last, even if from quite a long way from the stage. We were led to expect a long performance with an all-star jam afterwards but it was all over before we knew it. I particularly remember the long, dark walk back to the ferries in the early hours of the morning, and a sense of disappointment. At the ferry terminus some people tried to jump the queue and the seamen used their hoses to stop them. I certainly do not regret going and look back now with great nostalgia.

I WAS THERE: JOHN LENNON

We went to the Dylan show, and if there had been a jam, we would have got up. It was killed before it happened. It was so late by the time he got on. We would have jammed if it had been earlier. The crowd was dying on their feet by the time he got on.

He came over to our house with George after the Isle of Wight and I had just written 'Cold Turkey'. I was trying to get him to record. We had just put him on piano for 'Cold Turkey' to make a rough tape but his wife was pregnant or something and they left.

I WAS THERE: TOM PAXTON, MUSICIAN

I went with Dylan and The Beatles to the farmhouse where he was clearly in a merry mood because he had felt it had gone so well. The Beatles had brought a test pressing of *Abbey Road* and we listened to it and had quite a party.

I WAS THERE: TONY REED, AGE 19

I was 19 that year, and travelling through Europe, as middle-class North American kids did then in the summer. Airfares were cheap for students, and you could go almost anywhere, including Algeria and other places I wouldn't dream of going now. I met Australians who were taking the 'overland route' home; I doubt that that route still exists.

I got to the site on the Isle of Wight about, I don't know, five days or so before the concerts, with something like £10 in my pocket, and got a job digging toilets and putting up concession tents. All the good jobs, like building the stage, for instance, had been taken by Americans (and, yeah, by guys with carpentry skills). I met a bunch of people working there and we all lived in a small encampment we called Desolation Row. What else were we going to call it?

We even got semi-famous, and had a journalist from *The People* stay overnight who then went back to London and wrote a nasty piece about us. We got our pictures in various local and London newspapers and on the telly smashing up an old piano that the farmer gave us. I don't know why he gave it to us or why we smashed it up. It made some kind of sense at the time. Later, we got mentioned in Scaduto's bio of Dylan, although he got it wrong: I was the only North American in the group, which included a guy from the Midlands, some middle-class London kids, and a genuine Scottish tramp.

After the concert, that Monday morning, we were all going to stay and make some money helping with the big clean-up. Except that it was so truly desolate with the concert over and everyone just gone away and mountains of garbage all over that we just went home and forgot about it. Later, when I was back at University of Berkeley, California, I got a letter from one guy who was actually promoting a rock show of his own. He must have learned something while he was there, I guess. I have no idea what happened to the tramp. I don't have the pictures that appeared in the papers any more, or the Moroccan wallet that I kept for years with that 'Help Bob Dylan Sink the Isle of Wight' thing pasted into it.

I WAS THERE: FRANK BATTEN

We arrived at Southsea in 1969 too late for the last ferry, and ended up sleeping on the seafront. We could hear (we thought) The Who playing on the island. I can't work out what night that would have been – we saw The Who live (that must have been on Saturday) but we also saw The Bonzo Dog Doo-Dah Band (and the wonderful Viv Stanshall RIP).

One thing has always stuck in my mind about Dylan's set – one of the newspapers said that the crowd booed and threw bottles at Dylan because he was so late on stage. The booing and bottle throwing was aimed at the people in the press compound at the front, who stood up when Dylan came on stage, so none of us paying punters behind them could see anything. Peace and Love was one thing, but we still wanted value for money. The fact that Dylan was late didn't matter at all – he was there and that was all that mattered.

I WAS THERE: TONY PHELPS, AGE 18

This was my first festival but perhaps the best and most memorable. I had just turned 18 and some of my favourite groups were to be performing – The Nice, The Who, The Bonzo Dog Doo-Dah Band, Julie Felix, Tom Paxton, Moody Blues, Family – I had albums by all of them. And of course the greatest songwriter of the twentieth century was headlining – this was unmissable. The tickets were ridiculously cheap by today's standards – £2-10s for the full pass (though my wages were only £8 a week as a trainee draftsman). But cost was unimportant; I would have sold my soul to be there. People had started gathering at the site more than a week before the concert began and the newspaper articles and TV reports on the aptly

named Desolation Row only served to excite me further – I knew this was where I belonged. The week leading up to the concert I was holidaying with my family and cousins in Cornwall so I only had to catch the coast train to Portsmouth and from there it was a quick ferry ride to Ryde, with it's more than mile long pier. It was almost a homecoming for me as I had spent three years growing up on the IOW at a boarding school in Ventnor run by nuns for children with severe asthma (country air and all).

I arrived at the site on the Thursday in the clothes I wore, no tent or blanket and the remains of my holiday money in my pocket – so I spent a bit of it buying a large plastic sheet and a Mexican blanket, found a couple of sticks and draped the plastic over it to form a makeshift tent. Luckily it never rained and wrapped up in my blanket I was actually quite warm and comfortable for the duration. I don't actually remember eating anything much at the site, though on the morning of the Saturday I took a bus into Ryde and had lunch at a Chinese restaurant. I didn't stop long in Ryde as I didn't want to miss a minute of the stage activity, but I do remember seeing *Nashville Skyline* on sale for the first time and wondering if Dylan would be performing any tracks off it.

Apart from Dylan and The Band there were some very memorable performances and this is where I heard and became an instant fan of Third Ear Band (one of the most underrated bands of the era in my opinion). Other acts I have great memories of were The Bonzo Dog Doo-Dah Band with their inimitable stage performance, the Moody Blues, and the Nice (who I was a great fan of). I was also a great fan of The Who at the time and their set just blew me away. Apart from a few songs at the start and end the main body of the concert was given over to an almost complete performance of *Tommy*. Fantastic!

I was pretty close to the stage for the final evening. I was really looking forward to seeing Richie Havens as I wasn't very familiar with his music, but someone had told me that his appearance was one of the conditions laid down by Dylan before he'd agree to come. Whether there was any truth in this I have no idea but it was a great performance either way. I had just struck up a bit of a friendship with an American couple who had come across on a charter flight just to see Dylan and this is where I had my first taste of cannabis (which I took to like a duck to water). The Band followed Richie

Havens and then suddenly it was time for the culmination of three great days of music, fun and festivity. An hour or so later and it was all over and I was left with this overpowering feeling of what now? Suddenly my home-made tent didn't seem so appealing and I just wanted to get home to a warm bath and bed.

So I abandoned my plastic sheet, wrapped my blanket round my shoulders (I still have it) and joined the great mass of humanity wending it's way to Ryde pier. Ryde pier is so long that there is a train station at both ends of it. I was told that people were queuing the entire length of the pier but I decided to see for myself so caught the train to the end. Sure enough, for as far as I could see the pier was just jammed. The word was going round that it was going to take over 24 hours to clear even though ever ferry available was running. Some people from the train tried to jump the barriers to the head of the queue and were unceremoniously turfed back out. I had just decided to walk back into Ryde and find somewhere to doss when I was asked to help a girl back out over the barrier as she was about to faint. To my eternal shame, while helping her I managed to get one leg over the barrier. I stood straddling the barrier until ten minutes later someone else needed helping out and in the process my other leg made it over. I didn't get on the next ferry, but the one after I just made. From there a quick train ride to London where I slept on the platform along with about a thousand others until the police woke us and the first train to Derby saw me safely home.

I emigrated to Australia the following year so missed the Jimi Hendrix concert. I must have been to around 30 open-air concerts since then, but Isle of Wight '69 was my first, and to my mind, still the best one ever.

I WAS THERE: ERIC GRIFFITHS, AGE 16

I was a shy young lad from West Wales, just starting an apprenticeship in Plymouth and this was my first festival and first trip to the island. Memories? Well, there I have a problem – I remember the journey there, and part of the journey back, but the bit in between is a bit of a haze to say the least! This was due, I am sure, to what I smoked and drank and, of course, the lack of sleep. I was only 16 and some of my favourite groups, household names these-days, were performing – Moody Blues, The Who, Julie Felix, Joe Cocker, Free – among others. Then, of course, there was Bob Dylan, I was so looking forward to seeing him.

From memory, a number of us, all around the same age, got a train from Plymouth to Lymington, (I believe) on the Thursday and then a ferry to the island – and that's where it gets hazy! We were new friends and looking forward to what was a totally new experience for us all. I know that I carried a few spare clothes and a sleeping bag and that we shared an improvised tent of sorts – more like a big plastic bag! We walked and hitchhiked to the site; the tickets were just under half a week's wages at the time, but worth it to see the line-up and remember, this was my first time away. Spent all the weekend on site, eating, drinking and smoking what was available. I remember being wet at some time over the weekend, so either I ended up in a ditch or it must have rained! I remember a huge canvas dancehall of sorts and overall, the event seemed to be quite well organised. The music? Well, a lot of it went in one ear and out the other I'm afraid, but I do remember bits of The Who and Moody Blues. Dylan? I must have been 'asleep' at the time!

The trip back was uneventful except for arriving back at Plymouth station, dirty and tired and thinking I was one of the 'flower people'. That lasted a day until I was able to remove all the grime in a hot bath and catch up on some quality sleep; then it was time to get back to work. Ah, happy days!

I WAS THERE: DAVID KOHN, AGE 19

August 1969, and I was barely 20-years-old. I had been wandering around the UK, Paris, and finally Amsterdam for a month after a less-than-wonderful experience working on a kibbutz earlier in the summer. It was toward the end of August and I had to get back to London to catch my charter flight back to Chicago the first week in September. No sooner had I gotten back to London than I began to see all sorts of notices about the IOW festival in Ryde. I got on a train and headed down there. One of the people in my compartment was a reporter for the *Montreal Gazette*, and he suggested that he would get me press credentials as his photographer. We got off the train, got on the ferry, and headed straight to the place Dylan was to be having his press conference (where he didn't say much of anything).

After it was over, one of the other people in the pressroom offered to let me crash for the evening in his hotel. In the middle of the night I was awakened by this guy making some sort of pass at me. I'm a naive kid from the suburbs, so this kind of stuff I was only vaguely aware of by rumour. I just got out of there fast and headed over to the concert area where I met up with some kids from Scotland who were building a little shelter out of hay bales and tarps. I helped them finish and we had a nice comfortable house.

The first morning of the concert things were fairly sane in the little press section in front of the stage. I think we had two or three rows of seats and some space between the seats and the stage for taking photos or sitting on the ground. I was wearing my press pass in a full top hat I'd picked up at the Amsterdam flea market. I remember some celebrities up there in the press section – Jane Fonda with Roger Vadim a few seats down from me and Keith Richards further on.

Into the afternoon, the press section got ever more crowded. Evidently quite a few people (like me) who were not formally members of the press had managed to get passes. The event managers then decided to stop honouring our passes and reissue new ones on a much more selective basis. It looked like I was going to be shit out of luck until I saw Dylan's manager Albert Grossman standing off to the side. He happened to be the brother of one of my mom's best friends, so I walked over to him, introduced myself, and mentioned that I had spent some time with his nephew in the East Village just before I'd left New York a few months back. Although he didn't seem all that interested in the family small talk, he was gracious enough to make sure I got one of the reissued press passes.

For the most part the concert was kind of a blur. My clearest memory is looking up at Marsha Hunt's thick legs, which were hanging out of her black leather shorts. The Band was great, Dylan less so. Other high points were The Who, Joe Cocker, and the Bonzo Dog Doo-Dah Band.

As the concert ended I recall walking back to Ryde, but I have no recollection of the return ferry or train. A day or two later I was at Gatwick and on my way back my junior year of college.

The IOW festival attracted an audience of approximately 150,000

I WAS THERE: DAVID IAN ROBBINS, AGE 16

I lived as an Army brat, all over the world until 1969 when we retired. I had a sense of restlessness that was part of my genes by that time and a strong energy for Bob Dylan. I left work in Wiltshire early that Friday, August 29, and made it to the Festival along with a number of people who were fellow Fest-goers who I had met on the ferry. I was 16 then. I lay down on my sleeping bag in campsite one and listened to The Nice and other acts through the night. Saturday was cold but surreal. All the bands had an impact. The Moody Blues were great but a little too perfect. I met up with some homeboys, though that wasn't a current phrase then. We got stoned together and shared a campfire later.

Sunday was warm and later in the day there were hundreds, as I remember, of square feet of foam pumped onto an area of grass. I waded around blissfully and of course got soaked, so stripped down to skin and laid my clothes on the ground to dry, there were many of us naked or nearly so but we were generally ignored. A photo showed up on the front page of the *Daily Express* of a couple of bare bodies but too distant to see if one of them was me.

I wished for more from Bob, but was happy and made my way to Ryde to sleep in the parking lot of the ferry building until the first Monday morning boat took us back to the mainland. The trip over the Solent was more than just physical. I felt like I was leaving a place where for maybe the first time in my life I was home. Walking from the bus stop to our house in the Army camp of Tidworth, where we still lived during the last army year, I felt very transformed from two days before when I had left walking in the opposite direction.

I went to the following festival in 1970, a different me and another story. For 28 years now, I have lived in Sonoma, California and it was so long ago but still an energy that comes back to me when I relive that weekend in 1969.

I WAS THERE: MALCOLM COLTON

I had the unforgettable pleasure of attending the 1969 IOW festival along with my good friend Pete. We travelled down from Chesterfield in Derbyshire the night before, on the train to Southampton, and then the ferry to Cowes. We got there very early and I remember looking at the festival posters on the station taking in all the fantastic bands and even Bob Dylan! What made it funny was a poster next to it saying, 'Jesus Christ is coming' and Pete saying; 'Wow I thought Bob Dylan was hard to get!'

We arrived at the site and set up the tent and noticed an upturned burned out wreck of a fish and chip van that has been selling fish and chips at outrageous prices. But what really struck me was the quiet in the arena before the start. There must have been a few thousand people there and everyone spoke in whispers out of respect for the rest of the audience. A huge crowd in the field and before the music started there was hardly a sound! We felt proud that everyone spoke with great respect to each other and we all felt comfortable in each other's company as if we were all part of the same society. I saw one guy running after another who'd just dropped his wallet and the 'theft' of a leather jacket when announced on the PA concluded with the jacket being returned and a large cheer from the crowd.

Even though we got into the arena fairly late in the morning, we still had time to choose a spot fairly close to the front (the picket fence) and later even closer, where I got some great shots of The Who, Blodwyn Pig, and Marsha Hunt. The available festival food was basic, reasonably cheap and sustaining. Sadly the toilet facilities were, let's face it, basic! During Pentangle's performance a helicopter circled, drowning out the their music and everyone stood up giving it the 'V' sign – it could have been The Who arriving but there were many planes sightseeing that afternoon too. Halfway through their set there was someone who had decided to start evangelising at the back of the arena with a megaphone, much to the crowds disdain. When I went to the wall/toilet later, I passed by the spot where he had been shouting. All that was left was a crumpled megaphone a few banners and a large depression in the ground. A case of people voting with their feet then?

We all enjoyed the 'Swizzprick' inflatable and I remember thinking how clever the organisation was to get people to stretch their legs and join in the carnival spirit. In front of me, to the left of the stage, a young lady decided to lose all her clothes and dance around, which all added to spectacle of the event. Suddenly all the press photographers were looking away from the stage!

The music was amazing and virtually nonstop. Highlights for me were The Moody Blues, the Bonzo Dog Doo-Dah Band, Gypsy, (I think Gypsy performed twice and I remember their song 'Ringing the Dong'), The Who, Bob Dylan, The Band, Tom Paxton – who provided some great comic relief in his songs and knew exactly how to work the crowd. Sadly, Marsha Hunt did not appear topless, as was rumoured. The Who arrived by helicopter and the unpredictable Keith Moon shouted; 'Ricky Farr's an old queen' offstage! Then they played the whole of *Tommy* that afternoon. I heard later that their co-manager Kit Lambert told them after the

The picket fence around the front of the stage didn't work in keeping the crowds at bay

performance they had played it even better live than on record.

They were very happy because Charlie Watkins of Watkins Electric Music had put together the largest PA system known to man at the time – 4,000 watts I believe, I remember Ricky Farr 'OK people, here's a band that blew my mind, I know there gonna blow yours', berating the press by reading out the Sunday paper headlines concerning the IOW residents furore over hippy invasion etc. and throwing the screwed up papers into the press enclosure saying something like 'You do write some shit!' Following that outburst and obviously feeling hurt at the attack on their talents, the Fiery Creations allowed one of the press on stage to play some amazing classical guitar (could have been a piece called 'Romance'); he was brilliant and the audience loved it. Ricky Farr also announced that because of the sheer body mass of the audience we were keeping the rain away – apparently it was raining in Southampton. Such was the power of the festival. We were pioneers and indestructible, we all cheered! Overlaying everything was that haunting version of 'Amazing Grace' by The Great Awakening. That was our anthem.

Bob Dylan was worth the wait and the crowd loved the older material 'Mighty Quinn', etc., even though the music press had criticised his Johnny Cash white suit and *Nashville Skyline* voice! At the end, we caught the bus back to the ferry where the local residents couldn't have been more friendly and helpful. What a fabulous festival.

I WAS THERE: FRANK DEVLIN, AGE 18

I went to IOW in '69 with two pals of mine, we were all 18 and from Dublin, Ireland. Our trip began Dublin to Holyhead in Wales by boat, Holyhead to Euston in London by train, Euston to Waterloo, Waterloo to Portsmouth and then the ferry to the Isle of Wight. Some journey!

We arrived on the island around 11pm and pitched a tent along with thousands of other kids. I remember the tickets cost a fiver for the weekend. My pals were into a lot of the bands that were playing but I had come to see Dylan. I remember the weather was great, (unlike Woodstock).

On the Sunday morning, hundreds of us went to the beach, which was over the hill, everybody went in naked which was very daring for three innocent Irish lads. The compere of the show was a fella called Richie Farr, who all weekend said that The Beatles were in the crowd, and maybe they would play with Dylan at the end.

Dylan was supposed to come on stage at 8pm on Sunday to close the festival. He eventually came on at 11pm – three hours late. He played for 40 minutes and was gone. The crowd assumed he was taking a break, but he never came back. The crowd went nuts and broke up the fence around the site.

Myself and my pals decided to try and reach the stage, which we eventually did by crawling under the canvas. We found Richie still on the stage and had an argument with about how let down we felt with Dylan and all the bullshit from Farr himself all weekend. He asked us where we were from and counted out 15 pounds which he gave us to cover our outlay for the weekend and told us to go into the tent backstage and have a drink. Once in the tent, the only person we recognised was Jack Bruce from Cream.

The next day the site looked like a bomb had hit it. We were asked if we would help clear it for a few bob, and as we were not in any hurry, we helped clear up. Apart from Dylan, the gig was brilliant and we met loads of great people. We returned in 1970 to see Jimi Hendrix in what would be his last gig. That's my story of a great time in my life.

I WAS THERE: ANDREW STREET

I was there. I live on the Island but was in the Army at the time. The festival was in Wootton, which always seemed a strange place to have it but much more convenient than the 1970 one at East Afton, which was miles away from anywhere. As a local, I got a day pass and slept at home; I got paid for sleeping under canvas as a soldier so did not want to do it for free. The next year I was out of the Army and working for Southern Vectis, the bus company, taking folks to the 1970 festival. I made an amazing amount of money working overtime, ferrying punters to the site at East Afton but I never did get the time to go to the gig: so 1969 was my only experience of an Isle of Wight Festival. Bob Dylan plus the rest was good enough for me.

I WAS THERE: TED TUKSA

Just before Bob Dylan came on, they set out seats for all the guests in the press arena, when they poured in to sit down, I jumped over the barrier, which was non existent in those days, it was a fence about two feet high. I sat down in a seat on the third row right in the middle. I couldn't believe all the guests were sat down all around me, Ringo Starr was on the front row in the middle, behind him was George Harrison, and on the third row I had John Lennon and Yoko sat next to me.

At the time John and Yoko were the big new, and all the press were taking hundreds of pictures, with Ringo being on the front row, all the photographers were leaning and more or less climbing over him, after a few minutes, Ringo got annoyed and ordered all the press to stand a couple of feet in front of him and in line, and he said 'right, I will take all your photographs of John,' he then proceeded to take the camera off each photographer, lean over George and asked John and Yoko to smile and snapped away, and he did this with every photographer.

I WAS THERE: DAVID HALSTEAD

Unfortunately I didn't get to see Bob Dylan play. Neither did my friends who were trying to live the Sixties dream, but without the 'bread' man. Lemmy did the deals, Tony had the wheels and I was born to follow. I can't remember anything in any detail, but there were some snapshots that I have kept in my head to this day.

The car, which was a clapped out Standard 10 filled with hippies, sleeping bags, camping equipment and a two sleeper tent, went downhill at over 70 mph and uphill at barely more than walking pace. But it made it to the ferry and we bought a ticket to Ryde, and had to sing the song, of course! On the ferry was a groovy white car painted over in pop art fashion with pictures, symbols and on the front it said, 'Dylan or Bust'. I really hope they made it to see Bob.

I like to think my first single was 'Like a Rolling Stone', though in all probability it was probably something embarrassing to admit to today. I played it endlessly on my radiogram trying to write down the words and reckoned I'd cracked it and recited it to anyone who would listen. Many years later a kind friend let me know, between fits of laughter, that, 'Once upon a time you dressed so fine, you did the monkey time in your prime' wasn't what Dylan wrote. For decades I thought she was a great dancer and the 'monkey time' was some hip dance.

I listen to Dylan more now than I did then. For us, the big attraction was The Who. Although we were freaks (we preferred to be called heads), it wasn't that far back when we were Mods. The movement from Mod culture to Love & Peace was accompanied by our change from speed and mandies and alcohol to cannabis and acid. At the IOW we couldn't get any 'shit' ... but we did have a supply of black bombers!

During this time I worked in a dairy and lived in 'digs' with a milkman called Geoff and his overweight wife, Anne. In her medicine cupboard there was a large bottle of amphetamines prescribed by her doctor to make her more lively, less hungry and lose weight. Lemmy emptied the capsules into a handkerchief, replaced the contents with flour and put the bottle back. We huddled over the opened hankie in a marquee, provided free for those who didn't have a tent, licked our fingers and dipped into the pile of powder until it was all gone.

Another image remains of a beautiful young hippy chick smiling and gliding by with 'FUCK ME' written across her forehead. I had read about 'free love' but this shocked me.

Next problem was to get in without a ticket, or the means to buy one. We walked round the whole perimeter looking for a way in for free. Lemmy collected some cash and gave it to a 'guard' who turned a blind eye while we went under the fence. I can't honestly remember much about the Saturday evening or even any of the songs, but I do remember seeing the finale of the set by The Who and Roger Daltrey in his iconic fringed, brown suede jacket.

Later on things started to turn really weird. The high from the speed wore off and we started experiencing anxiety and paranoia as we came down to the ground. Later we found ourselves wandering aimlessly outside the fence between huge generator trucks that I'd seen before at fairgrounds. The thrum of the throbbing trucks mixed with the music fading and gaining in the wind was punctuated by announcements to the effect that there was some 'bad acid' out there man, and if you were having a bad trip then go to the medical tent. BAD TRIP, BAD TRIP! The effect of this magnified our paranoia, and probably thousands of others too. The last thing anyone wanted to hear was 'bad trip'. It took an eternity to get our heads straight and then the announcements started again. I wonder how many peaceniks had their serenity broken and their trip spoiled by this idiot. I imagine the medical tent filling up with freaked out heads and this spurring him to believe there was even more bad acid than first imagined and further cranking up their nightmare. We couldn't find the medical tent. We were lost and remained so.

By Sunday evening we were hallucinating. What made it worse was we saw the same figments of our collective imagination. It had to be real, didn't it? The fiery cross 50 feet high in the cliff, the man in a cape with a cat on his shoulder? Was it a full moon, the lights from the arena and/or the sun low on the horizon that cast surreal shadows over the camping area? Somehow we managed to score some black, the quality and strength of which we rarely see nowadays, and sat cross-legged in the small tent and smoked it all. Not a good idea! The shadows got more sinister and we could feel vibrations from the earth approaching the tent from all sides.

Memories for me tend to be visual or auditory, but what happened next was physical. Our backs were tight against the outside of the tent when I felt a hand press down on me from outside. Sheer panic propelled me to dive out of the tent. So did everyone else. The tent pole buckled and the canvas belly nearly burst with us inside screaming and scrabbling to get out. That horror moment of being trapped inside the tent like kittens about to be drowned is my most vivid memory of the summer of '69.

We could hear the music from the stage clearly from where we finally pitched ourselves on Sunday, but I can't remember a single song, except for one. In the evening we bumped into some beautiful Taunton chicks, one of whom took pity on me and I spent the rest of the evening in her sleeping bag in a platonic state of bliss. The sweetest moment, and final memory of the decade, was feeling peaceful and safe, listening to 'Lay Lady Lay' phasing, swirling and curling away into the night.

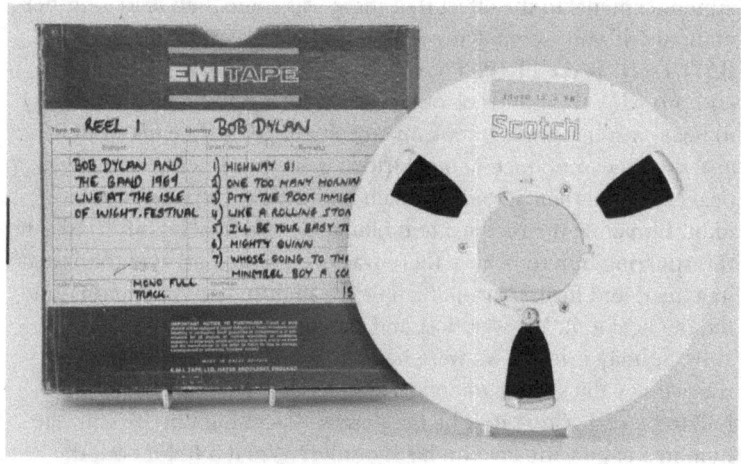

I WAS THERE: JOHN LENNON

One of the main points is that the media, being encouraged by the Establishment, or whatever way to – mind you, the Woodstock thing, we learned what really happened through the underground or through the grapevine. I was at the Isle of Wight gathering, at a Dylan concert, and there weren't as many people; so it was the biggest European gathering ever, and it was a beautiful experience, this calm – there wasn't a breath of air or vibration disturbing the atmosphere from any of the people there.

It was written up as if it was a holocaust, and that established in the minds of the people already decided, of the other generation, what's going on. It reaffirmed their fears of this generation with its haircuts, and its nakedness, and its pot smoking. The first thing we have got to do is to break through the media and get them to talk sense, and the only way they'll do that is if they are directed because they are directed on everything else, and they must be directed on what is happening because that's establishing a fear in the adult world that this generation is going to kill them or frighten them or, you know, go insane, like the 'Satan' guy, and to make the 'Satan' guy – that killer, to expunge – to use him as the leader or the image of this generation is as insane as saying everybody in the thirties was Hitler, and I don't know how we break that.

WOODSTOCK

LATE 1969, NEW YORK

I WAS THERE: LESLIE WEST, GUITARIST, PRODUCER

I didn't appreciate how great he was when I was with the Vagrants. I didn't really listen to his early albums. I wasn't a fan of his voice but I sure liked his lyrics, my God.

After I played Woodstock, I was going to buy a house in Woodstock. I got my first big royalty check. So I buy a Bentley and I go into this big driveway and in the distance about a quarter of a mile up the driveway, I see this gigantic log cabin. It was more like a mansion.

I had no idea whose house it was. And I go inside and on one of these screened-in porches I see a strip of photos. You know those photo booths where you can take four pictures for a dollar? I see a strip of John and Yoko.

I said, 'whoa, it's not their house, they don't live here.' And I go in the living room and on the whole wall is the picture of Bob Dylan from *Nashville Skyline*. Holy shit, it must be Bob's house. I got so scared and nervous, I ran out of the house, got in the car and drove away.

1970

COLUMBIA STUDIOS

JUNE 1970, NEW YORK CITY, NEW YORK

I WAS THERE: RON CORNELIUS, GUITARIST

I had said, 'wouldn't it be great if we could do an album with Dylan with just about five guys, and let him do his thing.' The way the West Coast players work, unlike LA and New York, when you're doing it our way, it demands each player to set up, get on the edge of his chair and give it what you've got. Right here, right now, the red light it's on. I told producer Bob Johnston, if we could ever do that with this guy Dylan I'd pull my shoes off and walk from California to New York if I could play on a record like that. One day a few months later I got a phone call and he said, ' Have you got your shoes on?' I'd forgotten even saying that.

We all arrived in New York City, we all called it the 'Black Rock', that was what we called Columbia Studios and we spent many, many days and nights recording sessions for what would become the *New Morning* album. In fact they made other albums from those sessions. But the *New Morning* sessions were very special to me; it was just like what I'd dreamed about. It was crazy too. Dylan would play a song on his own acoustic guitar and we would all get around and try and get our minds around what he was trying to do and chart the thing on how each one of us wanted it to look and play. And pretty soon he would get it to the stage where he would say, 'OK, you guys ready to try one? Well, here we go'.

We had a killer band; we had me and Charlie Daniels, Al Kooper on keyboards, David Bromberg on guitar, and the drummer Russ Kunkel. It was really a handful of guys who were the right people to have there.

Bob would say, 'Lets try one' and would count the song off in a completely different time then what you had just done. And that would make you have to play from scratch, because it wasn't like we just did. And if any one 'fell off' that time, we'd stop and start again, and he would count it in again in a completely different time as the last take! And if anyone fell off on that third take he would say, 'OK next song!'

About half way through these sessions the actual song 'New Morning' came up and I hooked up a pretty good solo on it, and Dylan came over to me later in the afternoon and said, 'Man, you've been giving me 110 per cent here. Is there anything I can do for you?' And I thought, mmm, I might have to think about that. And he said, 'OK, think about it'.

So, we went on and on for days there and I found out that on the Friday evening at 6 o clock, we're going to be done, and this was on the Wednesday. So I said to Bob, 'You know you said if there's anything you could do for me?' I said, ' You can hang around after we get done on Friday night, after everybody's gone, just me and you.' Now I'm from San Francisco, so he kind of looked at me funny!

And then said, 'OK cool.' So on the Friday, he said, 'What do you want?' And I have to say, if I'd said to him there's a really nice guitar I've seen on Broadway, he would have bought it for me, because he was really sincere. And we would say during those sessions, every day when Dylan walked in, it was like meeting a brand new person, a different guy, every day, and he'd have the weirdest people with him too.

Anyway, he said, 'OK, what do you want?' and I said, 'I want to go out in that main room, and I want to take a pillow and lay down on the floor, and I want you to sit at the piano and put your guitar on your lap. And I want to lay there and yell out Bob Dylan titles that I have always just been in love with. And if you wrote it on the guitar you play it on the guitar, and if you wrote it on the piano, then play it for me on the piano, and when I've had enough of that song I'll clap my hands and I'll yell out another title.' So for about 30 minutes I got to lay there on that floor, just me and him, and got my own Bob Dylan concert! And I tell you, it was one of the best gifts I ever had.

I WAS THERE: DAVID BROMBERG, GUITARIST

The *Self Portrait* sessions were the first time I played with Dylan. At first, when I got a phone call from him, (he called me himself) I thought it was a joke, somebody playing a trick. But I realised fairly swiftly that it actually was Bob Dylan on the phone. He'd come to various clubs in the Village where I was playing guitar for Jerry Jeff Walker, and I'd always assumed he was only there to hear Jerry Jeff. But I guess he was listening to me, too.

Most of what I remember is that it was just Bob and me in there. For several days straight, maybe even a couple of weeks, just the two of us, sitting across from each other playing and trying things. I had some really nasty cold thing going on all through that – I had a fever, and I'd work all day, come home and fall asleep in my clothes, wake up, take a shower and then head back into the studio and do it all over again. The songs that I did with him, as much as I can recall, were mostly folk songs. I'm not sure I remember seeing any *Sing Out* magazines, but *Sing Out* published a couple of songbooks, and I remember that Bob had one or two of those. But he knew those songs. He might have referred to the *Sing Out* books just to get a lyric here and there, but he knew those songs. Bob, as we all know, came up through the folk clubs, and he was really great at singing this music.

There was not a whole lot of discussion or direction. I think he liked how I played, and wanted to see what I'd come up with. Then he listened to the results, and what he really liked he used, and what he didn't, he saved.

Dylan's tenth studio album *Self Portrait* was released on June 8, 1970, by Columbia Records. His second double album (after *Blonde on Blonde*) features many cover versions of well-known pop and folk songs as well as four tracks recorded at the 1969 Isle of Wight Festival.

PRINCETON UNIVERSITY

9 JUNE, 1970, NEW JERSEY

I WAS THERE: DAVID CROSBY, MUSICIAN

Sara was trying to get Bob to go to Princeton University, where he was being presented with an honorary doctorate. Bob did not want to go. I said, 'C'mon, Bob it's an honour!' Sara and I both worked on him for a long time. Finally, he agreed. I had a car outside, a big limousine. That was the first thing he didn't like. We smoked another joint on the way and I noticed Dylan getting really quite paranoid about it. When we arrived at Princeton, they took us to a little room and Bob was asked to wear a cap and gown. He refused outright. They said, 'We won't give you the degree if you don't wear this.' Bob said, 'Fine. I didn't ask for it in the first place.' Finally we persuaded him to wear the cap and gown.

New Morning is the eleventh studio album by Bob Dylan, released on October 19, 1970, by Columbia Records. Coming only four months after the controversial *Self Portrait*, the more concise and immediate *New Morning* won a much warmer reception from fans and critics.

George Harrison had sat in on a session for *New Morning* on May 1, 1970, at Columbia's Studio B in New York, where he had played on an early take of 'If Not for You'. News of the collaboration between Dylan and the recent ex-Beatle caused great excitement in the music press. Over the following months, Harrison thought enough of the song to record it in London for his *All Things Must Pass* triple album set.

I WAS THERE: AL KOOPER, MUSICIAN

When I finished that album I never wanted to speak to him again. I was cheesed off at how difficult the whole thing was. He just changed his mind every three seconds. We'd get a side order and we'd go in and master it and he'd say, 'No, no, no. I want to do this.' And then, 'No, let's go in and cut this.' There was another version of 'Went to See the Gypsy' that was really good. It was the first time I went in and had an arrangement idea for it and I said, 'Let me go in and cut this track and then you can sing over it.' So I cut this track and it was really good... and he came in and pretended like he didn't understand where to sing on it.

> **I didn't say, 'Oh my God, they don't like this, let me do another one,' It wasn't like that. It just happened coincidentally that one came out and then the other one did as soon as it did. The *Self Portrait* LP laid around for I think a year. We were working on *New Morning* when the *Self Portrait* album got put together.**
>
> **BOB DYLAN**

1971

The Concert for Bangladesh was two benefit concerts organised by George Harrison and Indian Sitar master Ravi Shankar. The concerts were held at 2.30 and 8.00 pm on Sunday, August 1, 1971, at Madison Square Garden in New York City. The shows were organised to raise international awareness and fund relief efforts for refugees from East Pakistan (now Bangladesh), following the Bangladesh Liberation War-related genocide. The concerts were followed by a bestselling live album, a boxed three-record set, and Apple Films' concert documentary, which opened in cinemas in the spring of 1972.

MADISON SQUARE GARDEN

1 AUGUST, 1971, NEW YORK CITY, NEW YORK

I WAS THERE: PHIL SPECTOR, PRODUCER

It was chaos setting up at Madison Square Garden – we had three hours to mic the band, then the audience came in, and we didn't know how to mic the audience. And rather than a standard 'band', this was a full Wall of Sound orchestra: two drummers (Ringo Starr and Jim Keltner), two keyboard players (Billy Preston and Leon Russell), six horn players (led by Jim Horn), three electric guitarists (Harrison, Eric Clapton and Jesse Ed Davis), a trio of acoustic guitars to be 'felt but not heard' (Badfinger's Pete Ham, Tom Evans and Joey Molland), the seven members of Don Nix's Soul Choir, together with bassist Klaus Voormann and a dedicated percussion player, Mike Gibbins of Badfinger.

I WAS THERE: DON McADAM

I was young when Dylan first came on the scene. I had four older brothers so I got introduced to him at a young age, 9 or 10. My whole family was into music, and we all (about 20 of us) would get together and sit around and sing. 'Blowin' in the Wind' and 'Mr. Tambourine Man' were on the list of songs to sing and we would always sing those. Those were pretty popular back in the Sixties. When I learned to play guitar in the late Sixties I learned to play 'Don't Think Twice', 'The Times They are a-Changin'' and of course 'Mr. Tambourine Man'.

I saw him at the Bangladesh concert in 1971. It was quite a surprise because nobody really thought he was coming. When George Harrison introduced Dylan the crowd went crazy. My brother was a big Dylan fan and was jumping and waving his arms. It was like he just won a million dollars. It was great watching my brother.

Dylan was awesome. He only played five songs that night – 'A Hard Rain's a-Gonna Fall, 'Blowin' in the Wind', 'It Takes a Lot to Laugh, It Takes a Train to Cry', 'Mr. Tambourine Man' and

'Just Like a Woman'. They were all great and the crowd gave him a standing ovation. Dylan was awesome that night with George Harrison and Leon Russell.

I WAS THERE: JEFFREY BECK

I first saw Bob live in 1971 at the Concert for Bangladesh and have been enthralled by the many live performances I have witnessed thereafter, in excess of 100. I love the feeling of recognising a song from its introduction. I am never an observer at a Dylan show, I am always a participant. I cannot help but sing with him, they feel like my songs, I know them so well.

I WAS THERE: MARC CATONE

Not seeing the Concert for Bangladesh wasn't an option for Marc Catone

There was a large void in my life when The Beatles called it quits in 1970. During the next year, I tried to fill the emptiness with bootleg recordings of Beatles' concerts. By the summer of 1971, not only had The Beatles been gone for over a year, but Jimi Hendrix, Janis Joplin, and Jim Morrison were dead. It seemed like the Sixties were over... prematurely. I was spending most of my days and nights in a marijuana haze, but my senses became focused when a story began circulating in the New York City media in late July. George Harrison was organising a benefit concert for the people of Bangladesh at the request of his friend, Ravi Shankar.

The original name of the concert was 'Harrison and Friends', but was changed to the 'Concert for Bangladesh'. At first, this musical event was scheduled for the evening of Saturday, July 31, but based on anticipated ticket sales it became two performances on the afternoon and evening of Sunday, August 1. There was much speculation on who the performers would be.

Not seeing the Concert for Bangladesh wasn't an option for me. I had to see it. However, in the days before Ticketron and Ticketmaster, when one had to line up in front of the ticket office window at the concert venue, I was at a severe disadvantage. The concert was in a few days at Madison Square Garden in New York, and I was stuck in Danbury, Connecticut without a ticket. My good friend, Gilberte Najamy, who went with my sister Sara and me to see The Beatles at Shea Stadium, found a ticket agency in Stamford CT that still had a few remaining tickets. We were supposed to get two tickets for the both of us, but Gilberte remembered that she had a work commitment the same day. Still, she accompanied me on the hour drive to the ticket agency in Stamford where I became acquainted with the term, 'scalping'. What I paid for my ticket to the Concert for Bangladesh was cheap by today's standards. However, the actual price was $7.50, and the ticket agency charged me $18.00 – more than twice the cost. I didn't have much money in those days, but I handed over my cash, grabbed the ticket, and waited for the big day to arrive.

My ticket, which had the original name of the concert and a date of July 31 printed on it, was for the first performance in the afternoon. Not owning a car in those days, I took a bus from Danbury to the Port Authority terminal in Manhattan, and got a cab to Madison Square. By then, I knew who some of the performers would be – George Harrison, Ringo Starr, Eric Clapton, Klaus Voorman, Leon Russell, and Billy Preston. Earlier in the week, there had been talk about all four Beatles appearing on stage, but that rumour ended quickly. Still, there was faint hope that John Lennon might show up.

I hadn't been to many large concerts since seeing The Beatles in 1966. During my late high school and early college years, I saw The Doors, Grass Roots, Blues Magoos, and Rare Earth in Danbury, but the Concert for Bangladesh was the biggest concert I had attended in five years. Most of the people in the audience were close to my age of 21, with a few younger people, and many folks in their late 20s and early 30s. The gathering was a cross-section of the New York City area with nearly an equal number of males and females in attendance as well as people of colour – though there were more white faces than black.

I had an aisle seat in the Loge section, stage right, with a good view. I wore my 1971 'uniform' which consisted of a blue denim work shirt, and bell-bottom jeans. I sat next to two girls around my age, both wore army jackets and jeans. We talked quite a bit in the beginning, but not much during the show.

And then there was light, and it was shining down upon George Harrison as he introduced Ravi Shankar and his ensemble. Ravi knew the crowd had come to hear Harrison and his friends, but he asked us to listen to and absorb the more complex attributes of his Indian music. His portion of the show drew attention to the reason for the concert – to raise money for the ravaged people of Bangladesh. Although I listened respectfully to the Indian music, I was impatient for rock 'n' roll to take the stage.

After the Indian musicians finished, a crew set up microphones, and made their sound checks. The stage went dark for a few minutes. The lights came back on, and the band launched into 'Wah-Wah'. I had never heard so many guitars and horns playing at once. The song sounded remarkably like it did on Harrison's *All Things Must Pass* album from the previous year – except much louder. It was a glorious introduction to the concert, and the crowd was on its feet for the entire number. George and company did two more songs in a row from that album, 'My Sweet Lord' and 'Awaiting On You All'.

Harrison looked great in his white suit and orange shirt. His voice sounded strong, and the back-up singers, especially on 'My Sweet Lord', added quite a punch to the songs. Eric Clapton kept a low profile during the entire concert, sometimes standing with his back to the audience. Years later, we learned that he was in the midst of a heroin addiction, and had been very ill before the start of the performance.

One of the things that made the concert so great was the diversity of music – rock, folk, gospel, soul, R&B – it was all there. Billy Preston, who could arguably be called the fifth Beatle, had the crowd rocking with his soulful tune, 'That's The Way God Planned It'. Towards the end of the song, he walked away from the organ and did a wild stomping dance in front of George, running back to his chair just in time to play the ending.

Unlike the frenzied Beatles concerts, where one had to struggle to hear the band, this concert was different. Technology had taken a giant leap during the previous five years, improving the sound of vocals and instruments. Girls weren't screaming non-stop. The crowd was noisy, but the band could be heard very well.

Then came Ringo's turn. He was alternately all smiles, or seriously focused on his drumming, throughout the afternoon. The familiar guitar hook from 'It Don't Come Easy' was instantly recognisable. Again, the crowd rose to its feet. We were seeing two Beatles on stage together, and hearing a song in which both of them had played on record. That was one of two moments during the concert in which I almost had to pinch myself to make sure I wasn't dreaming. Ringo's voice was a little shaky, and he messed up the lyrics twice (during the line, 'And this love of mine keeps growing all the time'). Was he nervous? Probably. Was he Ringo? Yes, and his fans appreciated him.

Slowing down the pace, George sang the last of the afternoon's songs from *All Things Must Pass*. A somber tune a cautionary tale – telling us not to let sadness take over our lives, George's 'Beware Of Darkness' again showed him in good voice, with Leon Russell singing one of the verses. I always liked the song, but found it a bit maudlin. It wasn't until I saw the tribute *Concert for George*, and heard 'Beware Of Darkness' performed by Eric Clapton, that I realised how much the song reminded me of George, and how much I missed him. He was often criticised for 'preaching' in some of his songs, but all he was doing was sharing. Today, I can't listen to that song without getting a lump in my throat – the words ring true.

There hadn't been too many introductions to songs up until that point in the concert. Then George introduced the individual band members. I found this to be one of the most enjoyable parts of the show as George told us that people had 'cancelled a few gigs' to be in the concert. Clapton, Voorman, and Russell received loud applause, but it was Ringo (the first one to be introduced) who received a sustained ovation – ending with an impromptu organ snippet from 'Yellow Submarine' played by Leon Russell. Anyone who has ever seen the concert film remembers George turning to the band and inquiring if he had forgotten to introduce anyone. After a few seconds, he announces, 'We've forgotten Billy Preston'. Next time you watch the movie, listen carefully after George asks 'have we forgotten anyone?', and you will hear a female voice answer loudly, 'You'. I am now email buddies with the woman who yelled that out. Years after the Concert for Bangladesh, she became friends with George's sister, Louise, who got a real kick out of that story.

Shortly after the intros, without any announcement or fanfare, the assembled band played the beginning notes to a song which the audience knew right away, 'While My Guitar Gently Weeps'. This was the first of three Harrison songs performed during the course of the concert that George recorded with The Beatles. For me, it was a very emotional moment, the only time I envisioned what the concert would have been like had John Lennon and Paul McCartney been on stage. George, Ringo, and Eric had been on the original *White Album* recording of 'While My Guitar Gently Weeps'. Therefore, it wasn't much of a stretch to imagine all four of The Beatles on stage. I was only 21-years-old, and not given to public displays of emotion, but my eyes were wet during that number. I was not alone, people all around me had tears on their faces during the song. George sang the lines of one verse out of order, but no one cared. His voice sounded like it did when he sang the song on *The Beatles*.

As if to knock us out of our nostalgic stupor, George said into the microphone, 'Here's another number from Leon,' which heralded the hardest rocking songs of the concert. Leon Russell performed a medley of The Rolling Stones' 'Jumpin' Jack Flash', and the oft-covered Fifties rocker, 'Young Blood' (originally done by the Coasters). What I remember most is the incessant tom-tom beat by Ringo Starr and Jim Keltner. The audience kept time with their stomping feet. The entire Loge rocked in rhythm with the drums. I could feel the pulse-like pounding throughout my body. Leon's woeful sing-song tale of leaving his lover for a younger girl was the connection between the two songs. When he returned to 'Jumpin' Jack Flash' at the end of the set, the vibration in the floor was even stronger than the first time. Many concert attendees cite Russell's performance as the best of that day.

I don't know how the set list for the concert was planned, but the acoustic version of 'Here Comes The Sun', which Harrison and Pete Ham of Badfinger performed, was quite a counterpoint to Leon's raucous medley. Note for note, it was a perfect rendition of one of George's most acclaimed Beatles' tunes.

There was a lot of movement on stage, and a brief period of silence, as George leaned into his microphone and said, matter-of-factly, 'Here's a friend of all of us, Bob Dylan'. I couldn't make out what he said it first, then I began hearing people near me say, 'Oh my God, it's Bob Dylan'. Just when I thought the concert couldn't get any better...it did. When Dylan walked up to the microphone, it was a total surprise – the second time I thought about pinching myself. Was it real or was I dreaming?

Dylan sang 'A Hard Rain's a-Gonna Fall', 'It Takes A Lot To Laugh, It Takes A Train To Cry', 'Blowin' in the Wind', and 'Just Like a Woman'. I was not that familiar with 'It Takes A Lot To Laugh, It Takes A Train To Cry', despite owning the *Highway 61 Revisited* album from which it came, but I knew the other three songs quite well. I was quite impressed by the familiar antiwar favourite, 'A Hard Rain's a-Gonna Fall'. I knew 'Blowin' in the Wind' by heart, learning it first in a junior high music class. It was the only song during the concert in which I heard people singing along. However, my favourite from the Dylan set was 'Just Like a Woman'.

Standing side by side on 'Just Like a Woman' was Ringo Starr, George Harrison, and Bob Dylan. There are times when one knows they are seeing history in the making. I told myself, 'don't forget this moment – two of The Beatles and Dylan are on stage together – this might not ever happen again.' And there it is still in my mind's eye, Ringo with tambourine in hand, George Harrison playing guitar and singing back-up vocals to Bob Dylan's lead. As quickly as he entered, Dylan walked off the stage and was gone.

My memory of the next song, 'Something' is a bit hazy. Although I can't state this with absolute certainty, 'Something' may have been my 'bathroom song' out of necessity. The concert had been going on for almost three hours, and I had a bus to catch back to Danbury. For the first time all day, I became a clock watcher. Fortunately, the encore song was next, the recently penned George Harrison song, 'Bangladesh', in which he tells us why he decided to put on the concert for the poverty-stricken people of that war-torn nation.

I said a quick good-bye to the people sitting next to me, ran down the stairs, and made a hasty retreat to the streets outside. It was raining on that early Sunday evening, and yet I was able to get a taxi right away. The driver asked me, 'So, what's going on at the Garden today?' As I told him about the concert, he kept repeating, 'Wow, you're kidding me.'

Although I wished for a Beatles reunion that day, I realise now that the Concert for Bangladesh was better off without their competitive egos, and the legal rancour that existed among them at the time. What made the Concert for Bangladesh unique was the humanitarian purpose of the concert, the many artists who participated, the diversity of music performed, and a very loving audience who appreciated it all.

COLUMBIA STUDIOS

OCTOBER 1971, NEW YORK CITY, NEW YORK

I WAS THERE: HAPPY TRAUM, MUSICIAN

In October of 1971 I got a call from Bob Dylan asking me if I'd like record some songs with him for his Greatest Hits, Volume II compilation. Could I do it tomorrow, and would I bring my guitar and banjo and, oh yeah, how about a bass, too? (Never mind that I didn't own a bass and had never played one in public. I borrowed one fast.)

Now, for most fair-to-middlin' guitar fingerpickers the odds of getting a call like this are about as likely as John Glenn calling to see if you'd like a seat on the next space shuttle, but I tried to be fairly casual about the whole thing. You see, I had been friends with Bob since the early Sixties, and had already recorded 'Let Me Die in

My Footsteps' with him on a Folkways recording called Broadsides. (Bob was using the pseudonym Blind Boy Grunt in deference to his new Columbia contract.) By now, of course, he was the best-known singer/songwriter in the world, but as friends and neighbors in Woodstock, NY we often socialized and played together informally. So it wasn't a great leap to take what we had been doing in the living room into the studio. Was I excited? You bet I was!

So, laden with armloads of instruments, I took the bus from Woodstock to New York City and made my way to the Columbia Studios on West 54th Street. To my surprise the entire session consisted of just Bob, me and the engineer in a cavernous, nearly-empty studio. The first song Bob suggested was 'Only a Hobo,' one of the tunes he had recorded eight years earlier on the 1963 Broadsides session. The machines were turned on, Bob started playing, and I picked a clawhammer-style part on my banjo and sang a high harmony to his melody. After two takes it seemed that it wasn't coming together, so Bob moved on to another song. (For many years I was under the impression that 'Only a Hobo' hadn't worked out to Bob's satisfaction and was lost on the proverbial cutting room floor. Happily, it wasn't gone forever. Forty odd years later it finally appeared on Bob's bootleg release, Another Self Portrait, and I was surprised and delighted at how good it sounded.)

The next one we cut, 'I Shall Be Released,' immediately caught the right spirit and we relaxed into the music. We started the song with a slightly more bouncy feel than I had heard on The Band's famous recording, and it fit right into the bluesy fingerpicking style that I have always favored. Bob played it in A, so I capoed up to the fifth fret and played out of the E position, accenting the ends of lines with bass note hammer-ons and sliding 6ths and pull-offs in the treble. I joined in singing on the chorus, and before I knew it Bob was grinning and we were on to the next song. Now I was starting to have a good time!

I had heard 'Down in the Flood' in bits and pieces during the Basement Tapes sessions, but the version that we did at this recording was totally impromptu at least for me. It's a blues in G, so it wasn't hard to find some things to play. Again, Bob was strumming the rhythm with his flatpick, so I just tried to compliment his singing with some sliding licks and bluesy, fingerstyle fills on the high strings. The whole thing went by so fast that I didn't realize it was a take until we played it back.

Finally, we cut what turned out to be my favorite of that day's (or just about any day's) session, 'You Ain't Going Nowhere.' Bob set the pace with a strong rhythmic strum, and I tried to give the tune a rollicking, joyous feel with a frailing banjo part. We nailed it in two takes, singing and playing together, again with no previous rehearsal. After listening to it we decided it needed a little extra kick, so I made my debut as a bassist. I must admit it was a pretty visible way to start playing that instrument in public, but Bob and the engineer seemed to like what I did so my part stayed in. Not long after that session, Bob invited me to play bass on a date he was producing for Allen Ginsberg, so my career as a bassist stayed high-profile for a little while longer before disappearing into merciful obscurity.

As I re-listen to these recordings today, I can still hear the informal, home-style picking that so many listeners have told me they like about those particular performances. There's a relaxed intimacy there that I like to think is partly due to our friendship and to the many occasions in which we sat around the house playing the old songs. Of course, much of it was due to Bob's studio technique at the time: establish a good 'feel,' play the song as if you really mean what you're singing about, and get it in one or two takes. If you need more than that, it's not happening, so move on. It's a way of working that has created some unbelievably great recorded performances over the years, and I have always been incredibly proud to have been a part of four of them.

ACADEMY OF MUSIC

31 DECEMBER, 1971, NEW YORK

I WAS THERE: SUE SMALL McLACHLAN

I attended a Band concert at the New York Academy of Music. At the end of the concert, just moments after midnight, Bob Dylan suddenly appeared and performed songs with The Band, including 'Like a Rolling Stone'. It was a great surprise, a great way to start the year and a great memory to have 45 years later!

1972

ROGER'S RESTAURANT

SUMMER 1972, EAST HAMPTON, NEW YORK

I WAS THERE: BRUCE HARRY

Someone said, 'Bob Dylan's sitting in the dining room.' We had other famous people dropping in from time to time. I remember Cheryl Tiegs, Marlo Thomas, Craig Claiborne, and a bunch of other people.

I always try to perfect what I do, so I tried to make a perfect order of flounder for Mr. Dylan. After the meal he popped his head in and said, 'Thank you very much, that was a great meal.' I was all dirty and greasy, so I didn't shake his hand.

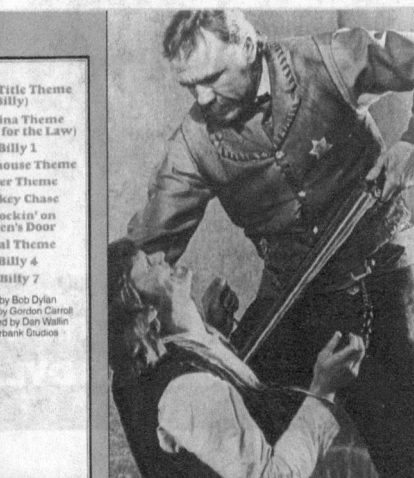

Pat Garrett & Billy the Kid became the twelfth studio album and first soundtrack album by Bob Dylan, released on July

13, 1973, by Columbia Records for the Sam Peckinpah film, *Pat Garrett and Billy the Kid*. Dylan himself appeared in the film as the character 'Alias'.

The soundtrack included 'Knockin' on Heaven's Door', which gave Dylan a No 12 hit on the US chart. The song was later covered by acts such as Eric Clapton, Dolly Parton, Bryan Ferry and Guns N' Roses.

1973

SHANGRI-LA STUDIOS

AUGUST 1973, MALIBU, CALIFORNIA

I WAS THERE: ROBBIE ROBERTSON, MUSICIAN

The idea of touring again seemed to really make sense. It was a good idea, a kind of step into the past. The other guys in The Band came out to Malibu and we went right to work.

We sat down and played for four hours and ran over an incredible number of tunes. Bob would ask us to play certain tunes of ours, and then we would do the same, then we'd think of some that we would particularly like to do.

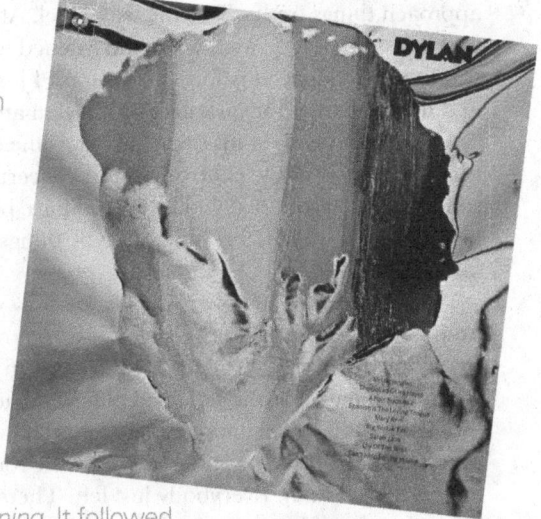

Dylan the thirteenth studio album by Bob Dylan was released on November 19, 1973, by Columbia Records. Compiled and issued by the label with no input from Dylan himself, it contains no original Dylan songs, the material consisting of two outtakes from *Self Portrait* and another seven from *New Morning*. It followed the artist's departure from Columbia for Asylum Records, and the announcement of his first major tour since 1966.

VILLAGE RECORDER

NOVEMBER 1973, LOS ANGELES, CALIFORNIA

I WAS THERE: ROB FRABONI, PRODUCER

A few weeks before we started the album, Bob went to New York by himself. He stayed there for two and a half weeks and wrote most all the songs. One of the classic songs, 'Forever Young,' he told me he had carried around in his head for about three years. He gets an idea for a song sometimes, he said, and he's not ready to write it down. So he just keeps it with him and eventually it comes out.

They initially came into the studio on Friday, November 2, to get set up and to get a feel for the studio. We did use one song that we recorded that day. They cut three or four things for the album on Monday. Just came in and knocked them off.

Then on Tuesday, they cut about four more things, and we used about three of them. We took two days off. Then they came in Friday and we cut the balance of the album that day. You've got to approach things fresh; that's the way I feel. After we mixed the album and it was all done, then I went and listened to his records. I didn't want to be influenced before the sessions. I just wanted to do it fresh, and that was what they wanted, too, Dylan and The Band.

The room was right for them. As far as the size, they really liked that. And as far as the control room is concerned, they just wanted something that sounded good. It could have been done at a number of places, but we had a combination of things: the room, the security and the location.

We only did one complete take of the slow version of 'Forever Young.' This take was so riveting, it was so powerful, so immediate, I couldn't get over it. When everyone came in nobody really said anything. I rewound the tape and played it back and everybody listened to it from beginning to end and then when it was over everybody sort of just wandered out of the room. There was no outward discussion. Everybody just left. There was just a friend and me sitting there. I was so overwhelmed I said, 'Let's go for a walk.' We went for a walk and came back and I said, 'Let's go listen to that again.' We were like one minute or two into it, I was so mesmerised by it again I didn't even notice that Bob had come into the room. So ,when we were assembling the master reel I was getting ready to put that take on the master reel. I didn't even ask. And Bob said, 'What're you doing with that? We're not gonna use that.' And I jumped up and said, 'What do you mean you're not gonna use that? You're crazy! Why?' Well, during the recording Lou Kemp and this girl came by and she had made a crack to him, 'C'mon, Bob, what! Are you getting mushy in your old age?' It was based on her comment that he wanted to leave that version off the record.

They liked the idea of being out of town (The Village Recorder is situated in West Los Angeles, about 10 miles from Hollywood). When we actually got down to the mixing, Robbie Robertson was comfortable with what he was hearing, and that was the really important thing. There was no producer on this record. Everybody was the producer. Robbie was the one who gives a lot of direction, although they all have something to say about the music, and are all really involved.

Robbie came in that first morning and said to me, 'There are going to be no overdubs. We're doing it live. This is it, what's happening here is it.' Bob doesn't overdub vocals. The record was really a performance, as far as I'm concerned. It wasn't like we were 'making a record.' It was more of a performance, and Bob wanted it to sound right, to come across. When he starts playing, there's nothing else happening but that, as far as he's concerned. I don't think I've seen anyone who performs with such conviction.

They had started rehearsing for the tour before we began recording. They only knew two of the songs on the album before coming in. The balance of the songs on the album they never heard until they were right here in the studio. Bob would just run it down, and they'd play it once. Then they'd come in to the control room and listen. That's another thing that really astounded me.

Nobody was saying, 'You ought to be doing this' or 'You ought to be playing that.' They just all came in and listened to hear what they should do, and then they'd go out into the studio. That would usually be the take, or the one following. That was pretty much the way it went. The other thing was, if that wasn't the take, they'd do a few more. Sometimes, they would change the arrangements from take to take because it was still so fresh. Then they'd choose the one that felt best.

Then we were assembling on Saturday, the next day, and Bob, myself, Nat Jeffrey (assistant engineer on *Planet Waves*) and Bob's friend were here. We put together the master reels.

Then around noon, Bob said, 'I've got a song I want to record later,' and I said fine. He said, 'I'm not ready right now. I'll tell you when.' We were doing what we were doing, and all of a sudden he came up and said, 'Let's record.' So he went out in the studio, and that was 'Wedding Song,' the cut that ends the album.

He just went out and played it. It was astounding. I hadn't heard him do anything that sounded like his early records. Lou Kemp, his old friend from Minnesota, was there. He also came on the tour with us. Anyway, Bob went out to record, and I put up some microphones, and I was going to get a sound. But usually he wouldn't sing unless we were recording. That's the way he was. You couldn't get him to go out and just sing, unless he was running something down with The Band.

Well, I said I was going to get a sound. He asked, 'Is the tape rolling? Why don't you just roll it?' So I did, and he started singing, and there was no way in the world I could have stopped him to say, 'Go back to the top.' It was such an intense performance.

If you listen to the record, you can hear noises from the buttons on his jacket. But he didn't seem to care. Lou and I were both knocked out by the song. We listened to it a few times and didn't think about it again until we got down to mixing. I mentioned re-cutting it to eliminate the button sounds, at one point, and Bob said, 'Well, maybe.' But he never said yes, so we let it go.

The final recording happened during the mixing. We had mixed about two or three songs, and Bob, Robbie, Nat and I were there. Bob went out and played the piano while we were mixing. All of a sudden, he came in and said, 'I'd like to try 'Dirge' on the piano.' We had recorded a version with only acoustic guitar and vocal a few days earlier.

We put up a tape and he said to Robbie, 'Maybe you could play guitar on this.' They did it once, Bob playing piano and singing, and Robbie playing acoustic guitar. The second time was the take. It was another one of those incredible, one-time performances.

Bob wanted certain types of sounds. He wanted a kind of bar room sound from the piano on 'Dirge' rather than a majestic sound. He also wanted a raunchy vocal sound. We actually mixed 'Dirge' immediately after we recorded it that night. Robbie and I listened to it once and I said,

'Let's mix it right now.' So we took a mix and that's what's on the record. It had a unique character. The sound of that particular mix made a lot of difference and was important to him. We did another mix later going for a more 'polished' sound, but didn't use it. That's the kind of stuff he was sensitive to, how the mixes affected the character of the music. That might have been more important to him than the sound quality.

We came in and mixed a few songs. We would work a day or two and take a few days off. And we always worked from noon to about eight, really good hours. One of the songs, 'Hazel,' we used the way we first mixed it. But we remixed the other two because we felt we could do better.

Once we got into doing them, we mixed the whole album in about three or four days. But then we spent more time than it took to record or mix just to sequence the record. Bob wanted to live with a few different sequences, until he found one that was just right.

After the mixes were done, they virtually turned the whole thing over to me. They let me decide on the spacing between songs, and everything regarding mastering. I cut sets of refs for them for approval when I was satisfied, and then they gave me the final go-ahead.

1974

The 40-concert, 30-date, 21-city North American tour began at Chicago Stadium on January 3, 1974, and ended with two nights at Inglewood Forum California on February 14, 1974. Many stars attended the final show including; Ringo Starr, Jack Nicholson, Carole King, Neil Young, Helen Reddy, Eric Burdon, Ramblin' Jack Elliott, Dory Previn, Warren Beatty, Joan Baez and David Crosby.

The tour reunited Dylan with The Band on stage after the release of Dylan's Band-backed *Planet Waves* album. It was reported that six million fans tried to get tickets. The 658,000 available seats for the six-week tour were sold almost immediately.

This was Dylan's first real tour in eight years, performing with The Band. As The Hawks, the then little-known group had backed him on his previous tour, the exhaustive 1966 world tour, between the releases of *Highway 61 Revisited* and *Blonde on Blonde.*

The set lists changed and evolved nightly, but mostly they included the old songs fans wanted to hear. The opening show was packed with classics like 'All Along the Watchtower,' 'Ballad of a Thin Man,' 'The Times They Are a-Changin'' and 'Like a Rolling Stone.' The Band also played some of their songs, including 'The Night They Drove Old Dixie Down' and 'Stage Fright.'

> We were doing exactly the same thing we'd done on the earlier Dylan-goes-electric tour, when people were booing us. They absolutely hated us. So it was good to find out that we were right, and that the world had come around to what we had been doing all along.
>
> **ROBBIE ROBERTSON**

I WAS THERE: ROB FRABONI, PRODUCER

I ended up working at The Record Plant just after Jimi Hendrix made *Electric Ladyland* there. I ended up working with Bob Dylan and John Lennon on an Alan Ginsberg session and one thing lead to another. I then went back to visit my parents' house for Christmas and there was an ad in *Billboard* for the studio called the Village Recorder which I'd always wanted to get a job at because it was in Westwood and not in Hollywood, where all the other studios were and I had seen that Eric Clapton had done his first record there. So I went and applied for the job but no luck.

Then I went to visit my parents again after I'd been in New York for a couple of years and I decided I would go and drop into the Village Recorder again and put in another job application. Two weeks later I got a call and they asked if I was interested in coming to work there. I ended up taking the job and moving from New York to Los Angeles, which ended up in me working on *Planet Waves* as well as records with Joe Cocker, The Beach Boys and The Rolling Stones.

I was driving around in my VW in Los Angeles and heard 'Up on Cripple Creek' on the radio and I thought to myself, man I would give anything to work with The Band. Then oddly enough, two weeks later the studio manger said to me Bob Dylan's coming in to do a record and I said, 'Really?' Also at this time we had Seals and Crofts coming in to the studio at the same time and I was thinking should I do Seals and Crofts or Bob Dylan, not knowing at this time that The Band were coming in.

Then I found out that it wasn't just Bob Dylan but Dylan and The Band and that settled it for me. It was like 'Wow!' The group who I'd idolised all my life since I knew of their existence I thought well that I'm not going to pass up.

That relationship then went on for 10 years, culminating in *The Last Waltz*. Things led up to that, I did *The Basement Tapes*, not the original recordings but the compilation of it and making it suitable for release, I did *Planet Waves, Before The Flood*, I did *Northern Lights Southern Cross* with The Band and another couple of records. We got really, really close, all of us. The relationship was really tight.

Then what happened was after *Planet Waves* was when they did the Dylan and The Band tour in '74 Robbie Robertson called me and said we're doing a sound check with Bill Graham's PA system at The Forum and Bob wants you to come and check it out with us, so I went. They were on stage playing and the forum was empty. Bob was walking around the room with me and Bill Graham and we were listening and I went over to the sound guy and said this doesn't sound very good, maybe we could this that and another, so I messed around with it for five minutes and got it sounding a lot better. Bob walked up to me and said, 'Do you want to go on the tour with us?' I said, 'Well I'd love to but I'm the chief engineer at the Village Recorder, and I just can't walk away.' Bob said, 'Well you should talk to them, get a leave of absence or something', so I did and I went out on the whole tour with them. When I came back I was a different person than the guy that went on the tour. I'd met everybody I'd ever wanted to meet in the music business because Bob hadn't toured for eight years since the motorcycle accident. I had a little notebook and would write down details of everyone I met on that tour.

They started rehearsing for the tour three to four weeks before recording the *Planet Waves* album. I was told they only did three of the songs at the rehearsal and the rest they followed Bob's hands at the session. They didn't even write down chord charts. They were that attuned to him that they could just watch him and follow him.

The first show was in Chicago, Illinois. They all went on stage together and the first song was Bob and he played a couple. Then, The Band played a couple then Bob played a couple. Sometimes, there were one, two or three songs and it was back and forth. At the end of the show, we really knew it wasn't right.

So, here I am, a young kid, and said, 'you know what I think we should do?' I said, 'I think The Band should open the show, then Bob should do a set with The Band, then, The Band should come out and join him and they should play together another set and the show is over.'

They did it the next night and it worked really well. That became the template for the rest of the tour. So, the record sequence isn't necessarily the way the shows were played.

I remember from the tour, 'Most Likely You Go Your Way' and 'I'll Go Mine', I always liked, it was a good start to the tour. I liked the way he went into 'Lay Lady Lay'. It was always kind of a moment to take a breath and he'd say, 'It's great to be here'.

I really liked the acoustic set. It was always very riveting and you could hear a pin drop, very powerful stuff.

The Band stuff was just the normal Band stuff, same arrangements, very well played as per usual. The rest of it, I mean, was just real interesting. I thought they were really great electric versions of some of these songs because The Band was so good. Every time they brought something to the situation, they'd make it really good.

I love the cover to the album. People started holding their lighters up at the end of this tour, it just started spontaneously. Photos would appear in newspapers and it just became a thing that people started to do. I thought it was very astute of the album cover photographer. One of the first times it happened, he said, 'Wow man look at that it is so incredible'. All those people with lighters was really quite awe inspiring.

Another strange Dylan related tale; my dad's sister lived in Illinois and she was from Minnesota. They had a house and sold this house to Bob Dylan's parents when Bob left home to go to New York to become Bob Dylan. Bob's folks wanted a smaller house so they bought my dad's sister's house.

When we started working on *Planet Waves*, my aunt heard through my parents that I was working with Bob. She said, 'Oh I sold his parents my house.' She sent me these five photographs, three of inside, two of outside. They were black and white with crinkled edges on the top and bottom. I thought I can't show Bob these pictures or he'll think I am AJ Weberman and think I've been digging in his trash. So, I ended up keeping them with me.

I think we'd been on the tour for about four weeks and so one day, Bob and I happened to be the only two people who were awake on the plane. I went over and sat next to Bob and said, 'Here's something I want to show you'. He said, 'What's that?' so I handed him the pictures He had them in his hand and he looked at it and stared up at me. He looked at the next one and stared at me with each one. He said, 'Where'd you get these?' I told him it's not like that. My dad's sister sold your parents their house. The pictures are from her. I showed him the letter, he was fascinated and that was that. But at first, he was taken aback.

We had some great times, I remember one night – you know The Band song 'Strawberry Wine', the woman who made that wine brought two gallons of the stuff to the after show party. We all had these small paper cups and all we drank was this moonshine, this rocket fuel all night out of these small paper cups. Everybody got plastered, from two gallons of this stuff. The next day we all had to fly out to North Carolina and everybody slept in late, and barely got up and made the plane. When we did get on board the private 707 plane, and everybody was really bleary eyed and we noticed that the stewardesses were all watching the porn film *Deep Throat* on the video screens on the plane as we boarded and we are all thinking this can't be possible, this is mad! So we all had a laugh on the flight, we landed and went to the gig, and when Bob went on stage in the evening he couldn't remember where was. He would always open with 'You go Your Way, I'll go Mine', and then before starting the second song 'Lay Lady Lay' he would always say, 'Its great to be here' where ever we were and name the city. And on this night he made the now famous comment, when he said, 'Its great to be here…. It's great to be anywhere!'

CHICAGO STADIUM

3 JANUARY, 1974, CHICAGO, ILLINOIS

I WAS THERE: PAUL JOHNSON

I've seen Dylan three times. The first was a story for the ages. January 1974, in Chicago, the first or second show of his first tour after the motorcycle accident. I rode from Cedar Falls, Iowa in a van with a group of people that included a young woman who went into labour on the way. Well, it was a story. A great show with The Band. Epic. Historic. I've seen him two more times but how could those experiences measure up to this one? This was the only time on this tour that Dylan played during The Band's set.

SET LIST:

Hero Blues
Lay Lady Lay
Tough Mama
The Night They Drove Old Dixie Down
Stage Fright
Share Your Love With Me
It Ain't Me, Babe
Leopard-Skin Pill-Box Hat
All Along The Watchtower
Holy Cow
King Harvest (Has Surely Come)
Ballad of a Thin Man
Up On Cripple Creek
I Don't Believe You (She Acts Like We Never Have Met)
The Times They Are a-Changin
Song To Woody
The Lonesome Death Of Hattie Carroll
Nobody 'Cept You
It's Alright, Ma (I'm Only Bleeding)
Life Is A Carnival

The Shape I'm In
When You Awake
Rag Mama Rag
Forever Young
Something There Is About You
Like a Rolling Stone
The Weight
Most Likely You Go Your Way (And I'll Go Mine)

THE SPECTRUM

6 JANUARY, 1974, PHILADELPHIA, PENNSYLVANIA

I WAS THERE: STEVEN BROOKS, AGE 21

Growing up in New York City, one of our neighbours was a record distributor for London Records. He always gave me 45s of new artists but could also get any album I wanted if I gave him a list. In the Sixties, I became a Dylan fan after *Blonde on Blonde*. I was too young to see him in the Village but I loved his music. Early on I preferred songwriters to singers. One of my friend's older sister went to Queens College with Art Garfunkel so we became fans.

In 1969, I worked at a camp about six miles from Woodstock. It was the summer of 'Lay Lady Lay', which is still one of my favourites.

The oddest thing about this show was that it was on a Sunday and I think it was in the afternoon. I was attending Drexel University and I think it was 1974. I remember getting a call from a good friend who had tickets and would I want to go. We were big fans of The Band and didn't expect to have the opportunity to see Dylan.

Dylan was amazing. Even though he had The Band as his backup. I don't remember very many Band songs being played. It was almost like Dylan's greatest hits, being played with The Band's unique style (big drums, big piano and Robbie singing). We had really good seats just off the stage to the right so the sound was outstanding. Dylan was a master, his singing was clear and strong, not garbled or hushed, as he is known to do. I remember him playing just about every hit and crowd favourite.

THE FORUM

11 JANUARY, 1974, MONTREAL, CANADA

I WAS THERE: DAVID LAWRENCE

I saw Bob Dylan with The Band in 1974 at the Montreal Forum. During the Dylan solo set, I swear to this day my friends and I were approached by The Band's drummer, Levon Helm. He joined us in finishing off the joint we were smoking!

SET LIST FROM BOSTON GARDEN:

Rainy Day Women #12 & 35
Lay Lady Lay
Just Like Tom Thumb's Blues
It Ain't Me Babe
I Don't Believe You (She Acts Like We Never Have Met)
Ballad of a Thin Man
Stage Fright
The Night They Drove Old Dixie Down
King Harvest (Has Surely Come)
This Wheel's On Fire
I Shall Be Released
Up On Cripple Creek
All Along The Watchtower
Ballad Of Hollis Brown
Knockin' On Heaven's Door
The Times They Are a-Changin' (Incomplete)
Don't Think Twice, It's All Right
Gates of Eden
Just Like a Woman
It's Alright, Ma (I'm Only Bleeding)

CAPITAL CENTRE

15 JANUARY, 1974, LANDOVER, MARYLAND

I WAS THERE: ROGER LATHBURY

Roger Lathbury gets the message across on his t-shirt

I saw Dylan again on his first big comeback tour, heralded on the cover of *Newsweek*, in 1974. It was the time of the Watergate Hearing, when Richard Nixon was under fierce attack. I had a job, and I wasn't the same, nor was Dylan. I had read his book *Tarantula*, and even managed to get it autographed by sending it to him (the naiveté!) and I was more of a fan than ever – but of the songs up to *Blonde on Blonde*. Although I liked and tried to like the music that followed, my heart wasn't in it, soul and fibre, as it was in the Sixties. I felt that Dylan wasn't giving himself as fully as he used to. Of course, he has a right to do what he wants to do, but I have a right to feel as I feel.

By that time I was living in Washington, DC I duly sent a certified check for $25.00 for the show and received the ticket(s). The Capital Centre (since demolished) was the venue; Dylan refused to let the video cameras be used, which independence elicited a huge round of applause from the audience.

The acoustic and band-accompanied parts were mixed. He started out with 'Most Likely You Go Your Way and I'll Go Mine,' a wonderful song that was, I felt, artificially energised by his effort to emphasise unexpected and not always suitable words. He ad-libbed a single remark, 'Good to be in DC' (though the Capital Centre was in Maryland), and at one point had to begin a song when a guitar string broke. It may have been during 'It's All Right Ma, I'm Only Bleeding.' This song contains the line 'even the President of the United States must sometimes have to stand naked.' Huge enthusiasm, applause, shouts, and whistles from the Washington DC area audience at this. He's still relevant!

This concert ended also with 'Like a Rolling Stone.' It was still a good experience, but it was not like the one eight years previous; he had moved into a safer place, I felt, and I was less taken.

You can't go home again.

Or, as an even greater writer put it, 'to live outside the law you must be honest'.

The innovative Capital centre, which opened in 1973, was a test bed for new technology including massive tv screens. It was demolished in 2002

I WAS THERE: KATHY GRALEY

I was a freshman in college at the time and received the tickets after sending in a money order and a self addressed envelope. One of my friends came down from NYC last minute because I didn't know I had gotten tickets until I returned to school from the Christmas break and checked the mailbox.

The concert was in January 1974 at the newly constructed Capital Centre in suburban DC which had the worst public transportation I've ever experienced.

We ended up taking a taxi out there, walking though ditches (I guess parking lots in progress). Needless to say, the show was spectacular. I remember looking through someone's binoculars and Dylan had a great tan. Nixon was still president at that time so the lyric 'but even the President of the United States sometimes has to stand naked' got a roar from the crowd especially in DC.

My all time favourite lyric is 'I'm going back to NYC, I do believe I've had enough' was especially significant for me then. I've seen Dylan a few more times over the years, and he's always brilliant with great musicians, so this particular show stands out because The Band was the backup band.

We got on the wrong bus after the show and ended up at the bus depot in Shirley, Virginia. Going from Maryland, passing the exit for DC and ending up in Virginia. Too funny, when we passed that exit. We were asking the driver, 'What state are we in?' We were so lost. The bus driver felt sorry for us and took us back to Wisconsin Ave in the Georgetown area of DC where he was going to meet his girlfriend. On his car radio was Marvin Gaye 'What's Going On?'. So now for all these years I have Marvin Gaye and Bob Dylan entwined in my memory.

Dylan's fourteenth studio album, *Planet Waves*, was released on January 17, 1974, by Asylum Records in the US and Island Records in the UK. The album was a hit, enjoying a brief stay at No 1 on the US *Billboard* charts (a first for Dylan) and No 7 in the UK.

The album was originally set to be titled *Ceremonies of the Horsemen*, a reference to the song 'Love Minus Zero/No Limit', from the 1965 album *Bringing It All Back Home*, (another, earlier working title was Wedding Song). *Planet Waves* release was delayed two weeks when Dylan decided to change the title at the last minute.

HOLLYWOOD SPORATORIUM

19 JANUARY, 1974, PEMBROKE PINES, CALIFORNIA

I WAS THERE: DEBORAH WILLIAMS, AGE 23

Deborah Williams was addicted to 'Lay Lady Lay'

I became a fan of Dylan in 1965 when 'Mr. Tambourine Man' came out, but when he released 'Lay Lady Lay' I found a new favourite song. I do believe I was addicted to that song and I still listen to it now all the time.

I remember how excited I was because it was my birthday present to myself. My 24th birthday was the following week. I flew for the first time by myself (and was scared to death) to go and see Bob Dylan and The Band in Pembroke Pines. Of course Dylan was not very talkative but when he played 'Lay Lady Lay' it didn't matter to me. I remember walking into the auditorium and it was dark except for the stage. When Dylan walked out and hit that harmonica everyone went crazy.

I'm a 68-year old hippie at heart and it was the greatest concert of my hippie days and still is. It was one of the best concerts I have ever been to and I have been to plenty, starting with Elvis Presley in 1956 at Pontchartrain Beach in New Orleans. Dylan and The Band could never be beaten.

MID-SOUTH COLISEUM

23 JANUARY, 1974, MEMPHIS, TENNESSEE

I WAS THERE: BRAD WARTHEN

Brad Warren was surprised to hear that it wasn't Matt Dillon from Gunsmoke singing Mr. Tambourine Man

Here's how I first heard of Dylan: My family had been living in Ecuador for two and a half years and I had been starved for American pop culture – I soaked it up like a sponge that spring and summer of 1965 when we returned, and loved all of it. I had a lot of catching up to do. One night, The Byrds were on TV doing 'Mr. Tambourine Man' and my uncle (only six years older than me) explained to me that that was cover of a Bob Dylan song. Except I thought he was saying Bob DILLON, since I knew about Matt Dillon on *Gunsmoke* but had never heard of Dylan Thomas.

My uncle, being a wise old man of 17, told me that this Dillon guy was a great songwriter but not such a good singer, so other people who sang better had hits with his songs. And for a while, that's about all I knew about him.

I was 20-years-old and a student at Memphis State University (now called University of Memphis). The tour took on a standard formula: an opening six-song Dylan/Band set, a five-song Band set, three more Dylan/Band performances, a five-song Dylan acoustic set, a three to four-song Band set, and a joint finale.

I was there to see The Band as much as Dylan, if not more, but this show got me much more into him than I had been.

I hadn't really been into Dylan at all for very long, maybe about a year. I had the *Greatest Hits* album and a companion book of guitar chords that I had been teaching myself to play. I had been a fan of The Band longer. I started listening to them my senior year of high school. I got interested in them about the time they were on the cover of *Time*, to which I subscribed, that was the issue of January 12, 1970. I think the first album I bought was *Stage Fright*, followed by the brown album. I was a big fan right away.

But visually, the part of the show I remember best was that solo acoustic set Dylan did, it was in a blue light with the harmonica and all, and I remember having a sense of unreality because it looks so much like the cover of the greatest hits album. I had to tell myself, 'No, this is real; that's actually Dylan a few yards away.'

While I'd only been a Dylan fan for a year or so, I'd been aware of him since 1965, but way back then (I was 11), I thought of him as someone for older people.

I shot this photo at the Mid-South Coliseum in Memphis, Tennessee on the night of January 23, 1974. The show was everything a fan could wish for – lots of Band material, plenty of Dylan. Dylan even did an acoustic set with guitar and harmonica, in a sort of bluish spotlight, and I remember having this weird disconnect looking at him: He looked so much like the cover of the greatest hits album that I couldn't quite convince myself that this was real, and I was here. It was odd.

MADISON SQUARE GARDEN

31 JANUARY, 1974, NEW YORK CITY, NEW YORK

I WAS THERE: CHRIS CHARLESWORTH

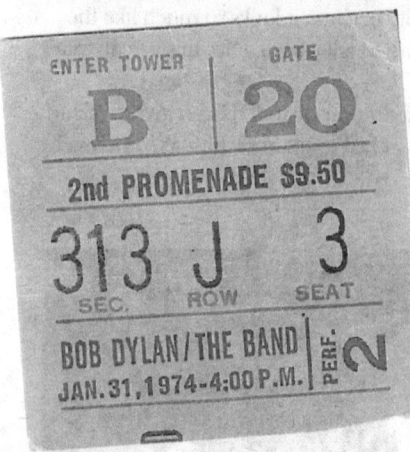

They cheered and clapped and waved for 15 minutes even though the house lights were up and 'Greensleeves' was playing through the PA system and Bob Dylan had already played a couple of numbers for encores. Bill Graham, at the rear of the stage, looked perplexed and wondered when in hell the 20,000 Madison Square Garden crowd was ever going to leave. Then Dylan returned, on his own and looking slightly sheepish. He'd discarded his black suit and was wearing a blue sweater with a white Maple Leaf on the front which indicated that the wearer was a supporter of a Canadian football team.

The cheering reached greater heights as Dylan walked to the microphone and looked as if he wanted to say something. Then he changed his mind and walked across the stage, smiling and holding his arms aloft like a prizefighter who's just knocked out Cassius Clay. Then he went back up to the mike and said somewhat briskly, 'Thank You. See you next year.' Then everyone knew it was over.

Bob Dylan's return to New York will doubtless be the highlight of his current 21-city tour of America. He played four concerts at the Garden, selling out each one. It would have been fitting, I think, if the tour had closed in New York but instead it closes at the Los Angeles Forum on February 14.

I attended the Thursday afternoon concert and was lucky enough to witness the first time that Dylan had actually walked back on to the stage after the encore to thank the audience. My luck, however, extended even further than that; I was sitting in the front row of the 20,000 seat stadium within 10 feet of Bob Dylan. A friend – an Irishman had obtained four tickets on the front row by mail order. The luck of the Irish is not just a proverb.

It was section A, row 1, seat eight which is slightly to right of the centre of the stage which also happens to be where Bob Dylan stands during the performance and at the close of the show I was pressed hard up against the stage in the throng who joined Dylan in the chorus to 'Blowin' in the Wind'. I was also asked by a member of the road crew to stop taking photographs: the practice was annoying the performer.

Dylan ignored the huge ovation that greeted his arrival on the stage. Dressed in a black jacket and waistcoat, black suede trousers, check shirt with brown boots, he strapped on a sunburst Fender Stratocaster and went straight into his opening song 'You Go Your Way And I'll Go Mine' which had been the regular opener on the tour.

The audience were still cheering his actual presence as the first chords were heard. To his right was Robbie Robertson, looking younger without his beard and glasses, dressed also in a black suit and picking on a red Strat. To his right was Rick Danko in check jacket and white trousers plucking on a fretless bass. Richard Manuel's grand piano was even further right, next to a battered old couch and at the rear of it all was Garth Hudson's swirling organ and Levon Helm at a drum kit small by today's rock excess standards.

Other furniture littered the stage: there was a hat stand to Dylan's left and a fake unlit lamp hanging to his rear. All the action took place on a red carpet over which a couple of roadies made hesitant sorties to straighten mikes, adjust controls and provide different instruments when required.

Dylan's next song was 'Lay Lady Lay', a different version from that on *Nashville Skyline*. Gone was the country flavour and in its place a jerky, almost rhythm and blues tempo over which the singer stretched out the syllables in all their sensuality. Dylan was stabbing at chords, playing an unheard rhythm guitar, which appeared slightly hesitant, but his voice was perfect.

'Rainy Day Woman #12 And 35' was greeted with a standing ovation and Dylan allowed himself his first smile of the evening as the crowd responded to the chorus each time it came around. Then it was 'It Ain't Me Babe', the second different arrangement he played.

Before the song Dylan, Robertson, and Danko huddled together around Helm's kit for a quick conference. The variation of the opening chords was such that the audience didn't recognise the song until the opening line; this time it was a simple rock beat instead of the folksy version on record.

'Ballad of a Thin Man', with Dylan at the piano, followed, before he left the stage for The Band to play four numbers without him. Up to this point no-one from the stage had spoken to the audience. They played 'Stagefright' which seemed particularly apt in the circumstances, and Danko's vocals were clear enough for all to understand the implications of the song. Next it was 'The Night They Drove Old Dixie Down' with a tremendous flow on the chorus line, 'King Harvest' and the jaunty 'Up On Cripple Creek' which seemed to satisfy a voice to my rear that had been requesting this song for 20 minutes.

The Band was on top form, and while it was obvious that it was Dylan's show, Robbie Robertson came close to stealing the limelight. His guitar runs were a joy, effortlessly played and perfectly executed time and time again.

Dylan returned for 'All Along The Watchtower', playing electric guitar again, then 'The Ballad of Hollis Brown' taken at an easy volume so the lyrics (he remembered them all) were heard before the first half closed with 'Knockin' on Heaven's Door'.

'Back in ten minutes,' said Dylan as he and The Band unstrapped their guitars and prepared to move off. It was the first time he'd spoken to the crowd.

The opening of the second half was probably the crux of the whole show; Dylan alone with acoustic Martin and harmonica strapped around his neck. He re-appeared to another standing ovation, had a quick word with one of the road crew, sipped from a paper cup and went straight into 'The Times They Are a-Changin''. It was after this song that the roadie came down to ask me to stop taking pictures.

Without hesitation Dylan went quickly through his acoustic set, playing next 'It Ain't Me Babe', then 'Don't Think Twice', 'Gates of Eden', 'Just Like a Woman' and ending on 'It's All Right Ma (I'm Only Bleeding)' which – in the light of Richard Nixon's fall –

contains the unusually appropriate words 'but even the President of the United States must have to stand naked'. At every concert on the tour this line brought a standing ovation. The Garden was no exception and Dylan, predicting the reaction, grinned ruefully.

This last song, in fact, was undoubtedly the highlight of this segment of the show, taken at a frantic pace and demonstrating what a powerful performer Dylan can be and it struck me then and there that in an era where singer songwriters seems to emerge almost daily, Dylan was the first, setting the pattern for them all and that on this tour he demonstrates an incredible superiority over the rank and file in both material and delivery. Any sceptics who predicted Dylan's era was over were mistaken; here in the Seventies, eight years after many of these songs were written, Dylan is still as important as ever in setting standards which others must look towards.

The acoustic set completed to another standing ovation, Dylan raised his arms in the now typical gesture of the winning sportsman, one arm holding the Martin and the other with a clenched fist that reflected strength now blended with maturity.

The Band re-appeared for four more songs – 'Rag Mama Rag' (superb), 'This Wheels On Fire', 'The Shape I'm In' and 'The Weight' all of which were played with clinical perfection.

Dylan re-appeared with electric guitar to play the only new song of the evening, 'Forever Young', with its opening line that sounds rather like the blessing at the end of a church service. Then it was all down to rock 'n' roll and 'Highway 61', another taken at a furious pace.

'Like a Rolling Stone' closed the act proper and by now Dylan was beaming with delight. The house lights were raised, an invitation for all to rush to the front and I was caught up in the melee of delighted faces who swayed with the music and joined the singer on his choruses. A girl behind me was screaming for her idol, a youth to my right lit a roll-your-own and tried to offer it to Dylan and a man to my left produced a box of photographs of Dylan and tried to show him them.

But Dylan remained calm and sang on, glancing up occasionally at the swaying arms, then down again to concentrate on the chords he was playing. Occasionally he allowed himself a grin, and even visibly laughed at us all during one break. By the end of the song his face was beaming and as he left the stage, his arms were again raised like a footballer who's scored in the last minute of an important match.

Five minutes later he re-appeared and sang 'Maggie's Farm' closely followed by 'Blowin' in the Wind', another song which invited full audience participation. He re-appeared with mirror sunglasses and from where I was standing the reflection of the audience could clearly be seen in his eyes. It was the reflection of gratitude for the music Bob Dylan has shared with the world, of gratitude for his decision to re-appear from seclusion and of gratitude to an artist who had just put on the best concert New York is likely to get this year or next.

'Thanks. Me and The Band enjoyed it,' he said before leaving. Fifteen minutes later we were still there and he came back to thank us again. See him next year? I damn well hope so.

I WAS THERE: MIKE BODAYLE, AGE 18

Mike Bodayle gets some light refreshment before seeing Dylan at Madison Square Garden

In 1974, I was an 18-year-old college freshman who still lived at home with his parents in New Jersey. Fortunately, a challenging high school made college easy for me, and most of my college memories are about partying with friends, listening to music and going to concerts. Several evenings a week, I worked at a part time job of delivering liquor which was quite helpful in providing both money for my music habit and a discount on beer.

As my high school days were coming to a close, I abandoned the Top 40 hits of AM radio and moved over to the free format of

FM radio. New York City's WNEW-FM 102.7 was my sole spot on the dial. Listening on the car radio during my daily commute to and from college was sandwiched by early morning and late evening listening in my bedroom. Legendary disk jockeys like Dave Hermann, Pete Fornutale, Scott Muni and Alison Steele were my surrogate college professors during these formative years of my musical education. It was through their hand-crafted playlists that I would become introduced to the music of Bob Dylan.

My musical development was quick, and I soon learned there was much more than just Top 40, The Beatles and The Monkees. Neither of these paths had lead me to much Dylan. His singles were seldom heard on WABC-AM with 'I Want You' conspicuously absent and 'Like a Rolling Stone' just too damn long to get much airplay. There eventually came a time when I learned of Dylan through the songs covered by Peter, Paul and Mary ('Blowin' in the Wind') and The Byrds ('Mr. Tambourine Man'). However, I sadly had heard very little sung by the actual 'protest singer' himself.

But, my schooling through my FM radio slowly brought me up to speed as I started to hear Dylan's classic songs performed by their author. My Dylan history lesson was further advanced through my fondness for the country rock and folk genres and my love for two of Bob's best interpreter's, The Byrds and The Band.

Around this time, I also started going to live concerts. This was a time when music news travelled at a snail's pace. I was still a neophyte and relied mostly on monthly or bi-weekly music publications to get information, which was often too late. I do remember an old girlfriend telling me that someone told her Dylan and The Band would soon be touring. Eventually, a full-page ad in the Sunday *New York Times* announced the 1974 New York shows at Madison Square Garden.

For some reason, I just wasn't up for the call. It was a given that this would be a tough ticket to come by. The nationwide use of a mail order-only lottery process created an even greater challenge. Fortunately, a college friend scored a pair and offered me one. It was a well-spent $9.50 on what would be the 30th concert I would attend.

Dylan's 1974 tour ended a self-imposed, eight-year absence from the road. This much-heralded return was even more special because he chose to bring along his best-known backing band. Formerly known as The Hawks, his supporting players had since become stars in their own right as The Band.

Midway through the tour, were three sold-out shows over two days at New York City's famous Midtown arena, which seated 19,500. My chance was the late afternoon matinee show on the second day. A thing of the past, many major acts were given this cost-effective method of squeezing in another show. Most fans either had to miss a class or two like me, or cut out work early to make the early 4:00 show time.

Just two weeks prior to this show, Dylan released his *Planet Waves* record on David Geffen's Asylum Records. This wound up being only a one album diversion from Columbia Records since Bob would return to the famous red label a year to the day later with *Blood on the Tracks*. Although the new record was recorded with his tour mates, this night's set list included only one of its songs, my favourite, 'Forever Young.' (Not much of a musician myself, I recently stretched and sang this song to my sons at my sixtieth birthday bash.)

Overall the set list was fabulous and I got to hear most of the songs I wanted to hear. I also got to discover some old songs that were new to me such as 'Ballad of Thin Man' which Bob rocked on the piano, and the odd choice of 'Most Likely You Go Your Way and I'll Go Mine' as the show's opener. This song also closed the main set most nights, but for some reason was left out of this show.

Looking back at this first time I saw Dylan, it was by far the best show of his that I have ever seen. A simple listen through his live records attests to the fact that in 1974, his voice was still strong and melodic – perhaps at its peak. Likewise, The Band has always served Bob best, and being a big fan of their music their two brief segments within the show were a huge bonus for me.

Outside of the intensity and brilliance of the performance, I have two memories from this show. First, is the surprise of seeing Dylan do the arena rock encore thing by playing his biggest hit, 'Blowin' in the Wind,' while the lighted disco mirror ball spun. The other is when the continued applause brought him back to the stage: he was wearing a Toronto Maple Leafs' hockey jersey and uttered his only words of the night, 'See you next year!' His long absence from the stage surely had everyone doubting his words. Who would have thought back then that he would eventually travel incessantly on what has been called the 'Never-Ending Tour?'

The 1974 tour was perfectly documented later that June on the live release *Before the Flood*. This parting shot to Asylum Records is in my book as one of the greatest live albums of all time.

This show was pivotal in my becoming a die-hard Dylan fan. *Planet Waves* was my first Dylan LP purchase, and I slowly backtracked on the older catalog. A year later, I would become totally mesmerised by *Blood on the Tracks*, which remains my all-time favourite record of his.

Since then, I bought each new record as it came out, and I devote substantial shelf space to the archival *Bootleg Series*. I try to catch every tour when he comes through Nashville where I have lived since 1998. While Dylan's live shows today are an acquired taste and don't live up to the magic I witnessed in 1974, they are nonetheless enjoyable. And like someone once told me, 'It's like getting to be in the same room as Shakespeare.' That's an opportunity I refuse to miss.

CRISLER ARENA

2 FEBRUARY, 1974, ANN ARBOR, MICHIGAN

I WAS THERE: JOE HALL

I was working security for Universities Activities Centre (UAC) -Daystar. At first I was keeping aisles clear, helping way too high folks find their seats, etc. We had all been promised a good posting and that the uniformed security would take care of the heavy stuff. However, a bunch of us got reassigned to do outside door security just before the concert began, (the venues doors were notoriously easy to pop).

The crowd trying to get in free (tickets were a whopping $7-$15) was about five deep and my partner and I spent a merry half hour yanking back glass doors that had been popped open. At some point Gary, my partner, was reaching out to pull a door shut when somebody clubbed him with a beer bottle crushing his cheek. As the medics were carrying him off, and the crowd poured in I decided that this was way above my pay grade. I went into the arena, sat on a step in the upper section and listened to the concert. The music was good, despite the shine having been taken off of it.

ASSEMBLY HALL

3 FEBRUARY, 1974, BLOOMINGTON, INDIANA

I WAS THERE: GARRY VALENTINE

I went to see Bob Dylan with my then-wife Nancy on February 3, 1974, at Indiana University's Assembly Hall in Bloomington, Indiana. Our seats were near the back of the hall, directly in the centre, viewing the stage.

A drawing Garry Valentine made after seeing Dylan in Bloomington

Dylan came out to thunderous applause, and when the noise died down he said, 'Thank you. It's nice to be here. It's nice to be anywhere.' The Band was his backup band. They played for about 45 minutes or so, and then Dylan sat on a stool in the middle of stage, just him and his guitar and harmonica, and played another 40 minutes or so. These times are all guess-work, as we were under the influence at the time. But the set with just him and his guitar I remember to be the best part of the show. The band came back out to finish the night. I remember when he sang, 'but even the President of the United States must sometimes stand naked' the crowd went wild. Mr. Nixon was not popular on campus in those days of Watergate.

Bob Dylan on stage at the Assembly Hall, Bloomington 1974

I WAS THERE: JOHN SPRADLIN

I saw Dylan in concert in 1974 at Indiana University. He was touring with The Band. I was a grad student up at Purdue at the time. I grew up with Dylan's music through the Sixties. Anti-war, civil rights and hypocrisy in general and to see the craziness in most things and not take life too seriously. Very formative stuff. By 1974 I'd been to lots of concerts, at college, at the Fillmore East, Central Park, etc. But never imagined I'd get to see Dylan live. I'd stopped following his career when he went into seclusion. At the time I was surprised he was touring with The Band. I was unaware of their relationship. The concert was amazing. I think he was just exiting seclusion at that point. I remember commenting (loudly) to the guys I was with, 'I wonder what it feels like to know that everywhere you do a show you're just knocking people out?'

ST LOUIS ARENA

4 FEBRUARY, 1974, ST LOUIS, MISSOURI

I WAS THERE: ED HERNANDEZ

The Band opened the show, Dylan came on about 40 minutes later and they never missed a beat. Leon Russell came on stage at the end – he never played I think, as he was a little bit too loaded. Bottom line, it made my top 15 concerts that I've seen and I've seen some heavies. I still have goosebumps.

DENVER COLISEUM

6 FEBRUARY, 1974, DENVER, COLORADO

I WAS THERE: NANCY ROGERS, AGE 16

Must have been 1974 – I was 16 and had bought tickets with my boyfriend at the time, but we broke up before the show. There was no way was I missing Bob and The Band at the Denver Coliseum! I will never forget listening to and singing along to 'how does it feel...to be on your own...Like a Rolling Stone...'

CENTER COLISEUM

9 FEBRUARY, 1974, SEATTLE, WASHINGTON

I WAS THERE: BILL WHITE

There were few things I looked forward to as much as the Arts and Entertainment section of the *Seattle Times*. There was always news of something to look forward to, but a very special surprise greeted me in a quarter page ad on December 2, 1973. Bob Dylan and the Band were coming to the Coliseum. I was never one to patronise the big shows at the Coliseum, and had been there only once before, to see Donovan in 1967, but I'd have gone anywhere to see Bob Dylan, who I had seen in 1966 at a much smaller venue. It had been eight years, and I had given up on the hope of ever seeing him again live, although I faithfully devoured every bootleg and legitimate album that I could get my hands on, and has been particularly enthusiastic about the recent release of *Planet Waves*.

Getting the tickets was another matter. Things had changed since 1966, when I showed up at the box office half an hour before showtime and got a fairly good seat for three dollars. This time around tickets were eight dollars, and were to be sold by lottery. You had to send in your money and hope you were lucky enough to receive a ticket. I sweated it out for a while until a letter came informing me that I had been selected to receive a ticket, and that it would arrive in the mail presently. But the ticket never came. The day before the show, I went to the box office at the Bon Marche and frantically told my story. After some tense moments of delay they gave me a ticket to the matinee show.

Bill White would go anywhere to see Bob Dylan

I had a good seat, near the stage up about 20 rows from the floor on the left side of the arena. I sat there trembling with anticipation until the lights went down, and Dylan and The Band tore into the loudest, fastest, and meanest version of 'Most Likely You'll Go Your Way and I'll Go Mine' imaginable. After six songs, he left the stage and The Band played five songs alone. Although I was a big fan of The Band, I wasn't interested in hearing their solo sets, not with Dylan in the house. I just waited impatiently for his return. His rendition of 'Knockin' on Heaven's Door', with an added verse, brought me to tears, as the memory of the death scene it accompanied in *Pat Garrett and Billy the Kid* was still fresh in my mind.

Dylan's acoustic set was fabulous. His voice was just as big as it had been with the electric backing, and I was absolutely mesmerised from start to finish. The songs blasted out like the proclamations of an Old Testament prophet, and chilled me to the bone. The Seventies were an era during which many of us younger people looked to popular culture for an understanding of the confused world we lived in. Others were just there for a good time, and the clash of sensibilities came to the fore during 'Like a Rolling Stone', when Dylan put the crowd to the question of how it felt to be a desolate, alienated, homeless non-entity and the crowd responded that it felt really good, as they lit their matches and roared with delight. Here was the prophet castigating them and they responded with warm cheers. It was disconcerting, to say the least. But that is the paradox of fame. So many people are so enamoured of the legend that they are deaf to the messenger.

FRIENDS OF CHILE BENEFIT

9 MAY, 1974, FELT FORUM, NEW YORK CITY, NEW YORK

I WAS THERE: CAROLE KLEIN

I've seen Dylan on a number of occasions; the most memorable was at the old New York Felt Forum back in the early Seventies. It was a fundraiser for something, I don't even think they called them fundraisers back then. He was singing solo with an acoustic guitar. I had cameras and he had taped a spiral bound sheet of paper to the microphone stand right near the microphone, with the lyrics to 'Blowin' in the Wind'.

I have the negatives from a few rolls of Tri-X I shot that day somewhere. I guess I should find them. You can clearly read the handwritten words on a few of the headshots. I don't remember much else about that event. I suppose if I dig out the photos it will reveal a lot more. But I do remember that he was not the headliner, but was on the bill.

Bob Dylan and The Band released the live double album *Before the Flood* on June 20, 1974. The seventeenth album by Dylan and the seventh by The Band, it documents their joint 1974 American tour and was the first live album that Dylan released.

Recordings were made at New York at Madison Square Garden, the Seattle Center Coliseum, the Alameda County Coliseum and the Los Angeles Forum in Inglewood, California.

Before the Flood peaked at No 3 on the *Billboard* chart in the US and No 8 in the UK.

A&R RECORDING

SEPTEMBER 1974, NEW YORK CITY, NEW YORK

I WAS THERE: ERIC WEISSBERG, MUSICIAN

I got the distinct feeling Bob wasn't concentrating, that he wasn't interested in perfect takes. He'd been drinking a lot of wine; he was a little sloppy. But he insisted on moving forward, getting onto the next song without correcting obvious mistakes. He couldn't have cared less about the sound of what we had just done. We were totally confused, because he was trying to teach us a new song with another one playing in the background. I was thinking to myself, 'Just remember, Eric, this guy's a genius. Maybe this is the way geniuses operate.' If it was anybody else I would have walked out. He put us at a real disadvantage. If it hadn't been that we liked the songs and it was Bob, it would have been a drag. His talent overcomes a lot of stuff.

I WAS THERE: GLENN BERGER, ENGINEER

Phil Ramone chose Eric Weissberg, banjo and guitar player extraordinaire, and his 'Deliverance Band,' a bunch of top session players. I set up for drums, bass, guitars, and keyboard. I placed Dylan's mics in the middle of the room. In the midst of the hubbub, Dylan skulked in. He grunted hello and retreated to the farthest corner of the control room, keeping his head down, ignoring us all. No one dared enter his private circle.

He called off a tune. 'Let's do 'If You See Her, Say Hello." He barely rehearsed the song when he told us to record. The players were just beginning to figure out the changes and what to play. On the third try, he threw everyone off by playing a different song. The musicians stumbled. Barely having recovered from the shock, after a run-through or two of the new song, Dylan changed songs midstream, again, without letting anyone know. One by one, the musicians were told to stop playing. This hurt. You could see it in the musicians' eyes as they sat silently behind their instruments, forced not to play by the mercurial whim of the guy painting his masterpiece with finger-paints. We cut an entire album's worth of material like that in six hours.

1975

Blood on the Tracks became the fifteenth studio album by Bob Dylan, released on January 20, 1975, by Columbia Records. The album marked Dylan's return to Columbia after a two-album stint with Asylum Records.

A version of the album that was recorded in New York City was finished and even pressed as a test acetate before Dylan grew displeased with it at the last minute. He decided to postpone the release by a month so he could re-record half the songs.

The album reached No 1 on the *Billboard* 200 charts and No 4 on the UK Albums Chart.

WITH EACH NEW ALBUM, IT WAS A DIFFERENT DYLAN. AND THE QUESTION WAS ALWAYS POSED: WHICH IS THE REAL ONE? BUT OF COURSE THEY ALL WERE REAL. THEY WERE FILLED WITH THE TRUTH. BUT WHO WAS THE MAN WHO MADE THEM?

WE STUDIED HIS ENIGMATIC PHOTOGRAPHS, BUT THERE WERE NO CLUES IN THAT BRITTLE STARE. IN HIS INTERVIEWS, HE PUT US ON. IN HIS FILM, HE PUT US DOWN. HE WAS KING OF BAD BOYS, AND HE WAS ALWAYS IN IMPERIAL SECLUSION.

EVERY SO OFTEN HE'D COME OUT OF THE SHADOWS IN SOME BOLD NEW INCARNATION: WOODY G. DYLAN, COWBOY BOB, WOODSTOCK BOB, THE LEGEND-KILLER, THE LEGEND, AND THEN HE'D DISAPPEAR AGAIN.

NOW, SUDDENLY, HERE'S THIS STARTLINGLY *EXPOSED* FIGURE STANDING IN THE SUNLIGHT. COULD THIS BE "THE REAL BOB DYLAN"? WE STILL CAN'T KNOW.

BUT WE DO KNOW THERE'S SOMETHING PROFOUNDLY DIFFERENT ABOUT THIS ALBUM.

WE DON'T KNOW WHAT CHANGE HAS COME ABOUT IN DYLAN'S LIFE. MAYBE EVEN HE DOESN'T. IN ANY CASE, HE ISN'T SAYING.

BUT THERE'S EVIDENCE. AND YOU CAN JUDGE FOR YOURSELF.

BOB DYLAN BLOOD ON THE TRACKS

ON COLUMBIA RECORDS AND TAPES

Dylan's sixteenth studio album *The Basement Tapes* was released on June 26, 1975, by Columbia Records. The songs featuring Dylan's vocals were recorded in 1967, eight years before the album's release, at Big Pink and other houses in and around Woodstock, New York, where Dylan and The Band lived.

After Dylan was injured in a motorcycle accident in July 1966, while Dylan was out of the public's eye during an extended period of recovery in 1967, he and the members of The Hawks recorded more than 100 tracks together, incorporating original compositions, contemporary covers, and traditional material.

I WAS THERE: ROBBIE ROBERTSON, MUSICIAN

We had moved up to Woodstock because in New York City we couldn't find a place where we could work on our music without it being too expensive or bothering people. So we went up there and found this ugly Pink house out in West Saugerties, on the outskirts of Woodstock.

I have a friend who knows all about acoustics, recording and microphones and I asked him to go and take a look in the basement where we were going to set up - we just know this is going to work. At this time, no one else was doing this. If you were going to make a record, you would go to a place that made records. So he comes back to me after looking and said, 'This is a disaster, this is the worst situation. You have a cement floor, you have cinderblock walls, and you have a big metal furnace. These are all things that you can't have if you're trying to record something. It won't work, you'll listen to it and you'll be depressed. Your music will sound so bad, that you'll never want to record again.' So I said, 'What if we put down a rug?' And he said, 'A rug! You need everything down here.' So I thought, well this is depressing, we'd already rented the place, so I was thinking should we set up in the living room? What should we do here? Then I thought well, to hell with it, we don't have a choice, we don't have the flexibility, so we did put a rug down, we had some microphones and a small tape machine so we set up and started writing and working on our new record.

Then Bob Dylan comes out and sees all this and says, 'This is fantastic! Why don't we do some stuff together? I need to make up some songs for the publishing company for other people to record.' Bob had been taking care of us all this time, we owe him to do something – the idea was we were going to do another tour but he broke his neck in a motorcycle thing and we couldn't do that, so we're still on the payroll and its like going on and on and on, so it was a way to something, a gesture back. So I said yes, we'll do these things and we'll work on our stuff, but he keeps coming out all the time. And we love it, we're laying down these things on tape and in their own way they're like field recordings – they sound fantastic in their own way.

There is something about bringing the recording experience to you in your own comfort zone as opposed to going into some studio with the huge clock on the wall and the guys in the union there saying hey, its about dinner break – you make your own atmosphere, there's something very creative about this. So we did all the stuff with the Bob, we do all kinds of stuff ourselves, and we think well no ones ever going to hear this and it becomes the first huge bootleg, rock 'n' roll record ever. And it was like, that wasn't the idea, it was only for the publishing company and artists that might want to record that particular song. Anyway, it became a whole other phenomenon.

I WAS THERE: GARTH HUDSON, MUSICIAN

Richard did the cooking, I did the vacuuming, and Rick did the outside work. We'd be around doing what ever we did and then Bob would come over and sit around and talk about serious stuff, like the local characters, local wise men and pretty ladies, and then he would go to the typewriter and tap on that for a while, and then someone would go downstairs and check the equipment in the basement and then finally everyone would go down the pink stairs.

Bob Dylan met Patti Smith for the first time when her group played at The Bitter End on June 26, 1975. Smith had yet to record an album, but she was attracting a lot of attention from the music press and industry. Dylan was out and about, looking for ideas and musicians and he would certainly have known about her.

THE BITTER END
26 JUNE, 1975, NEW YORK CITY, NEW YORK

I WAS THERE: PATTI SMITH, MUSICIAN

I first met Bob Dylan backstage at The Bitter End. We didn't have a drummer yet. It was just the four of us, we hadn't been signed yet.

Somebody told us he was there. My heart was pounding. I got instantly rebellious. I made a couple of references, a couple of oblique things to show I knew he was there. And then he came backstage, which was really quite gentlemanly of him. He came over to me and I kept moving around. We were like two pit-bulls circling. I was a snot-nose. I had a very high concentration of adrenaline. He said to me, 'Any poets around here?' And I said, 'I don't like poetry anymore. Poetry sucks!'

I really acted like a jerk. I thought: that guy will never talk to me again. And the day after there was this picture on the cover of the *Village Voice*. The photographer had Dylan put his arm around me. It was a really cool picture. It was a dream come true, but it reminded me of how I had acted like a jerk.

And then a few days later, I was walking down 4th Street by the Bottom Line and I saw him coming. He put his hand in his jacket – he was still wearing the same clothes he had on in the picture, which I liked - and he takes out the *Village Voice* picture and says, 'Who are these two people? You know who these people are?' Then he smiled at me and I knew it was all right.'

Recording sessions for what would be Dylan's seventeenth studio album *Desire* were held between July and October 1975.

COLUMBIA RECORDING STUDIOS

28 JULY, 1975, NEW YORK CITY, NEW YORK

I WAS THERE: EMMYLOU HARRIS, MUSICIAN

There was a fellow at Columbia that was a fan, who was like an executive producer, and I think Dylan told him 'I need a girl singer.' Don DeVito was his name. I got a call that Dylan wanted me to sing, but that wasn't true because he just wanted a girl singer. I mean, we basically shook hands and started recording. I didn't know the songs, the lyrics were in front of me, and the band would start playing and he would kind of poke me when he wanted me to jump in. Somehow I watched his mouth with one eye and the lyrics with the other. You couldn't fix anything. What happened in a moment was on the record.

I WAS THERE: SCARLET RIVERA, MUSICIAN

I had left my apartment in Lower East Side when some ugly green car comes up and cuts me off. The guy driving asked me if I really knew how to play the violin. Actually, he had this woman next to him ask me, who it turns out was his companion, percussionist Sheena Seidenberg. He asked her to ask me for my phone number, but I told her to tell him that I didn't give out my number to somebody stopping me on the street. Then Dylan said, 'Come downtown and rehearse with me'.

I have perfect pitch, and I know exactly how to follow keys even with nobody telling me where it's going. That's just something I know. I will say in the recording studio he gave me a couple of takes, but literally only a couple. At one point he said, 'Play under,' play more under him, meaning the lower end, and then at one point he was going to do his harmonica solo and I stopped and didn't play, and he actually said, 'No, go ahead and play with me.' And I was just stunned that he asked me to play with his harmonica, and, you know, just went into complimentary mode, and fortunately I didn't have too much time to think about it.

I've gone on to work with many different songwriters and artists over the years, and I feel I bring a piece of what I created on *Desire* and the Rolling Thunder Revue to each situation. It is the wellspring that I perpetually draw new inspiration from. While I work with musicians of all ages, it seems many young musicians have sought me out. For example, I was hired by a young rock group in Japan to be on their record and when I played live with them in Tokyo to thousands of their fans, we performed 'Hurricane' together! I felt Bob would be pleased to see me perform 'Hurricane' to a new young audience in Japan.

The Rolling Thunder Revue tour kicked off on October 30, 1975, in Massachusetts at the Plymouth War Memorial Auditorium. The tour included 57 concerts in two legs – the first in the American Northeast and Canada in the fall of 1975, and the second in the American South and Southwest in the spring of 1976.

With a travelling caravan of musicians, including Joan Baez, Roger McGuinn, and Ramblin' Jack Elliott, Bob Neuwirth assembled the backing musicians, including T-Bone Burnett, Mick Ronson, David Mansfield, Steven Soles, and from the *Desire* sessions, violinist Scarlet Rivera, bassist Rob Stoner, and drummer Howie Wyeth.

Dylan led the way in a red Cadillac convertible. His plan was to arrive unannounced in any town that had a stage available, have people give out fliers for a show that night, and entertain a bemused but excited audience for hours.

I WAS THERE: ROB STONER, MUSICIAN

Bob Dylan was very challenging to work with and the most talented and intelligent person I've ever met. He always kept me in suspense because you never knew what surprises he would pull.

He's very enigmatic, very mercurial, unpredictable, a dynamic personality. He has an amazingly quick mind, a great intellectual. He knows about everything, every subject. He's very moody. He's sometimes hard to work for, therefore.

I was the musical director during my years with him. He would communicate most of his musical decisions to the band through me. Dylan would make the basic decisions about material, keys and tempos and leave it to the musicians to come up with parts.

During rehearsals, sometimes he wouldn't show up for days at a time, so I would sing his parts for the run-throughs. I would conduct most of the rehearsals or sound checks and he would give final approval of what we did. Other times he was very hands-on about arrangements, so he really kept us on our toes.

He'll go through a lot of trouble to prepare a certain song and rehearse it. Once in a while, he'll work meticulously at an arrangement. And then he'll go onstage and sing it in a different key and at a totally different tempo than he worked on.

I think part of it is an act. It's to keep people guessing. It's sort of a put-on. That's why he calls himself 'Joker Man.' And I think part of it is genuine. His mind is working so fast, he's thinking about so much, he's going through the motions while he's thinking about something else.

I WAS THERE: DAVID MANSFIELD, MUSICIAN

I think at the time I was still in that band, Quacky Duck, which was in a limbo period because we were without a recording contract and trying to hang tough playing the college circuit. I got involved with the Rolling Thunder Revue through the infamous Bobby Neuwirth gig at the Bitter End.

My girlfriend at the time was working as a waitress at the Bottom Line and she heard about this almost free-for-all jam session for Bobby's gig over at the Bitter End. There were a lot of people sitting in. Some of them were well known, some of them weren't. But each night it was growing by leaps and bounds. She dragged me down there by my ear and said, 'They don't have a fiddle player. You should go and sit in with these guys.' She was the one that actually pushed her way backstage and said, 'My boyfriend is a really great violin player.' Neuwirth said something like 'Make me cry,' or something equally ridiculous and profound. Whatever it was, I just went right on stage with the next set and joined the fray.

Somebody was talking about Dylan hanging out with Neuwirth.

I didn't know what was going on. I don't think I was all that aware of it. It was enough for me being involved with Mick Ronson, Roger McGuinn and just the exotic nature of some of the other people he invited down like T-Bone Burnett from Texas, who was a young man at the time and looked like a drawling Big Bird with a Les Paul guitar.

It was only in hindsight that I knew all the pieces of the puzzle and realised those guys had been carousing all night and hanging out. I can only imagine how it came about. I don't know whether Dylan had the idea for doing something like this or whether it was a matter of hanging out with Bobby in their sort of drunken reveries after the gigs, or whatever. But the atmosphere at the Bitter End was such that it wouldn't take much to say, 'Hey, this would be great. Let's just take this out on the road and we'll make it like a revue and when we get tired we'll get somebody else to take over for us.' That was the original concept actually – that it would be a self-perpetuating thing and when Dylan, or whoever, got tired of it someone else of similar stature would take it on and keep it going.

There were rehearsals at Studio Instrumental Rentals (SIR) in New York. I don't remember how long they lasted. They could have lasted a week. Then there were more rehearsals up near where we started the first gig in Plymouth, Massachusetts. We were holed up in a hotel at the beginning of the cape? We rehearsed in a dress rehearsal kind of way so they could get the sound and lights up and stuff like that. The SIR rehearsals were a bunch of musicians plugged into small amps in a room playing songs. Nothing like a dress rehearsal for a show.

I WAS THERE: IAN HUNTER, MUSICIAN

What happened was, it was the strangest thing. We always used to hang out at the same bar as Tony Defries was hanging out and I was so fed up with going because it was all posing and the rest of it, I said why don't we go down this place, The Bitter End, Paul Colby's place in the Village and there was a restaurant and then you could walk down into a small club room with a stage.

So me and Mick Ronson are sitting there having a drink with the girls, when in walks Bob with Bobby Neuwirth, sits down, pulls a guitar out and proceeds to play the whole of his live album to Bobby

Neuwirth. There were only the four of us in the room. We're just sat there gaping.

About four hours later, the place is mobbed. I remember Mick was drunk and the owners had thrown him out three times. But the next night, Bob decided to take some people on the road and anyone who was there could have joined. Bob's very hippy how he does things. There's no manager comes up and officially says, 'You're in the band' or anything like that. It didn't work like that. People just walked in and started playing and Mick got up but I never did.

I wasn't living in the City, but Mick was. What happened next was Suzi Ronson started talking to Neuwirth and the next thing you know she's ringing me up the next Wednesday saying he was in the band, why don't you come down. I said, 'I can't come down, nobody's asked me to.' Mick said, 'It doesn't work like that, just come down.' But I just couldn't.

I WAS THERE: MICK RONSON, MUSICIAN

I didn't know any of the Dylan material, so I was kind of lost for a while. But it was great figuring it out. It was a circus and Dylan was funny, too, because he changes things right in the middle of playing. He'll change key or play the bridge a bit longer than it's supposed to be – I loved it when he did that. You've got to listen and you've got to watch, if you're going to survive as a sideman.

I WAS THERE: LARRY SLOMAN

Onstage it was like a carnival. Bobby Neuwirth and the back-up band warmed up the audience. Next, Dylan ambled on to do about five songs. After intermission, the curtain rose to an incredible sight, Bob and Joan Baez, together again after all these years.

After a few numbers, Baez took centre stage for a dynamic six-song set, followed by a solo set from Bob. Then he was joined by The Band for a few numbers, and the finale, Woody Guthrie's 'This Land Is Your Land,' featuring everyone on stage from Allen Ginsberg to Bob's mother Beatty, one night.

The spirit was so amazingly warm that when Joni Mitchell flew in to play one concert, she wound up staying for the remaining three nights of the tour. And it all came to a dramatic finale on December 8, in Madison Square Garden where, with the help of Muhammad Ali, Roberta Flack and 14,000 screaming partisans, Dylan performed a benefit concert for imprisoned boxer and Dylan's latest cause, Rubin Carter. That concert was known as The Night of The Hurricane.

I WAS THERE: RONEE BLAKLEY, MUSICIAN

I was set to tour with my band, and when Bob Dylan invited me to come on Rolling Thunder Revue, I turned him down and flew down to Alabama to rehearse with my band, to whom I had a commitment. But they said, 'No! Go! Tell him you can go! Go back and tell him!' So I went back to my motel and called New York information for the hotel, and sooner or later got the hotel, and Bob got on the line and he said, 'Come back!' So he sent a car for me and a ticket for me, and I went back. We recorded 'Hurricane' that night, and I had just met him 24 hours earlier, maybe 30 hours earlier, at The Other End in Greenwich Village!

In that time, I'd gone out, we'd all partied afterward, and then I went to the airport, got on the plane, went to Huntsville, went to Muscle Shoals, talked to the boys, went back to the hotel, went back to Huntsville, got back on the plane, went back to New York, a car picked me up and took me to the recording studio, and we recorded 'Hurricane' that night. And from there, I was on the road with Bob.

I WAS THERE: ROGER McGUINN, MUSICIAN

We had about 100 people on the road; it was an entourage. We toured in these busses. Back in the Byrds' days, we toured in these busses that had all of the seats in them. Frank Zappa figured out

ROGER McGUINN

Roger McGuinn enjoyed Frank Zappa's tour bus on the Rolling Thunder tour

that it would be much more comfortable if you take out all of the seats, and put in beds and couches and TVs and things. So, Bob rented Frank Zappa's bus; it was a bus called Phydeaux.

It's the greatest thing I've ever done in my life. It was a paramilitary commando team, going out and just taking on the country. Everybody was really tight and together. Nobody was making any errors. I mean, you'd break a guitar string and somebody would change it in 10 seconds. The lights were perfect, the sound was perfect. We covered everything.

COSTELLO GYMNASIUM

2 NOVEMBER, 1975, UNIVERSITY OF MASSACHUSETTS, LOWELL

I WAS THERE: PAUL MARION

The Rolling Thunder Revue was really something in Lowell, Massachusetts. Dylan, the singing poet troubadour, sang all night. Joan Baez and Bob played as two. Bob sang a song for Sara; Joan sang one for him: 'Diamonds and Rust,' for 'the original unwashed vagabond phenomenon.' Roger McGuinn played 'Chestnut Mare.' Joan Baez sang maybe 10 songs, each a wonderful choice: 'Please Come to Boston,' 'The Night They Drove Old Dixie Down,' 'Swing Low, Sweet Chariot,' 'I Dreamed I Saw Joe Hill.' Joan and Bob played 'Blowin in the Wind' – starting with the lights out behind a sheer curtain, and the audience went wild.

Dylan sang and played with enthusiasm and energy, looking like he loved every minute, bouncing around the stage and dancing and stamping his foot, his whole leg, in time to the beat. Bob played 'It Ain't Me Babe,' 'Hurricane,' 'Just Like a Woman,' 'I Shall Be Released'. He dedicated 'A Hard Rain's a-Gonna Fall' to Jack Kerouac. Ramblin' Jack Elliott had earlier dedicated 'Me and Bobby McGee' to Kerouac. Bobby Neuwirth played an 'on the road' song. Dylan played a batch of new songs, sounding like a Mexican balladeer on some. The show ended with the whole troupe, including poet Allen Ginsberg on tambourine, singing Woody Guthrie's 'This Land Is Your Land.'

It was a classic night of music. Dylan, in flower-plumed, broad-brimmed hat and yellow bell-bottom pants, wore white make-up with reddened cheeks, a kind of clown face. In his dark leather jacket he looked small and thin, but full of life. He played acoustic and electric guitar and harmonica. We were told that the concert was being recorded and filmed for a movie. The audience stood for 15 minutes, applauding and cheering, at the end of the show.

I WAS THERE: ANN-LOUISE HARRIS

I don't remember a lot of publicity for the Rolling Thunder Revue tour concert, just a small van with posters. My roommates and I all went, of course.

SPRINGFIELD CIVIC CENTER

6 NOVEMBER, 1975, MASSACHUSETTS

I WAS THERE: CHRIS CHARLESWORTH

Chris Charlesworth reviewed the Springfield show for Melody Maker

In an era when tickets for concerts by major rock stars go on sale anything up to nine months before the show, it beggars belief that on Thursday, November 6, 1975, two hours before it commenced, I bought two tickets at face value ($7.50) for a 5pm Bob Dylan show from the box office at the 10,000-seat Civic Center in Springfield, Massachusetts, and two tickets from a tout outside for an 8pm show for $10 each, opting to pay the extra $2.50 in order to get seats closer to the stage.

Dylan was leading his Rolling Thunder Review on the fifth stop on the tour, the dates of which weren't announced in advance and advertised only locally. One ticket at Springfield — which was actually the tour's biggest venue — was for myself, the other for my friend and photographer, Bob Gruen, who'd driven north with me for four hours from New York. Before both shows Bob stripped down to his briefs in our car and taped his camera equipment to himself, then dressed again in loose fitting dungarees and a sweater so the bulges wouldn't show. Photographers weren't allowed in, but this was never going to stop Bob, six of whose pictures accompanied my lengthy report on the shows, stretched across three pages of *Melody Maker* of November 15, 1975.

'You need more than a weatherman to know which way Bob Dylan blows,' was my opening line in a review that, sentence for sentence, was the longest show review I ever wrote for *MM*. The concerts were, after all, 'reviews' in the accepted sense of the term which meant everyone got a go, and the bill also featured Joan Baez, Roger McGuinn, Mick Ronson, Ramblin' Jack Elliott, Arlo Guthrie and others, all of whom played at least one song of their own alongside the band that accompanied Dylan who, naturally enough, grabbed the lion's share of stage time, both solo and in combinations with the others.

He was magnificent too, playing and singing not to make money or even to promote a new record, but simply because he wanted to. After the hullabaloo surrounding the previous year's tour with The Band, which was Big Corporate Rock, Dylan had opted for something completely different, a folksy down-home feel, almost like a hootenanny, and he was happy to chime along with everyone else though there was no doubt who was the star of the show. Some of the songs he sang would appear on *Desire*, not yet released, and I was spellbound by 'Sarah', his homage to his former wife. The shows ended with the ensemble gathered round several microphones for 'This Land Is Your Land', Woody Guthrie's alternative National Anthem, a fitting finale to an evening of music in which Dylan explored his roots, mused on his past and offered a glimpse into the future. Unquestionably two of the best shows I ever saw.

PATRICK GYM

8 NOVEMBER, 1975, BURLINGTON, VERMONT

I WAS THERE: DOUG COLLETTE

You know you have got a good friend when he knows you so well that he does on instinct what you would do yourself, under similar circumstances. I was lucky enough to have such a friend in the fall of 1975 when my former classmate saw a crowd gathered at the University of Vermont's Patrick Gym and inquiring accordingly, was told tickets were being sold for an upcoming Bob Dylan concert. Impulse buying ruled the day and to great effect in both short term and long.

The day in question was obviously past the point of only vague rumours circulating on what would come to be known as The Rolling Thunder Revue. But given that Dylan had only just toured for the first time in eight years since his reunion with The Band early in 1974 (and my buddy having been awestruck with that show at the Montreal Forum that January), buying a pair of tickets was as much of a no-brainer for him as it would've been for me.

The look of envy on the faces of those who I advised about having those tickets was almost worth the price of admission (which I forget at this point but reckon were in the $12-15 ranges as designated for Dylan/Band shows). The experience of the concert itself, in a sweltering gymnasium in early November, was absolutely priceless. Not that there weren't some down times during the course of the two hours, but those were certainly relative and hardly the fault of the other artists on the roster with Dylan.

Striking enough in white face and feathered hat, Bob became all the more so as the concert ensued, displaying a startling level of engagement in his performance whenever he was on stage. There had been a certain disconnect between Bob and his former accompanists when they got back together the previous year, so much so the most memorable segments of the show, as accurately documented on the live double album, *Before the Flood*, were those when the two were playing apart. But Dylan meshed with the Rolling Thunder band and they in turn aligned behind him, if a bit sloppily, winging it much of the way as their charismatic leader as always been wont to do, here though to unusually theatrical effect.

The audience and the performers seemed equally excited, all the more so because, in addition to new material like 'Isis' and 'One More Cup of Coffee (Valley Below)' (from the album *Desire* yet to be released in the first month of 1976), the setlist included songs that, only a decade or so prior, Bob Dylan had deemed obsolete. The socially relevant likes of 'The Lonesome Death of Hattie Carroll' rang true in the context of Rubin 'Hurricane' Carter's jailing (more on that later), while 'A Hard Rain's a-Gonna Fall' and 'Blowin' in the Wind' vividly evoked the author's days as conscience of the folk music protest movement.

Accordingly, while that particular aspect of the concert echoed in the familiar personage of Joan Baez, the presence of Byrds' founder Roger McGuinn reminded of the breadth of Dylan's influence on popular culture. Such figures got their due acclamation, but it was nothing compared to the electricity in the air when Dylan took the stage, commanding it with perhaps the most authority he ever had to this point in his career because there were no naysayers, as on the raucous tour that yielded The Real Royal Albert Hall Concert 1966 and no unwieldy expectations as in 1974.

Unusual for the time, the format of the show in two sets made practical sense, giving the performers, as well as the audience, a break, not just from the heat in the college venue, but a respite from the intensity of the show itself. Baez's appearance for a protracted segment was as comparable a nod to her roots as Dylan's and it also offered a fitting nod the folk tradition represented by Ramblin' Jack Elliott (and the homage to same and its author Woody Guthrie with the ensemble encore of 'This Land Is Your Land'). The fact the tour was turning into a campaign on behalf of the (seemingly) wrongly imprisoned boxer Carter, lent a weight of righteous social justice to the proceedings.

But there were even greater dynamics involved in this Rolling Thunder presentation, such as the quick interludes with figures such as the embodiment of a non-sequitur in the form of Bowie sideman/guitarist Mick Ronson or front man's comrade-in-arms Bob Neuwirth. The latter Greenwich Village contemporary of Dylan's and who may have been no more recognisable than violinist Scarlet Rivera, he was hardly the wraith-like enigma of this itinerant musician. Reportedly encountered by Dylan on the streets of New York, the violinist added as much exotic mystery to the proceedings with decidedly gypsy-styled accoutrements as the sound of her instrument on songs including 'Oh, Sister.'

Nothing seemed exactly rushed during the course of this extended performance, but there was nevertheless a sense of the troupe as a whole riding the crest of a wave of inspiration. On a more broad scale, that sensation furthered the idea of Rolling Thunder as an impromptu sequence of events, an extended immersion in the moment on behalf of all involved, including the audience; as the tour extended into the fall then early winter, the swift turnaround of show announcements, ticket sales, and appearances was expert execution of the practical aspect of this dynamic, proportionately applied.

The spontaneous tone set by Bob Dylan's own unselfconscious approach to performing - in contrast to his often stilted approach in 1974 and notwithstanding his film-making of *Renaldo & Clara* during the tour – was a rare commodity indeed. The massive administration of roadworks we know today wasn't yet common even though The Rolling Stones' Exile on Main Street tour three years prior inaugurated the concept and the Dylan/Band reunion in 1974 had furthered it.

And, as on so many fronts (with many such instances in his past and yet to come), here was Bob Dylan going against the grain of expectations to great effect, on what turned out to be history-making even before (and arguably to greater degree than) the appearance at Madison Square Garden on behalf Hurricane Carter later in the year. Often overlooked in the historical arc of Rolling Thunder is the evolution of the band down to the core personnel that appeared with Dylan for the *Hard Rain* television concert of September 1976, much of which was released on the eponymous album and constitutes to many one of the highlights of the man's live releases.

Yet it's the early days of the tour by The Rolling Thunder Revue, like this unheralded stop in the Green Mountains, that, even more so that the 1966 with The Hawks near 20 years before that, as represented on *The Bootleg Series Vol. 5*, posits the most indelibly memorable example of how deeply Bob Dylan enjoys performing his music live on stage.

I WAS THERE: JOEL THOMPSON

Best concert I ever saw, although tickets were $8.25, which was more than twice the cost of concert tickets back then. I saw Bruce Springsteen in Burlington in 1974 for $3.50.

I remember the Gym was sweltering hot that night. Dylan's singing and phrasing was incredible. He was on fire with the new songs from *Desire* and played great versions of his older stuff. It also happened to be the first time in concert that he played 'Simple Twist of Fate'.

I do remember some trouble outside, with fans throwing bottles at the doors of the Gym, maybe they didn't have tickets? I think there was an announcement that if they didn't leave the show would be cancelled.

CONVENTION CENTER

15 NOVEMBER, 1975, NIAGARA FALLS, NEW YORK

I WAS THERE: BILL ARNOLD

My first Dylan concert was the evening show of the Rolling Thunder Revue in Niagara Falls, New York on November 15, 1975. A specific moment that I remember was when someone yelled 'Dylan!' Bob said something like 'That's not me. He isn't here tonight.' At the time, no one was aware that he might be playing the Renaldo character. (This may have been two nights later in Rochester, New York, where I also went to the evening show.)

At Niagara Falls, we were in row 23. Apparently, no one had cleaned up after the afternoon show, where beer had been sold. Under a seat in the row in front of us when we went in was a large pool of puke. While we were watching, a girl came in, sat down, slid her purse under her seat into the vomit, then hooked her toes over the metal rung near the bottom of the seat, sticking her toes into the mess which had been pushed back slightly by the purse.

WORCESTER MEMORIAL AUDITORIUM

19 NOVEMBER, 1975, WORCESTER, MASSACHUSETTS

I WAS THERE: RAY UPPSTROM

I was kind of broke and hanging out with a young lady who I eventually married. He was playing at the Worcester Memorial Auditorium. Melissa and I walked up to the back entrance and I told the guard we were low on funds and did not have a ticket but really wanted to see the concert. He looked at us for a second and said, 'follow me'. He brought us right up front of the centre stage and we sat on the floor with several others! We could not believe it! The band came out and the first number they played was 'You Don't Need a Ticket to Ride This Train'. It was unbelievable! Still get a rush thinking of this all these years later!

I WAS THERE: DEAN HASS JR. AGE 24

I saw the Rolling Thunder Revue, November 19, 1975, at the Worcester Memorial Auditorium (MA), with an entourage of iconic artists. He did the last half solo, all his classics. Because JFK, Jr was in the front row, with Caroline Kennedy, he did a special version of his then-new song, 'Hurricane', with a plea to free Rubin Carter. It was an awesome show!

I was 24, married, and a fan since the Sixties. I saw him once before, a few years earlier in a concert in Boston. He didn't tour much back then, so anytime you got to see him was a big deal. At the Rolling Thunder Revue, it was an incredible, and ambitious tour – he was bringing some of his closest friends all over the country. The line up was kind of fluid, depending on their schedules. In Worcester, Joan Baez, Bob Neuwirth, and several others performed both solo and with him, in the first half of the show, which lasted around an hour and a half. The second set featured Bob doing an acoustic set of his greatest hits – many early classics, and it was heaven. After about a half hour of that, he brought out everyone, and played his (then) new stuff, like 'Hurricane', and much of the mid-Seventies material, like off *Desire*. All in all, one of the top concerts I've ever been to.

Dylan had a lot to say...he did a special intro to 'Hurricane', pleading for Rubin Carter's release from jail.

Actually, here is the lineup at this concert – it changed at different venues – Joan Baez, Roger McGuinn, and Ramblin' Jack Elliott. Bob Neuwirth assembled the backing musicians, including T-Bone Burnett, Mick Ronson, David Mansfield, Steven Soles, and from the *Desire* sessions, violinist Scarlet Rivera, bassist Rob Stoner, and drummer Howie Wyeth. Although Joni Mitchell had performed at a previous one in Plymouth, Massachusetts before this one, and was rumoured to perform this night, she had another commitment.

MUSIC HALL

21 NOVEMBER, 1975, BOSTON, MASSACHUSETTS

I WAS THERE: GORDY BOWMAN

Local reviews of the show mention 'washed up relics of the Sixties,' 'con-men,' and wonder if Dylan can move forward from what is felt to be too narrow a view in his newer songs. The reviewers have been falling all over themselves to have the final word on this magical mystery tour. This tour effectively ducked the press by barring cameras and recorders and not even announcing ticket-sales until thirty minutes before they were to go on sale. This low-profile approach caught most people off-guard, and tickets were available for only two days.

Critics, who had already written their last Dylan review, pulled out their old material and misfired, hitting the Dylan myth and missing the artistry of the actual performance. Because this was excellent music, executed in a remarkably tension-free atmosphere.

Only two tickets were sold to a customer and tickets were going for $50 on the street the night of the show. A downpour had ticket-holders heading to the Music Hall at a near gallop. Inside, a curtain proclaiming The Rolling Thunder Revue hung over the stage.

When it was finally hoisted, an unfamiliar and unlikely looking band took the stage. Guitarist Mick Ronson, an English rocker in the Jeff Beck mould, stood out among a collection of country rollers. Bob Neuwirth, a Dylanite from the Sixties, joined the basic band of Ronson, Steve Soles, T-Bone Burnett, Scarlet Rivera, Rob Stoner and a percussionist named Luther. Rivera's electric violin proved more than adequate at trading off with Ronson's leads. After one month of playing together, they had become a really tight band. A few members of the band performed songs of their own and while some folks couldn't resist the urge to scream 'we want Bobby,' the audience had time to sit back and relax.

Band-leader Neuwirth confidently promised 'a few surprises.' The evening's first surprise walk-on was Ronee Blakley of *Nashville* Fame. She sang a couple of original songs and accompanied herself on piano and then, as she was leaving the stage, a rumour materialised in the person of Joni Mitchell, who drifted out by herself. The audience blew its top. She had joined up with the tour on Thursday night and hadn't worked anything out with the band. After two numbers, she vacated the spotlight, ignoring the carnivorous roar calling for her return. She had set the assembled hundreds off on their first full-blown adrenalin-rush of the night.

Ramblin' Jack Elliott emerged dressed in cowboy chaps and crowned with a ten-gallon hat. The air was over-ripe with an air of anticipation. Roger McGuinn anonymously plucked out a little banjo accompaniment. Ramblin' Jack sagely added a humorous mood with a long talking-blues.

Dylan finally appeared at centre stage. He was wearing a brown and white pinto-patterned shirt, black vest and on his head sat the hat he had worn in *Pat Garrett and Billy the Kid*. As he began an energetic 'When I Paint My Masterpiece,' I was struck by his pronounced and peculiar pallor. Wait a minute! His face was painted white. Was that really Dylan? I remembered 'The Duke of Earl' recording from the *Masked Marauders* album. Who else could it be? Only one person could hammer out his phrases like that. Whatever was on that particular clown's mind, he wasn't clowning around. He was getting down.

He played a few oldies making them sound better than ever. A reggae-laced beat to 'It Ain't Me Babe' gave the tune a brand new shine. He began to talk to the audience.

'Sam Peckinpah,' he called out. 'Are you out there Sam? This is all I gotta say – Goooooood luck.' His voice dripped thick with cynicism. He responded to a cry for a protest song – 'This is a protest song.' Later he added, 'This song is a true story ... they're all true stories.' He remained sphinx-like with his white face as oceans of applause flooded the hall. 'This is an autobiographical song,' he said and with his harmonica between his hands he blew into 'It Takes A Lot to Laugh, It Takes a Train to Cry.' The hardest rock of the night, this eerie old song was transformed into a supersonic twister. The sheer power pushed the audience back in their seats. No one since Jimi Hendrix died, has wielded such onstage presence. Dylan leapt and blew and rocked and stomped and before the vandals even beheld the handles, there were no more jams left to kick.

During the intermission, I wondered about the incongruity of Dylan's appearance and performance. His hat looked like it had a bunch of plastic carrots or some sort of dinner table centrepiece hanging on the band. And the white paint on his face? Was it an allusion to the Al Jolson-minstrel show era? A bad skin condition? A case of mistaken identity? A protective layer? Halloween? The return of the ghost rider? The jester? An addition for Mt Rushmore? Prisoner in disguise? In any case, he was delivering the goods.

The audience was privileged to be on the receiving end of a tour which had been designed for maximum music and maximum mellowness instead of maximum money. The Revue had been conceived on a wine-drenched night in New York City, when Dylan began recruiting any and everyone he ran into. This impulsive desire to perform generated an almost amateur-night ambience at times. The sites were originally going to be intimate clubs; however it's obvious that small halls offered the golden mean between audience size and the quality of the music. Everyone in the theatre could hear and see and feel the performance. The stage was close enough so that a real sense of movement was obtained without circus elephants. It was obvious that the performers were really in the groove and this was the only half-way point.

When the lights dimmed, 'Blowin' in the Wind' could be heard. The curtain stayed in place, but no one had to be told this was Dylan and Joan Baez. And when the curtain began to rise, you could see these two old lovers leaning over a single mic. Joan sang with Bob in a way no one else can ever hope to equal. Their voices and styles, seemingly so disparate, flowed, lifted and ran together. Bob joined her for a few more numbers, including a memorable rendition of 'I Shall Be Released,' and then left Joan onstage.

She sang 'Diamonds and Rust,' a song she had written about Bob. 'Yes, I've loved you dearly and if you're offering me diamonds and rust, I've already paid.' She responded to a cry for the Boston University song with the comment, 'I was only at BU for about four days. All I learned was how to be Jewish if I had to.' Then she broke into a snide version of the old Sam Cooke tune: 'Don't know much about history, don't know much trigonometry ... .'

She sang 'Do Right Woman' without accompaniment and brought down the proverbial house with 'The Night They Drove Old Dixie Down.'

Roger McGuinn came out in a red velvet jacket with a bow-tie and sang 'Chestnut Mare,' which may or may not be alluded to on Dylan's scathing 'Idiot Wind.' Then in a truly well-timed move, the folksy atmosphere was blown out the tubes with a loose-as-a-goose playing of 'Eight Miles High.'

Dylan reemerged and it was clear that while he hadn't exactly removed his coat of white paint, he had managed to at least smear most of it off, leaving only lines of war paint. 'Here's a good one for you,' he announced as request upon request bounced up from the crowd. Whereupon he performed 'Isis,' a yet-to-be-released, powerful, driving, haunting in a minor-key way, hard-rocker about the Egyptian goddess.

Dylan soloed on 'Tangled Up in Blue' and 'I Don't Believe You.' He kept running to get a drink, pawing about the stage like a big cat. He hunched down over the mic hesitantly, stalking the mic stand, looking like a moth zig-zagging towards a candle flame. His singular intensity was the cornerstone of the night. This was one of the few times a superstar would perform and an audience would be so sublimely satisfied.

He drove through 'Just Like a Woman,' 'Oh, Sister,' 'Knockin' on Heaven's Door,' and his new protest song – 'Hurricane.' At one point he paused, 'I want to dedicate this to my old friend Larry,' he said.'Larry? You still out there? Not you Larry ... the other Larry...you Larry.' Are you kidding?' No one had left. There was a river of communication flowing from the stage into the hall. An umbilical cord of rapport had been established. How would it be cut? How else? The entire cast and a few extras took the stage for a hootenanny version of Woody Guthrie's 'This Land Is Your Land,' a novel thought lately, but it sounded real.

That's it, Dylan made it real. There were no hassles for the

As a symbol of his gratitude Bob Dylan gifted each member from the Rolling Thunder Revue with a special necklace

audience, except for one poor dude who lost his smoke to a security guard. The assembled entourage provided an excellent framework to highlight the true superstar. The mixed-up kid, coffee-house refugee, motorpsycho punk, Dylan has grown into the consummate songwriter/performer of our times. This Zimmerman fellow, the devil-driven artist of Anthony Scaduto's 'Intimate Biography,' still has the drive and the power and now he's shown that he means to use it and not lose it. His super-ego is finally held to earth and his reborn creativity is a gift to us all.

Walking from the Music Hall into the morning rain, I couldn't help but feel that, yes, under that outrageous hat that he wore all night was a true Mad Hatter, his madness firmly checked by the other side of a thin line bordering true genius. Slightly humbled by the experience, the audience went away without the myth, but with the man. That's a concert.

Bob Dylan gifted each member from the Rolling Thunder Revue a special necklace at the end of the first leg of the tour as a symbol of his gratitude for being on tour. The chained necklace measures 1.5 inches in diameter and on one side is adorned with symbolic gemstones and an American eagle. The other side of the medallion is lettered 'Rolling Thunder Revue 1975,' amidst a symbolic design.

MAPLE LEAF GARDENS

2 DECEMBER, 1975, TORONTO, CANADA

I WAS THERE: COLIN BARLOW

I saw how engaged Bob was during the show. Watching him prowl around the stage like a tiger during 'Isis' (which was a new song, not yet released) is something I will never forget. It was very intense. And while he did work really well with the band, I found that they speeded through a lot of the songs very aggressively.

We had guest spots from both Joni Mitchell and Gordon Lightfoot making the entire show over four hours long. We all left the place totally exhausted but fully aware that we witnessed something truly special.

MADISON SQUARE GARDEN

8 DECEMBER, 1975, NEW YORK CITY, NEW YORK

I WAS THERE: SCARLET RIVERA, MUSICIAN

I got to meet Muhammad Ali afterwards and that was just incredible. But also what led up to that concert was we went into the prison, and did a prison concert at Rikers Island where Rubin Carter was, it was an amazing experience. It was a maximum-security prison and that preceded Madison Square Garden. So there was a huge amount of energy that went into that concert and a lot of rising of consciousness I think to champion for him to champion the injustice that happened to Rubin.

1976

Released on January 5, 1976, by Columbia Records between the two legs of Dylan's Rolling Thunder Revue tour, *Desire* became Dylan's seventeenth studio album and one of Dylan's most collaborative efforts. The album features the same caravan of musicians as the acclaimed Rolling Thunder Revue tours.

Most of the album was co-written by Jacques Levy, best known for 'Chestnut Mare', a collaboration with Roger McGuinn. The opening track 'Hurricane', tells a passionate account of the murder case against boxer Rubin Carter, whom the song asserts was framed. Carter was released from prison in 1985, after a judge overturned his conviction on appeal.

I WAS THERE: JACQUES LEVY

I wrote with Roger McGuinn from The Byrds before I worked with Bob, and I believe I first met Bob briefly in California when I was with McGuinn probably after a concert. I knew who he was of course, but he had no idea who I was. But it turned out later that he did know who I was because he'd gone to see a couple of things I'd directed.

The second time we met was complete serendipity. I walked out of my house and Bob walked passed me on his way somewhere. I said, 'Bob!' and he turned and looked at me and say, 'Hi' and we chatted and I asked him where he was going and it turned out he was going to a place that I often hung out – a little bar on Bleeker Street called The Other End. So we went and had a drink together and that's how the two of us connected.

After a couple of drinks Bob came back to my place and we wrote 'Isis'.

He had heard the lyrics I'd written for McGuinn for 'Chestnut Mare' and I think he liked the idea that I could tell a story. Bob is really not that good at telling stories, he doesn't go from A to B to C to E, so they don't usually end up as a story.

He asked me if I had any interest in Hurricane Carter and as it turned out I knew all about Hurricane's story and was well aware of what had been going on with him, so it made it very easy to write a song about him. Bob had read his book, was planning to go and see him and wanted to write a song about him. He thought he was an innocent man and I agreed with him.

First of all it got me a little nervous, and I said to him you know I write the lyrics, I don't write music. And he said, 'Yeah I know'. We were sat in my living room on the sofas and we talked a little more and decided to meet up the following day to start working on the song. I wasn't 100 per cent sure he would come over, I thought it might be one of those passing things and he wouldn't show.

But sure enough, he arrived the next day at the time arranged with his guitar and told me that during the summer he'd been to Europe and hung out with some gypsies where he'd written a couple of new songs and preceded to play them for me. One was 'One More Cup of Coffee' and he had part of the song 'Sara' written. I thought 'One More Cup of Coffee' was just fantastic! And I can only recommend to you that someday if you're very lucky you'll be three feet away from him when he plays it! It's quite an extraordinary experience. And then we got to work.

He didn't have a tune for anything and I didn't have any words, there was nothing prepared. He would play a couple of chords and I might come up with a couple of words or a phrase or what ever, and we just kept going back and forth that way. Sometimes I might have a couplet, three of four lines, sometimes he would throw something in and say, 'How about this?'. I would take it or not take it. That was an interesting moment when the first time I said, 'No I don't think that's right.' You have to do that otherwise you can't collaborate.

I have to say, I was always a big fan of Bob's but I wasn't a fan with a capital F. Every now and then he would play a bit of a song and I would say, 'What's that?' And it would turn out to be one of his songs and I didn't know it! And I think he liked that. He's not an egotistical guy at all and I think he loved the idea that I didn't know some of his stuff. That I wasn't one of these people that knew every detail about his life.

It turned out that we had a rather similar sense of humour and I think you can tell that in a number of the songs. He would get a big kick out of certain line that I wrote, he would just laugh!

So the two of us were really getting on well. The problem was that here we were sat in my apartment, out there was the city of New York and their was a bar round the corner so we would break off, go to the bar and hang out.

He told me he wanted to write a new album and I was delighted that he wanted to go on after we'd written this first song, so I said we need to get out of New York, go somewhere where we can really concentrate. We both had a place in the county, but he could get his opened up straight away so we went out to Lily Pond Lane in East Hampton, Long Island. We stayed out there for three weeks or a month. Some of it was really funny, like me and Bob walking down the isles in the supermarket pushing the trolley.

When we had finished the lyrics to a song, I would sit down at the typewriter and write down the lyrics and then Bob would continue to work on it. After we had finished that first song, we went out to a bar and Bob had this sheet with him and he went to the corner of the bar and said to this guy I'd like you to hear this new song I just wrote. Well, you can just imagine, my God, and Bob pulls out this lyric sheet and reads it really intensely to the person who just sat there nodding!

I really thought the album was wonderful sounding, I liked the idea that there was content in it that you could really chew on.

LAKELAND CIVIC CENTER

18 APRIL, 1976, LAKELAND, FLORIDA

I WAS THERE: ROBBIE MAC, AGE 17

I attended the April 18, 1976, Easter Sunday show at Lakeland Civic Center, the first night of the spring leg of the Rolling Thunder tour. I was 17-years old and at military school in St Petersburg, Florida. I talked a buddy of mine into going AWOL with me!

We took a cab to the Trailways station, rode a bus and got to Lakeland an hour before the show started. I squeezed my way through to the front, literally had my elbows on the front of the stage. Dylan & Co were magical, there was electricity crackling through the air on every song! David Mansfield was playing mandolin, flat-top guitar, pedal steel guitar, you name it. Bobby Neuwirth drank almost a whole bottle of Jose Cuervo Gold by himself and was still strumming his acoustic guitar like a champ! Joan Baez lead a stirring rendition of 'The Night They Drove Old Dixie Down,' everyone in the audience was singing it with her and there wasn't a dry eye in the house!

Dylan was the ringmaster, watching and playing with such intensity, all the while making history right there on the stage. It was well worth the 15 hours of marching duty I received when I got back to military school at 2am!

FLORIDA FIELD

25 APRIL, 1976, GAINESVILLE, FLORIDA

I WAS THERE: STEVE DERBY

I saw him on his Rolling Thunder Review tour with Roger McGuinn and Joan Baez and the incomparable Steve Martin et al. Incredible concert! Steve Martin was a humorous emcee and kept everyone in stitches. Outside at the University of Florida, the weather was perfect for a perfect performance by Dylan.

I WAS THERE: MARY COX

I saw him at the University of Florida football stadium. He was with Joan Baez. Tickets were thrown from the stadium to fans below. If I had to pay for my ticket it would have been $5.00. I also saw him again in July 11, 2009, at Eastlake, Classic Park. Willie Nelson and John Mellencamp were there too. Both were great concerts.

LSU ASSEMBLY CENTER
4 MAY, 1976, BATON ROUGE, LOUISIANA

I WAS THERE: STEVE ROBERTS

Steve Roberts memories from this particular concert are a bit fuzzy

I was a senior in high school, memories from this particular concert are a bit fuzzy... no idea why. He's not the showman onstage like a lot of other performers. Joan Baez was there, although I was never a huge fan of hers. What I do recall from this time is the amazing amount of great music we were treated to.

The Seventies was outstanding; The Who, Led Zeppelin, Pink Floyd, Crosby, Stills & Nash, Eric Clapton, Bruce Springsteen, Bob Dylan... it was a magical time.

One thing that really struck me about Dylan was his lyrics. Because of him, I became a fan of so much music that relied, not just on the music, but the lyrics and what the songwriter was trying to say. I grew to appreciate music that I had been listening to already in a completely new way. As I discovered more music, the lyrics became a real focal point. I would bring home a new album and listen to it, start to finish, reading the lyrics as it played.

It almost became a ritual. I had a real love for singer/songwriters like Randy Newman and Warren Zevon simply because their lyrics were so amazing. I had a new appreciation of older groups as well, like The Beatles and Pink Floyd. And I really think Bob Dylan gave me that.

The Last Waltz was a concert by The Band, held on American Thanksgiving Day, November 25, 1976, at Winterland Ballroom in San Francisco, California.

Advertised as The Band's farewell concert appearance, the show saw The Band joined by more than a dozen special guests, including Eric Clapton, Ringo Starr, Bob Dylan, Ronnie Wood, Muddy Waters, Neil Young, Neil Diamond, Van Morrison, Bobby Charles, Dr. John, Paul Butterfield, Emmylou Harris, Ronnie Hawkins, Joni Mitchell and, The Staple Singers.

I WAS THERE: ROB FRABONI, PRODUCER

I was with The Band one day and we were having lunch when Robbie Robertson said out of nowhere, 'You know, I think I've had it with being out on the road,' and the rest of the guys all looked at him and said, 'What are you talking about?'. Robbie said, 'This is too much for me, I think we should do a final concert,' and Rick Danko says, 'Well if we're going to do our final concert, then maybe what we should do is invite all our friends and make it a real event.' So everybody talked about it for while and then decided that this was a really good idea, and from that conversation the whole thing developed into calling various people to see if they were interested which they were so little by little the whole thing came together.

At this time The Band were on Capital and were about to change labels and they'd been talking to Warner Brothers and Mo Ostin. Robbie told Mo what they were thinking of doing and Mo said he would put up a million dollars of his own money to make this final show happen as long as The Band would sign to Warner Brothers, which they did.

The million dollars that Mo put up paid for all the equipment, and all the expenses. Then Robbie talked to Martin Scorsese who said he would have to pull in some favours to make the film happen and he did. All the cameramen he brought in worked just for expenses.

After the show, a short show reel was made with highlights of the concert and Martin Scorsese invited some big players to show them what he had including Jack Nicholson who sat next to Mike Medavoy from United Artists and all they way through the show reel Nicholson was saying to Medavoy, 'This is amazing! This is brilliant!' So by the end of the 15 minutes we had a deal for United Artists to have the film.

I WAS THERE: BILL GRAHAM

Bob Dylan was in the second half and there was an intermission and I was asked to come to the back in a hurry and Robbie Robertson said to me 'Oh my God, Bob has changed his mind at the last minute, the wind is blowing in the wrong direction and he's changed his mind. He says he doesn't want to be filmed.' So I went into Bob's room and he told me he doesn't want to be filmed, he'd changed his mind. I told him that Martin was filming this and that he was the key to the film, he was Bob Dylan, the best there was, and Martin Scorsese was beside himself.

A Martin Scorsese Film

THE LAST WALTZ

A MARTIN SCORSESE Film
The Last Waltz

It Started as a Concert

Starring
The Band
Rick Danko
Levon Helm
Garth Hudson
Richard Manuel
Robbie Robertson

Also Starring
Eric Clapton
Neil Diamond
Bob Dylan
Joni Mitchell
Neil Young
Emmylou Harris
Van Morrison
The Staples

Dr. John
Muddy Waters
Paul Butterfield
Ronnie Hawkins
Ringo Starr
Ron Wood

It Became a Celebration

Production Design by
BORIS LEVEN

Executive Producer
JONATHAN TAPLIN

Produced by
ROBBIE ROBERTSON

Directed by
MARTIN SCORSESE

PG PARENTAL GUIDANCE SUGGESTED DOLBY STEREO United Artists
A Transamerica Company

The Last Waltz

Everyone was ready to film and the instruction went out that Bob would play, but not to film him. So I went on stage to introduce Bob and then walked to the side of that stage where a camera man was standing and each camera man had a guy stood by him and I went over to each one of these guys and raised my voice rather high as I would in these situations and told each one of them to roll the film.

Bob Dylan, for me anyway, is the single greatest poet our industry has ever produced. And on any given night when he is on just with his guitar and his words, there is only one. The worst that could happen would they would destroy the film and he would never talk to me again.

I WAS THERE: ROBBIE ROBERTSON, MUSICIAN

We had to play 21 songs with other artists, going from Muddy Waters to Joni Mitchell. We played this five-hour concert and we didn't make a mistake.

Initially, we planned to invite just Ronnie Hawkins and Bob Dylan, because of their pivotal roles in The Band's formation. But the roster of guests kept expanding – Eric Clapton, Van Morrison and a whole crew of stars signed on to the project, including Martin Scorsese. It just kept going and going, and with Martin Scorsese becoming involved, it turned into something special, and it felt beautiful at the time. Bill Graham, the promoter for the Winterland Ballroom, had the idea to serve the crowd a big dinner. He said, 'We're going to serve Thanksgiving dinner to 5,000 people, and we're going to have a waltz orchestra playing while they dine.'

When I told Bob Dylan about the final concert, he said, 'Is this going to be one of those Frank Sinatra retirements where you come back a year later?'

'No,' I told him. 'The Band has to get off the road. It's become a danger zone, and we're afraid of what might happen.' Bob knew from all the car wrecks back in Woodstock and from his time with us on the road that it could be a delicate balance inside The Band keeping things from steaming off the tracks.

1978

RUNDOWN STUDIOS

JANUARY 1978, SANTA MONICA, CALIFORNIA

I WAS THERE: ALAN PASQUA, PIANIST

My first gig out of college was playing with Tony Williams, Miles Davis's drummer. While we were rehearsing at Studio Instrument Rentals Studios in New York, I met a guy in the hallway named Rob Stoner, who was Bob's bass player. We started talking and became buds. Later Rob called, and said: 'I'm starting to put together a band for an upcoming tour. Why don't you come over and play for a little while, and I'll give Bob a tape?' That's how it all started.

The Bob Dylan World Tour 1978 kicked off on February 20, 1978, with three nights at the Budokan, Tokyo. The year-long world tour, saw Dylan and his band performing 114 shows in Japan, the Far East, Europe and the US, to a total audience of two million people.

Concerts in Tokyo in February and March were recorded and released as the live double album, *Bob Dylan at Budokan* in April 1979. It was during the closing stages of this tour that Dylan experienced a 'born-again' conversion to Christianity. The 1978 world tour grossed more than $20 million.

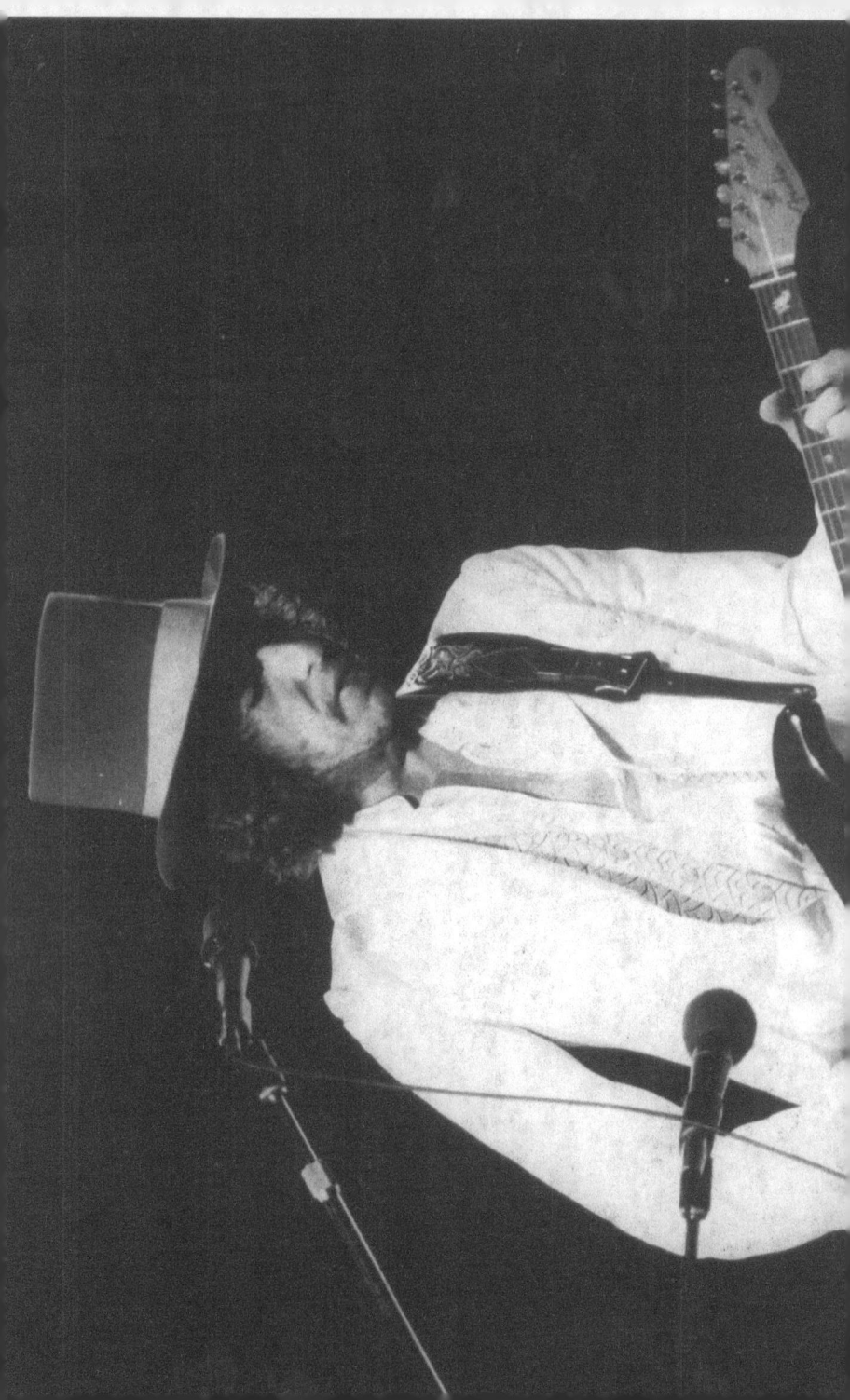

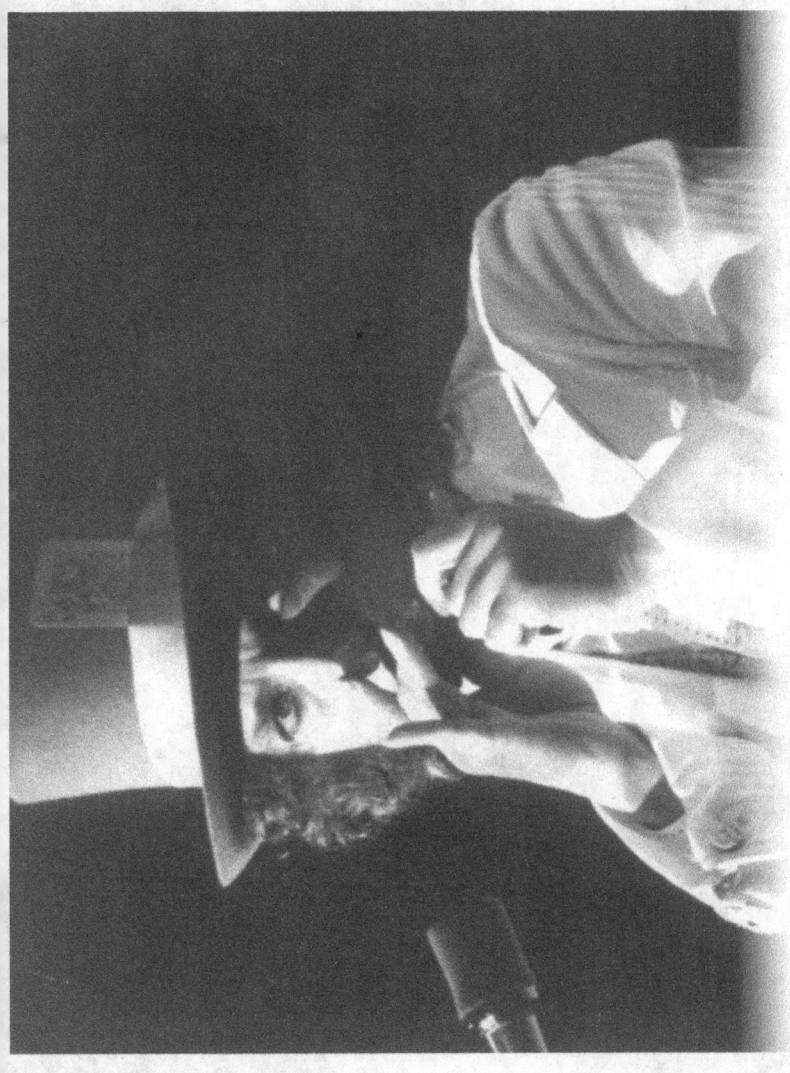

WESTERN SPRINGS STADIUM

9 MARCH, 1978, AUCKLAND, NEW ZEALAND

I WAS THERE: PAUL JUDGE, AGE 21

I have incredible and vivid memories of seeing Bob Dylan at Western Springs, Auckland, New Zealand, in 1978. It was the first time he'd been to our country and the expectation was immense. It truly was like seeing God, as Eric Clapton was famously called on a graffiti wall in England.

It was so momentous to see him that a large group near the front of stage just called out his name continuously, as though they were trying to convince themselves it was actually him. Dylan seemed slightly embarrassed at this, I recall, and tipped his hat sheepishly at them.

But here was Bob Dylan in a white suit, top hat, and with a queen of spades card stuck in its rim, and with an 13-piece band complete with girl chorus and playing his great songs in completely different ways to how we knew them.

There was a capacity crowd at the venue and I was quite close to the front of stage, close enough to see the card in his top hat. He played 'Like a Rolling Stone' just a few songs in and I remember the guitar player, Billy Cross, just playing this incredible riff that cemented the song into my brain, and then the momentous build up toward the end just carried people away. This was the most magnificent music I had heard to that point in my life. I was 21 years old and had been listening to Dylan since I was 13, but nothing had prepared me for this.

Bob's harmonica playing was a special highlight, and I remember the effect of this on songs like 'Love Minus Zero/No Limit'. Bob on stage blowing into his harp, with the most soulful sound imaginable. When I heard these songs later on the album *Bob Dylan at Budokan*, they didn't disappoint. This live album was recorded about two days before the Auckland concert, of course, during the tour of Japan.

A highlight was the solo version of 'Girl From the North Country'. He played this as though alone on stage, picking out the tune on his Fender Stratocaster but with a subtle accompaniment throughout from a stripped back band. Hearing this was a like a religious experience. His voice seemed to convey so much depth of feeling and the pain of lost love. But it was even more than that, this was our hero Bob Dylan, performing as though the folk musician of old, one of the key songs we grew up with. The emotion of this event, of just this one song, let alone the entire concert, was indescribable.

Bob Dylan in Auckland, New Zealand March 1978

I remember very clearly how Bob welcomed the Highway 61 Motorcycle gang as they cut a swathe through the centre of the crowd about 20 minutes into the concert.

I also remember the craziness of large numbers of people leaving the concert at half time (yes, there was a half time). Those of us overcome with the awe of seeing Bob in the flesh couldn't believe why, and people started talking about how the songs were different and it was not the Bob Dylan they expected and so on. We thought that this was just nuts. This was 1978. We had already heard the *Hard Rain* album and had figured out by this stage that Bob was not going to reproduce his hits as they sounded on the radio. Maybe the old folkies were alive and well and were looking forward to hearing the Freewheelin' album reproduced on stage. There is no other explanation as to why people were not happy. One comment

I remember hearing was that the concert was 'too loud'.

Bob was in another mode of entertaining. He was even listed as 'Entertainer' in the concert booklet we dutifully purchased at the gate. This became very clear during the performance of 'Ballad of a Thin Man'. Bob discarded his shoulder-strapped guitar and pranced around the stage like Tom Jones or somebody. We had never expected this from him and it was absolutely mind-blowing.

Years later I managed to score a very low quality bootleg recording of this show. It is certainly interesting to hear what order the songs were played in but it doesn't come close to capturing the sheer excitement and huge sense of occasion that this concert was in real life. I often play the *Bob Dylan at Budokan* album, though, and no doubt because of the superior audio quality this manages to bring back some of the excitement of hearing this wonderful and rich music as we heard it on the night.

I have seen Bob Dylan in concert about 30 times since, but as exciting and as brilliant as all of those concerts have been, none of them really compares to the incredible concert of 1978 when he played with his *Street-Legal* and Budokan band and where he was billed as 'Entertainer' and wore a white suit like Elvis and a black top-hat like Fred Astaire.

MYER MUSIC BOWL

20 MARCH, 1978, MELBOURNE, AUSTRALIA

I WAS THERE: PETER KRUSCHE, AGE 27

In some respects I travelled 12,000 miles to be there. My wife and I had come from London a couple of years before to travel around Australia. We overstayed our visas, which wasn't deemed such a crime back in those days. At the time we had no intention of staying, but here I am nearly 40 years later – legally. I was 27 at the time of the shows. The three shows were very similar, with just a few variations in the set lists. My abiding memory is the first show on March 20, which was actually the last to be announced. I could only afford general admission, which meant standing way back on the grass in the pouring rain. I remember quite a few people leaving before the end as it was so wet. I didn't care. It was Bob and, even if these days I don't particularly like the pseudo reggae 1978 big band arrangements, at the time it was great just to be there. The version of Ramona simply gave me goose bumps. I had tears streaming down my face such was the moment. In the rain it didn't matter. The following night I was with my wife and friends under cover, which is when I took the photos. For the third show, I was back up on the grass but finally the rain had gone. As you can see from the photo, he also sang without guitar. I don't recall which song but it was very early in the set.

Peter Krusche went to all three Melbourne shows in 1978

I don't have much of a tale to tell but when Bob Dylan announced he was touring Australia in March 1978 I was absolutely thrilled and queuing up literally all night for tickets in those pre-internet days was hardly a chore. I managed to get near front row centre stage seats at the Myer Music Bowl in Melbourne. In those days there were no restrictions on cameras without flash. I shot off two rolls in quick succession at the start of the show so I could enjoy the rest without distractions. I went to all three shows but could only afford seats to one of them. For the others I stood way up the back in pouring rain. The magic moment was his arrangement of 'To Ramona'.

ENTERTAINMENT CENTRE
27 MARCH, 1978, PERTH, AUSTRALIA

I WAS THERE: JANE ELIZABETH FRANCIS

I was right up the back – terrified because I suffer from vertigo. Somehow I made my way to the front and it was a wonderful show. My son's middle name is Dylan. I also went to see Dylan in February 1986 at the same place with Tom Petty and the Heartbreakers.

SYDNEY SHOWGROUND
1 APRIL, 1978, SYDNEY, AUSTRALIA

I WAS THERE: BOB HOWE, AGE 21

Although I had heard his songs as a kid during the Sixties (and being in the UK then, it would mostly have been the hit parade covers by Manfred Mann and the like) I became a real fan in 1971, when I was 14, pretty much the same time as I got my first guitar and started learning to play songs.

So I was 21 when I first saw Dylan in 1978. He was wearing a white suit with black edging and eye makeup. I don't honestly remember him talking much, let alone what he might have said. The outdoor acoustics wouldn't have been great in those days and with the new arrangements it was even hard to recognise some of the songs.

On April 1, 1978, I saw Bob Dylan. The concert was held at the Sydney Showground, which after several days of exceptional rainfall, was like a mud pit. The eight-piece band started off with an instrumental version of 'A Hard Rain's a-Gonna Fall', which I didn't recognise until my friend Ian exclaimed the title. This would set the tone for what was to follow. Dylan had only fairly recently begun the process of reinventing his repertoire by changing the arrangements and even the melodies of his well-known songs. While this seemed shocking at the time, listening now (check out *Bob Dylan At Budokan* recorded the previous month or the bootleg from the Adelaide show two weeks earlier) it was tame compared with what would come in the years ahead.

Bob Howe became a Dylan fan age 14, bought a guitar and started writing songs

I WAS THERE: RICK WALLIN

April Fools' Day 1978, the last leg of his Asia Pacific tour was at the Sydney Showgrounds. Other venues have been named for this concert: Randwick Park, Sydney Sportsground, but it was at the Showgrounds a week after the finish of the wettest Sydney Royal Easter Show on record.

The ground was churned up mud from all the earlier events at the Easter Show. A quarter of the ground was still under water. You walked in, most people were wearing trash bags with the holes cut out for their arms and head due to the rain and mud. You picked up a safety barrier plank and dropped it on the mud to sit on. Then you dropped another one cause the first one sank into the mud!

There was plenty of fun to be had as the crowd in the stands cheered on the mud people running and diving into the pools of muddy water.

Oh, the concert? This was my first Dylan concert as I wasn't old enough for his 1966 tour. Actually it was the first concert I ever attended. Dylan appeared in white leather and kicked off with 'A Hard Rain's a-Gonna Fall' and then continued with most of his better known material. But the track that I remember best is 'Maggie's Farm'. I have the bootleg vinyl from that time. I've seen him on all his later Australian tours. As long as he keeps coming back I'll keep coming back.

I WAS THERE: MARITA SAID, AGE 17

I was on my first blind date. I had borrowed a floor length leather coat from said date's sister-in-law. It was at the Sports stadium in Sydney, Australia, and it was a mud bath but I was smitten with the man on the stage and the one beside me! The reviews were not great but I had loved Dylan's poetry and his music since being small. I was thrilled just to be in the audience.

I do recall 'I'll Be Your Baby Tonight' as it was very apt for the occasion, though we were very innocent. I dated that guy for some time after, and never lost my love for Dylan. From memory I don't recall him talking much, but I loved the songs. By the way – the guy ended up being the one I should have never let go!

SET LIST:

A Hard Rain's a-Gonna Fall (instrumental)
Love Her With A Feeling
Mr. Tambourine Man
I Threw It All Away
Shelter from the Storm
Love Minus Zero/No Limit
Girl From The North Country
Ballad of a Thin Man
Maggie's Farm
I Don't Believe You
Like a Rolling Stone
I Shall Be Released
Going, Going, Gone
One Of Us Must Know (Sooner Or Later)
You're A Big Girl Now
One More Cup Of Coffee (Valley Below)
Blowin' in the Wind
I Want You
Don't Think Twice, It's All Right
Just Like A Woman
Oh, Sister
To Ramona
All Along The Watchtower
The Man In Me
All I Really Want To Do
It's Alright, Ma (I'm Only Bleeding)
Forever Young
The Times They Are a-Changin'
Knockin' On Heaven's Door
I'll Be Your Baby Tonight

UNIVERSAL AMPHITHEATER

1-7 JUNE, 1978, LOS ANGELES, CALIFORNIA

I WAS THERE: TOM PETTY

Growing up in Florida, we hadn't heard of Dylan until 'Like a Rolling Stone' came out as a single. And we loved that right away. We learned that, did it in the show. We learned all his singles. We didn't have Dylan albums until *Blonde on Blonde*. I had heard *Highway 61 Revisited*, a friend of mine had that. But I actually bought *Blonde on Blonde*. That's where I really got into Bob. And I started to really dig his thing.

He influenced my songwriting, of course. He influenced everybody's songwriting. There's no way around it. No one had ever really left the love song before, lyrically. So in that respect, I think he influenced everybody, because you suddenly realised you could write about other things.

TOM PETTY & THE HEARTBREAKERS

I met him in '77 or '78 in Los Angeles. We went to see him in concert. I and Bugs Weidel, longtime roadie got two comps. We left the Shelter studio, and we drove to the Universal Amphitheater, had a flat tyre, and both of us got out on the road trying to change the tyre. So we were just covered with grease and dirt. And we got to Universal, found our seats. The show had just begun. And then midway through the show, Bob introduced the celebrities in the audience, which was kind of unusual for Bob.

It was like 'Joni Mitchell's here' and there'd be applause. And then suddenly he said, 'Tom Petty's here.' And there was applause. And that was the first time it really hit me that people knew who we were, because I'd only made two records then. Then a guy came up to us where we were sitting in our seats, and said, 'Bob would like you to come backstage.' So we went backstage and had a brief conversation. Nothing of any substance, but I had met Bob.

I WAS THERE: RJ FUENTES

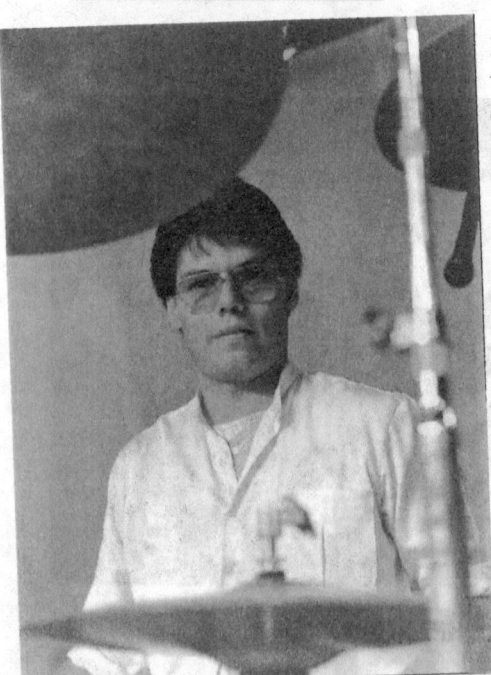

I remember exactly where I was when I first heard 'Like a Rolling Stone' and at that moment I became a devoted fan of Bob's. I have been in the music business most of my life. I've worked at Warner Brothers Records, Music Corporation of America, Universal Studios and various other studios from 1973-1988.

While working at Universal Studios in the royalty department in the black tower, we were always given tickets to all Universal Amphitheater events – well when tickets for Bob were offered...Duh!

It was a beautiful clear summer night, no roof on it yet, perfect seats dead centre and dead centre of theatre. Anticipation was way over the top, energy was thick, and the haze was thick green.

Then the lights go down and out he came. I don't remember the song list, except for some classics and of course 'Like a Rolling Stone'. I do remember just staring, feeling like I was being drawn in to something bigger than the actual music being played. His presence was magical. I don't know if it was the lighting but I could see a glow emanating from him, not on him. The crowd was in awe, they were all seeing and feeling what I was. Silent during songs and casual banter, and raising the roof that wasn't there yet, after each song! A couple of long encores too. Such a great experience that I still remember it 42 years later.

EARLS COURT EXHIBITION CENTRE

15-20 JUNE, 1978, LONDON

I WAS THERE: NED MALET de CARTERET

I was late into Dylan but he was my first ever gig – Earls Court June 1978. I was I think completely bowled over by his awesome presence. He played all his repertoire. I sat behind a seven foot giant in the stalls! I can picture him in my mind, black leather jacket, electric guitar. Just simply amazing.

I WAS THERE: SARAH ANN RICE

I first heard Dylan's music in the early Sixties but it was 1965 when I really started to listen to him seriously. A friend at that time loaned me his albums *The Freewheelin' Bob Dylan* and *Another Side Of Bob Dylan*. My favourite tracks were 'Girl From The North Country' and 'To Ramona'. Later when I could afford to, I bought all his albums going back to the first one.

I was training to be a nurse in the late Sixties and would drive all the other girls in the nurses' home crazy playing *Blonde on Blonde* over and over, especially tracks like 'Visions of Johanna' and 'Sad Eyed Lady of The Lowlands'. There were many more favourite tracks from albums in the years following, 'I Dreamed I saw St Augustine' from *John Wesley Harding*, 'Lily of The West' from *Dylan*, 'You're a Big Girl Now' from *Blood on The Tracks*. Apart from *Blonde on Blonde*, for me, no other albums have stood out until *Desire* and *Street Legal* were released. 'Hurricane', 'One More Cup of Coffee', 'Romance in Durango', 'Sara' from *Desire* then 'Changing of The Guard' and 'Señor (Tales of Yankee Power)' from *Street Legal*. There are many more tracks I love from all the Sixties and Seventies albums but they are too many to mention here. I had always wanted to see Dylan live but it was never possible until 1978 when he did his World Tour.

Friends of mine queued in Glasgow for tickets. We travelled down from Edinburgh to London on Monday June 19. On reaching Earls Court in the afternoon we had a while to wait until the concert. The feeling of excitement around the area was palpable, electric, buzzing! I remember after we had found our seats, fourth row from the front, I went back to the entrance hall to look at the merchandise. I heard the band strike up and everyone around started to run. Dylan was coming on stage. I got back to my seat just as he appeared. When you have loved an artist like Dylan for a long time and seeing them for the first time it is hard to describe the feeling.

Dylan's set could not have been better. He sang most of my favourite songs. Especially, 'Love Minus Zero/No Limit', 'Tangled Up in Blue', 'Rainy Day Women', 'You're A Big Girl Now', 'One More Cup Of Coffee', 'Señor (Tales of Yankee Power)' and 'Forever Young' with lighters being waved, which was the first time I had seen this at a concert. Another memorable moment was during his second set when he said, 'this is a song I wrote a while back for a friend of mine and she's in the house tonight so I'm gonna play it'. It was 'To Ramona'! I had always assumed the song was about a girl called Ramona. Over the years I have since found out it was an old folk melody to which Dylan added lyrics. Joan Baez has said Dylan called her Ramona and others have said he wrote the song for Nico. So, maybe it was either Joan or Nico in the house that night!

All I can say is, it was an unforgettable night – just fantastic!

I WAS THERE: BARBARA BOYD SHAW

I saw him in 1978 at Earls Court. We queued up overnight in Glasgow for tickets, (that was an experience – the Glaswegian Jamie's amused us). We travelled down to London in a transit van, eight of us with mattress in the back.

Dylan was amazing and our seats were four rows from the front. I saw him again that year at the Blackbushe festival. Joan Armatrading also played but again Dylan stole the show.

I WAS THERE: DAVE HARDING, AGE 29

I first became aware of Bob Dylan in the sixth form at school when I was 18 years old, but it was 1968 at the age of 19 before I could afford to buy an album. This was *John Wesley Harding*, which turned out to be very different from the singles I had heard on the radio, so I then started to invest in his earlier albums as funds permitted and became totally hooked.

My next ambition was to see Bob in concert, so when I heard in 1978 that he was appearing at Earls Court I made up my mind to try and obtain a ticket. This was easier said than done in those days especially as I had been working in Iran for five weeks, then the USA for four weeks, so by the time I returned to England the concerts had sold out. I then spotted an advert in the *New Musical Express* and having saved a fair amount of money from my working assignments, I replied to the advert and although the guy was asking about £40 for a £7.50 ticket I was desperate to see Dylan as at that time it was not known if or when he would play in the UK again. I sent my cheque in the post and patiently waited to find out if I would receive a genuine ticket or if I had been ripped off. Luckily, the ticket duly arrived for seat B 161 in Block 35 on Saturday, June 17, 1978, so at age 29 I would get to see Bob in concert for the first time.

Now at the time I had a Vauxhall Viva, but it was gradually falling to bits and had become unreliable so a couple of days before the concert I invested in a second hand Ford Capri in the hope that it would get me to London without any problems. It turned out to be fine and after finding a place to park I strolled to Earls Court full of eager anticipation.

Coming from Devon the crowd was quite overwhelming, but my excitement grew as we all waited for the doors to open, supposedly at 6.30pm but I am sure they kept us waiting a lot longer. Eventually they let us all into the hall and after a mad scramble I purchased a programme and found my seat.

When the group came on stage my first impressions were that Bob was a lot smaller than I had imagined and there seemed to be an awful lot of people with him, perhaps because all the previous concerts I had attended were either solo artists or groups containing four or five members. It was also the first concert I had attended where the artist received a standing ovation even before he had performed any songs.

As for the concert itself, I was in a trance most of the time just pinching myself that I was in the same place as someone I had admired and waited so long to see on stage.

The highlights I do remember were the slow rearranged version of 'Tangled Up in Blue' which I thought was the most powerful moment of the entire concert and the slow version of 'I Want You'. I also enjoyed hearing my favourites at that time 'Mr. Tambourine Man', 'All Along the Watchtower', 'Just Like a Woman' which ended with a harmonica solo,

'Simple Twist of Fate', 'Forever Young' and a strong performance of 'Like a Rolling Stone' which I think drew the most ecstatic response from the audience. Some of the other songs passed me by but I remember not being very keen on the new arrangement for 'Shelter from the Storm' with the girl singers very much involved.

As regards Dylan's comments to the audience, I think he said thank you to the audience quite a few times and when he played a new song he mentioned it was off his latest album, *Street Legal*, which had only been released a few days earlier. The only new one I remember making any impression on me was 'Señor (Tales of Yankee Power)'. He also introduced the band together with the names of the girl singers.

The atmosphere in the hall became electric towards the end of the concert and the hairs were standing up on the back of my neck; coming away from the concert I remember wanting to experience more of these events and couldn't wait for the next time. It was certainly the real deal as far as I was concerned and a long way from listening to *John Wesley Harding* on my record player.

I then had to find out if my car was still safe as I had parked in a make shift car park in a builder's yard where I think they charged me £5 which was quite a lot in 1978. However the car was fine and travelling the four-hour journey back to Torquay I tried to remember all the best bits of the concert before inserting a homemade tape of *Blood on the Tracks* to guide me safely home.

I WAS THERE: JOHN LINDLEY

John Lindley queued round the block to buy tickets for the Earl Court concerts

In 1969, aged 17, I first began paying attention to Bob Dylan – reading what I could about him and buying what I could afford of his albums. Attending the Isle of Wight Festival in August of that year was a little too early and never a possibility for me. Dylan might just as well have been playing Mars for all the chance I had of going there. I was not to know that it would be another nine years before the opportunity would arrive to see Dylan in the UK again.

Urgent and illicit phone calls were made from my office desk in 1978 on the day workmates first informed me that Bob Dylan would be coming to our shores for six London shows at Earls Court. From these hurried enquiries I learned the location of the nearest ticket outlet (Hime and Addison in Manchester) and the time and date they would go on sale (9am Sunday, May 7). On Saturday, May 6, I drove into Manchester from my hometown Stockport with my then wife, Celia, on no more than a shopping excursion. Around 11am, passing Hime and Addison, I saw a queue of what proved to be about 80 people beginning at the shop's doorway, continuing down the block and snaking around the corner. I screamed to be let out of the car, watched my wife drive off for home and joined those early punters for what I fully expected would be a 22 hour wait to be served.

Relationships were formed in that queue that have lasted to this day but, surprisingly pleasant as this pre-Ticketmaster experience was, it was with some relief that around 2am Sunday morning the record shop sensibly instructed a member of staff to get over there, open up and start selling tickets to a queue of people that was now in the hundreds. I'd instructed Celia as I leapt from the car 15 hours earlier to telephone a mate when she got home and tell him to join me as quickly as possible in my vigil. So it was that around 2.15 am, with my tickets for three shows stuffed in my jacket pocket, I climbed on the back of my friend's motorbike and we shot away before (I feared) we could be mugged for our haul.

The Earls Court residency commenced on a Thursday; my own mini-residency as an audience member was Saturday to Monday – shows three, four and five. The importance of Dylan's first visit to mainland Britain in 12 years was clearly not lost on those whose responsibility it was to populate the arena's inner perimeter until showtime. Where now we have the deadly procession of souvenir stand and rip-off food and drink bars repeated ad nauseam as concert-goers sleepwalk in circles before taking their seats, back then there were clowns, uni-cyclists, acrobats (were there really all these things?), at least for these shows. I was perched in the side balcony for my first live Dylan experience where my abiding memory prior to the lights going down was of multiple Bob Dylans on the front cover of the £1 programme ('A quid! How much?!)

peering up from their perch on people's laps through his (literally) handmade binoculars.

I remember too, my excitement as the backing band entered and briefly played before Dylan emerged from behind the drum riser, bouncing to stage front and joyfully pointing at random at the crowd. Despite owning all of his albums by this point, neither of his opening two songs that night, 'Love Her with a Feeling' and 'Baby Stop Crying', were familiar to me and I assumed both were from his new-about-to-be-released album, *Street Legal*; not so, as the first, I later learned, was, of course, a Tampa Red cover.

There was much to take in that evening, from that, 'This is the story of my life.' introduction to 'Shelter from the Storm,' the guitar-less (hard now to imagine how strange that looked then) rendition of 'Love Minus Zero/No Limit' with the first use of harmonica that night, to 'Like a Rolling Stone' and the standing ovation that followed it. The eventual transformation of Earls Court from concert venue to Cathedral came with the corny but undeniably moving display of raised matches for the closer, 'Forever Young' and then it was Dylan returning for the encores, stripping off his jacket and playing an anthemic 'The Times They Are a-Changin'' throughout which the ground floor crowd stood. (Yes, they were seated for most of the show!)

One song only changed in the set list on each of my two subsequent nights but each concert remained just as thrilling and memorable. Aided now by reference to a few brief notes I made at each of the shows I saw, I can recall from the Sunday night Dylan and lead guitarist Billy Cross leaning back to back on the opening song's guitar break, Dylan busting a string in 'Shelter from the Storm' and dispensing with his Strat mid-song to strap on a Telecaster, him playfully pretending (?) to fool with Cross's tuning as the latter played out 'Ballad of a Thin Man' and adding to his introduction of drummer Ian Wallace the mild admonition to the crowd 'C'mon, you can give him a bigger hand than that.' There was a double salute from Dylan before leaving the stage that night.

Monday's show was equally as spirited, belying Dylan's claim as the intermission approached that, 'We're gonna take a break after this one – go backstage and wake up.' Apart from the now familiar nightly shifting carousel of descriptions applied to each of his backing singers – 'Fiancée.' 'Current girlfriend.' 'Ex-wife's best friend', snippets of pithy between-song chatter punctuated the show: 'I wanna say hello to the

Riley family tonight – come down from Manchester.'; 'I wrote this a while back for a friend. She's in the audience tonight so I'm gonna play it.' ('To Ramona'); 'This is the song that started it all for me.' ('Maggie's Farm'. On Saturday he'd introduced it as 'the one that got me booed of the stage at Newport'.) He preceded 'I Don't Believe You' with the words 'Here's one of the very few songs (of mine) that's not been misinterpreted.' The last and lasting impression for me of my Earls Court adventure was of Dylan jabbing a pointed finger at who-knows-who to his stage right whilst singing the lines 'Come writers and critics who prophesise with your pen. Keep your eyes wide the chance won't come again.' Before leaving Dylan picked up a tartan scarf that had been hurled onstage, twirled it above his head and handed it to Ian Wallace. Then he was gone and out of my life (at least until Blackbushe a month later).

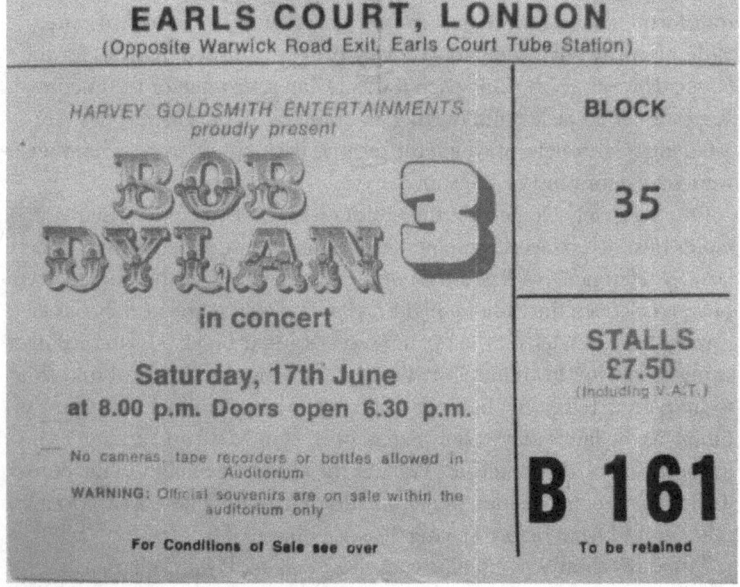

I WAS THERE: PATRICK CORLEY

The year was 1978 and the times they were a changin'. Punk rock had swept the country and the old guard was being pushed aside. It was announced that Bob Dylan was to arrive in Britain for five nights at London's Earls Court. The news was greeted with derision by the new wave but for anyone over 25 this was the best news in years. It was Dylan's first visit to Britain for nine years, since his legendary appearance at the Isle Of Wight festival in 1969. Excitement spread like wildfire throughout the land, the tickets were to go on sale at various venues around the country one Sunday morning at 9.00. Each person was allowed to buy four tickets. The nearest venue to us was the Colston Hall in Bristol.

The night before the tickets went on sale I began to get worried that we would be at the back of the queue and miss out on the tickets.

'I think we should be in the queue now,' I said to my friends. We set off for Bristol with our sleeping bags sure that we would be the first in line at the box office. When we got to Colston Hall we were surprised to see a line of people stretching from the box office to the corner of the street. To our horror when we got to the corner we found the queue stretched all the way along the next street as well. There were already thousands of people camped out to get Bob tickets. This was the amazing appeal of Bob Dylan in those days.

There was a fantastic atmosphere on the streets of Bristol that night as a mini Bob fest was held, people sat on the pavement drinking and chatting and listening to Dylan on tape recorders and the sweet smell of marijuana drifted up Colston Street. Next morning the bleary eyed revellers began to shuffle forward when the box office opened. Finally with a sigh of relief I had the precious tickets in my grasp. We were going to see Bob Dylan!

A few weeks later, we found ourselves in the vastness of Earls Court arena, Bob was just a tiny figure in the distance, this was before the age of huge video screens. If my memory serves me well he was wearing a top hat. The band were superb though and included three girl singers who were excellent. I think this was the best band Bob had in his career. It's so long ago now in the mists of time that I can't remember a lot about the concert apart from Bob getting a huge round of applause when he first played the harmonica on 'Love Minus Zero/No Limit', also the crowd gave a huge cheers when during 'Its Alright , Ma (I'm Only Bleeding)' Bob sang 'but even the President of the United States has to stand naked', this was only four years since Nixon resigned don't forget.

I think my favourite song that night was 'I Want You' which Bob had slowed right down to a haunting love ballad. There were also songs from his brand new album *Street Legal*, which were excellent. I think the last song he did was 'Forever Young' and during this song people started holding up cigarette lighters and candles until there were 15,000 little lights inside Earls Court. It was an amazing sight. The whole concert was a deeply moving spiritual experience.

Afterwards in a packed tube train the excitement of the evening had become too much for me and I got a really bad comedown and felt really claustrophobic, almost panicking. I hate tube trains anyway. I soon recovered though when I got in the fresh air.

Then it was announced that Dylan was to end his European tour with a huge outdoor concert at Blackbushe Aerodrome near Camberley in Surrey. It was to be known as the 'Picnic'. Some picnic this was! Once more we set off to see Bob. The official figure of the attendance that day was 165,000 but anyone who was there knows that the real figure was about three times that. It was vast, I think it is only rivalled by the Stones concert in Hyde Park as the biggest concert ever in Britain. As well as Bob, Eric Clapton was on and Joan Armatrading and Graham Parker And The Rumour who were a shit hot band in those days. All the glitterati were there, during Bob's set Ringo Starr and George Harrison could be seen at the side of the stage.

It took us five hours to find our car afterwards and it was dawn before we finally made it to the main road to head home. There would never again be a concert in Britain like Dylan's concert at Blackbushe, which was the hippies graveyard. For me it represented the end of an era.

The following winter was the winter of discontent and in 1979 Thatcher seized power, pestilence and blight spread throughout the land as she systematically stuck the boot into the working people. A darkness descended upon the country which she held in the grip of her icy claw. How could a country which was supposed to be known for its sense of fair play and support for the underdog have fallen into the hands of this mean spirited she-devil? I saw Dylan again in 1981, but it wasn't the same. By then I was disillusioned, if Bob Dylan was the voice of a generation how come someone like Thatcher got elected? For me it was only Glastonbury Festival which kept the flame of hope alive during those dark years of unemployment and poverty. I lost interest in Bob for a while especially when he reached his nadir with the *Saved* album and then his shambolic awful performance at Live Aid, but in recent years I have returned to playing Bobs records and there is no doubt to me that he is one of the greatest poets who ever lived and anyone who ever saw Bob perform live is privileged.

I WAS THERE: LESLEY CAMPBELL HUNTER

My love of all thing Bob arose way back in 1965 as a 13 year old listening to vinyl records belonging to my friend's older brother which included *The Freewheelin' Bob Dylan*.

My life at the time had revolved around Tamla Motown singles and learning all the words to be able to sing along to them. Threepenny bit on the arm of the stylus made it easier to lift up and put back down! No internet or any other way to have lyrics at hand in the good ole days! Things changed when I heard Bob's lyrics and tried to make sense of them. A past time I continue with today.

Lesley at the front with black hair and bell bottom jeans. Her cousin Christine's bare feet! Who could walk the streets of London barefoot today?

When I heard that Bob was playing in Liverpool (1966) my heart soared and was promptly plummeted back to earth by a cursory 'NO, YOU CAN'T GO!' from my mother.

By 1969 I had ingested all Bob's albums to date and was delighted he was set to appear at IOW festival that year. My heart soared and was promptly plummeted back to earth by a resounding 'NO, IT'S TOO FAR FOR A 17 YEAR OLD GIRL TO TRAVEL TO' from my mother, (how times have changed).

It took until 1978, the year I was engaged to be married (and yes, I delayed my wedding day until after Bob's gig!) I could see Bob in person for the very first time. By this time I owned a bright yellow Hillman Imp and I squeezed in my younger brother, aged 14, and three workmates for the journey down to London. No CDs or in-car cassette radios back then. We had a portable (large!) cassette player complete with six huge batteries to play Bob albums on. We still lived our lives in black and white back then. Life only began to be lived in colour for me after the Earls Court show, June 17, 1978. The stand out track for me was 'Forever Young' which is still one of my favourites today.

I have gone on to attend 75+ shows all over the world since, including three at the Beacon theatre in April 2005, with Merle Haggard supporting as well as Amos Lee. It was strange to me to see fans of Merle Haggard actually leave before Bob came on!

One of my favourite periods for Bob is the Gospel years, which at the time I had to defend. I remember attending the June 1981 London show and being spellbound by Bob's singing accompanied by such wonderful backing vocals. A real treat!

My all-time fave though is Rolling Thunder Revue. In recent years I am not too enamoured by the American song book phase and Bob singing Sinatra wears thin for me now. The fact that Bob is on stage with such poor lighting (40 watt bulb anyone!) and his lack of interaction makes me more nostalgic for past times unfortunately. Still, his mercurial sound is God-given and we love him for it!

ZEPPELINFELD

1 JULY 1978, NUREMBERG, GERMANY

I WAS THERE: RICKIE WOODRING

Saw him many times, but this was the best. This is the same field where Hitler used to give his speeches, and his stage was still there. Dylan refused to step foot on Hitlers stage, so they had to quickly build another one, directly across from Hitlers. The headline in the next *Stars And Stripes* said, 'Dylan Confronts Hitler'.

The highlights for me were 'A Hard Rain's a-Gonna Fall' (first song after intermission and my favourite), 'Señor' (brand new song at the time), 'Masters of War' (Dylan seemed to spit the words at Hitlers stage with a passion) and 'The Times They Are a-Changin'' where Eric Clapton joined him on stage for this encore. I read later that neo-nazis were throwing things at Dylan on stage, but after drinking warm German beer all day, I really can't say.

I WAS THERE: KEITH KENNEDY AGE 17

Keith Kennedy saw Dylan on Hitler's parade field in Nürnberg, Germany

I saw Dylan in 1978 in Nürnberg, Germany at Hitler's parade field! I was 17 years old. I had probably been listening to Dylan for two years at that time. I don't remember any one song standing out over the others, I just remember feeling overwhelmed by the fact that I was watching a musician who was already a legend at that time. He performed along with Eric Clapton, Nils Lofgren, and several others! It was a fantastic concert, and I will cherish the memory of that day!

There were approximately 70,000 people there that day, and you couldn't help but wonder what Adolf Hitler would think of Robert Zimmerman performing on Hitler's parade field!

SCANDINAVIUM
12 JULY 1978, GOTHENBERG

I WAS THERE: GERT ØRNBØLL

I was a fan of Bob Dylan's since I heard 'Like a Rolling Stone' on the radio. When I was 25 years old some friends and I went from Denmark to Gøteborg, Sweden, for a Bob Dylan concert. He and

his band played the good old songs and some new songs, but in a new way. He had a gospel choir in the background. It was a great concert. When I came home, I made this water colour painting of Bob, with some of his songs from the concert illustrated in his hair and jacket: 'Isis', 'Knockin' on Heavens Door', 'One More Cup of Coffee', 'Mr. Tambourine Man' and some others.

Gret Ornboll made the water colour painting below of Dylan, with some of his songs from the concert illustrated in his hair and jacket

Bob Dylan's show at the Blackbushe Aerodrome was his final show of his European tour that summer. Over 200,000 people attended including various celebrities (Ringo Star and Bianca Jagger). Eric Clapton was also on the bill and Clapton joined Dylan onstage for 'Forever Young'.

THE PICNIC AT BLACKBUSHE AERODROME

15 JULY, 1978, CAMBERLEY, SURREY

I WAS THERE: CARL STICKLEY, AGE 14

This was my first gig. We had a mate who lived in nearby Fleet so we stayed at his parents' house. We queued for hours to get in with our beer and fags – no ganja in those days! I remember going down the front for Graham Parker, (well, front and 100 yards to the right, up against the fence). 'Hey Lord Don't Ask Me Questions' was great and I remember thinking, 'Fuck. That's loud!' Having never been to a gig or stood next to a huge PA before I was a bit scared!

Most of the day was long and boring as we couldn't see anything and the sound was constantly blown around – it was a big, flat aerodrome. You'd think someone would have realised!

Eric Clapton got a big cheer and we recognised a few tunes like 'Cocaine'. Again, couldn't see much and the sound wasn't great. I remember seeing a 'Clapton is God' sign and not really getting it. Still don't.

After an enormous wait there he was! Bum Dildo!! That was the pet name we had. Ah, youth. Most of the songs I didn't know, until years later when I got into Dylan properly. Looking at the set list today it was a great Greatest Hits show! The only bit I remember with real clarity was the acoustic section when a German guy let me use his binoculars (damn, why hadn't we thought of that?). I remember 'Gates of Eden' and 'It's Alright, Ma (I'm Only Bleeding)' with Bob in his battered top hat. Weirdly the wind dropped so we heard these really clearly, especially the harmonica which did send a chill. For a brief moment I got a glimpse of why all these people were there and what Bob meant.

It took us hours to get back to our mate's house but the mince and mashed tatties that his Mum had waiting for us tasted magic!

Years later I got a dodgy cassette bootleg and it sounded much like the day... muffled.

I WAS THERE: CLIVE GREGSON, SINGER, SONGWRITER

My last summer living in Crewe, where I'd been sporadically attending teacher training college and getting my band Any Trouble together, we saw the ads for this one day festival and instantly thought, 'that's for us'... Dylan, Clapton, Joan Armatrading and Graham Parker & The Rumour. So many of our faves on one bill... tickets

Singer Songwriter Clive Gregson on stage with his band Any Trouble in 1977. Clive later worked with Dylan's drummer Ian Wallace

were ordered and duly arrived. If memory serves, we went team handed... band, girlfriends and a few pals all piled into the group Transit and headed south. We must have been a bit late getting there. I can't remember seeing anything of Merger, the first act up, at all. Can't remember much about Lake either. I started to pay attention when Graham Parker & The Rumour hit the stage. I was a big fan of Graham Parker and we'd actually seen him play a couple of nights earlier at a free concert in a park in Manchester. He and the band were working up material for what became my favourite album of his, *Squeezing Out Sparks*. The free gig was awesome; the Blackbushe show was much shorter and beset by sound problems.

I recall it was a warm, sunny day and I was still drinking back then. I suspect that we brought plenty of ale with us. I don't recall actually going to a bar. I do recall going to a portaloo at least once and it was a bloody long winded operation. I'm not a natural festival goer by inclination and don't get me started on my various Glastonbury experiences. But I remember this as a pretty mellow day out on the whole. Eric Clapton followed Graham Parker. Oddly enough, only Dylan had a current album out. Eric Clapton was between *Slowhand* and *Backless*, neither of which I was that crazy about. Loved the previous record *No Reason To Cry* though, but I'm pretty sure Eric Clapton didn't play anything from that. He definitely played 'Layla' though... well he would, wouldn't he?

Between the sun and the grog, I was definitely feeling very much the worse for wear by the time Joan Armatrading came on. *To The Limit*, the third of Joan's holy trinity of albums with Glyn Johns producing came out a couple of months after this gig, so I imagine she must have played some songs from that in with the earlier classics, but I'm damned if I can remember. I was well gone by this point and it is one of the great regrets of my life that I really was in no state to appreciate Joan that day. Any Trouble opened a European tour for Joan in 1982 and she was sensational every night as well as being kindness itself to the bunch of clueless, scruffy Herberts that was Any Trouble back then.

So, Dylan. He was plugging *Street Legal*, a record I really loved. It was the big band with the girl singers, sax, keyboards and quite a few guitars. Dylan wore a suit, a top hat, heavy makeup and mostly played a Strat. (This was in the period where he let his other guitarists play the solos, thankfully!) I can't remember whether there was an acoustic set. I don't think so. There was certainly an interminable section where it seemed like just about everybody onstage got to sing lead vocals on a song. In truth I couldn't tell you whether it was a good, bad or awful show and I've seen Dylan do all of the above. It was just a long day with too much sun and too much beer, and I was righteously too far out of it to have any understanding of the finer points of Dylan's gig.

I lived in Nashville, Tennessee between 1992 and 2005 and one of my best friends there was the wonderful Ian Wallace, native son of Bury and Dylan's drummer at this and many other gigs. He always talked fondly of his time with Bob, although I suspect it was often a rather bizarre gig. As Ian once said to me, 'Sometimes it was Sad Eyed Lady sometimes it was *Wiggle Wiggle*.' Ian died in 2007, way too soon. I miss him. I'm glad Bob is still with us and sometimes I miss him, too.

I WAS THERE: GILL MURRAY

It may be important to put this concert in the context of it Dylan's first visit to the UK for nearly a decade.

After news of his six-night residency at Earls Court broke in April, fans slept out on pavements for three nights to get tickets at outlets across the UK. The shows were so over-subscribed that the promoter Harvey Goldsmith decided to put on an extra show, expecting about 100,000 people but the attendance was at least double that. Harvey Goldsmith told me personally; 'Dylan was on fire during that tour and at Blackbushe we couldn't get him off the stage'.

This was a worry as 'local' residents had tried to stop the concert from taking place on noise pollution grounds and Goldsmith was worried about falling foul of the law.

Dylan's three hours and five minute performance was his longest ever continuous appearance on stage, though he did leave the vocals to backing singers and band members at one stage to 'make a telephone call'.

Bob Dylan and Graham Paker backstage at Blackbushe

I WAS THERE: MILES McCARRON

My best friend's family and I were on holiday from San Francisco, California that year. The first day we arrived in London we noticed tickets on sale for Blackbushe. Bob Dylan and Eric Clapton in about four weeks near, the end of our trip. We bought six tickets for about £12 pounds each, (I still have the stub).

We took several trains and buses from Sussex early in the morning. The closer we got to the festival the larger the crowds. It was a beautiful sunny day, and everyone was in great spirits. After the last bus ride everyone had to walk about two miles on a closed road to get to the site. Then a good mile or so on site. It was hard with camping gear, but nobody complained.

We were veteran concert/festival fans from the San Francisco Bay. We had been to many 60,000+ stadium shows, and a few 100,000+ shows in Golden Gate Park. This show felt like we were walking to Woodstock. We had just attended the Macroom Castle Festival, featuring Rory Gallagher near Cork, Ireland. So we had a taste of a euro-festival. But that was only about 25,000 people.

We put our camping gear at the camping site and went into the gig. We packed food, whiskey and water. Were surprised that they let large two litre cans of beer in. We made it right to the front fence dead centre. While the opening acts played, everyone sat down! This was the opposite of a US gig. We sat because we were tired, and wanted to have plenty of energy for Clapton and Bob Dylan sets. Joan Armatrading and Graham Parker & The Rumour both put on good shows.

Clapton started and Bianca Jagger and Ringo sat on fold out chairs within arms reach out of on the other side of the four foot high security fence. I still have a picture somewhere. So we stood up to see the show in all of its glory, like good Yanks do. People started throwing cans at us. The security told us to sit down which was not easy to do given the density of the crowd. We were confused about everyone sitting and being quiet at a rock 'n' roll show. Eric and his band were awesome as the late afternoon sun stayed warm. I really wanted to hear 'Key to the Highway', and yelled it quite a bit. Eric actually acknowledged me with some kind of funny mumble before he played it. They featured most of the *Slowhand* LP in perfect concert versions. The sound system was awesome.

BOB DYLAN STREET LEGAL

BLACKBUSHE JULY 15th, 1978

There was quite a long break after Clapton's set. The sun was going down. I played a portable handheld cassette player loaded with The Beatles' tune for Ringo. He gave me a thumbs up when he heard the tunes. All of sudden after they removed the gear from the stage, a motorised stage rolled out over the base stage. It had all of Dylan's gear on it. Amazing stuff for 1978. Instant Dylan. Tons of equipment for multiple guitars, horns, keyboards, mandolins, extra vocalists, and percussions.

Dylan came on at twilight. Top hat and coat and a focused look on his face. His band boomed. As darkness approached, everyone was standing, (we Yanks were happy!) The show was 30 songs plus. Almost all the greatest tunes he ever conceived in one show! He switched from acoustic to heavy electric tunes seamlessly. The band was hot. The lead guitar player had a screaming Les Paul gold top. His solos were big league. Horns, keys, and pedal steel and mandolin rocked too. Even a flute was played. Completely orchestrated and perfectly choreographed show. Clapton came out for one tune late in the show, but he was too high to play lead. He grinned from ear to ear just listening to Bob tell the story of the song.

I am sorry to hear the audience recordings of this show were not so good. I have been to many Dylan shows before and after this show. This one was the most sophisticated show in terms of setlist, arrangement, number of musicians, stage setup and sound quality.

We arrived home in the San Francisco Bay two days later. We saw The Rolling Stones' Some Girls tour at the Oakland Coliseum on Saturday, July 26 after the Blackbushe experience. The music from Blackbushe was still in our heads.

Bob Dylan at Budokan (February 28 and March 1, 1978) is the closest representation of the material played at Blackbushe. But the show at Blackbushe was more energetic than this recording.

PRESENTS

The Picnic

AT **BLACKBUSHE** AERODROME

BOB DYLAN
SPECIAL GUEST
ERIC CLAPTON
and his band
WITH
JOAN ARMATRADING
GRAHAM PARKER & THE RUMOUR
LAKE

BLACKBUSHE AERODROME, CAMBERLEY, SURREY
SATURDAY 15th JULY

I WAS THERE: JOHN WILSON, AGE 15

A date I wont forget. The first time I had a spliff and I lost my virginity the same night!

We took the train from London. The old Mary Jane was being passed around, people were talking about Jack Kerouac and the death of Keith Moon. I remember signs along the roadside which said, 'Hippies graveyard'.

Joan Armatrading was a good act and I remember Eric Clapton coming on with Dylan for a few numbers. I don't know if my memory is playing up but I was sure Clapton fell over during the set with Dylan. On the way back I spent a few hours in some woods with a girl I went with! Well, what else could a 15 year-old school boy ask for?

I WAS THERE: JOHN PEARCE

It was a hot, balmy July day in 1978 and someone had decided to organise a picnic. And 200,000 people turned up.

The venue was Blackbushe in Hampshire, once a significant commercial airport (where my father worked in the late Fifties/early Sixties) which had evolved into a thriving private/business airfield as Heathrow grew in size and importance. Just off the A30, it wasn't well served by public transport and the organisers set aside a massive area as car parks.

It was an all-day concert with some impressive support acts leading up to the 'main man', including former local petrol pump attendant (according to rumour) Graham Parker, Midlands guitarist and songbird Joan Armatrading, and someone called Clapton who seemed capable of stringing some chords together on his 'axe' in a meaningful way (and looked like a man with a future).

Dylan came on at around 8.00 pm, played an extended set of 2½-3 hours, which included the vast majority of his best known and most successful numbers from his extensive catalogue (noting only that that represented only 25% of his time as a major artist to date!) Dylan moved effortlessly between songs such as 'Shelter from the Storm' and 'Simple Twist of Fate' from the more recent and excellent album *Blood on the Tracks*, and the earlier seminal hits like 'Blowin' in the Wind', 'It's all over now Baby Blue' and 'Like a Rolling Stone'. A spot of research reveals that he encored with 'Changing of the Guards' and 'The Times They Are a-Changin'' (not that actually we saw him leaving the stage before them; see below). Something for everyone…

Where I said, 'looked like' above (in reference to Clapton), that must be qualified with the fact that most of the performers appeared tiny and unrecognisable, as one would expect when standing in the middle of a crowd of that magnitude. Nevertheless, it was a great atmosphere and occasion.

Melody Maker announce the triumph of Blackbushe

My parents still lived a mere half a mile from the airfield. Anticipating an evacuation exercise of Dunkirkian proportions, I and my two work colleagues left the concert while Bob was still in full flow and walked back along familiar paths across the common to their house, with the music still loud and clear. I must be one of very few people who can claim to have listed to Dylan performing live, and clear as a bell, from the relative comfort of their front garden.

I WAS THERE: MARK HANDYSIDE

We were just about half way from the front, just in front of these giant speakers that relayed the sound to the rest of the crowd. To be honest I can't remember a lot of the concert now. I remember my mate Todd who was in a wheelchair – when the concert finished we literally had to carry him out as it was impossible to push his wheelchair due to all the cans and bottles on the ground. I've been to a few outdoor concerts over the years but have never experienced such a large audience as this. It took us a good eight hours to get out the car park.

I WAS THERE: TERRY ROBERTS, AGE 15

I went with my girlfriend Jessica and her older sister and boyfriend and a few others. This was my first big festival gig, (I went to Reading Rock several weeks later). I remember the huge queue to get in, and the already massive crowd. We settled for a spot about 50 yards from the stage, between the two sound piers approximately in the middle. I remember Merger were first on stage, they were a steel drum – reggae band, and seemed to go down well. After them, I went to get some food (big mistake) and I didn't find it back to my friends until half way through Graham Parker's set.

Due to the 'Party Seven' beer can we'd already consumed (remember those?) I took that opportunity to go to the toilet. No chance, enormous queue, so I used the fence like 500 others festival goers.

Most of the crowd sat down pretty much all day until Eric Clapton came on. The sound wasn't that good but the guitar playing from Clapton was awesome, 'Layla' and 'Cocaine' (everyone sang that one!) unforgettable show, it energised all around us.

Joan 'Arma-plating' went down very well, everyone loved that song of hers, 'sing me a little love song, this time with a little dedication'.

Then later Bob Dylan came on, old shaky voice, he looked 190 years old back then, and that was over 40 years ago and he's still touring. At the time we thought, 'well this is probably his last tour,' How wrong we were.

My girlfriend's sister was a huge Dylan fan, and of course we'd all heard his latest studio album *Street Legal*. 'Is your Love in Vain?', 'Baby, Stop Crying' etc, well it was good, but he looked tired on stage, and after a short while I was thinking, 'Bob please stop singing'. I believe there's a famous Jimi Hendrix quote which applied that day, 'If Bob Dylan can sing, so can I'.

Later when he'd gone off stage, it was my first gig where everyone lit their cigarette lighters and held them above their heads. What's this all about I thought? There were about 100,000 lighters aloft. I didn't smoke, but not to be outdone (or feel left out) I grabbed a discarded programme, tore off the back cover and lit that up like a flaming torch. I've got the best flame there, then bits of it started to separate and float away still lit…oops! People were shouting at me to put it out!

Dylan came back on, and if I'm not mistaken 'Baby, Stop Crying' was played a second time as one of the encores.

Eric Clapton definitely stole the show, and if I'm not mistaken I think that was a headline in *Sounds* music magazine the following week.

I WAS THERE: JENNIE MCFIE

We had friends out front who were selling burgers to raise some money to pay their mortgage – they went on to have a small chain of successful restaurants in London, and become vegetarian. Possibly as a result of this day!

We went out front every so often to hang out for a while with them and to see a bit of the performances, but would retreat backstage sharpish as there were so many people there and it was so crowded. But backstage you couldn't see the performances, which is why I can't really remember any of the music; even looking at the line up now didn't prompt any memories.

I think we left before the end of Dylan's set as we wanted to get back before the rush. It wasn't the greatest festival ever, by any means. But it didn't rain, not that I remember anyway.

I WAS THERE: MEL DERBYS

It was my first big outdoor event, a great atmosphere, as all gigs are, and wonderful to see such an excellent line up.

The size was just too big. I don't remember there being any screens back them. We were close to the front which was like being at the back at Knebworth. It took about two hours to find the car, which we slept in while most other people queued all night to get off the site. Excellent memories.

I WAS THERE: PHIL HUGHES

I got a Blackbushe ticket because I couldn't get a ticket for the Earls Court concerts. I had seen Dylan only once before, in the Sixties in the old Capitol Cinema, Cardiff.

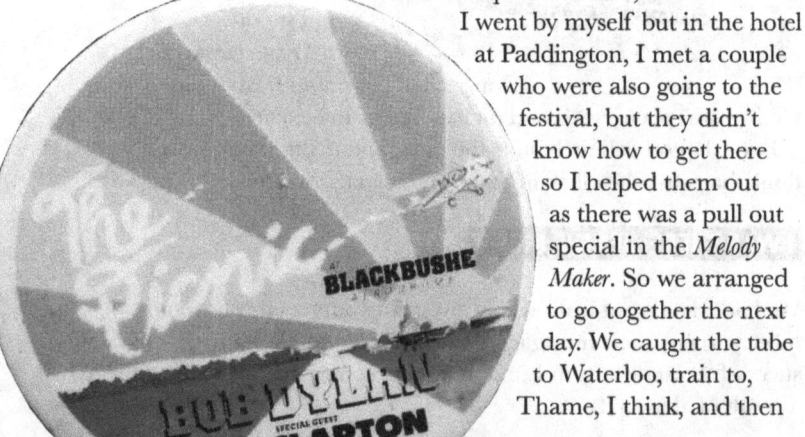

I went by myself but in the hotel at Paddington, I met a couple who were also going to the festival, but they didn't know how to get there so I helped them out as there was a pull out special in the *Melody Maker*. So we arranged to go together the next day. We caught the tube to Waterloo, train to, Thame, I think, and then think it was a mixture of taxi and walking to the site.

We were so far back, we could hardly see the stage but could make out Dylan in his borrowed top hat when people started passing binoculars around now and again.

It was a tremendous show on a hot day but you couldn't really wander around the site or you would never get back to your spot. I took some food with me so I survived.

The couple, from Manchester, I think, told me later that they got engaged during the concert!

Getting back to Paddington was difficult as there were huge queues for taxis when we got back to Waterloo. I think that in the end we got in a taxi with a cowboy female driver. I don't think she ripped us off but she didn't seem to know Paddington too well.

The couple did not show up for breakfast at the hotel the next day. We had arranged to have a drink in one of the local pubs but somehow we didn't meet up and I didn't see them again. And they had left some of their fruit in my bag during the concert!

I WAS THERE: PATRICK MARKS

I attended the day and will remember it with great affection. I managed to squeeze my way up to near the front and had a great view of Dylan whom I thought was in great form that evening! I have a few photos including one of me drinking from a large cider flagon! I still have the programme and the tee-shirt somewhere in the house. I always felt sorry it wasn't properly recorded for posterity.

I WAS THERE: TIM BETTERIDGE, AGE 19

I went with a group of friends in a hired minibus. In the previous May, I had broken my leg in a motorcycle accident and was in plaster from toe to thigh. My idea was to see Bob Dylan and be able to say that he was 'totally overrated' but I thought he was really something. It took all night to get out of the car park and it was broad daylight on Sunday morning when we got home and that was only about 50 miles away. It was only recently that I noticed Eric Clapton was on the same day – he did not make any impression on me.

I WAS THERE: ANDREW J ORR

A flat, featureless airfield is not the best place to hold any outdoor gigs, not only is the viewing difficult from 50 meters back without any video screens but the sound gets carried away on even the lightest of breezes. If I recall, of all the gigs and festivals I attended, this one had the worse sound balance for that reason.

Fans sat waiting for Dylan's appearance at Blackbushe

I WAS THERE: SUSAN RICHARDSON

Just found my ticket in a box of photos. £7 for that line-up! Unbelievable.

We were in the very front row, and I recall seeing Bianca Jagger and various celebrities of the time in the enclosure between us and the stage.

I remember Bob doing some standards but with different arrangements – 'It's All Over Now Baby Blue' being one of them? And of course lots from *Street Legal* which was just out that summer. And a loud version of 'Like a Rolling Stone'.

I remember falling off the train when it reached Liverpool St station. A tall American lifted me to my feet: I was exhausted.

I WAS THERE: ELAINE RAMWELL

My memories of the event are a little hazy, as you would expect! But I still hold some images in my mind's eye of the green fluorescent flashes all over the aerodrome whilst listening to Dylan in the dark. I recall a helicopter flying over and dropping loads of these fluorescent neckbands and wands which were being waved by whomever had been lucky enough to pick one up – the view from the helicopter must have been amazing and I also remember vividly the emotional response to the final song, 'Forever Young'.

I was lucky enough to have a great view of the stage and wish I'd had today's technology to take photos or videos. All I'm left with are some rather crumpled bits of paper and a badge.

The other abiding memory is the utter chaos of leaving the site and the desolation of being stranded when the shuttle train was cancelled. I slept on the grass verge for a few hours, being stepped over (and stepped on, occasionally) by others trying to get home, and spent the whole of the following day trying to return to Carmarthen, where I was living at the time. I was unable to get home in time to put in an appearance at the hospital where I worked nights, and was given a disciplinary interview and a written warning, despite having telephoned to explain that I was doing my best to get home!

To add insult to injury, that night on the damp and cold grass verge gave me a nasty chest infection, but I'd do it all again. It was a great gig and I feel privileged to have also seen Eric Clapton, Graham Parker and Joan Armatrading, who were terrific too, although I have no recollection of the others who played.

I WAS THERE: PAUL CARY

This is a ticket my brother Dave retained. Our stories differ, (age and substances no doubt!) but basically we drove down from Liverpool, in my 'Big Yellow Taxi', a big bright yellow Bedford van which we used for lots of festivals around this time. We must have taken about 20 people down all crammed in the back on mattresses and the odd sofa, some who had tickets, but the majority didn't. We arrived at some unearthly hour, some like myself the driver, crashed out, others wandered about surveying the scene.

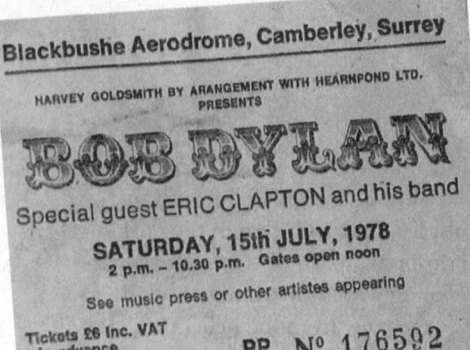

My recollection is that we gave one of our party all the cash to go and queue for the tickets at a sort of temporary box office outside the huge perimeter wall to save us all queuing.

Anyway, he bought from one of the touts of course and instead of being at the front of the compound as we had planned we were all marched into a police compound and kept there for hours watching as the best part of the reported 250,000 people went in before us. The guilty man was questioned by the police but Harvey Goldsmith eventually let us all in – but of course by this time – right at the back!

I remember the stage seeming like it was five miles away and the sound being poor and much like a transistor radio constantly blowing around (not surprising you might say). It was like watching ants in the distance. We did try and hustle our way closer to the front, but this crowd was enormous.

I also remember the security was very heavy, not just outside but also inside the compound, with lots of well built guys and flash Jeeps. A friend and I wrote complaining about this seemingly new level of heavy security at festivals to the music rags and *Sounds* (weekly music newspaper) printed the letter and a cartoon which took the piss out of the event on the whole of their back page.

I WAS THERE: DIANE LEGGO

When I was 11 years old I packed my bag and was heading to the Isle of Wight festival to see Bob Dylan. My parents kindly pointed out I was a bit young to go. I was devastated! In 1978 Bob Dylan was to play in the UK for the first time in a long time. I was at university in Southampton and was lucky to live with some fans. We decided we wanted to go to the Blackbushe festival and also Earls Court. The way to gain tickets was via the box office at the Southampton Gaumont. We queued all night, singing songs and I drank a bottle of Stones ginger wine – thinking it would keep me warm. Instead I got very merry and nodded off in my sleeping bag. At about 6am some horrible people charged the queue and it was chaotic. Luckily I got tickets and enjoyed every minute of the one day festival and the concert. Coincidentally I now live five minutes from Blackbushe and it will be 40 years next year – maybe there will be a reunion.

I WAS THERE: NEIL FLETCHER, AGE 16

I was working in a hotel in North Devon with a few people who were absolutely hooked on Dylan (amongst other things!). Before the concert we would hear snatches of *Street Legal* played on Radio One, these were the days before iTunes, so hearing new tracks was a rare treat and we would huddle around the radio shouting at people to be quiet.

We hired a small VW Van which just about took a double bed mattress in the back (which was inserted) and an unbelievable 17 of us travelled from Lynmouth, North Devon to Blackbushe. Things didn't go great as the van wouldn't go up Porlock Hill – a very steep one in four, so we had to get out and walk, picking up the van at the top! As we exited the van a large cloud of suspicious smoke followed us out – we really laughed at that.

We were innocent teens really, which was made obvious by the fact that we spent our hard-earned cash on, what turned out to be, forged tickets and were promptly refused access. We were all shown into a giant holding pen – however the organisers decided to let us all in! Amazing result, thank you Harvey!

My memory of the concert is 'Lay Down Sally', 'Cocaine' and then, finally Dylan. Superb, mind blowing, almost life altering to a young 16-year-old. I also remember the hours it took to get to the lavatories and the difficulty in finding our little group again.

Some people were peeing into bottles, I was too shy at that age to attempt such a thing. But it took hours to gently tread over thousands of people. But it was worth it. 'Where Are You Tonight' is still fresh in my mind.

Street Legal is still a favourite album, I don't listen to it much, but when I do it brings back those distant memories of giant wigwams, a tightly packed VW Van, nothing to eat, no sleep, early morning departure – so many memories, life seemed so different then and so much has flowed under all of our bridges.

FOUR-PAGE MM REPORT. PICTURES BY BARRY PLUMMER

By the time we got to Blackbushe we were a quarter million strong...

CHRIS BRAZIER SETS THE SCENE

RIGHT: ERIC CLAPTON jams with BOB DYLAN

I WAS THERE: ANDY MACDONALD

I arrived with a group of mates, some of us had tickets, but I didn't. I didn't have the money to buy one, even if I had met a tout. I thought I could find some way in for free, but was confronted by a site that was surrounded by high corrugated iron fencing that looked impossible to get over. My friends either went in or went home, but I scouted round the site, thinking there might be a chink somewhere, but there was no break in the fence.

Then I noticed the band buses, parked up outside the fence, but near the stage (on the left of the stage as you looked at it). I saw that it wouldn't be difficult to climb up the buses and drop over the fence from the top of one of them. So that is what I did. Once at the top, I didn't really look to closely, just checked I wasn't going to land on anyone and then jumped down. It was just a bit scary and a bit of jolt landing, but I was OK.

I picked myself up and started wandering, as casually as possible, away. Nobody seemed to notice me, or didn't think anything of it. After a few moments, I realised I wasn't in the main section of the crowd. I was in a section that had a side on view of the stage and that there was another iron fence between me, and the rest of the crowd. I cottoned on that I had landed in some kind of VIP enclosure! There were quite a lot of folk there, but obviously I didn't know anybody, so I thought maybe I could get over the second fence and into the main crowd to find my friends. I found a chair and stood on it next to the fence and I could just see over the top into the main crowd. What a sight! A huge crowd, packed in so tight that most people couldn't sit down if they wanted to. It was immediately apparent that I would have great trouble finding my friends in that crowd, but also that it was much more pleasant in the VIP enclosure.

So I spent the time in there. I'd like to say I made friends with famous stars, but I didn't. I think I managed to bum a smoke and maybe some drink off some folk in there. As I remember it, Bob was rather disappointing but Joan Armatrading turned in a great set. But on the whole rather boring without any mates. Another lesson in what is important in life, I guess.

I WAS THERE: FRANCIS B

I was 18, and having just arrived from Dublin to spend a student summer working in London, had found myself at a superb Bowie concert in Earls Court on my first night. I travelled out to The Picnic by myself, looking forward mainly to Joan Armatrading and Eric Clapton.

They were great, even though I needed binoculars to see them. I remember being amazed by the age range of the crowd, including babies and grandparents (or so they seemed to me). I made friends and shared food and beer, etc. with others sitting nearby, most of whom were there for Dylan. I wasn't that interested in him, as to me he represented my big sister's generation, but stayed on, happily enjoying the atmosphere.

He came on at dusk, and I remember the stage lights glowing warm colours in synch with the brass section for the 'Changing of the Guard' and other *Street Legal* songs. I was utterly bowled over, and found to my amazement that, like almost everyone around me, I knew the words of almost all the songs, having been brought up with them playing in the background! It was close to how I imagine a religious experience must be, an epiphany made even more intense by Dylan's apparent ability to look right into my eyes (through the binoculars) as he sang! (I have noticed this about him several times since at other concerts in Ireland, the USA and Spain – it must have something to do with his make up, or maybe it's just 'great presence'.)

I joined in with the backing singers (excellent) and choruses, etc., whenever I could, and danced like there was no tomorrow. The set just went on and on, and I was in seventh heaven!

I floated blissfully back to my crummy hostel in Gloucester Road, and stayed on a high for several days after, wrapping sausages at the end of a production line in Putney. I have been to many festivals since, but none to equal Blackbushe for intensity.

I WAS THERE: ANDREW DARLINGTON

He's laid spread-eagled on the grass, wrapped in a Union Jack, comatose. Blonde, and spaced to everything. You think… why? He's paid his £6 in advance, or maybe £7 at the gate for this once-in-a-lifetime event, what a joy it is to be alive at this moment, and he's too out of it to know. Gates open at noon, we arrive early. After staying overnight in Almondbury, we travel south with Dix behind the wheel, driving me, with Rita and Steve. Steve keeps pointing out 'hey, there's a picturesque country pub, we could stop for one,' and each time we do I'm thinking, 'yeah, we can visit quaint little country pubs anytime… but this is DYLAN!' Itching to move in a frantic kind of boring. Can you tell me where we're headin', Lincoln County Road or Armageddon? We're three miles from Camberley on the A30 London-Southampton Road, and start seeing itinerants for miles around. This is the year of Punk, there are splash-paint signs pointing 'HIPPIE'S GRAVEYARD', maybe they're right. But it's a great and groovy graveyard.

Eric Clapton plays a black-&-white Fender and tries to sing 'Cocaine' with a cig in his mouth-corner, 'Lay Down Sally' with Mercy Levy harmonies, and a blistering 'Badge'. He even does Dylan's 'Knockin' on Heaven's Door'. Later, he joins Dylan on-stage for 'Forever Young'. Strangely I have little memory of it. Not really been into anything he'd done since… um, since that Delaney & Bonnie record. Maybe punk conformity blanks him out, like the Union Jack guy? Or maybe we were in some country pub while his guitar gently weeps? I considered bringing a tape machine, but decided no, security won't let it through. But once inside there are batteries of them, some NASA-like mobile recording studios, tripod-mounted furry-mics spooling it all in. It's tempting to walk past them, one-by-one, declaiming enigmatic runic Dylanesque mutterings into each. Despite it all, the only Blackbushe 3CD bootleg I've found is pretty lo-fi (the German Wanted Man WMM 24/25/26, 1993). Atmospheric, but poor sound. Spliffs too. A low cumulus of dope. All you need do is walk and inhale. It later turns out there are 36 arrests, six for theft, six for bootlegging tickets, and 24 for drug offences. Joan Armatrading on stage now, lost in vastness as light laces higher. 'Love & Understanding' and 'Down To Zero' swelling like soap-bubbles bursting in the sun.

Driving into the 23-acre 'Dylanville' compound, in surreal juxtaposition there's a line of camouflage-grey World War II aircraft, huge Jurassic bombers rearing above grass, runway tarmac and rivers of assorted miscreants. Death-planes that refuse to turn into butterflies above our 200,000-strong nation. The biggest single-day event to date. Harvey Goldsmith Inc has lined up acts from 2.00pm – the jostling reggae of Merger licking like a friendly puppy then doing 'Biko' dedicated to the oppressed of Africa, the Anglo-German Lake running Crosby, Stills, Nash & Young harmonies over prog noodlings, Graham Parker & The Rumour roaring into 'Hey Lord, Don't Ask Me Questions' with sparks glinting on his heels. Ringo Starr is rumoured to be here, alongside Bianca Jagger, Billy Connolly, Susan George and Jennie Agutter, Martin Carthy and Woody Guthrie's widow, Marjorie. The south-wall toilet facilities are a tented water-sculpture constructed of dripping overflowing gutter-ways interconnected to slopping oil-drums marooned in a wetland of yellow mud. I find a trove of science fiction paperbacks squirrelled into the palisade – JG Ballard, Robert Silverberg, and stuff them in my jacket.

Back at the soundstage, visibility is less than good. Sight-lines confused by 'Desolation Row' pennants, big-hat picnickers with kids and miniature stoves. No video-screens. On the way out afterwards you sneak-hear, meaning-hungry people debating whether or not Dylan was wearing a hat. He was. A hat with a cockade, and 1966 shades to provide refuge. But it's telling that they couldn't tell. Everyone has a different perspective on it, but with footage playing over and over in your head, everything is heightened. Dylan's set opens with an instrumental 'My Back Pages', the man arriving virtually unannounced from the back-stage leading into a cover of bluesman Tampa Red's 'Love Her With A Feeling'. Then, glasses-off but eyes closed, he spits and slurs his new single 'Baby Stop Crying' which – on the back-of this event, climbs to No 13, making it his final UK Top 20 hit, so far. He doesn't speak much, little more than 'thank you, we're starting to get going'. Then ditches guitar, in favour of holding hand-mic and harmonica for 'It's All Over Now, Baby Blue'. Determinedly going 'over the top' I trek the near-half-mile through the carnage of sleeping-bags and body-clusters, fighting through to the front. To the post Rolling Thunder stage cluttered with snarls of tangled wiring. The closest to a Big-Band Dylan we're likely to get. Most personnel remaindered from the *Street Legal* sessions, Steve Douglas' wailing bluesy horns on 'I Want You', Billy Cross lead guitar, Alan Pasqua's keyboards, Bobbye Hall, percussion and Ian Wallace on drums.

The vocal back-up trio modelled on Bob Marley's 'I Three' – midpoint Dylan steps back for them to solo 'cause I'm getting tired', Carolyn Dennis does Sam Cooke's 'Change Is Gonna Come',

Helena Springs dances and moves around the stage as she does 'Mr. Tambourine Man', and Jo Ann Harris sings 'The Long And Winding Road' (earlier the girls repeat Dylan's lines ghosting 'Like a Rolling Stone'). 'And now the genius' says Dylan, and the Alpha Band's Steve Soles, on rhythm guitar, does a solo spot with 'Laissez-Faire'. After his long wilderness years, Dylan had re-established his mystique with *Blood On The Tracks* and *Desire*, with *Street Legal* impending, the set is strewn with its cuts. 'Señor (Tales Of Yankee Power)', and the smooth pure horns of 'Is Your Love In Vain' smearing into the air like warm oil, about as perfect as sound can get, 'can you cook and sew, make flowers grow, do you understand my pain?' Still amphetamine-skinny, scarecrow-haired and Rimbaudian, black jacket, a lightning flash down his twitching insectoid pants' leg. He plays electric Fender Strat, switching to acoustic with harmonica-harness for 'Gates of Eden' in blue spotlight pool. He's the postman, so he says. The guy who delivers songs. 'Ballad of a Thin Man' starts with his voice alone, before the band phase in, Billy Cross' demonic guitar kicking against the organ. In a natural light-show of spectacular sunset etching the stage-profile into the sky. Bonfire beacons across the enclosure. As Steve points out, he uses the Hendrix *Electric Ladyland* arrangement of 'All Along The Watchtower' – making him possibly the first artist to do a cover version of one of his own songs, albeit whipped up by David Mansfield's violin, Dylan replacing his previously discarded top hat. After the rasping nasal whine of 'All I Really Want To Do', Dylan does the band intro's, then into a cranked-up consciousness-stream 'It's Alright Ma, (I'm Only Bleeding)'. 'Forever Young' delivered, or interpreted as a defiant generational anthem. Closing with the wild high mercury sound of 'Changing Of The Guards' and 'The Times They Are a-Changin'.

Dix knows the new tracks already. I buy the album the next record shop I encounter. Heading back for the car, glancing at my notes, I've written 'blazing airships consuming the night, metallic dandelion-seeds spiralling down across the sky, two-tone siren horsemen howling, wading through elfin-pools of piss and tin-cans cranked up high on electric decibels' – what the hell does that mean??? Does Dylan himself get into similar conundrums with his own lyrics? As we leave, down moonlight lanes into a six-mile traffic tailback, the 'blonde and spaced' dreamer is still laid there, still wrapped in the Union Jack, tight shut lids, sleeping under strange –skies a-spin with glints of whirling seeds. And he's missed it all.

I WAS THERE: BARBARA ZOPPI

His voice is dreadful now – and he did a CD of Christmas Carols! I saw him about seven years ago at Nottingham Arena and he was dreadful. I was sat next to the sound engineer.

But in '78, I saw him at Blackbushe Festival with Clapton, Joan Armatrtading, Graham Parker, etc. It was a beautiful day. He was on very late and he was brilliant. It was just after the LP *Blood on the Tracks* came out and it will be in my mind forever, that concert. I've never seen so many speakers, standing as I do with my left ear next to the speakers which seemed to go on up to the sky. I lost a bit of hearing and my ears were ringing for two days after that.

To me, Dylan's 'Mr. Tambourine Man' is the best song ever.

I WAS THERE: JOHN LINDLEY

My memories of the Blackbushe festival are of a cracking set by Graham Parker, a stultifyingly dull one from Eric Clapton and a stunning and generously long performance by Dylan. The night culminated for me and a friend in a trek around the campsite in near pitch blackness for what seemed like hours, trying to locate our tent.

Three years later I was in London to see Dylan again and chatted with a doorman outside the Mayfair Hotel. (I was passing not staying.) He was wearing a top hat identical to the one that Dylan took to the stage in at Blackbushe and told me that Dylan had lifted the hotel uniform hat from his work colleague's head as he left the hotel for the show and carried it off. Apparently the Mayfair took it all in good spirit, although the doorman told me that didn't stop them from later billing Dylan's management for the hat.

The second leg of the North American 1978 tour kicked off on September 15, 1978, at the Augusta Civic Center, Georgia in front of 7,200 fans. The tour continued until the final date on December 16 at Hollywood Sportatorium.

NASSAU VETERANS MEMORIAL COLISEUM

27 SEPTEMBER, 1978, UNIONDALE

I WAS THERE: MARGARET MOORE, AGE 18

I was in the US visiting from Ireland for the summer. I had turned 18 in July. I was familiar with Bob Dylan, and I had never been at a rock concert before. There was no big concert venue in Ireland at that time. My main recollection was the size and scale of the venue. And the spectacle of thousands of lighters held high at the end of her concert. I've been told many times by 'aficionados' that the *Street Legal* album was not his finest work, but it will always be my first and favourite concert and my favourite album of his.

MAPLE LEAF GARDENS

12 OCTOBER, 1978, TORONTO, CANADA

I WAS THERE: GUY HOWORTH, AGE 22

I've been a fan since the early Seventies and bought all current at the time vinyls. I still have all of them in pristine condition.

Bob did about four acoustic songs including; 'It Ain't Me, Babe'. The rest of the concert was back up singers, very Vegas like. This was during his Christian phase. Someone yelled out a song to play and he said, 'I don't play that song since I found Jesus'. So I was disappointed. I still have the ticket stub and programme.

On October 18, 1979, Dylan and his new backing band appeared on the television show *Saturday Night Live*, performing three songs from the new album: 'Gotta Serve Somebody', 'I Believe in You', and 'When You Gonna Wake Up'. Two weeks later, on November 1, 1979, Dylan and his new band kicked off a new tour with a fourteen-concert engagement at the Fox Warfield Theatre in San Francisco.

CHICAGO STADIUM

17 OCTOBER, 1978, CHICAGO, ILLINOIS

WE WERE THERE: DAN KORTMANN AND JENNY TRIO

Dan and Jenny recount at how Dylan picked up her scarf and placed it around bassist Rob Stoner.

The first Bob Dylan concert for Jenny and me was in 1974 with The Band at the Chicago Stadium. Since then it's been over 30 Bob shows.

The concert story we have is from 1978. Again, it was at the Chicago Stadium and Bob had a big band consisting of Steve Soles, Rob Stoner, David Mansfield, and the wonderful voices of his singers I believe it included Helena Springs among others.

We were fortunate enough to get second row centre seats. We paid the price, it was worth it. At one point during the show someone threw a cowboy hat on the stage. Bob was in a playful mood that night and he picked it up and put it on one of the band members. Again, another hat hit the stage and again Bob tossed it to another band member.

We decided to join in. Jenny pulled off

her white silk scarf and I tossed it. It landed at Bob's feet. We started yelling, 'Put it on Bob, put it on'. He picked it up and put it on the bass player. I was able to snap this picture. See Jenny's scarf on Rob Stoner.

Proof that Dylan's bassist Rob Stoner wore Jenny's scarf

We had one more chance. I had on a red plaid wool scarf. I balled it up and tossed it and again it landed at Bob's feet. And again we started yelling, 'Put it on Bob, put it on'. He shrugged his shoulders and put it on! Wow! Oh Wow. I started snapping off the most jiggly blurry pictures I ever took. This was the best picture we got. He tossed it off to his left and someone in the front row grabbed it and put it around their neck.

What happened next was crazy on my part. The show was over and the house lights came up. I saw the guy with my scarf on in row one. I also noticed an envelope on the stage by Bob's microphone. I got a weird idea. I climbed over row one and from a first row seat I jumped onto the stage and picked up the envelope. (I'm guessing someone wrote Bob a letter.) I took the envelope and walked across the stage toward the guy who had my scarf on. He saw me as I extended my hand with the envelope down toward him. He reached up to accept the envelope from me. When he took the envelope from my hand I grabbed my scarf off his neck and dashed back toward Jenny, jumped off the stage and we quickly left the building. Not knowing if the guy who had my scarf for a few brief moments was coming after us or not.

So, my red plaid wool scarf went from my neck to Bob's neck to an audience stranger and back to my neck. And it's not over.

Two days later we were walking the halls of our school, Lake County College. We saw a guy walking toward us with a Bob Dylan concert t-shirt on. It looked brand new. We stopped him and asked if he was at the show. Yes, he was. We then regaled him with our scarf story. His eyes widened as he spoke and said that he was sitting stage left and saw the whole scarf incident. And, he happened to take a great picture of Bob wearing my red scarf. He said he would be glad to make a copy and bring it to school next week. He did and here is the picture he took of Bob wearing my red plaid wool scarf. I still have that scarf.

THE SUMMIT

26 NOVEMBER, 1978, HOUSTON, TEXAS

I WAS THERE: ALICIA GORSON, AGE 15

I had gone with a group of friends. We had a great time and Bob Dylan jammed his butt off! I'd always loved his very unique voice. He sang 'Precious Angel', 'Gotta Serve Somebody'. I loved it when he played his harmonica, but the truth of the matter is I just quite simply have a love for bluesy music and music in general.

Alicia Gorson (on the left) and friends

I've also seen both Bob Dylan and Tom Petty together at the Houston Summit.

LSU ASSEMBLY CENTER

29 NOVEMBER 1978, BATON ROUGE, LOUISIANA

I WAS THERE: SANDY MOORE

I still have the t-shirt that I bought at the concert. Dylan concerts are very different from the albums. The 1978 concert had a full orchestra and the songs and music sounded very different from the albums. My favourite album is *Blood on the Tracks*. I was hanging around New Orleans, Louisiana around the time that album came out. I especially loved 'Tangled Up in Blue'.

1979

Drummer Pick Withers first met Dylan after playing a gig with British band Dire Straits at The Roxy, West Hollywood, California. They were introduced at an upstairs private bar there. Dire Strait's 1978 self-titled debut LP featured the sprawling Dylan-esque hit 'Sultans of Swing.' Both Withers, a player with a crisp, nimble and jazzy touch, and Dire Straits guitarist Mark Knopfler, whose eloquent solos quickly became a hallmark of that band's sound, were brought in to play on Dylan's *Slow Train Coming*.

MUSCLE SHOALS SOUND

APRIL – MAY, ALABAMA

I WAS THERE: PICK WITHERS, DRUMMER

I guess The Roxy show was an informal audition as Jerry Wexler and Barry Beckett had recommended us. I wanted to do it but the prospect of failure was lurking in the shadows of my mind. So, in a way, I felt it was more to do with a crossing of the Rubicon and more significant than anything I achieved with Dire Straits.

He likes to have everyone there from day one. He doesn't do overdubs or guide vocals; the vocal he sings on the first take is the master vocal. I have tremendous admiration for him. That's why you get such wonderful energy on the tracks; but Jerry Wexler was determined we wouldn't do this and sent various people home. Dylan was quite suspicious of this but went along with it and eventually relaxed into it. There was one track about 15 verses long that Wexler wanted to edit. So we cut the tape down to about seven verses and Dylan overdubbed his new vocal, which he didn't like. So it was re-edited using the original vocal take and it was so much better as you could hear us responding to his voice. It was a bit jumpy in parts as they couldn't get the backing tracks as clean as the edit that he overdubbed vocals on; but it was a better overall feel. I was only with him for 10 days but I think he was pleased with what I did. I learnt something during that session about recording and keeping ones integrity.

I don't recall playing any drums until we had some kind of road map in our heads. What was interesting for me was that Dylan's vocals on those initial takes would be the master vocal. You had a maximum of three attempts before you moved on to another song. All of the album was recorded in this manner – the four basic rhythm section pieces and then all instruments as in Mark's solos, backups, organ, percussion, horns, etc., were recorded after.

I am particularly fond of 'Do Right to Me Baby' and reggae-flecked 'Man Gave Names To All The Animals.' Some of the other stuff was incomplete without those gorgeous gospel girl back-ups and the horns and extra keys, etc. I think those tracks blossomed as a result of the overdubs.

SCANDINAVIUM
11 JULY, 1979, GOTHENBURG, SWEDEN

I WAS THERE: OLE JORGEN FARSTAD

The first time I saw Dylan was at the Scandinavium in Gothenburg, Sweden in 1978. He played of course his classic songs from the Sixties and Seventies and from his new album *Street Legal*. My God it was great! I thought beforehand it was impossible for a Norwegian to meet Dylan at a concert in Scandinavia. This was in the time before the internet and Facebook but yes! The second time I went to see him was in Oslo, Norway in June 1995. A great concert in the Spektrum, but the greatest experience was the meeting with Bob after the concert. I met him at an outdoor restaurant after the show. We talked a little bit. I said, 'thank you for the concert' and good night. He was very friendly! I have seen him several times after that.

VINEYARD CHURCH
AUTUMN, 1979, SANTA MONICA, CALIFORNIA

I WAS THERE: CHERI PAULETTE DE LAAT-LIND, AGE 18

The year was 1979. I was 18 years old and I have always been a fan of Bob Dylan and his music. I would see him in the back of the church service in a long black jacket hat and shades. I was too shy back then to say hello to him. I was very inspired by Bob's album at the time! It encouraged my heart and faith in being a young Christian gal just out of high school. I was impressed that a folk-rock legend icon had a strong relationship with Christ and did such a bold album about it. I especially enjoyed hearing 'Gotta Serve Somebody' on his *Slow Train* album. I love all the songs on this album though!

FOX WARFIELD THEATRE

15 NOVEMBER, 1979, SAN FRANCISCO, CALIFORNIA

I WAS THERE: BILL WHITE

Backstage passes don't mean you get to meet the artist. They just get you through the back door. After that, it's a struggle with the security patrols to get anywhere. You wander through the corridors until somebody asks you where you are going. It doesn't matter how you answer; it's bound to be off-limits. So you are escorted to a holding area where people are grouped according to the access level of their passes. Eventually someone comes along and takes your group to its allowed destination.

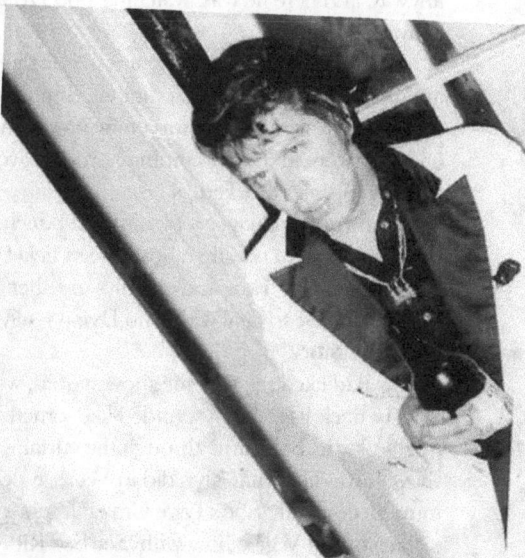
Bill White was lucky enough to hear Dylan jamming on some gospel tunes during the soundcheck

We got into the Forum a couple of hours before the doors were opened to the general public, but we were not allowed to go into the theater area because the band was doing a sound check. While my friend Stogie was hobnobbing with photographers, journalists, and radio personalities in the holding tank, the sounds from the auditorium caught my ear. The lyrics Dylan sang were unfamiliar and I had trouble making them out, I caught so many references to Jesus Christ that I figured they were jamming on some gospel tunes to get warmed up for the show.

It turned out that Stogie's passes were so worthless that they didn't even entitle us to seating. When the concert started, they had to watch it from a backstage riser that gave only a partial view of the stage. As for sound, all they could hear was an echo of the onstage monitors. So here they were, with enviable passes, and worse conditions for seeing and hearing the concert than those with the crappiest seats in the house.

Billy wasn't complaining. He couldn't have afforded the cheapest ticket anyway, and here he was, watching Bob Dylan from the wings. He was in heaven.

It is funny how some people are so quiet in a crowd, but get them alone and there is no end to their opinions. Sitting next to Stogie during the concert, Billy assumed he was enjoying the show. Once it was over, though, and they were in the car coming home, he wouldn't shut up about how much the concert sucked.

'Dylan's new manager took him to a bunch of Neil Diamond concerts to show him how to remain a hot concert ticket even with bad record sales,' Stogie surmised. 'Fans and enemies together are digging this tour because they don't have to deal with who Dylan really is. They are just bowing down to history.'

Billy had liked the way the show started, with an instrumental version of 'My Back Pages' that sounded like something Doc Severinson's band might play as Bob came through the curtains to join Johnny on the *Tonight* show. It was like what Elvis did in Vegas, especially when he followed the introduction with 'She's Love Crazy,' a move that reminded Billy of Elvis kicking off his Vegas show with 'See See Rider.'

Dylan himself was looking forward to the end of the tour, which had started last summer in this very same arena. That was before he met the woman who led him to Jesus Christ when he was being driven crazy by too many different ideas he had of himself. He was sick of all the earth goddesses and sky mothers that visited him in the person of ordinary sluts who wanted a pound of his flesh for the mantle to put next to their husband's bowling trophy. More than ever, he just wanted to be a singer, but the song had gotten the better of him, so he had to change the song, find something that would open up his heart, his voice, and free him from all the images that had held him stupefied.

Before singing 'Ballad of a Thin Man,' he explained to those in the crowd who had never seen *Nightmare Alley* what a geek was. Then he talked about a geek he had known who explained that he was able to get through life by seeing other people as freaks, and that had helped him deal better with people.

'He has never seemed so dated to me as he was tonight,' Stogie continued. 'Back in 1974, he breathed some new life into his old material. The new arrangements were pretty much confined to one approach, but his phrasing was so unpredictable that is was always exciting. Tonight there was a lot of variety in the arrangements, but his singing was boring. I sat there wondering was coming next, instead of listening to what he was singing in the moment.

'I never thought I'd see the day when Bob Dylan would take a scarf from an outreached hand, wipe the sweat from his forehead, and throw it back into the crowd, as if he had given the most precious souvenir a person could hope to take home from the concert. Who does he think he is? Tom Jones? And why did he keep throwing his index finger into a salute, or kneel into his amplifier pretending to look for feedback? Some might say he has a looser stage manner than before, but really it's just a tightly choreographed pile of shit.'

There was some truth in what Stogie was saying, but he had missed the bigger picture. Great as the 1974 tour with the band had been, it wasn't all that different from what they did together in 1966. The eight years had brought about improvements in concert sound, so the words could be heard above the ruckus, but there was too much of the sense that Dylan was trying to prove that he could still do what he had done before. Tonight's show, four years later, offered brand new arrangements and more varied singing.

Not all of it worked. 'The Times They Are a-Changin'', which opened the second half, had a truly awful arrangement, fully deserving Stogie's scorn as a Hallmark greeting card version of the original. But 'Changing of the Guards' was just about the best thing Billy had ever heard in his life. As Dylan sang, Billy could almost see the demons and the angels fighting for his soul, rendering him carrion for both heaven and hell. This was truly a man in agony; hijacked on a heroic journey by the treachery of beloved maids, renegade priests, and the souls of previous times. His voice as ragged as his wounds of love, shooting through the clouds like a bolt of lightning hurled back at the god whose shoes he had shined.

'Thanks for bringing me along,' Billy told Stogie when they got back to the Grove. 'It was fun hanging out with you.'

'Yeah. We ought to check out some more concerts. I get a lot of free tickets to stuff.'

Even though Stogie came across as a name-dropping nobody who boasted about his past, Billy liked him for what he was, a Hollywood version of the old-fashioned nerd who had spent his adolescence alone in his bedroom with a ham radio set, listening to broadcasts from foreign countries in languages he didn't understand. This clumsy, overweight child had grown into a creature that could never expect anything normal out of life, yet hadn't crawled into the conformity of freakdom with the rest of the losers. He was still just a kid who stared out at the adult world passing by, knowing there was no place for him in it.

Mace was watching *Terror in a Texas Town* when Billy got home. He wanted to hear about the concert, but the movie was too good to interrupt. Billy kicked his shoes off, boiled water for Top Ramen, and sat down to watch the picture. He couldn't pay attention to it though, because his head was still buzzing with the concert. He was thinking about the second half, which started poorly but picked up with a burning version of 'We Better Talk this Over' that boosted the intensity of the record without departing from the arrangement. Billy liked it when the singers punched up the ends of the lines, before a smoking 'Masters of War,' he said something about Phil Specter being a bigger genius than himself, and 'Tangled Up in Blue' sounded like something off an Edith Piaf record.

'You know what was disappointing?' Billy said to Mace when the movie ended. 'Since I saw him four years ago he has put out three great albums. And, out of the 28 songs he played, there were only two from *Blood on the Tracks*, one from *Desire*, and three from *Street Legal*. And all those, except for a crummy 'Shelter from the Storm,' were the best songs of the night.'

'Well, I saw him two years ago, at the Hurricane Carter benefit, and he did all the *Desire* stuff then, so he's probably sick of all those songs.'

'Was that the tour that they filmed for the *Hard Rain* special on TV?'

'Not really. The band was the same, but it was a lot later. He was burned out on the whole thing by then.'

'Because I saw that show, and something seemed off.'

'Did you see *Renaldo and Clara*?'

'No, I wanted to, but they pulled it before the first week was out.'

'Shit, man, it's playing in Pasadena this week. We ought to take a bus out there.'

'Really?'

'Yeah. It's at the Rialto. And it's fucking great. It catches that tour at its best.'

They watched a couple more movies before falling to sleep, and got up around noon. Neither had anything to do, so they caught a bus to Pasadena, and hung out in some donut shops to kill time before the movie. Mace told every story he knew that had anything to do with the Rolling Thunder Revue, so when the theatre finally opened, Billy was primed for the opus to come.

The movie was mostly concert footage of the tour, with random bits of Dylan, the band, their friends, and girlfriends either sightseeing or acting out scenes. Mace was showing signs of irritation throughout, but held his temper until the lights came up.

'I can't fucking believe it, man. They chopped out half the movie! At least they kept all the concert stuff, but none of the rest of it makes any sense now. I'm sure that, to the people who cut it, it didn't make any sense in the first place, and they thought they were doing a salvage job, and maybe they were, but some of the most interesting movies are made by people that aren't filmmakers, but are artists in another field. Look at Norman Mailer. Doesn't know the first thing about making a movie, but he's a motherfucker of a novelist. And *Maidstone* is a masterpiece. There's nothing else like it!'

Billy was stunned by the performances in the movie. As he and Mace took the long bus ride home from Pasadena, he was thinking about how Shakespeare had created Hamlet, the first modern man, a man who reflected, not only on himself, but also on the nature of mankind. It was almost like when Shakespeare created us when he created Hamlet.

And there was a similar thing with Bob Dylan. He created himself out of all the things he wanted to be, and that person he created was like nobody who had come before. Now, everybody had a guitar and notebooks full of songs. If it hadn't been for Dylan, every last one of them would have been somebody else. Nobody would be writing songs and trying to make records.

PHOTO CREDITS:

Jens Christian Berg and Anna Adamczewska, Blackbushe photos, David Hersk photo courtesy of minniepaulmusic.com, Sony Legacy, Don Hunstein, Auckland 1978 photos, Robin Morrison, The NZ Herald, Malcolm Colton for the IOW photos

CREDITS:

I consulted the following magazines, web sites and organisations and for this I remain truly grateful. Thanks to Richard Houghton, The Rock and Roll Chemist, Beatles Bible, Michigan Today, The Guardian, CMT, Matt Wake and Al.com, Street Photography.com, Houston Chronicle, The Village Voice, Gibson.com, Pioneerproductions.com, The Dissolve.com, Eight Miles Higher, Planet Waves FM, Visions of Pat, MTV.com, Vintage Vinyl News, The Sunday Times, Stuart Penny's account first appeared on the Empty Mirror website. Thanks to Marc Catone the author of Until The Birds Chirp: Reflections On The Sixties, Ultimate Classic Rock, The University of Chicago Magazine, Gordy Bowan account from Joni Mitchell.com, Ray Connolly for his IOW, Nick Lauro for Pick Withers, Growing Old With Rock & Roll, For Bass Players Only, Muff Winwood interview was reprinted in 'Wanted man: in search of Bob Dylan'. Keith Clark from Pro Sound Web for the The Planet Waves Sessions article. Etcetera for the Bonnie Dobson account, The Bob Dylan Fan Club. Bruce Langhorne the interview was done for the two-part Sixties folk-rock history Turn! Turn! Turn!/Eight Miles High, now combined into the ebook Jingle Jangle Morning by Richie Unterberger, Bob Dylan Roots, American Songwriter, BBC online, YouTube, The Blues Mobile.com, The Prisim Archive, Snap Galleries, Ryko, The Daily Freeman, Sound On Sound, Steve Hoffman forums, Gaslight Records, The Independent, The Band. com, Beatlefan Magazine, Glide Magazine, Reverend Barker from UK Rock Festivals.com, The Prince Blog, Bob Dylan's Musical Roots, Tape Op magazine, Doug Collette, RichardWilliams.net, Paul Judge, Westbridgfordwire.com, witleysoralhistory.org, Expecting Rain, The Woodstock Whisperer, Richard Howe, HiddenGlasgow.com, RockCellarMagazine.com and Frank Mastropolo, The Never Ending Pool, Steve Barker and special thanks to Chris Charlesworth, ISIS Magazine and all the Bob Dylan fan sites, Happy Traum, 1999 and 2017. Used by permission

www.ingramcontent.com/pod-product-compliance
Lightning Source LLC
Chambersburg PA
CBHW012000090526
44590CB00026B/3799